Communications
in Computer and Information Science 995

Commenced Publication in 2007
Founding and Former Series Editors:
Phoebe Chen, Alfredo Cuzzocrea, Xiaoyong Du, Orhun Kara, Ting Liu,
Krishna M. Sivalingam, Dominik Ślęzak, Takashi Washio, and Xiaokang Yang

More information about this series at http://www.springer.com/series/7899

Patricia Pesado · Claudio Aciti (Eds.)

Computer Science – CACIC 2018

24th Argentine Congress
Tandil, Argentina, October 8–12, 2018
Revised Selected Papers

 Springer

Editors
Patricia Pesado (iD)
National University of La Plata
La Plata, Argentina

Claudio Aciti
National University of Buenos Aires Center
Buenos Aires, Argentina

ISSN 1865-0929   ISSN 1865-0937   (electronic)
Communications in Computer and Information Science
ISBN 978-3-030-20786-1   ISBN 978-3-030-20787-8   (eBook)
https://doi.org/10.1007/978-3-030-20787-8

This Springer imprint is published by the registered company Springer Nature Switzerland AG
The registered company address is: Gewerbestrasse 11, 6330 Cham, Switzerland

Preface

Welcome to the proceedings of the XXIV Argentina Congress of Computer Science (CACIC 2018), held in Tandil, Buenos Aires, Argentina, during October 8–12, 2018. CACIC 2018 was organized by the National University of the Center (Buenos Aires) on behalf of the Network of National Universities with Computer Science Degrees (RedUNCI).

CACIC is an annual congress dedicated to the promotion and advancement of all aspects of computer science. Its aim is to provide a forum within which the development of computer science as an academic discipline with industrial applications is promoted, trying to extend the frontier of both the state of the art and the state of the practice. The main audience for and participants of CACIC are seen as researchers in academic departments, laboratories, and industrial software organizations.

CACIC 2018 covered the following topics: intelligent agents and systems; distributed and parallel processing; software engineering; hardware architecture; networks and operating systems; graphic computation, visualization, and image processing; computer technology applied to education; databases and data mining; innovation in software systems; computer security, innovation in computer science education; signal processing and real-time system; digital governance and smart cities.

This year, we received 155 submissions. Each submission was reviewed by at least two, and on average 3.2, Program Committee members and/or external reviewers. A total of 116 full papers, involving 368 different authors from 52 universities, were accepted. According to the recommendations of the reviewers, 26 of them were selected for this book.

During CACIC 2018, special activities were also held, including two plenary lectures, one discussion panel, four invited speakers, a special track on Digital Governance and Smart Cities, and an International School with six courses.

Special thanks are extended to the members of the different committees for their support and collaboration. Also, we would like to thank the local Organizing Committee, reviewers, lecturers, speakers, authors, and all conference attendees. Finally, we want to thank Springer for their support of this publication.

April 2019   Patricia Pesado

Organization

The XXIV Argentine Congress of Computer Science (CACIC 2018) was organized by the School of Computer Science of the National University of the Center (UNICEN) on behalf of the Network of National Universities with Computer Science Degrees (RedUNCI).

Editors

Patricia Pesado (RedUNCI Chair)	National University of La Plata, Argentina
Claudio Aciti	National University of Buenos Aires Center, Argentina

Editorial Assistant

Pablo Thomas	National University of La Plata, Argentina

General Chair

Claudio Aciti	National University of Buenos Aires Center, Argentina

Program Committee

Maria Jose Abásolo	National University of La Plata, Argentina
Claudio Aciti	National University of Buenos Aires Center, Argentina
Hugo Alfonso	National University of La Pampa, Argentina
Jorge Ardenghi	National University of South, Argentina
Marcelo Arroyo	National University of Río Cuarto, Argentina
Hernan Astudillo	Technical University Federico Santa María, Chile
Sandra Baldasarri	University of Zaragoza, Spain
Javier Balladini	National University of Comahue, Argentina
Luis Soares Barbosa	University of Minho, Portugal
Rodolfo Bertone	National University of La Plata, Argentina
Oscar Bria	National University of La Plata, Argentina
Nieves R. Brisaboa	University of La Coruña, Spain
Carlos Buckle	National University of Patagonia San Juan Bosco, Argentina
Alberto Cañas	University of West Florida, USA
Ana Casali	National University of Rosario, Argentina
Silvia Castro	National University of South, Argentina
Antonio Castro Lechtaler	National University of Buenos Aires, Argentina
Alejandra Cechich	National University of Comahue, Argentina

Edgar Chávez	Michoacana University of San Nicolás de Hidalgo
Carlos Coello Coello	CINVESTAV, Mexico
Uriel Cuckierman	National Technological University, Argentina
Armando E. De Giusti	National University of La Plata, Argentina
Laura De Giusti	National University of La Plata, Argentina
Marcelo De Vincenzi	Inter-American Open University, Argentina
Claudia Deco	National University of Rosario, Argentina
Beatriz Depetris	National University of Tierra del Fuego, Argentina
Javier Díaz	National University of La Plata, Argentina
Juergen Dix	TU Clausthal, Germany
Ramón Doallo	University of La Coruña, Spain
Domingo Docampo	University of Vigo, Spain
Jozo Dujmovic	San Francisco State University, USA
Marcelo Estayno	National University of Lomas de Zamora, Argentina
Elsa Estevez	National University of South, Argentina
Marcelo A. Falappa	National University of South, Argentina
Pablo Rubén Fillotrani	National University of South, Argentina
Jorge Finocchieto	CAECE University, Argentina
Daniel Fridlender	National University of Cordoba, Argentina
Fernando Emmanuel Frati	National University of Chilecito, Argentina
Carlos Garcia Garino	National University of Cuyo, Argentina
Luis Javier García Villalba	Complutense University of Madrid, Spain
Marcela Genero	University of Castilla-La Mancha, Spain
Sergio Alejandro Gómez	National University of South, Argentina
Eduard Groller	Vienna University of Technology, Austria
Roberto Guerrero	National University of San Luis, Argentina
Jorge Ierache	National University of Buenos Aires, Argentina
Tomasz Janowski	Danube University Krems, Austria
Ramiro Jordan	University of New Mexico, USA
Horacio Kuna	National University of Misiones, Argentina
Laura Lanzarini	National University of La Plata, Argentina
Guillermo Leguizamón	National University of San Luis, Argentina
Fernando Lopez Gil	University of Zaragoza, Spain
Ron P. Loui	Washington University, USA
Emilio Luque Fadón	Autonomous University of Barcelona, Spain
Maria Cristina Madoz	National University of La Plata, Argentina
Maria Alejandra Malberti Riveros	National University of San Juan, Argentina
Maria Malbrán	National University of Buenos Aires, Argentina
Cristina Manresa	University of Baleares Islands, Spain
Javier Marco	University of Zaragoza, Spain
Mauricio Marin	National University of Santiago de Chile, Chile
Ramon Mas Sanso	University of Baleares Islands, Spain
Orlando Micolini	National University of Cordoba, Argentina
Alicia Mon	ITBA, Argentina
Regina Motz	University of the Republic, Uruguay

Sponsors

RedUNCI

SECAT
Secretaría de Ciencia, Arte y Tecnología

Network or Universities
with Careers in Computer
Science (RedUNCI)

Secretary of Science, Art
and Technology
National University
of Center (UNICEN)

National University
of Center (UNICEN)

COMISIÓN DE
INVESTIGACIONES CIENTÍFICAS
Ministerio de Ciencia, Tecnología e Innovación

cessi
ArgenTina

MunicipiodeTandil
Lugar Soñado

Commission for Scientific
Research Province of Buenos
Aires (CIC)

Chamber of Business of
Software and Information
Service (CESSI)

Municipality of Tandil,
Buenos Aires,
Argentina

Contents

Software Engineering

Databases and Data Mining

Hardware Architectures, Networks, and Operating Systems

Innovation in Software Systems

Signal Processing and Real-Time Systems

Computer Security

Innovation in Computer Science Education

Digital Governance and Smart Cities

Agents and Systems

Solving the Multi-Period Water Distribution Network Design Problem with a Hybrid Simulated Anealling

Carlos Bermudez[1], Carolina Salto[1,2], and Gabriela Minetti[1(✉)]

[1] Facultad de Ingeniería, Universidad Nacional de La Pampa, Calle 110 Nro. 390, General Pico, La Pampa, Argentina
bermudezc@yahoo.com, {saltoc,minettig}@ing.unlpam.edu.ar
[2] CONICET, Buenos Aires, Argentina

Abstract. This work presents an optimization technique based on Simulated Annealing (SA) to solve the Water Distribution Network Design problem, considering multi-period restrictions with time varying demand patterns. The design optimization of this kind of networks is an important issue in modern cities, since a safe, adequate, and accessible supply of potable water is one of the basic necessities of any human being. Given the complexity of this problem, the SA is improved with a local search procedure, yielding a hybrid SA, in order to obtain good quality networks designs. Additionally, four variants of this algorithm based on different cooling schemes are introduced and analyzed. A broad experimentation using different benchmark networks is carried out to test our proposals. Moreover, a comparison with an approach from the literature reveals the goodness to solve this network design problem.

Keywords: Water Distribution Network Design · Optimization · Metaheuristic · Simulated Annealing

1 Introduction

A water distribution network consists of thousands of nodes with nonlinear hydraulic behaviour, linked by thousands of interconnecting links. The inherent problem associated with cost optimisation in the design of water distribution networks is due to the nonlinear relationship between flow and head loss and the discrete nature of pipe sizes. As a consequence, the solution concerning the layout, design, and operation of the network of pipes should result from good planning and management procedures. In this way, this problem known as Water Distribution Network Design (WDND) requires to manage an important number of variables (pipes, pipe diameters, demand nodes, water pressure, reservoirs, etc.), and constraints (water velocity, pressure, etc.). This problem, even for simple networks, is very difficult to solve, in particular it is classified as NP-hard [1].

Early research works in the WDND optimization area were focused on the single-period, single-objective, gravity-fed design optimization problem.

© Springer Nature Switzerland AG 2019
P. Pesado and C. Aciti (Eds.): CACIC 2018, CCIS 995, pp. 3–16, 2019.
https://doi.org/10.1007/978-3-030-20787-8_1

The first research works applied linear programming [2,3], and non-linear programming [4,5]. After that, the metaheuristics have been used to solve these problems, such as the trajectory-based ones: Simulated Annealing [6,7] and Tabu Search [8]. Also population-based metaheuristics were applied, for example, Ant Colony Optimization [9], Ant Systems [10], Genetic Algorithms [11–13] Scatter Search [14], and Differential Evolution [15].

Recently, the single-period problem was extended to a multi-period setting in which time varying demand patterns occur. Farmani et al. [16] formulated the design problem as a multi-objective optimization problem and apply a multi-objective evolutionary algorithm. In [12], a Genetic Algorithm was used to solve six small instances considering velocity constraint on the water flowing through the distribution pipes. This constraint was also taken into account in [17], but the authors used mathematical programming on bigger, closer-to-reality instances. A Differential Evolution (DE) algorithm was proposed in [18] to minimize the cost of the water distribution network. Another version of a DE algorithm to solve this problem was presented in [19]. An Iterative Local Search [20] was specifically-designed in order to consider that every demand node has 24 hrs water demand pattern and a new constraint, which imposes a limit on the maximal velocity of water through the pipes.

Based on the problem formulation given by De Corte and Sörensen [20], we propose an optimization technique, based on Simulated Annealing (SA), in order to improve and optimize the distribution network design. Thus, this SA is designed to obtain the optimal type of pipe connecting the supply, demand, and junction nodes in the distribution network. This proposal incorporates a local search procedure in order to improve the layout of the network, arising the Hybrid Simulated Annealing (HSA). The HSA's performance is compared with algorithms present in the literature. This work constitutes an extension of a previous work [21] and includes new content regarding an study and analysis of the main control parameter of the HSA, known as temperature. Moreover, we introduce and statistically compare four HSA's variants, taking into account different schemes to schedule the cooling process. We test the performance of our proposals with a set of networks with different sizes expressed by number of pipes and characteristics. The evaluation considers relevant aspects such as efficiency and internal behavior.

The rest of this article is organized as follows. In Sect. 2, we introduce the problem definition. Section 3 explains our algorithmic proposal, HSA, to solve the WDND optimization problem and the four HSA's variants. Section 4 describes the experimental analysis and the methodology used. Then, we analyze the results obtained by the variants and compare with the obtained by the ILS [20] in Sects. 5 and 6, respectively. Finally, we present our principal conclusions and future research lines.

2   Multi-Period Water Distribution Network Design

The objective of the WDND problem is to minimize the total investment cost (TIC) in a water distribution network design. The problem can be characterized as: simple-objective, multi-period, and gravity-fed. Two restrictions are considered: the limit of water speed in each pipe and the demand pattern that varies in time. The network can be modeled by a connected graph, which is described by a set of nodes $N = \{n_1, n_2, ...\}$, a set of pipes $P = \{p_1, p_2, ...\}$, a set of loops $L = \{l_1, l_2, ...\}$, and a set of commercially available pipe types $T = \{t_1, t_2, ...\}$. The TIC is obtained by the formula shown in Eq. 1,

$$\min TIC = \sum_{p \in P} \sum_{t \in T} L_p IC_t x_{p,t} \tag{1}$$

where IC_t is the cost of a pipe p of type t, L_p is the length of the tube, and $x_{p,t}$ is the binary decision variable that determines whether the tube p is of type t or not. The objective function is limited by: physical laws of mass and energy conservation, minimum pressure demand in the nodes, and the maximum speed in the pipes, for each time $\tau \in T$. These laws are explained in the following paragraphs.

Mass Conservation Law: It must be satisfied for each node N in each period of time τ. This law establishes that the volume of water flowing towards a node in a unit of time must be equal to the flow that leaves it (see Eq. 2),

$$\sum_{n_1 \in N/n} Q_{(n_1,n),\tau} - \sum_{n_2 \in N/n} Q_{(n,n_2),\tau} = WD_{n,\tau} - WS_{n,\tau} \quad \forall n \in N \quad \forall \tau \in T \tag{2}$$

where $Q_{(n_1,n),\tau}$ is the flow from node n_1 to node n at time τ, $WS_{n,\tau}$ is the external water supplied and $WD_{n,\tau}$ is the external water demanded.

Energy Conservation Law: It states that the sum of pressure drops in a closed circuit in an instant of time τ is zero. These drops can be approximated using the Hazen-Williams equations with the parameters used in EPANET 2.0 [22] (the hydraulic solver used in this paper), as indicated in Eq. 3.

$$\sum_{p \in l} \left[\frac{10.6668 y_{p,\tau} Q_{p,\tau}^{1.852} L_p}{\sum_{t \in T} (x_{p,t} C_t^{1.852} D_t^{4.871})} \right] = 0 \quad \forall l \in L \quad \forall \tau \in T \tag{3}$$

In Eq. 3, $y_{p,\tau}$ is the sign of $Q_{p,\tau}$ that indicates changes in the water flow direction relative to the defined flow directions, $Q_{p,\tau}$ is the amount of water flowing through pipe p in time τ, L_p is the pipe length, C_t is the Hazen-Williams roughness coefficient of pipe type t, and D_t is the diameter of pipe type t.

Minimum Pressure Head Requirements: for each node n in each period of time τ, it must be satisfied (see Eq. 4),

$$H_{n,\tau}^{min} \leq H_{n,\tau} \quad \forall n \in N \quad \forall \tau \in T \tag{4}$$

being H^{min} the minimum node pressure and $H_{n,\tau}$ the node's current pressure.

Maximum Water Velocity: The water velocity $v_{p,\tau}$ can not exceed the maximum stipulated speed $v_{p,\tau}^{max}$. Equation 5 shows this relationship.

$$v_{p,\tau} \leq v_{p,\tau}^{max} \quad \forall p \in P \quad \forall \tau \in T \tag{5}$$

Table 1. Different solutions or network designs in vector representation.

Solution	Pipe ID	1	2	3	4	5	6	7	8	Feasibility
	Length (m)	31	20	35	37	24	50	12	65	TIC
1	Diam. (mm)	150	150	80	80	100	60	60	80	Feasible
	Cost	1550	1000	1225	1295	912	1100	264	2275	9621
2	Diam. (mm)	150	150	80	60	100	60	60	80	Infeasible
	Cost	1550	1000	1225	814	912	1100	264	2275	9140

3   Our Proposal for the Multi-Period WDND Problem

Simulated Annealing (SA) [23], a simple trajectory-based metaheuristic, is based on the principles of statistical thermodynamics, whereby the annealing process requires heating and then slowly cooling the physical material until it solidi-fies into a perfect crystalline structure. The SA algorithm simulates the energy changes in a system subjected to a cooling process until it converges to an equi-librium state (steady frozen state), where the physical material states correspond to problem solutions, the energy of a state to cost of a solution, and the tem-perature to a control parameter.

At the beginning (with a high temperature), SA accepts solutions with high cost values under a certain probability in order to explore the search space and to escape from local optima. During the annealing process this probability decreases according to temperature cooling; intensifying the search and reducing the exploration in order to exploit a restricted area of a search space.

Simulated annealing evolves by a sequence of transitions between states and these transitions are generated by transition probabilities. Consequently, SA can be mathematically modeled by Markov chains, where a sequence of chains is generated by a transition probability, which is calculated involving the current temperature.

The proposal consists in adapting and hybridizing the SA algorithm to solve the Multi-Period WDND optimization problem, arising Hybrid Simulated Annealing (HSA) algorithm. A solution to this problem is a network, as shown in Fig. 1(a) and (b). A network or a solution is represented by a vector, where each element is the diameter selected for that pipe, as can be seen in Table 1. In this table the vectors that represent the candidate solutions in Fig. 1(a) and (b) are shown. The total investment cost for each solution is calculated by the Eq. 1, using the input data from tables (c) and (d) of Fig. 1. The first solution is hydraulically feasible (satisfying all constraints mentioned in Sect. 2) and the second one is infeasible (violating the minimum pressure constraint in node 7).

In Algorithm 1, we show a pseudo-code of the HSA algorithm to solve the WDND optimization problem. HSA uses the EPANET 2.0 toolkit [22] to solve the hydraulic equations, since this hydraulic solver is applied in most existing works. HSA generates a feasible initial solution S_0 applying both HighCost and Lowcost mechanisms proposed in [20] (line 2). After the evaluation of the initial

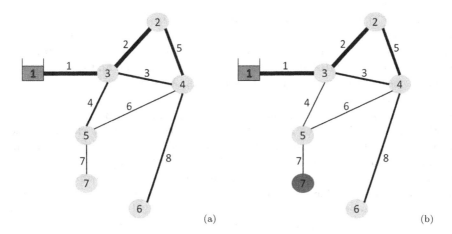

Fig. 1. Different solutions or network designs. (a) Solution 1; (b) solution 2; (c) pipe lengths; (d) available pipe types with their corresponding costs.

Pipe ID	Length (m)
1	31
2	20
3	35
4	37
5	24
6	50
7	12
8	65

(c)

Diam. (mm)	Roughness unitless	Cost
60	130	22
80	130	35
100	130	38
150	130	50
200	130	61

(d)

Algorithm 1. HSA Algorithm to solve the WDND optimization Problem

---

```
 1: k = 0;
 2: initialize T and S₀; {temperature and initial solution}
 3: evaluate S₀ in TIC₀;
 4: repeat
 5:    repeat
 6:       k = k + 1;
 7:       generate S₁ from S₀ applying the MP-GRASP Local Search;
 8:       evaluate S₁ in TIC₁;
 9:       if TIC₁ < TIC₀ then
10:           S₀ = S₁; TIC₀ = TIC₁
11:       end if
12:       generate S₂ from S₀ applying the perturbation operator;
13:       evaluate S₂ in TIC₂;
14:       if (TIC₂ < TIC₀) or (exp((TIC₂ − TIC₀)/T) > random(0, 1)) then
15:           S₀ = S₂; TIC₀ = TIC₂
16:       end if
17:    until (k mod MCL) == 0
18:    update T;
19: until stop criterion is met
20: return S₀;
```

solution (line 3), an iterative process starts (lines 4 to 19). As a first step in the iteration, the hybridization is carried out in order to intensify the search into the current region of the solution space. In this way a feasible solution, S_1, is obtained by applying the MP-GRASP local search [20] to S_0 (line 7), and then a greedy selection mechanism is performed (lines 9–11). As a consequence, S_0 can be replaced by S_1 if this is better than S_0. In the next step a perturbation operator is used to obtain a feasible neighbor, S_2, from S_0 (line 12), in order to explore another areas of the search space. This perturbation randomly changes some pipe diameters. If S_2 is worse than S_0, S_2 can be accepted under the Boltzmann probability (line 14, second condition). In this way, at high temperatures (T) the exploration of the search space is strengthened. In contrast, at low temperatures the algorithm only exploits a promising region of the solution space, intensifying the search. In order to update T, a cooling schedule [23] is used (line 18) and it is applied after a certain number of iterations (k) given by the Markov Chain Length (MCL) (line 17). Finally, SA ends the search when the total evaluation number is reached or the $T \neq 0$.

Most features in SA, such as search space, perturbation operator, and cost (evaluation) function, are fixed by the problem definition. The only feature that is variable during the process is the temperature. Therefore one of the most important features in simulated annealing is the choice of the annealing schedule, and many attempts have been made to derive or suggest good schedules [24]. In this work, we study the behavior of the most known cooling process in the literature to solve the Multi-Period WDND optimization problem, arising three new HSA variants as explained in the following.

– HSA_{Prop} applies the proportional cooling scheme, also called geometric schedule [23], in order to reduce the temperature, as the Eq. 6 shows:

$$T_{k+1} = \alpha * T_k \tag{6}$$

where α is a constant close to, but smaller than, 1. Particularly, we calculate α as follows:

$$\alpha = \frac{k}{k+1} \tag{7}$$

This scheme is the most popular cooling function because, the temperature decay is not too slow neither too fast allowing to achieve an equilibrium between exploitation and exploration.

– HSA_{Exp} uses the exponential cooling scheme [23] to produce the temperature decay. The Eq. 8 describes these process, where the constant $\alpha^k < 1$ is calculated in the Eq. 9. This schedule quickly cools the temperature reducing the required time and iterations to converge to a good solution. In big and complex problems, this becomes in a disadvantage, given that the equilibrium between the exploitation and exploration is broken.

$$T_{k+1} = T_k * \alpha^k \tag{8}$$

$$\alpha^k = \frac{e^k}{e^{1+k}} \tag{9}$$

Table 2. Information on the HydroGen networks.

Network	Meshedness coefficient	Pipes	Demand nodes	Water reservoirs	Network	Meshedness coefficient	Pipes	Demand nodes	Water reservoirs
HG-MP-1	0.2	100	73	1	HG-MP-9	0.1	295	247	2
HG-MP-2	0.15	100	78	1	HG-MP-10	0.2	397	285	2
HG-MP-3	0.1	99	83	1	HG-MP-11	0.15	399	308	2
HG-MP-4	0.2	198	143	1	HG-MP-12	0.1	395	330	3
HG-MP-5	0.15	200	155	1	HG-MP-13	0.2	498	357	2
HG-MP-6	0.1	198	166	1	HG-MP-14	0.15	499	385	3
HG-MP-7	0.2	299	215	2	HG-MP-15	0.1	495	413	3
HG-MP-8	0.15	300	232	2					

– **HSA_{Log} employs the logarithmic cooling scheme** [25], which modifies the temperature, as shown in Eq. 10. In this Equation, the chain converges to a global and minimal energy value, where the constant C is computed as the Eq. 11 shows. This schedule is too slow to be applied in practice but has the property of the convergence proof to a global optimum [26].

$$T_{k+1} = C * T_k \tag{10}$$

$$C = \frac{ln(k)}{ln(1+k)} \tag{11}$$

Furthermore, we propose a fourth HSA variant, named HSA_{Rand}. This new variant combines the three previous explained cooling schemes in only one schedule process. In each iteration, HSA$_{Rand}$ randomly selects one of these schemes in order to reduce the temperature. In this way, we try to enhance the HSA by aggregating the advantages of these three schemes and mitigating their disadvantages.

4   Experimental Design

In this section, we introduce the experimental design used in this approach, the execution environment, and the result analysis. In order to evaluate HSA, the HydroGen instances of WDND optimization problem [27] are solved. These instances, HG-MP-i, arise from 15 different distribution networks (see Table 2). A set of 16 different pipe types is used and their characteristics and costs can be found in Table 3. The demand nodes are divided into five categories (domestic, industrial, energy, public services, and commercial demand nodes), each one with a corresponding base load and demand pattern[1]. In this way, five different instances are considered for each HG-MP-i network, totalling 75 instances.

The computational environment used in this work to carry out the experimentation consists of computers with INTEL I7 3770 K quad-core processors 3.5 GHz, 8 GB RAM, and the Slackware Linux with 3.2.29 kernel version.

---

[1] The base loads can be found in the EPANET input files of the instances.

Table 3. Available pipe types and their corresponding costs.

Number	Diam. (mm)	Roughness	Cost	Number	Diameter	Roughness	Cost
1	20	130	15	9	200	130	116
2	30	130	20	10	250	130	150
3	40	130	25	11	300	130	201
4	50	130	30	12	350	130	246
5	60	130	35	13	400	130	290
6	80	130	38	14	500	130	351
7	100	130	50	15	600	130	528
8	150	130	61	16	1,000	130	628

Because of the stochastic nature of the algorithms, we performed 30 independent runs of each instance to gather meaningful experimental data and apply statistical confidence metrics to validate our results and conclusions. As a result, a total of 9000 executions ($75 \times 4 \times 30$) were carried out. Before performing the statistical tests, we first checked whether the data followed a normal distribution by applying the Shapiro-Wilks test. Where the data was distributed normally, we later applied an ANOVA test. Otherwise, we used the Kruskal–Wallis (KW) test. This statistical study allows us to assess whether or not there were meaningful differences between the compared algorithms with a confidence level of 99%.

5   Analysis of the Results Obtained by Our Proposals

In this section, we summarize and analyze the results of using the four proposed HSA's variants (HSA_{Prop}, HSA_{Exp}, HSA_{Log}, and HSA_{Rand}) on all the problem instances, following the next methodology. First, we analyze the behavior of these variants considering the results shown in the Table 4. The columns 2–5 show the average of the best cost values found by these four variants for the 75 instances grouped by their corresponding distribution network. The minimal cost values found by each group are boldfaced. In the last column, the results of the Kruskall-Wallis test are summarized, where the symbol "+" indicates that the behavior of the four HSA's variants are statistically similar, while the symbol "-" specifies that these behaviors are significantly different. Secondly, we analyze the temperature decay for each proposed HSA taking into account the variation of the temperature parameter during the search, as shown in the Fig. 2.

Regarding the quality point of view, HSA_{Prop} finds the best cost in many more instances than the rest of variants, i.e. HSA_{Prop} achieves the best solutions in eight instances, followed by HSA_{Exp} with three, HSA_{Rand} with two, and HSA_{Log} with only one instance (see the boldfaced values in the Table 4). These differences between the behaviors are supported by the KW results, which indicate that the cooling schemes drive the search in significant different ways,

Table 4. Averages of the best cost values found by each proposed variant, which are grouped by network.

Network	HSA$_{Prop}$	HSA$_{Exp}$	HSA$_{Log}$	HSA$_{Rand}$	KW
HG-MP-1	**335882,80**	338817,60	338223,00	338250,60	–
HG-MP-2	298842,40	304934,80	298651,80	**297241,60**	–
HG-MP-3	387088,80	**371490,40**	386142,80	386133,60	–
HG-MP-4	**690033,40**	698058,60	691564,60	697496,40	–
HG-MP-5	722217,60	722878,00	**718754,80**	724301,00	–
HG-MP-6	**741638,20**	747825,80	751994,80	742786,60	–
HG-MP-7	817261,80	825763,40	831011,80	**812428,20**	–
HG-MP-8	**855478,60**	862003,00	867300,00	866820,20	–
HG-MP-9	**834821,40**	841512,20	842372,60	845829,40	–
HG-MP-10	**788422,20**	796010,80	801549,60	809821,60	–
HG-MP-11	**909037,80**	915537,80	915997,20	912114,80	–
HG-MP-12	1046426,00	**1043728,20**	1054274,40	1058030,60	–
HG-MP-13	**1179568,00**	1196634,00	1190972,00	1189460,00	–
HG-MP-14	**1085194,80**	1092782,40	1087786,20	1087889,40	–
HG-MP-15	1161200,00	**1155254,00**	1166694,00	1170664,00	–

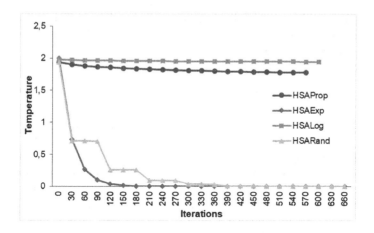

Fig. 2. Average temperature decay during the search.

strengthening the search when the proportional scheme is used. This scheme produces a temperature decay that allow an adequate exploration at the beginning, enabling a greater exploitation at the ending of the search.

If the Fig. 2 is analyzed, no quick temperature convergence to zero is observed when HSA$_{Prop}$ and HSA$_{Log}$ are executed, but the temperature decay is greater in the first one. This last property is the reason of the HSA$_{Prop}$'s success to find the minimal cost values in more than 50% of the instances. Conversely, regarding

Table 5. Average of the best TIC values obtained by ILS and HSA$_{Prop}$ for all instances grouped by the corresponding network. The best values are boldfaced.

Network	ILS	HSA$_{\text{Prop}}$	Network	ILS	HSA$_{\text{Prop}}$
HG-MP-1	339200	**335883**	HG-MP-9	**831200**	834821
HG-MP-2	303800	**298842**	HG-MP-10	790600	**788422**
HG-MP-3	389200	**387089**	HG-MP-11	**907000**	909038
HG-MP-4	694200	**690033**	HG-MP-12	1022800	1046426
HG-MP-5	728200	**722218**	HG-MP-13	1190400	**1179568**
HG-MP-6	750400	**741638**	HG-MP-14	**1070200**	1085195
HG-MP-7	818000	**817262**	HG-MP-15	**1122600**	1161200
HG-MP-8	**851600**	855479			

HSA$_{Exp}$ and HSA$_{Rand}$, the temperature converges quickly to values close to zero restricting the exploration at the beginning of the search, although HSA$_{Exp}$ outperforms HSA$_{Rand}$ when the solution quality is analysed. It is remarkable that, the stop condition is achieved by all HSA's variants when the number of evaluations (EPANET calls) is equal to 1,500,000 but the temperature remains greater than zero.

Summarizing, the proportional cooling scheme allows HSA$_{Prop}$ outperforms the remaining HSA's variants, by balancing the exploitation and exploration during the search. As a consequence, HSA$_{Prop}$ obtains the best networks designs doing the same computational effort than the others variants.

6   Comparison of HSA$_{Prop}$ and the Literature Approaches

Regarding that HSA$_{Prop}$ obtained the best results, we select this variant to compare its performance with the ILS proposed in [20]. This metaheuristic is chosen from literature for this comparison, since its authors also used the HydroGen instances to test it. In this way, our results can be compared with ones of the state-of-the-art, allowing to know the level of quality reached by our proposal.

The methodology used to analyze the results is described in the following. First, we study the HSA behavior comparing the best cost values found by HSA$_{Prop}$ and ILS [20] for the 75 instances, grouped by their corresponding distribution network, as presented in the Table 5. Secondly, we analyze the HSA$_{Prop}$ convergence, in comparison with ILS, taking into account the cost values found at the 1e+05, 3e+05, 5e+05, 10e+05, and 15e+05 EPANET calls (evaluations), as shown in the Fig. 3. Besides, the HSA's execution times (in seconds) to carry out the maximum number of evaluations for each test case, grouped by network, are shown in the Fig. 4. Note that, we only present the HSA's total execution time for all test cases, because no data about this metric are reported by De Corte and Sörensen in [20].

Analyzing the Table 5, we detect that HSA_{Prop} finds solutions with less TIC values than the ones of ILS in nine networks. As a consequence, in 60% of the problem instances better cost values are found when they are solved by HSA_{Prop}. The HSA advantage arises out of the Boltzmann probability application to accept high TIC values, which allows to diversify the search to escape from local optima.

From the convergence point of view, we observe that HSA_{Prop} finds solutions with TIC values near to the best ones in 80% of the instances, with only 1e+05 evaluations. Instead, ILS needs at least 3e+05 evaluations for that, besides this is achieved in only 66% of the test cases.

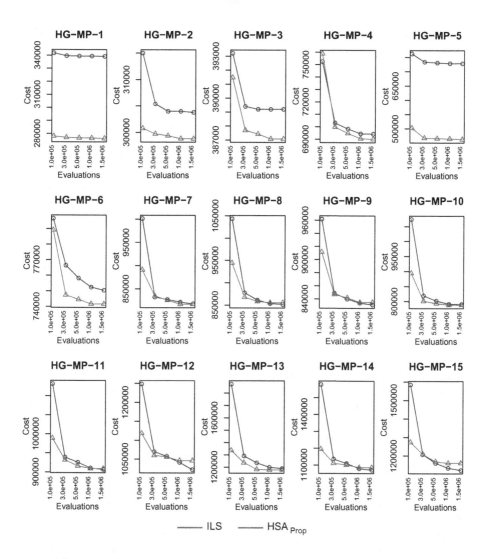

Fig. 3. Evolution of the TIC values during the search for all instances.

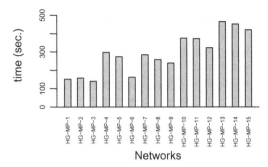

Fig. 4. Average of the total HSA$_{Prop}$ execution times for all instances grouped by the corresponding network.

Evaluating both the Fig. 4 and the Table 2 together, we notice that the HSA's execution time is affected by the number of pipes and demand nodes. In this way, five groups of three networks can be formed exhibiting similar execution times. These instances have consecutive numbers, e.g. the set of the HG-MP-1, 2, and 3 networks have similar number of pipes and demand nodes, and so on. Being the set formed by the HG-MP-13, 14, and 15 networks the most expensive cases to solve. Furthermore, analyzing what happened into each set of networks, the network with more demand nodes consumes less execution time than the other two, since more feasible solutions exist and HSA needs less time to find one of them.

Summarizing, HSA$_{Prop}$ outperforms ILS for the 60% of the problem instances when the result quality is considered. Moreover, a quick convergence to good solutions is also evidenced by our proposal in most of the problem instances. Furthermore, the HSA's runtime is affected by the growing and combination of the number of pipes and demand nodes.

7   Conclusions

In this paper, we have proposed water distribution network designs considering the multi-period settings with time varying demand patterns. The technique proposed to obtain these network designs is a hybrid Simulated Annealing algorithm, called HSA, which solves the hydraulic equations by using the EPANET 2.0 toolkit. HSA combines an WDND-adapted SA with the MP-GRASP local search [20]. Furthermore, four different HSA's variants (HSA$_{Prop}$, HSA$_{Exp}$, HSA$_{Log}$, and HSA$_{Rand}$) have been created by applying the proportional, exponential, logarithmic, and random cooling schemes respectively. For this study, we have tested 75 instances that come from 15 different HydroGen networks.

An important point is that all the proposed HSA's variants had an equivalent computational effort, because all of them carried out the same number of evaluations. In this context HSA$_{Prop}$, the algorithm that uses the proportional cooling scheme to reduce the temperature, found the best networks designs outperforming the remaining proposals.

Moreover, HSA_{Prop}'s results were compared with the obtained by the ILS proposed in [20] to solve this problem. As a consequence, we observed that this HSA variant also outperformed the results obtained by ILS in more than half (60%) of instances. Additionally, HSA achieved a better exploration than ILS, because of the Boltzmann probability application to accept solutions that can explore new areas of the search space. This advantage combined with the local search allowed HSA to converge quickly on the best solutions.

For future works, we will improve the HSA to solve the multi-period WDND optimization problem, by introducing changes in the initialization method of the temperature. We are also interested in testing larger dimension instances, as close as possible to real scenarios.

Acknowledgments. The authors acknowledge the support of Universidad Nacional de La Pampa and the Incentive Program from MINCyT. The second author is also funded by CONICET.

References

1. Yates, D.F., Templeman, A.B., Boffey, T.B.: The computational complexity of the problem of determining least capital cost designs for water supply networks. Eng. Optim. **7**(2), 143–155 (1984)
2. Alperovits, A., Shamir, U.: Design of optimal water distribution systems. Water Resour. Res. **13**(6), 885–900 (1977)
3. Kessler, A., Shamir, U.: Analysis of the linear programming gradient method for optimal design of water supply networks. Water Resour. Res. **25**(7), 1469–1480 (1989)
4. Fujiwara, O., Khang, D.: A two-phase decomposition method for optimal design of looped water distribution networks. Water Resour. Res. **26**(4), 539–549 (1990)
5. Duan, N., Mays, L.W., Lansey, K.E.: Optimal reliability-based design of pumping and distribution systems. J. Hydraul. Eng. **116**(2), 249–268 (1990)
6. Loganathan, G., Greene, J., Ahn, T.: Design heuristic for globally minimum cost water-distribution systems. J. Water Res. Plan. Manag. **121**(2), 182–192 (1995)
7. da Conceicao Cunha, M., Sousa, J.: Hydraulic infrastructures design using simulated annealing. J. Infrastruct. Syst. **7**(1), 32–39 (2001)
8. da Conceicao Cunha, M., Ribeiro, L.: Tabu search algorithms for water network optimization. Eur. J. Oper. Res. **157**(3), 746–758 (2004)
9. Maier, H.R., et al.: Ant colony optimization for design of water distribution systems. J. Water Resour. Plan. Manag. **129**(3), 200–209 (2003)
10. Zecchin, A.C., Simpson, A.R., Maier, H.R., Nixon, J.B.: Parametric study for an ant algorithm applied to water distribution system optimization. IEEE Transact. Evol. Comput. **9**(2), 175–191 (2005)
11. Dandy, G.C., Simpson, A.R., Murphy, L.J.: An improved genetic algorithm for pipe network optimization. Water Resour. Res. **32**(2), 449–458 (1996)
12. Gupta, I., Gupta, A., Khanna, P.: Genetic algorithm for optimization of water distribution systems. Environ. Model. Softw. **14**(5), 437–446 (1999)

13. Bi, W., Dandy, G.C., Maier, H.R.: Improved genetic algorithm optimization of water distribution system design by incorporating domain knowledge. Environ. Model. Softw. **69**, 370–381 (2015)
14. Lin, M.-D., Liu, Y.-H., Liu, G.-F., Chu, C.-W.: Scatter search heuristic for least-cost design of water distribution networks. Eng. Optim. **39**(7), 857–876 (2007)
15. Vasan, A., Simonovic, S.P.: Optimization of water distribution network design using differential evolution. J. Water Resour. Plan. Manag. **136**(2), 279–287 (2010)
16. Farmani, R., Walters, G.A., Savic, D.A.: Trade-off between total cost and reliability for anytown water distribution network. J. Water Resour. Plan. Manag. **131**(3), 161–171 (2005)
17. Bragalli, C., D'Ambrosio, C., Lee, J., Lodi, A., Toth, P.: On the optimal design of water distribution networks: a practical MINLP approach. Optim. Eng. **13**(2), 219–246 (2012)
18. Uma, R.: Optimal design of water distribution network using differential evolution. Int. J. Sci. Res. (IJSR) **5**(11), 1515–1520 (2016)
19. Mansouri, R., Mohamadizadeh, M.: Optimal design of water distribution system using central force optimization and differential evolution. Int. J. Optim. Civil Eng. **7**(3), 469–491 (2017). http://ijoce.iust.ac.ir/article-1-310-en.html
20. De Corte, A., Sörensen, K.: An iterated local search algorithm for water distribution network design optimization. Network **67**(3), 187–198 (2016)
21. Bermudez, C.A., Minetti, G.F., Salto, C.: SA to optimize the multi-period water distribution network design. In: XXIX Congreso Argentino de Ciencias de la Computación, CACIC 2018, pp. 12–21 (2018)
22. Rossman, L.A.: The EPANET Programmer's Toolkit for Analysis of Water Distribution Systems (1999)
23. Kirkpatrick, S., Jr, C.G., Vecchi, M.: Optimization by simulated annealing. Science **220**, 671–680 (1983)
24. Talbi, E.-G.: Metaheuristics: From Design to Implementation. Wiley, Hoboken (2009)
25. Hajek, B.: Cooling schedules for optimal annealing. Math. Oper. Res. **13**(2), 311–329 (1988)
26. Geman, S., Geman, D.: Stochastic relaxation, Gibbs distributions, and the Bayesian restoration of images. IEEE Trans. Pattern Anal. Mach. Intell. **6**(6), 721–741 (1984). https://doi.org/10.1109/TPAMI.1984.4767596
27. De Corte, A., Sörensen, K.: Hydrogen. http://antor.uantwerpen.be/hydrogen. Accessed on 27 June 2018

Distributed and Parallel Processing

Checkpoint and Restart: An Energy Consumption Characterization in Clusters

Marina Morán[1]([✉]), Javier Balladini[1], Dolores Rexachs[2], and Emilio Luque[2]

[1] Facultad de Informática, Universidad Nacional del Comahue,
Buenos Aires 1400, 8300 Neuquén, Argentina
`marina@fi.uncoma.edu.ar`
[2] Departamento de Arquitectura de Computadores y Sistemas Operativos,
Universitat Autònoma de Barcelona, Campus UAB, Edifici Q,
08193 Bellaterra (Barcelona), Spain

Abstract. The fault tolerance method currently used in High Performance Computing (HPC) is the rollback-recovery method by using checkpoints. This, like any other fault tolerance method, adds an additional energy consumption to that of the execution of the application. The objective of this work is to determine the factors that affect the energy consumption of the computing nodes on homogeneous cluster, when performing checkpoint and restart operations, on SPMD (Single Program Multiple Data) applications. We have focused on the energetic study of compute nodes, contemplating different configurations of hardware and software parameters. We studied the effect of performance states (states P) and power states (states C) of processors, application problem size, checkpoint software (DMTCP) and distributed file system (NFS) configuration. The results analysis allowed to identify opportunities to reduce the energy consumption of checkpoint and restart operations.

Keywords: Checkpoint · Restart · Energy consumption · Power ·
Fault tolerance methods

1 Introduction

High Performance Computing (HPC) continues to increase its computing power while increasing its energy consumption. Given the limitations that exist to supply energy to this type of computers, it is necessary to know the behavior of energy consumption in these systems, to find ways to limit and decrease it. In particular, for the exaescala era, a maximum limit of 20 MW is estimated [6].

The fault tolerance method most currently used in HPC is the rollback-recovery method by using checkpoints. This, like any other fault tolerance

This research has been supported by the Agencia Estatal de Investigación (AEI), Spain and the Fondo Europeo de Desarrollo Regional (FEDER) UE, under contract TIN2017-84875-P and partially funded by a research collaboration agreement with the Fundacion Escuelas Universitarias Gimbernat (EUG).

P. Pesado and C. Aciti (Eds.): CACIC 2018, CCIS 995, pp. 19–33, 2019.
https://doi.org/10.1007/978-3-030-20787-8_2

method, adds an additional energy consumption to the execution of the application [6]. Due to this, it is important to know and predict the energy behavior of fault tolerance methods, in order to manage their impact on the total energy consumption during the execution of an application.

The objective of this work, which is an extension of [15], is to determine the factors that affect the energy consumption of checkpoint and restart operations (C/R), on Single Program Multiple Data (SPMD) applications on homogeneous cluster, contemplating different configurations of hardware and software parameters. A cluster system has compute nodes, storage nodes, and at least one interconnection network. We have focused on the energetic study of computing nodes, and we have extended the previous work contemplating, on the one hand, a second experimentation platform, and on the other hand, the storage node, in particular when studying the impact of checkpoint files compression. The energy consumption of the network is not considered in this article.

The contributions of this article are:

- A study of the system's own factors (hardware and software) and of applications factors that impact the energy consumption produced by checkpoint and restart operations.
- The identification of opportunities to reduce the energy consumption of checkpoint and restart operations.

Section 2 presents some related works, while in Sect. 3 the factors that affect the energy consumption are identified. Section 4 mention the experimental platform and the design of experiments, whose results and their analysis are presented in the Sect. 5. Finally, the conclusions and future work can be found in the Sect. 6.

2   Related Work

[5] and [4] evaluates the energetic behavior of the coordinated and uncoordinated C/R with message logs. In [4] they also evaluate the parallel recovery and propose an analytic model to predict the behavior of these protocols at exascale. In [3] they use an analytic model to compare the execution time and the consumed energy of the replication and the coordinated C/R. [1] and [7] presents an analytic model to estimate the optimal interval of a multilevel checkpoint in terms of energy consumption. They do not measure dissipated power but use values from other publications. In [16] they measure the power dissipated and the execution time of the high level operations involved in checkpoint (coordinated, uncoordinated and hierarchical) varying the number of cores involved. They do not use different processor frequencies, nor do they indicate whether the checkpoint is compressed or not. In [8], [9] and [10] a framework for energy saving of the C/R are presented. In [8], many small I/O operations are replaced by a few large, single-core operations to make the checkpoint and restart more energy efficient. They use RAPL to measure and limit energy consumption. [9] propose to have a core to execute a replica of all the processes of the node in order to avoid

re-execution from the last checkpoint and analytically compare the energy consumption of this proposal with the traditional checkpoint. In [10] a runtime that allows modifying the clock frequency and the number of processes that carry out the I/O operations of the C/R are designed, in order to optimize the energy consumption. Another work that analyze the impact of the dynamic scaling of frequency and voltage on the energy consumption of checkpoint operations is in [2]. They measure the power at the component level while writing the checkpoint locally and remotely and compare variations in remote storage: NFS using the kernel network stack and NFS using the IB RDMA interface. [11] evaluate the energy consumption of an application that uses compressed checkpoints. They show that when using compression, more energy is spent but time is saved, so that the complete execution of the application with all its checkpoints can be benefited from an energy point of view.

Our work focuses on coordinated C/R at the system level. The dissipated power of the checkpoint and restart operations are measurements obtained with an external physical meter. We have not found papers that evaluate the impact of C states and NFS configurations on the energy consumption of C/R operations.

3 Factors that Affect the Energy Consumption

Energy can be calculated as the product between power and time. Any factor that may affect one of these two parameters should be considered and then analyze how it affects energy consumption. These factors belong to different levels: Hardware, Application Software and System Software.

3.1 Hardware

The Advanced Configuration and Power Interface (ACPI) specification provides an open standard that allows the operating system to manage the power of the devices and the entire computing system [17]. It allows managing the energy behavior of the processor, the component that consumes the most energy in a computer system [12]. ACPI defines Processor Power States (Cx states), where C0 is the execution state, and C1...Cx are inactive states.

A processor that is in the C0 state will also be in a Performance State (Px states). The status P0 means an execution at the maximum capacity of performance and power demand. As the number of state P increases, its performance and demanded power is reduced. Processors implement P states using the Dynamic Frequency and Voltage Scaling technique (DVFS) [13]. Reducing the voltage supplied reduces the energy consumption. However, the delay of the logic gates is increased, so it is necessary to reduce the clock frequency of the CPU so that the circuit works correctly. In certain multicore processors, each core is allowed to be in a different P state.

When there are no instructions to execute, the processor can be put in a C state greater than 0 to save energy. There are different C state levels, where each of the levels could turn off certain clocks, reduce certain voltages supplied to idle components, turn off the cache memory, etc. The higher the C state number, the lower the power demanded, but the higher the latency required to return to state C0 (execution status). Some processors allow the choice of a C state per core.

As both states, C and P, have an impact on power and time, it is necessary to evaluate their impact on energy consumption during C/R operations.

The GNU/Linux kernel supports frequency scaling through the subsystem CPUFreq (CPU Frequency scaling). This subsystem includes the scaling governors and the scaling drivers. The different scaling governors represent different policies for the P states. The available scaling governors are: performance (this causes the highest frequency defined by the policy), power save (this causes the lowest frequency defined by the policy), userspace (the user defines frequency), schedutil (this uses CPU utilization data available from the CPU scheduler), ondemand (this uses CPU load as a CPU frequency selection metric) and conservative (same as ondemand but it avoids changing the frequency significantly over short time intervals which may not be suitable for systems with limited power supply capacity). The scaling drivers provide information to the scaling governors about the available P states and make the changes in those states[1]. In this work we use userspace and ondemand governors.

3.2   Application Software

Basically, a checkpoint consists in saving the state of an application, so that in case of failure it can restart the execution from that saved point. The larger the problem size of the application, the longer the time required to save its state. Its incidence, at least over time, converts problem size into a factor that affects the energy consumption of C/R operations.

3.3   System Software

There are two types of system software highly involved in C/R operations. On the one hand, the system that carry out these operations. On the other hand, since the checkpoint file needs to be protected in stable and remote storage, it is necessary to use a distributed file system. In our case, the system software we use is Distributed MultiThreaded CheckPointing (DMTCP) [14] and Network File System (NFS). Both have configuration options that affect the execution time and/or power, and therefore are factors that affect the energy consumption of the C/R operations.

In the NFS case, folders can be mounted synchronously (sync option) or asynchronously (async option). If an NFS folder is mounted with the sync option, writes at that mount point will cause the data to be completely downloaded to the NFS server, and written to persistent storage before returning control to the client[2]. Thus, the time of a write operation is affected by varying this configuration.

In the case of DMTCP, it is a tool that performs checkpoints transparently on a group of processes spread among many nodes and connected by sockets,

---

[1] https://www.kernel.org/doc/html/v4.14/admin-guide/pm/cpufreq.html.
[2] https://linux.die.net/man/5/nfs.

as is the case with MPI (Message Passing Interface) applications. DMTCP is able to compress (using the gzip program) the state of a process to require less disk storage space and reduce the amount of data transmitted over the network (between the compute node and the storage node). The use or not of compression impacts the time and the power required, therefore it is another factor that affects energy consumption.

4   Experimental Platforms and Design

4.1   Experimental Platform

The experiments were carried out on two platforms. Platform 1, on which most of the analysis of this work is carried out, is a cluster of computers with a 1 Gbps Ethernet network. Each node, both computing and storage, has 4 GiB of main memory, a SATA hard disk of 500 GB and 7200 rpm, and an Intel Core i5-750 processor, with a frequency range of 1.2 GHz to 2.66 GHz (with the Intel Turbo Boost[3] disabled), four cores (without multithreading), 8 MiB of cache and 95 W TDP. The clock frequency range goes from 1.199 GHz. to 2.667 GHz. Platform 2 is a compute node connected to a storage node with a 1 Gbps Ethernet network. The compute node has an Intel Xeon E5-2630 processor, a frequency range of 1.2 GHz to 2.801 GHz (with the Intel Turbo Boost mechanism disabled), six cores (with multithreading disabled), 16 GiB of main memory, 15 MiB of cache and TDP of 95 W. It uses a Debian 9 Stretch operating system. The storage computer has an Intel Core 2 Quad Q6600 processor, four cores (without multithreading), 8 GiB of main memory and 4 MiB of cache memory. The clock frequency range goes from 1.2 GHz to 2.801 GHz.

The nodes of Platform 1 and the computing node of Platform 2 use the GNU/Linux operating system Debian 8.2 Jessie (kernel version 3.16 of 64 bits), OpenMPI version 1.10.1 as an MPI message passing library, and the tool checkpoint DMTCP version 2.4.2, configured to compress the checkpoint files. The network file system used to make the remote writing of the checkpoint files is NFS v4 (Network File System).

For power measurements we use the PicoScope 2203 oscilloscope (whose accuracy is 3%), the TA041 active differential probe, and the PP264 60 A AC/DC current clamp, all Pico Technology products. The electrical signals captured by the two-channel oscilloscope are transmitted in real time to a computer through a USB connection. The voltage is measured using the TA041 probe that is connected to an input channel of the oscilloscope. The current of the phase conductor, which provides energy to the complete node (including the power source) is measured using the current clamp PP264, which is connected to the other input channel of the oscilloscope.

The selected application[4] for system characterization is a SPMD heat transfer application written in MPI that uses the float data type. This application

---

[3]   https://www.intel.com/content/www/us/en/architecture-and-technology/turbo-boost/turbo-boost-technology.html.

[4]   https://computing.llnl.gov/tutorials/parallel_comp/#ExamplesHeat.

describes, by means of an equation, the change of temperature in time over a plane, given an initial temperature distribution and certain edge conditions.

4.2 Experimental Design

Two compute nodes are used (unless otherwise specified) and each compute node writes to a dedicated storage node through an NFS configured in asynchronous mode (unless otherwise specified). The sampling rate used for both channels of the oscilloscope was set at 1000 Hz. The power measurements correspond to the power dissipated by the complete node including the source. The tests were performed with the processor C states option active (unless otherwise specified). For the measurements of the checkpoint and restart time we use the option provided by DMTCP. To change the frequency of the processor, the userspace governor is used. The same frequency is used in all cores at the same time.

Each experiment consists of launching the application with one process per core, letting it run during a preheating period (20 s), performing a checkpoint manually, aborting the application from the DMTCP coordinator and re-starting the application from the command line with the script generated by DMTCP. The experiment is repeated three times for each frequency and problem size due to the low variability of the measurement instruments used.

5 Experiments and Results Analysis

In this section we show the experiments and analyze how the mentioned factors influence power, time, and energy consumption of CR operations.

The first Subsect. (5.1 to 5.4) analyze the effect of clock frequency (see Subsect. 3.1) and problem size (see Subsect. 3.2) on Platforms 1 and 2. As there are no significant differences between the two platforms for these factors, we have carried out the study of the remaining factors, NFS configuration and compression of the checkpoint files (Subsects. 5.5 and 5.6) only on Platform 1. We understand that these last factors are influenced mainly by the network, which is the same in both platforms.

5.1 Real Power

In order to know the energy we need to know the average power dissipated of each operation. Figure 1 shows the real power on both Platforms, obtained with the measurements delivered by the oscilloscope, when an application is executed, a checkpoint is done, a fault is injected, and a restart is initiated. These power measurements are averaged over the duration of the checkpoint and restart operation. In the rest of the work, when referring to dissipated power, we refer to the average dissipated power.

Platform 2, unlike Platform 1, has two high phases and two low phases during the checkpoint. To know what happened in those phases we measured the CPU and network usage in both platforms, which is shown in Fig. 2. When observing

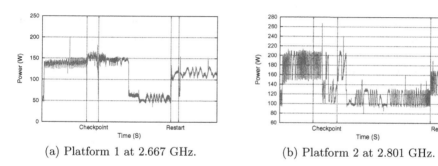

(a) Platform 1 at 2.667 GHz.   (b) Platform 2 at 2.801 GHz.

Fig. 1. Power dissipation during checkpoint and restart.

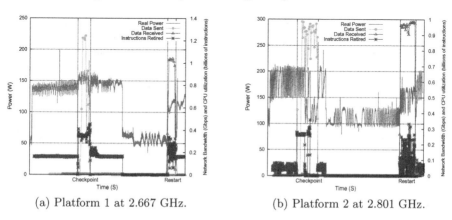

(a) Platform 1 at 2.667 GHz.   (b) Platform 2 at 2.801 GHz.

Fig. 2. Power dissipation, network bandwidth and CPU utilization during checkpoint and restart.

the use of CPU, we see that the high power phases coincide with a higher CPU usage, and that low phases coincide with a low CPU usage. During a checkpoint, the CPU is used to compress. From this it follows that in Platform 2, DMTCP, at times, stops compressing. When observing the use of the network, we see that on both platforms the transmission begins a few seconds after the checkpoint has started and continues until the end of the checkpoint. We also note that in the first low phase of Platform 2, the transmission rate drops by half, causing inefficient use of the network. Studying these inefficiencies could be part of future work. In the case of the restart, the transmission rate remains stable throughout its duration, on both platforms.

5.2   Processor's P States

The impact of processor's P states on the C/R operations energy consumption was evaluated. The Figs. 3 and 4 show the average dissipated power (a) and time (b) for different frequencies of the processor, on both platforms. It is observed that as the clock frequency increases, the dissipated power increases and the time decreases. The functions obtained are strictly increasing for the case of dissipated power and strictly decreasing for the case of time. It is also observed that the checkpoint is more affected by clock frequency changes, both in the power dissipated and in time.

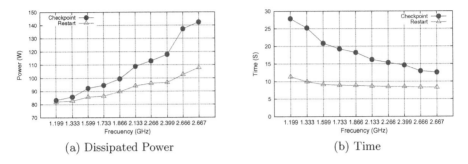

(a) Dissipated Power   (b) Time

Fig. 3. Influence of P states on Platform 1.

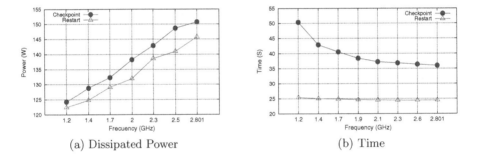

(a) Dissipated Power   (b) Time

Fig. 4. Influence of P states on Platform 2.

5.3   Processor's C States

During the writing or reading of a checkpoint file it is possible that the processor has idle moments and therefore transitions between C states can occur. These transitions can affect the power dissipation of the processor. To study its behavior, C/R operations were performed with the C states enabled and disabled, for several frequencies of the processor, on Platform 1 and 2. The results are shown in the Figs. 5 and 6.

In both platforms it is observed that the power measurements with the C states enabled show greater variability, especially in the restart at Platform 1. It is also observed how the difference between the power dissipated with C states enabled and disabled increases with the increasing frequency of the processor. On Platform 1, this difference becomes approximately 9 % for the checkpoint (at the maximum frequency), and 10% for the restart (at the frequency 2.533 GHz).

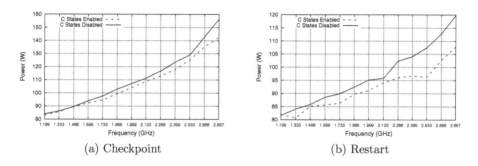

(a) Checkpoint   (b) Restart

Fig. 5. Influence of C states on power dissipation - Platform 1.

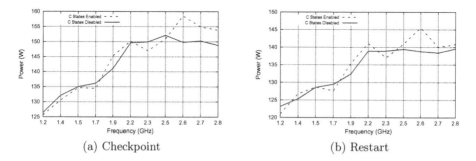

(a) Checkpoint   (b) Restart

Fig. 6. Influence of C states on power dissipation - Platform 2.

In Platform 2 these differences are smaller, 6% for the checkpoint, and 5% for the restart, in the frequency 2.6 GHz in both cases.

The consumption of energy is mainly benefited by the use of C states. On Platform 1, for the checkpoint case, the consumption is up to 13% higher when the C states are disabled, and in the restart case, up to 20% higher. On Platform 2 these differences are smaller, up to 5%, except for the 1.4 GHz frequency, where the differences are greater than 15%, both for checkpoint and restart.

In any case, the best option is to keep the C states enabled since they reduce the energy consumption by up to 13% for the checkpoint, and up to 20% for the restart, at certain CPU frequencies. Times showed no variation when enabling or disabling the C states.

5.4   Problem Size

The impact of the problem size on energy consumption of C/R operations was evaluated. The power dissipated and the time of the checkpoint and restart were measured, for different problem sizes, on both platforms.

Problem sizes do not exceed the main memory available in the compute node. In the Figs. 7(a) and 8(a) it is observed that the power dissipated almost does not vary when varying the problem size (the differences do not exceed 4% in any case). In the Figs. 7(b) and 8(b) it is observed that the time increases as the problem size increases, as expected.

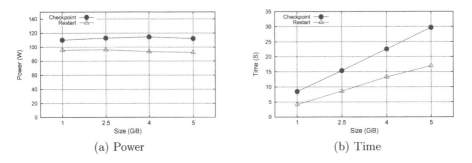

(a) Power   (b) Time

Fig. 7. Influence of problem size on Platform 1

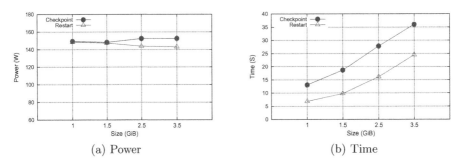

(a) Power   (b) Time

Fig. 8. Influence of problem size on Platform 2

5.5   NFS Configuration

The impact on energy consumption of the use of the NFS sync and async options was evaluated. The Fig. 9 compares the dissipated power, time and energy consumed by a checkpoint stored on a network file system mounted with the option sync and async, for three different clock frequencies (minimum, average and maximum of the processor), on Platform 1. For the three frequencies, the dissipated power is greater and the execution time is shorter when the asynchronous configuration is used. The shortest time is explained by the operating mode of the asynchronous mode, which does not need to wait for the data to be downloaded to the server to advance. The greater dissipated power may be due to the fact that the asynchronous mode decreases idle times of the processor, and therefore C states of energy saving does not activate (see Subsect. 3.1). However, for the minimum and average frequency, these differences are small, resulting in a similar energy consumption, as shown in Fig. 9(c). The asynchronous mode consumes 1.5% more energy at the minimum frequency. It could be said that this configuration of the NFS does not affect the energy consumption when using this frequency. In the medium frequency, the asynchronous mode consumes 7% less energy. If we now observe what happens at the maximum frequency, we see that the asynchronous mode consumes 25% less energy. Although the dissipated power is 37% higher, the time is 85% lower, and this means that at the maximum frequency, it is convenient to use the asynchronous mode for lower energy consumption.

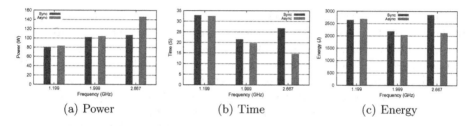

(a) Power   (b) Time   (c) Energy

Fig. 9. Influence of sync/async configuration on power, time and energy consumption during checkpoint

5.6   Checkpoint File Compression

The impact of checkpoint files compression on the energy consumption of the computation node was analyzed, and in this work, we added the study of the storage node. The experiments were performed on a single computation node writing on a storage node, for three different clock frequencies (minimum, average and maximum available in the processor) and for the governor ondemand (see Sect. 3.1), on Platform 1.

The Fig. 10 shows the power and time of checkpoint and restart, with and without compression of the checkpoint files.

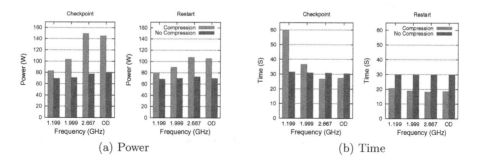

(a) Power   (b) Time

Fig. 10. Influence of compression on power and time.

The results obtained show the following:

- The dissipated power, both in checkpoint and restart, is greater when using compression. This is due to the higher CPU usage that is required to run the compression program (gzip) that DMTCP uses.
- Without compression, checkpoint and restart times almost do not vary for different clock frequencies.

Figure 11 shows the energy consumption of computation and storage nodes. In the case of the storage node, the clock frequencies indicated are the frequencies used by the computing node. Because the application does not share the storage node with other applications, the energy considered for the storage node is calculated using the total dissipated power (base power plus dynamic power). In the computation node, the energy consumption of the checkpoint is always greater when using compression (up to 55% higher in the minimum frequency). In the storage node, the energy consumption of the checkpoint is always lower when using compression, except for the minimum frequency. The energy consumption of the restart is always lower when using compression (up to 20%), both in computing and storage node.

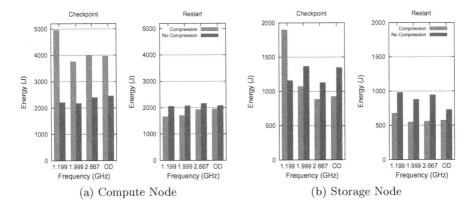

Fig. 11. Influence of compression on energy consumption.

Let's see the total energy consumption, considering both nodes (computation and storage), in Fig. 12. For the checkpoint case, it is never advisable to compress, and even less at the minimum frequency. Although, when no compression is used, the minimum frequency is the most convenient, because it is the one with the lowest energy consumption. In any case, the energy consumption when no compression is used is similar for all frequencies studied, with differences that do not exceed 12%. For the restart case, it is always convenient to compress. When using compression, the lowest energy consumption is obtained with the frequency 1.999 GHz. However, by not using compression, the lowest energy consumption is obtained with the ondemand governor. Studying this behavior can be part of future work.

Taking into account that, in general, more checkpoint operations than restart operations are carried out, it is advisable not to use compression to reduce energy consumption.

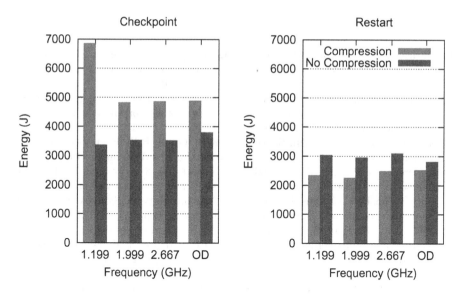

Fig. 12. Total energy consumption: compute node and storage node

6   Conclusions and Future Work

This work shows, from a series of experiments on an homogeneous cluster executing an SPMD application, how different factors of the system and the applications impact in the energy consumption of the C/R coordinated operations using DMTCP. The impact of the P and C states of the processor was studied. It was found that checkpoint operations are more sensitive to changes in P states than restart operations. On the contrary, the changes of the C states of the processor affect more the restart. In the evaluated platforms, the use of C states allows energy savings (up to 15% for the checkpoint and 20% for the restart). The increase in the application problem size under study always results in an increase in energy consumption, due to its high incidence in the time taken by the operations. It was found that by using the maximum clock frequency, up to 25% energy savings was possible when using the asynchronous mode in the NFS configuration. The compression of the checkpoint files is beneficial for the restart. When considering only the computation node, up to 20% of energy saving was registered when using compressed files. However, compression negatively impacts the checkpoint operation, with a 55% higher energy consumption when using the minimum clock frequency. Among the future works it is expected to evaluate other factors that may affect the energy consumption of checkpoint and restart operations, such as the compression program used for checkpoint files, the parallel application programming model and the fault tolerance tool used.

References

1. Amrizal, M.A., Takizawa, H.: Optimizing energy consumption on HPC systems with a multi-level checkpointing mechanism. In: International Conference on Networking, Architecture, and Storage (NAS). IEEE (2017)
2. Mills, B., Grant, R.E., Ferreira, K.B.: Evaluating energy savings for checkpoint/restart. In: Proceedings of the 1st International Workshop on Energy Efficient Supercomputing. ACM (2013)
3. Mills, B., Znati, T., Melhem, R., Ferreira, K.B., Grant, R.E.: Energy consumption of resilience mechanisms in large scale systems. In: 122nd Euromicro International Conference on Parallel, Distributed, and Network-Based Processing. IEEE (2014)
4. Meneses, E., Sarood, O., Kalé, L.V.: Assessing energy efficiency of fault tolerance protocols for HPC systems. In: 2012 IEEE 24th International Symposium on Computer Architecture and High Performance Computing, pp. 35–42. IEEE (2012)
5. Diouri, M., Glück, O., Lefevre, L., Cappello, F.: Energy considerations in checkpointing and fault tolerance protocols. In IEEE/IFIP International Conference on Dependable Systems and Networks Workshops (DSN 2012), June, pp. 1–6. IEEE (2012)
6. Bergman, K., et al.: Exascale computing study: technology challenges in achieving exascale systems. Defense Advanced Research Projects Agency Information Processing Techniques Office (DARPA IPTO), Technical report, 15 (2008)
7. Dauwe, D., Jhaveri, R., Pasricha, S., Maciejewski, A.A., Siegel, H.J.: Optimizing checkpoint intervals for reduced energy use in exascale systems. In: 2017 Eighth International Green and Sustainable Computing Conference (IGSC), October, pp. 1–8. IEEE (2017)
8. Chandrasekar, R.R., Venkatesh, A., Hamidouche, K., Panda, D.K.: Power-check: an energy-efficient checkpointing framework for HPC clusters. In: 2015 15th IEEE/ACM International Symposium on Cluster, Cloud and Grid Computing, May, pp. 261–270. IEEE (2015)
9. Cui, X., Znati, T., Melhem, R.: Adaptive and power-aware resilience for extreme-scale computing. In: International IEEE Conferences on Ubiquitous Intelligence & Computing, Advanced and Trusted Computing, Scalable Computing and Communications, Cloud and Big Data Computing, Internet of People, and Smart World Congress (UIC/ATC/ScalCom/CBDCom/IoP/SmartWorld), July, pp. 671–679. IEEE (2016)
10. Saito, T., Sato, K., Sato, H., Matsuoka, S.: Energy-aware I/O optimization for checkpoint and restart on a NAND flash memory system. In: Proceedings of the 3rd Workshop on Fault-Tolerance for HPC at extreme scale, June, pp. 41–48. ACM (2013)
11. Ferreira, K.B., Ibtesham, D., DeBonis, D., Arnold, D.: Coarse-grained energy modeling of rollback/recovery mechanisms (No. SAND2014-2159C). Sandia National Lab. (SNL-NM), Albuquerque, NM (United States) (2014)
12. Silveira, D.S., Moro, G.B., Cruz, E.H.M., Navaux, P.O.A., Schnorr, L.M., Bampi, S.: Energy consumption estimation in parallel applications: an analysis in real and theoretical models. In: XVII Simposio em Sistemas Computacionais de Alto Desempenho, pp. 134–145 (2016)
13. Le Sueur, E., Heiser, G.: Dynamic voltage and frequency scaling: the laws of diminishing returns. In: Proceedings of the 2010 International Conference on Power Aware Computing and Systems, October, pp. 1–8 (2010)

14. Ansel, J., Arya, K., Cooperman, G.: DMTCP: transparent checkpointing for cluster computations and the desktop. In: 2009 IEEE International Symposium on Parallel & Distributed Processing, May, pp. 1–12. IEEE (2009)
15. Morán, M., Balladini, J., Rexachs, D., Luque E.: Factores que afectan el consumo energético de operaciones de checkpoint y restart en clusters. In: XIX Workshop Procesamiento Distribuido y Paralelo (WPDP), XXIV Congreso Argentino de Ciencias de la Computación, CACIC 2018, pp. 63–72 (2018). ISBN 978-950-658-472-6
16. Diouri, M., Glück, O., Lefevre, L., Cappello, F.: ECOFIT: a framework to estimate energy consumption of fault tolerance protocols for HPC applications. In: 13th IEEE/ACM International Symposium on Cluster, Cloud, and Grid Computing, May, pp. 522–529. IEEE (2013)
17. ACPI - Advanced Configuration and Power Interface. http://www.acpi.info

Energy Consumption Analysis and Time Estimation Model in GPU Cluster and MultiGPU in a High Computational Demand Problem

Erica Montes de Oca[1]($\boxtimes$), Laura De Giusti[1,2], Armando De Giusti[1,3], and Marcelo Naiouf[1]

[1] Computer Science Research Institute LIDI (III LIDI),
School of Computer Science,
National University of La Plata (UNLP) - CICPBA, La Plata, Argentina
{emontesdeoca,ldgiusti,degiusti,
mnaiouf}@lidi.info.unlp.edu.ar
[2] Scientific Research Agency of the Province of Buenos Aires (CICPBA),
La Plata, Argentina
[3] Consejo Nacional de Investigaciones Científicas y Técnicas (CONICET),
La Plata, Buenos Aires, Argentina

Abstract. In this article, the energy used in two GPU clusters and MultiGPU to solve the n-body problem is analyzed. A time estimation model is developed and validated. Solutions are described and results shown, together with a performance and energy consumption analysis for the case study.

Keywords: GPU · GPU cluster · MultiGPU · N-Body · Green Computing · Energy consumption

1 Introduction

The deep changes that came with the progress of technology have impacted the ways in which we communicate. Computer Science and the industry in general have spared no efforts to develop quickly albeit, in most cases, at the expense of environmental deterioration [1].

Nowadays, the generation of large volumes of data requires runtime reductions for the applications processing such data. However, speeding up data processing increases energy consumption [2]. GPUs (Graphics Processing Units) are an option to speed up computation [3]. GPU manufacturers have substantially improved energy efficiency in their graphics cards, even with increased speeds [4]. According to Sumit Gupta, general manger of the Tesla accelerated computing business at NVIDIA, "... *Energy efficiency has become the defining element of computing performance...*" [5].

In recent years, software programmers have grown awareness about the importance of developing algorithms that are more efficient and require a smaller number of resources to execute functions, decreasing energy consumption as a direct consequence [6, 7].

© Springer Nature Switzerland AG 2019
P. Pesado and C. Aciti (Eds.): CACIC 2018, CCIS 995, pp. 34–46, 2019.
https://doi.org/10.1007/978-3-030-20787-8_3

In [8], the performance and energy consumption of the n-body simulation in a GPU cluster and MultiGPU was studied, carrying out one- and three-step simulations. Based on the results obtained, we are proposing here a time estimation model for the case study. Simulation input samples were expanded, which allowed analyzing the energy used by the different architectures tested.

In Sect. 2 below, the basic concepts of Green Computing are introduced. Section 3 describes the simulation of the n-body gravitational attraction problem. Section 4 shows the results obtained in the experiments carried out. Finally, in Sect. 5, our conclusions and future lines of work are presented.

2 Green Computing

The effect of human activity on the environment is reflected on the climate change our planet is undergoing. Indiscriminate greenhouse gas emanations are responsible for global warming [9]. The industries that generate the highest volumes of carbon dioxide (the most common greenhouse gas) are electric power generation, production industries, transportation, commerce and housing [10].

Faced with this environmental challenge, scientists continue to search for alternatives that are not harmful for the environment, focusing on clean technologies [1]. "*Green*" has become a popular term to describe things that are "good" for the environment. The computer science community, computer users in particular, have popularized [11] the concept of *Green Computing,* which involves the efficient use of resources. Its goals are reducing the use of hazardous materials, maximizing energy efficiency during the production life cycle, and promoting product and factory wastes recycling or biodegradation [12].

Either to protect the environment or to reduce energy expenses, energy consumption reduction is present in both the technological and communications industries. Towards this end, a computer system should not only be scalable and reduce processing times, but it should also be efficient as regards energy consumption, reducing power expenses and decreasing environmental impact.

3 GPU Architecture

As a way to reduce application response times, in recent decades General Purpose Graphics Processing Units (GPGPU) have become popular. A GPU is a parallel architecture from its inception, and each new generation doubles the number of cores and increases the number of floating point operations per second [12–14].

CUDA (Compute Unified Device Architecture) is a C-based software-hardware architecture that came to be thanks to NVIDIA in 2007; it was aimed at helping developers work on these architectures.

Nvidia GPU architectures consist of a set of Streaming Multiprocessors (SM) that are in turn formed by several Streaming Processors (SP). Nvidia [14] changes the number of SMs in each new generation, making their performance scalable, and changes the number of DRAM as well, escalating capacity and memory bandwidth.

Each SM provides enough threads, cores and shared memory to run one or more blocks of CUDA threads. The components that are really responsible for the execution are the SPs, which run multiple threads concurrently. Threads are organized into blocks, and in each SM there are one or more blocks running concurrently. Thread organization can be seen by level or hierarchically: Grid, Blocks and Threads.

3.1   GPU Cluster

A GPU cluster is a heterogeneous architecture that has a subsystem consisting of several CPU cores and a memory and I/O system on the one hand, and a GPU subsystem with its on- and off-chip memories on the other. These two subsystems communicate over PCI-E at a low bandwidth speed compared to communication speeds in memory systems. Thus, communication between both subsystems becomes a bottleneck [15].

3.2   MultiGPU

MultiGPU architecture involves using one or more graphics cards on the same PC. In this case, GPUs are easily programmable through CUDA using SLI (Scalable Link Interface), provided by Nvidia [16]. The communication between CPU and GPU occurs via PCI-E, the same as in Sect. 3.1.

4   N-Body: High Computational Demand Problem

The n-body problem was one of the first problems in the scientific world for which a computer was used to find a solution [17]. It consists in simulating the behavior of n bodies in a workspace. In particular, this study is based on gravitational attraction calculation [18].

Newton proposed his *Law of Universal Gravitation* based off the *Theory of Gravitational Attraction*, which states that each body has a mass, an initial position and a speed. Gravity causes bodies to accelerate and move through a force of attraction between them. The magnitude of the gravitational force between two bodies is expressed by Eq. (1):

$$F = \frac{G * m_i * m_j}{r^2} \tag{1}$$

being m the mass, r the distance, and G the gravitational constant ($6,67 \times 10-11$).

4.1   Using a GPU to Solve the Problem

To carry out the simulation, N-sized vectors are used, representing forces, positions, speeds and masses. The algorithm performs the following actions:

1. Calculating the force of attraction for body i, which is determined with N-i bodies. These N-i bodies will in turn be affected by the force of gravity from i.
2. The position of body i is modified, depending on its force of gravity.
3. Steps 1 and 2 are repeated as many times as simulation steps are desired.

Since calculating the force of attraction for each body is an independent process, this can be run in a GPU. Basically, the algorithm for a GPU carries out the following steps:

1. From the CPU, GPU memory is reserved;
2. Data are transferred from the CPU to the GPU;
3. The *kernel* responsible for calculating gravitational attraction forces is executed;
4. Processed data are transferred from the GPU back to the CPU.

4.2   Using a GPU Cluster to Solve the Problem

Running the simulation on a GPU cluster requires using a combination of MPI with CUDA. For each MPI process created, there is an associated GPU. Using a master/slave scheme, the master process is in charge of initializing the information of the bodies to be distributed among the slave processes. The N bodies are distributed to P processes, meaning that each process has to compute a total of N/P elements. Additionally, each process uses PCI-E to send these data to their GPU, which is where the actual computation occurs, since MPI processes merely communicate data between them. Once the GPU has calculated the force of attraction for the bodies assigned to it, it sends the resulting data to the CPU. Then, the MPI process communicates these data to the other processes [6, 19].

4.3   Using a MultiGPU to Solve the Problem

When using MultiGPU, the volume of data that will be processed by each GPU is divided in equal parts. CUDA provides the function `cudaSetDevice(i)` (where i ≤ *T*, *T* being the number of GPUs in a PC) to set GPU affinity in a PC [18]. The calculation of the gravitational attraction force for each of the bodies in the workspace is done following the same method as in the solution explained for a single GPU [20].

5   Experimental Work

The environment used for testing includes the following equipment:

- Multicore cluster with Quad Core Intel i5-2310 2.9 GHz processors, 6 MB cache; each node has one GeForce TX 560TI GPU. CUDA 8.0
- Multicore cluster with Quad Core Intel i5-4460 3.2 GHz processors, 6 MB cache; each node has one GeForce GTX 960 GPU. CUDA 8.0
- PC with Quad Core Intel i5-2310 2.9 GHz processor with two Tesla C2075 GPUs. CUDA 4.2

Using an input size of N = 128000, 256000 and 512000 bodies, a time estimation model is proposed (1) for simulating the calculation of gravitational force attraction on the GPU architectures mentioned above. Measurements were recorded for one, three, and six simulation steps. For the tests, thread blocks with 256 threads each were used for all GPUs. The data obtained are the result of an average of ten runs of the algorithm and measurements of the energy consumption. A set of three scenarios corresponding to the three input sizes was used, repeating the simulation ten times.

Each step of the simulation receives a number of bodies that is constant throughout the process of calculating the gravitational attraction force. The amount of computation carried out during each step is the same. Then, knowing the time required to simulate the calculation of the gravitational force for an input size of N, the simulation time needed for x number of steps will be given by (2).

$$\text{Time}(N) = \text{Time\_1Step}(N) * x + v \tag{2}$$

Being:

N = number of bodies in simulation
Time(N) = simulation execution time, in seconds
Time_1Step(N) = execution time for a step, in seconds
x = number of steps
v = variable term corresponding, for instance, to communication, synchronization delay, etc.

To corroborate the estimation model (1), the times measured are compared to times calculated using the estimation model. Pearson Correlation Coefficient [21] is used to establish the relation between the models.

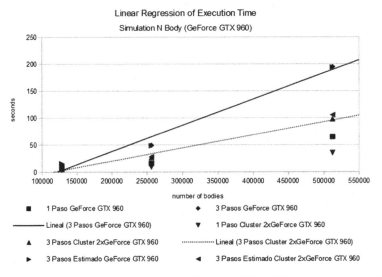

Fig. 1. Execution time linear regression in GeForce GTX 960 and a cluster with two GeForce GTX 960.

As seen in Figs. 1, 2 and 3, the time estimation model is linearly correlated with the times measured, the correlation coefficient being 0.99 in all three cases. To validate the time estimation model (1), execution time was calculated for the 6-step simulation and then compared to the times measured for that number of steps. Table 1 shows the times measured and the times estimated, in seconds, for the simulation using one GPU, the

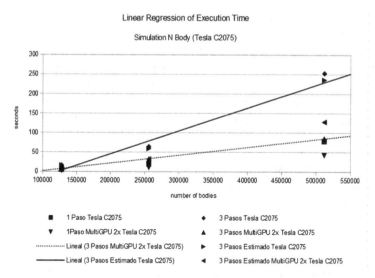

Fig. 2. Execution time linear regression in a Tesla C2075 and a MultiGPU with two Tesla C2075.

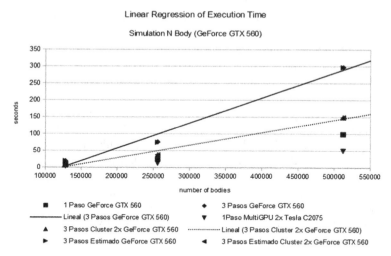

Fig. 3. Execution time linear regression in GeForce GTX 560 and a cluster with two GeForce GTX 560.

clusters and the MultiGPU. In [8, 22], execution times and energy consumption measurements for the same architectures as the ones used here are presented, for simulations with one and three steps.

Table 1. Execution Measured Times (MT) and Estimated Times (ET) for the N-body simulation, measured in seconds for 6 steps, using one GPU, a cluster with two GeForce GTX 960, a MultiGPU with two Tesla C2075, and a cluster with two GeForce GTX 560.

GPU architectures	128000		256000		512000	
	1 GPU	2 GPU	1 GPU	2 GPU	1 GPU	2 GPU
GeForce GTX 960 (MT)	26.08	18.61	97.84	55.11	386.59	203.50
GeForce GTX 960 (ET)	31.38	22.14	96.90	56.52	387.78	211.08
Tesla C2075 (MT)	32.18	16.15	127.77	64.41	505.76	255.52
Tesla C2075 (ET)	32.16	16.14	136.44	64.38	545.70	255.48
GeForce GTX 560 (MT)	38.17	17.19	149.47	74.87	594.71	298.69
GeForce GTX 560 (ET)	35.52	20.76	149.22	74.88	594.48	298.50
Correlation Coefficient	0.99					

Table 1 shows that there is a correlation between the measured times and the estimated times obtained with (1). Therefore, it can be concluded that the number of steps in the simulation is not dependent on time. Below, the results obtained for input sizes N = 128,000, N = 256,000, N = 512,000 and N = 1,024,000 for a simulation step are presented. Energy measurements were obtained for the simulation runs using the sizes of N mentioned above.

For these measurements, a clamp ammeter (for measuring electrical current, sensibility of 1 A/100 mv, 1 A/10 mv and 1 A/1 mv) and a transformer (measuring voltage at the current outlet) were used. Voltage was measured directly from the power line to which the multicore cluster and the MultiGPU are connected. Both devices are connected to the input channels of an oscilloscope (Rigol DS1074Z, sampling rate of 1GSa/s [23]). To measure consumption, 2 channels were used (one for current and one for voltage), storing 12 Mpts in memory.

To analyze the samples obtained for each scenario, the energy consumption analysis application called energyAnalyser [24] was modified.

Using the current and voltage data obtained with the oscilloscope, instant power is calculated. Once obtained, the average power and the Joules used to run the N-body algorithm are calculated.

Table 2 lists simulation execution times for the input sizes of N = 128,000, N = 256,000, N = 512,000 and N = 1,024,000, for one step of the simulation, for one GPU GeForce GTX 960, one Tesla C2075, one GeForce GTX 560, one GPU cluster and the MultiGPU.

Table 2. Execution times for the N-body simulation, measured in seconds, using one GPU, a cluster with two GeForce GTX 960, a MultiGPU with two Tesla C2075, and a cluster with two GeForce GTX 560.

Number of bodies	GeForce GTX 960	Tesla C2075	GeForce GTX 560	Cluster of 2 GeForce GTX 960	MultiGPU of 2 Tesla C2075	Cluster of 2 GeForce GTX 560
128000	5.23	5.36	6.42	3.69	2.69	3.46
256000	16.16	19.66	24.87	9.42	10.74	12.48
512000	64.64	78.64	99.08	35.18	42.59	49.75
1024000	259.12	337.33	396.04	135.62	168.58	198.17

It can be noted that GeForce GTX 960 requires the least amount of time to run. However, all three GPUs are able to speed up algorithm computation. In previous works, a significant speedup was obtained using GPUs vs. shared memory, distributed memory and hybrid memory models [3, 6].

Parallel algorithms use *speedup* as a performance measurement to measure the behavior of an increased number of processors compared to using only one. The architectures used for these tests are inherently parallel [25]; therefore, this is not the best metric to measure their performance. For this reason, the concept of *speedup* (3) is defined as metric to measure performance when using more than one GPU [6].

$$Aceleración = \frac{Tiempo_{1GPU(N)}}{Tiempo_{+GPU(N)}} \tag{3}$$

In the case of the MultiGPU with two Tesla C2075, Fig. 4 shows that a superlinear speedup is obtained. This is usually due to data splitting: with N data to be processed by one GPU, when there are two GPUs available, data are split into two groups with N/2 data each, i.e., the volume of data to be processed by each GPU is lower, and a superlinear result is obtained.

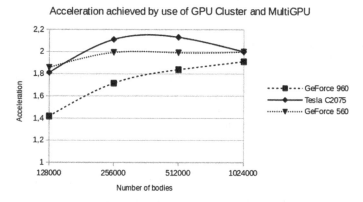

Fig. 4. Speedup achieved with the simulation using GPU clusters and MultiGPU

Nowadays, speeding up computation considering only performance in system scalability is not enough. For this reason, application energy consumption studies have gained relevance.

Average power is defined as the average energy required that is delivered to or absorbed by an element. This means that the power needed to process a piece of data is the same regardless of the piece of data and the volume of data to process. Table 3 lists the average power, measured in watts per second, when using one GPU, the GPU clusters, and the MultiGPU to run the N-body algorithm.

Table 3. Average power for the N-body simulation, measured in watts per second, using one GPU, a cluster with two GeForce GTX 960, a MultiGPU with two Tesla C2075, and a cluster with two GeForce GTX 560.

Number of bodies	GeForce GTX 960	Tesla C2075	GeForce GTX 560	Cluster with two GeForce GTX 960	MultiGPU with two Tesla C2075	Cluster with GeForce GTX 560
128000	160.48	276.74	191.87	306.85	376.4	382.29
256000	160.91	276.96	193.01	315.62	375.94	390.88
512000	162.36	278.51	202.77	321.13	378.39	394.64
1024000	163.54	278.37	209.09	325.86	398.84	407.76
Average	161.77	277.64	199.18	317.36	382.39	393.89

As it can be seen in Table 3, the average power does not change significantly. The variations observed may be due to data movement within GPU memory hierarchy or to cooling, for instance. Thus, a mean value can be calculated for the average power values measured to obtain a mean power that characterizes each GPU and GPU cluster/MultiGPU.

At this point, an accurate assessment of the ideal energy consumption for each architecture used to run the simulation is not possible. This is due to the measurement method available, which allows measuring "from outside" the equipment, which means that the value obtained includes the power used by the GPU as well as all other PC components. To compare architectures, measurements at rest were carried out to obtain the static power for each of them. Table 4 shows the static power values, in watts per second, for the architectures used for testing.

Table 4. Static power, measured in watts per second, for one PC or a cluster with two GeForce GTX 960, a MultiGPU with two Tesla C2075, and a cluster with two GeForce GTX 560.

GPU	One PC	Cluster/MultiGPU
GeForce GTX 960	69.4	120.2
Tesla C2075	132	132
GeForce GTX 560	97.6	122.1

Table 5 shows the average power values excluding the corresponding static power, in watts per second, for one GPU, GPU clusters, and MultiGPU.

If average power values for each architecture are normalized in relation to the corresponding mean static power, the consumption corresponding to each simulation run on each experimental platform can be established. In average, one GeForce GTX 960, one Tesla C2075, one GeForce GTX 560 and the cluster with two GeForce GTX

960 have a consumption that is twice as high. On the other hand, the MultiGPU with two Tesla C2075 and the cluster with two GeForce GTX 560 have a consumption that is three times as high. Table 6 shows how much higher consumption is on one GPU, one cluster of GPUs or one MultiGPU running the simulation.

Finally, Fig. 5 shows the power, in Joules, used by the simulation with one GPU.

Table 5. Average power excluding static power for the N-body simulation, measured in watts per second, using one GPU, a cluster with two GeForce GTX 960, a MultiGPU with two Tesla C2075, and a cluster with two GeForce GTX 560.

Number of bodies	GeForce GTX 960	Tesla C2075	GeForce GTX 560	Cluster with two GeForce GTX 960	MultiGPU with two Tesla C2075	Cluster with two GeForce GTX 560
128000	91.01	144.74	94.22	186.64	244.4	260.27
256000	91.44	144.96	95.36	178.97	243.94	268.86
512000	92.89	146.51	105.12	185.45	246.39	272.62
1024000	94.14	146.37	111.49	205.66	266.84	285.66

Table 6. Normalized average power used for the N-body simulation using one GPU, a cluster with two GeForce GTX 960, a MultiGPU with two Tesla C2075, and a cluster with two GeForce GTX 560.

Number of bodies	GeForce GTX 960	Tesla C2075	GeForce GTX 560	Cluster with two GeForce GTX 960	MultiGPU with two Tesla C2075	Cluster with two GeForce GTX 560
128000	2.31	2.09	1.96	2.55	2.85	3.13
256000	2.32	2.10	1.98	2.50	2.85	3.20
512000	2.34	2.11	2.08	2.56	2.87	3.23
1024000	2.35	2.10	2.14	2.71	3.02	3.33

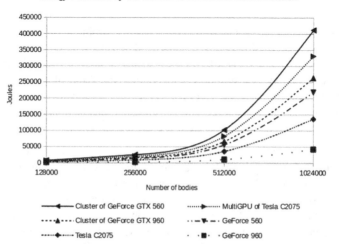

Fig. 5. Power, in Joules, used by the simulation for each GPU architecture

As it can be observed, the power used by GeForce is the same, but work time is reduced when a node is added. In the case of the MultiGPU, working with two graphics cards reduces computation time, but with a higher energy consumption.

6 Conclusions and Future Work

The benefits obtained with GPUs, either as regards costs or features, have turned them into a highly viable option when choosing a parallel architecture. However, computation speedup comes with a side effect – higher energy consumption. In this article, three different graphics cards and their energy consumption were analyzed when running a solution for the high computational demand N-Body problem. A comparison was made using a single GPU, two GPU clusters and a MultiGPU.

Based on the performance and energy consumption measurements presented in the previous section, it can be concluded that:

- A time estimation model was proposed for simulating the N-Body problem for the GPU architectures used for testing. Using linear regression and Pearson coefficient, it was shown that there is a correlation between measured and estimated times, with a Pearson coefficient of 0.99. This means that simulation time depends on input size and not on the number of steps in the simulation.
- As regards execution time, the GeForce GTX 960 GPU requires the least amount of time to solve the problem. However, all three GPUs are able to speed up algorithm computation.
- The speedup obtained with any of the three GPU architectures used is close to optimal speedup.
- The conclusions reached in [26] were also corroborated, where it was found that the average watts required by a single GPU, a cluster of GPUs or a MultiGPU is independent from input size, and that the variations observed in the values measured is insignificant. This variation could be due to data movement and/or card cooling.

Based on the results obtained for the N-Body problem, and considering the experimental scenarios used, it can be concluded that using a single GeForce GTX 960 GPU or a cluster of GeForce GTX 960 GPUs achieves the best results both as regards performance and energy consumption. Considering the costs of the different GPUs used, the best option is still the GeForce GTX 960. The card that has the lowest consumption, in general, is GeForce 960 for all tested problem sizes.

In the future, the following lines of work will be explored:

- Proposing an energy estimation model for this problem, which would allow predicting energy consumption when adding a GPU or increasing input size.
- Using the same N-Body algorithm, measuring energy consumption in more than two nodes for GPU clusters with GeForce GTX 560 and GeForce GTX 960.
- Studying and using NVIDIA Management Library (NVML), which allows monitoring and managing various states of NVIDIA GPU devices. It allows direct access to queries and commands exposed through nvidia-smi. Queries include card energy

management. It is available for Tesla C2075 (but not for the other cards, GeForce GTX 560 and 960). The query returns the value for the instant power used by the graphics card.

- Analyzing energy consumption for other types of simulations, such as individual-oriented simulations.

References

1. Porcelli, A.M., Martínez, A.N.: La nueva economía del siglo XXI: análisis de los impactos de la informática en el ambiente. Tendencias actuales en tecnologías informáticas verdes, un compromiso con la sustentabilidad. Quaestio Iuris, Rio de Janeiro, vol. 08, no. 04, Special Number, pp. 2174–2208 (2015)
2. Francis, K., Richardson, P.: Green maturity model for virtualization. Arch. J. **18**, 9–15 (2008)
3. Montes de Oca, E., De Giusti, L., De Giusti, A., Naiuof, M.: Comparación del uso de GPU y cluster de multicore en problemas con alta demanda computacional. In: XI Workshop de Procesamiento Distribuido y Paralelo, CACIC 2012, Bahía Blanca, Buenos Aires, Argentina (2012)
4. Nvidia. www.nvidia.es/graphics-cards/geforce/pascal
5. Nvidia. https://nvidianews.nvidia.com/news/nvidia-gpu-accelerated-supercomputer-sets-world-record-for-energy-efficiency
6. Díaz, J., Ambrosi, V., Castro, N., Candia, D., Vega, E., Rodriguez, A.: Experiencia de la enseñanza de Green IT en la currícula de carreras de Informática de la UNLP. In: XI Congreso de Educación en Tecnología y Tecnología en Educación (2016)
7. Montes de Oca, E., De Giusti, L., Chichizola, F., De Giusti, A., Naiouf, M.: Utilización de Cluster de GPU en HPC. Un caso de estudio. In: IVX Workshop de Procesamiento Distribuido y Paralelo. CACIC2014, La Matanza, Buenos Aires, Argentina (2014). ISBN 978-987-3806-05-6
8. Montes de Oca, E., De Giusti, L., De Giusti, A., Naiouf, M.: Análisis de consumo energético en Cluster de GPU y MultiGPU en un problema de Alta Demanda Computacional. In: XXIV Congreso Argentino de Ciencias de la Computación (CACIC) 2018, Tandil, Buenos Aires, Argentina, October 2018
9. Valdés Castro, E.: Tecnologías de información que contribuyen con las prácticas de Green IT. Ingenium **8**, 11–26 (2014)
10. González, C., Pérez, R., Vásquez Stanescu, C., Araujo, G.: Eficiencia energíetica. Uso racional de la energía eléctrica en el sector administrativo. In: Ministerio del Poder Popular para la Energía Eléctrica. Municipio Libertador, Distrito Capital República Bolivariana de Venezuela (2014)
11. Talebi, M., Way, T.: Methods, metrics and motivation for a green computer science program. In: SIGCSE 2009, Chattanooga, Tennessee, USA (2009)
12. Represa Pérez, C., Cámara Nebreda, J.M., Sánchez Ortega, P.L.: Introducción a la programación en CUDA, Universidad de Burgos, Área de Tecnología Electrónica (2016). http://riubu.ubu.es/bitstream/10259/3933/1/Programacion_en_CUDA.pdf
13. Silvestein, M., et al.: GPUnet: networking abstractions for GPU programs, transactions on computer systems. ACM Trans. Comput. Syst. **34**(3), 9 (2016). ACM 0734-2071/2016/09, 2016
14. Nvidia. www.nvidia.com/object/what-is-gpu-computing.html

15. Nvidia   Development.   https://devtalk.nvidia.com/default/topic/808106/question-abount-cudasetdevice-and-multiple-host-threads
16. Nvidia. nvidia.com/object/tesla-features-la.html
17. Bruzzone, S.: LFN10, LFN10-OMP y el Método de Leapfrog en el Problema de los N Cuerpos. Instituto de Física, Departamento de Astronomia, Universidad de la República y Observatorio Astronómico los Molinos, Uruguy (2011)
18. Nvidia CUDA Programing. https://docs.nvidia.com/cuda/cuda-c-programming-guide/index.html
19. Tsuyoshi, H., Keigo, N.: 190 TFlops astrophysical N-body simulation on cluster of GPUs. Universidad de Nagasaki. IEEE (2010). 978-1-4244-7558-2
20. Montes de Oca, E., De Giusti, L., Chichizola, F., De Giusti, A., Naiouf, M.: Análisis de uso de un algoritmo de balanceo de carga estático en un Cluster Multi-GPU Heterogéneo. In: XV Workshop de Procesamiento Distribuido y Paralelo. CACIC2016. San Luis, San Luis, Argentina (2016)
21. Restrepo, L.F., Gonzalez, L.J.: De Pearson a Spearman. Rev. Colombiana de Ciencias Pecuarias **20**, 183–192 (2007)
22. Montes de Oca, E.: Análisis de consumo energético en Cluster de GPU y MultiGPU en un problema de alta demanda computacional. In: Trabajo Final Integrador para la carrera de Especialización en Cómputo de Altas Prestaciones y Tecnología Grid (2018). http://sedici.unlp.edu.ar/handle/10915/69719
23. Rigol: RIGOL User's Guide MSO1000Z/DS1000Z Series Digital Oscilloscope (2018). http://beyondmeasure.rigoltech.com/acton/attachment/1579/f-050a/1/-/-/-/-/MSO1000Z%26DS1000Z_UserGuide.pdf
24. Tool developed by Dr. Balladini J., National University of Comahue
25. Nvidia GPU Computing. www.nvidia.com/object/what-is-gpu-computing.html
26. Pousa, A., Sanz, V., De Giusti, A.: Análisis de rendimiento de un algoritmo de criptografía simétrica sobre GPU y Cluster de GPU. Instituto de Investigación en Informática LIDI, Fac. de Informática, UNLP. HPC La TAM 2013 (2013)

Technology Applied to Education

Advances in Test Personalization and Adaptation in a Virtual Learning Environment

Marcela Gonzalez[2(✉)], Delia Esther Benchoff[1,2],
Constanza Huapaya[1,2], Cristian Remon[1], Guillermo Lazzurri[1],
Leonel Guccione[1], and Francisco Lizarralde[1,2]

[1] Artificial Intelligence Applied to Engineering Research Team,
Mathematics Department, Engineering Faculty, Mar del Plata National
University, J.B. Justo Av., 4302 Mar del Plata, Argentina
benchoff@mdp.edu.ar, constanza.huapaya@gmail.com,
remoncristian@gmail.com, guillesky@gmail.com,
leonel.guccione@gmail.com,
francisco.lizarralde@gmail.com

[2] Basic Applied Psychology Institute and Technology (IPSIBAT),
Psychology Faculty, Mar del Plata National University and CONICET,
Funes St – Building 5 Level 3, 3280 Mar del Plata, Argentina
mpgonza@mdp.edu.ar

Abstract. This paper states the analysis of an experience of personalization and adaptation for the learning of university students. The experience presents tests of formative evaluation, personalized and adapted in a Virtual Learning Environment, as a complement on site teaching. The objective of this communication is exposing, as a contribution, our adaptive methods for the learning experience. The personalization of the tests was based on the identification of the learning styles and the levels of previous knowledge of the students. The experience started in the year 2014 and still continues. The results of the analysis show that our techniques of personalization and adaptation, which have been refined as time went by, improve the students' learning and guide the professors in the decision-making that have an impact in the optimization of the pedagogical proposal.

Keywords: Personalized tests · Adaptation · Virtual Learning Environment

1 Introduction

From the educational paradigm focused on the student, the research about the personalization and adaptation of the learning nowadays guides many developments, particularly in Virtual Learning Environments (VLE). In this context, both concepts can seem similar. However, they show evident differences. Personalization in education considers the suitability of pedagogy, curricula and learning environments, the needs and learning styles of the students as individuals [1]. Personalized learning involves any action that both a professor and software put into action to teach a topic to an

© Springer Nature Switzerland AG 2019
P. Pesado and C. Aciti (Eds.): CACIC 2018, CCIS 995, pp. 49–61, 2019.
https://doi.org/10.1007/978-3-030-20787-8_4

individual student. Personal characteristics that differentiate one individual from the rest of the group are identified: cognitive abilities, unlike levels of knowledge, preferences and learning styles, among others. The personalization can be applied to exercises, explanations, tests according to the individual profile.

On the one hand, the adaptation of the learning is related to the adaptive functionalities available in the learning management systems (LMS). These systems provide the student with predefined actions to select the ones that guide his learning process [2, 3]. From the professor's viewpoint, the LMS provide the possibility of planning the configuration of contents, the interface, the evaluation and/or feedback and in this way, improve the general performance of the learning environment focused on the student [4] and, on the other, advise and provide effective feedback [5].

In this paper we present the advances of an experience that shows personalized designed formative evaluations for university students. The main guide of our paper is the integrated adaptation in the modeling of the user. The spheres of analysis inquired were the aspects associated to the interaction human-computer in the teaching and learning process. We focused on the technologies and materials used and mainly, on one of the aspects less dealt with in literature, design and use of the self-evaluation personalized tests.

2 Personalization and Adaptation Techniques

In order to design the personalization techniques, it was necessary to clarify the actions of the participants that take part in the teaching and learning process, students and professors. To do so, we considered the differences that exist between three concepts that are used in an almost interchangeable way: individualization, differentiation and personalization, according to the considerations of students and professors' actions [6].

Individualization identifies different students' learning needs and guides the actions carried out by the professor to accompany them, that is, as each student takes his own way to reach the common objective for all the class.

The differentiation recognizes the learning preferences in different groups of students and orientates the teaching according to those trends. The learning objectives are the same for all the students, but what is important here is he teaching method applied to reach the objective in common. This method is different according to the preferences of the groups.

The personalization is based on the student. It aims the teaching to follow the learning needs, to adjust to the preferences and interests of different students; in this way the personalization involves the differentiation and individualization. A LMS is personalized if the techniques used for the teaching vary according to students' characteristics.

According to the definition of personalization previously mentioned, the techniques developed for such process and the adaptation one were based on attributes inherent to the student (for the personalization), in dynamic attributes of the student/VLE interaction (for the adaptation) and in topics of domain.

Particularly, for the personalization were examined the individual preferences by means of learning styles and the previous knowledge about the domain, using surveys. For the adaptation, it was analyzed the dynamic interaction with the students in a virtual learning environment. The prevailing learning styles in the group of students and the most difficult contents to be learned were studied. Based on the attributes just mentioned, the personalization and adaptation techniques were built based on Moodle Questionnaires working on the access, timing and feedback, as well as the offering of material and personalized assistance. Bellow there is a brief description of the students' attributes and formative tests.

2.1 Learning Styles

From a cognitive perspective, the *learning styles* concept implies, that the students process the information in different ways: they manifest particular ways of selecting, absorbing and internalizing new information, creating individual learning patterns, flexibly stable [1]. Knowing the learning styles can ease these processes and, in the same way, adapt the pedagogical practices according to student styles, contributing to ease a meaningful learning.

Actually, many perspectives, classifications and controversies coexist around this topic. It is argued if the styles are dispositions biologically desemesterined, or if they have flexible characteristics with a strong influence of personal and environmental factors. According to literature, there have been empirical tests about flexibility and dynamics, characteristics that would let students adapt their styles to the context and learning requirements [7].

Its considerations state the personalization and adaptation that evidence a positive influence as shown in several studies [8]. In this project the instrument called Index of Learning Styles (ILS) [9] proposed by Felder and Soloman was applied and directed to Engineering students. It has been translated into Spanish and validated in other areas of knowledge [10–12].

The ILS is a questionnaire of 44 multiple choice questions that evaluates the preferences of *learning styles* by means in four dimensions, each of them organized in two categories. The dimensions and their respective categories are: Processing of information: *Active* or *Reflective* students; Perception of information: *Sensing* or *Intuitive*; Reception of information: Students mainly *Verbal* or *Visual* and Comprehension of information, whose categories represent *Sequential or Global* students.

2.2   Previous Knowledge

Previous knowledge (PK) can be understood as a baggage of ideas and concepts that people previously have in their long semester memory, organized in a format of semantic nets. It is considered one of the influencing factors in the learning, as the implementation of the novelty and the PK, is essential in the development of the teaching and learning process.

According to Carretero [13], in every educational level it is necessary to take into account students' previous knowledge, as the new learning will be set upon the previous one. In this way, the possibility of learning will be related to the quantity and quality of the previous knowledge and the established connections among them.

2.3   Formative Tests with Questionnaires

Formative tests are activities that aim to provide the necessary information to improve the educational process, oriented to both professors and students. The concept of effective feedback is central both in the learning oriented assessment approach [14] and in the formative test. Carless states that the evaluation should effectively contribute to the learning improvement. The principles of this approach suggest that: (a) the adequacy between objectives, contents and testing tasks facilitates a deep learning experience; (b) the students' participation in the evaluation: self-evaluation, evaluation in pairs, peer feedback promotes a better comprehension of the learning objectives; and (c) appropriate feedback of the evaluation fosters the commitment of the student in his process and lets delimitate difficulties in the learning of specific topics and apply appropriate corrections.

Our tests were designed as a supplement on site teaching, blended-learning. We used LMS Moodle. We used LMS Moodle, because it is a management learning system in permanent development, open source, scalable and free of charge, with a variety of activities and resources that the professor can incorporate in his pedagogic proposal. We decided to build the tests using Questionnaires as they are the most accurate way to design self-evaluation formative tests. This tool allows the professor to design and state questions in different formats: matching, multiple choice, true – false, short answers and numeric answers, randomized or well organized access, with limited resolution time or without, with unlimited or restricted attempts for the response sometimes specific. We focused on the configuration of two relevant topics to reach our objective: the first related to the definition of the restrictions to the access, the second to the selection of the options of feedback according to the students' answer.

3   The Experience

The career of Computer Engineering at Mar del Plata National University was launched in 2014. The subject on which this paper has been performed is Informatics Foundations, taught in the second semester of the first year. It is taught in both semesters of the year.

Actually, we are in the cycle corresponding to the 9th cohort. Informatics Foundations is the first subject of the career with specific contents about computer and provides students with an introduction about most the contents that they will learn along the career.

The total number of enrolled students in the analyzed period was 111. The first implementation in the VLE was done for the students' cohort in the second semester 2015 (N = 33), when we identified the first advance. Then we continued with both semesters in 2016, (N = 31 and N = 47 respectively).

To ensure the best possible result of the experience, it was decided to work focusing on processes, applying the Cycle Deming PDCA: Plan, Do, Check, Act, for the continuous improvement [15].

During the first cohort, the teaching staff decided to incorporate services and digital resources to facilitate the access to study material (it was uploaded in Blogger and Google Drive and there was fluid communication via email). Even though we started the personalization task during the second semester of the year 2014, there was a substantial delay in the implementation of the LMS Moodle when collecting the main learning styles, due to the lack of availability of an own server in which we could install and/or set and give access to an VLE by means of a public IP. We could perform the adaptation of the personalized tests in the VLE for the students of the cohort in the second semester 2015. Taking as input the profiles of the learning styles of the first cohorts and more complex topics together with frequent errors detected, the personalization of the didactic design was started considering those topics: Assembler Language (CODE 2) and Logical Design, taken as inputs the learning styles profiles corresponding to the first cohorts, the more complex topics and the frequent errors detected [16]. In particular, the treatment of the Algorithmics topic was considered essential for the specific formation of a computer engineer. Without letting aside all the topics included in the subject, more effort was set in the development of self-evaluation exercises for the topic mentioned.

Figure 1 summarizes the advances performed by the team related to the personalization and adaptation of the VLE. Although the experience continues, in this communication we will present the first three advances showing the adjustments of the original design and the results that have been reached.

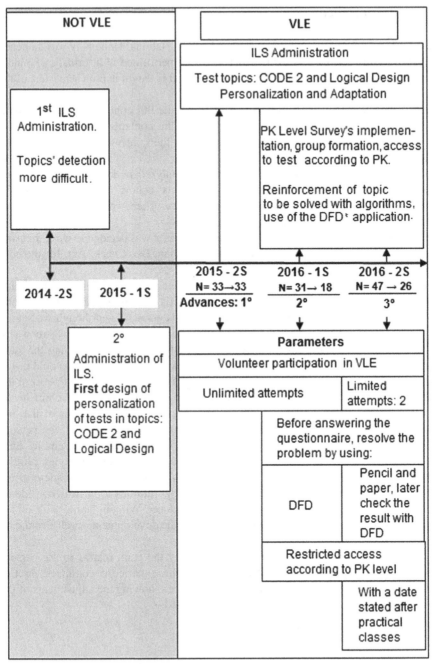

Fig. 1. Advances in test personalization and adaptation

3.1   Prevailing Learning Styles Profile

The beginning of the personalization was performed during the 2nd semester of the year 2014, period in which we began to identify the learning styles. In the context of the experience, we will detail the learning styles profile found in the cohorts being analysed. Eighty-eight full protocols were processed: 25 corresponding to the 2015 second semester, 24 to the 2016 first semester, and 39 students from the 2016 second semester. The results showed a balance in the active/reflective dimension, with a slight trend towards the active pole; a greater tendency towards the sequential and visual pole; and a clear balance in the sensing/intuitive dimension. Figure 2 illustrates the compiled trend.

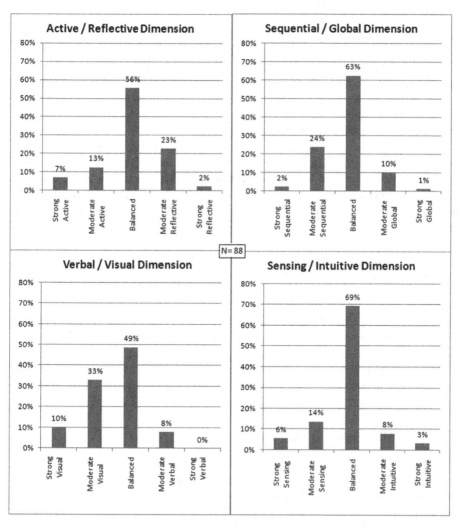

Fig. 2. Profile of learning styles, Cohorts: 2015-1st S., 2016-1st S. and 2016-2nd S.

These results showed the balance in the active/reflective dimension, indicating a dynamic learning modality: use of didactic material, group activities, and access to study materials for the reflective approach. There is an interest in the details and step by step problems resolution (sequential pole). The use of visuals representations, flow diagrams and videos, alludes to visual preferences.

3.2   The 2015 Cohort – 2nd Semester

Thirty-three students took part. The topics were Logical Design and Assembler Language, chosen according to the learning difficulties discovered in the previous cohorts. The participation of VLE was voluntary, although it was focused on the performing of tests as an instance of assistance and preparation for the first mid-term test.

The self-evaluation tests were designed based on the active, sequential and visual profiles. Two questionnaires were developed for each topic with two levels of difficulty. For the topic Logical Design, matching questions were implemented and multiple choice for Assembly Language. The students could attempt unlimitedly. In order to minimize the number of random hits, the Certainty-based marking (CBM) was chosen in the development of questions/answers. Apart from that, specific feedback was used according to students' answers, providing visual aids and extra texts according to the visual pole of the learning profile indicated.

The results of this first adaptation showed that even though all the students started their questionnaires, not all of them finished neither a sustained participation in the experience was maintained. In the low complexity questionnaires of both topics, the percentage of finishing them was higher: 94% of the students in the first topic and 76% in the second, in all the cases with good marks which included bonuses with CBM. In the complex tests, 54% of the sample finished the questionnaire of the first topic and as regards the second, the number of participants was reduced to 24 students, from which only 63% finished the questionnaire. In these higher complexity tests the number of resolution attempts was increased and the penalizations with CBM, data that lets infer doubts in the responses or less knowledge acquired.

Finally, the achievement of the extra practice as a formative evaluation could be also seen in the results of the first mid-term test that included the topics discussed. From a total number of 33 students, 28 sat for the first mid-term exam. 71% passed (20 students) and 29% failed (8 students). In the group of the students who passed, 70% (14 students) finished the adapted self-evaluation tests, including at least one of the high complexity exercises. The result showed that 9 students had a grading mark higher or equal to 7, and 5 students reached marks between 4 and 7 points.

3.3   The 2016 Cohort – 1st Semester

The total number of students enrolled in this course was 31. The analysis was made on the performance of 18 students who completed the questionnaire. The topic evaluated was Algorithmics, highlighted by being transversal to the main subjects of the career. For the personalization of the tests, we use the profiles learning styles and the results of a survey that enquired the topic's previous knowledge. Starting from these results, three levels of previous knowledge were established PK: Null (4 students), Low (11 students), and Medium/High (3 students).

The adaptation of the self-evaluation test was designed in the questionnaire, considering the learning styles and each level of previous knowledge in the following way: the questionnaire had 10 exercises, in a rising order of complexity and integration. By means of the configuration of a restriction access, the students of null PK had to do the complete questionnaire, being the expected result a total of 17 points. For the students of Low PK, the questionnaire had seven exercises, where the first corresponded to the fourth in the full questionnaire, which means that they were starting at a level of medium complexity, the score was 14 points. Finally, the students of Medium/High PK solved the three hardest complexity exercises of the original questionnaire, and the expected score was 6 points.

Attending to the active learning style, the activities were centred in the dynamic interaction with the material. The gradual presentation of the exercises with restrictions to their access and timing, was set up taking into account the preference of sequencing, and for the visual preference diagrams, videos, images and supplementary texts were provided. For the Low and Medium/High PK there were revision videos with the necessary contents for the resolution of the exercises.

The development of self-evaluation tests did not show difference in the results between the Null and Low PK. From a total number of 15 students belonging to these levels, 67% reached the expected score (10 students) and the 33% was under score (5 students). For the medium/High level, there were only 3 students: 2 of them got the maximum score and 1 got a scored below the expectations.

The follow up of the students in both mid-term exams was specifically performed to the item of the tested domain. Always taking into account the level of PK, the performance among groups of students that participated in the VLE and the ones who did not was compared. The general results of this follow up in both mid term indicate that the group of students of Null and Low PK in the VLE got better marks in the item: half of these students reached scores over 50% required for the item, whereas the group without participating in the VLE, just a 25% got equivalent marks. They also had a notorious absenteeism, having to make up the tests.

The Medium/High Level of PK (CP), in the VLE only had a better result in the item corresponding to the 1st mid term test, whereas in the 2nd the students that did not take part in the VLE got a slightly better development.

3.4   The 2016 Cohort – 2nd Semester

In this semester there were 27 enrolled students, 26 participating in the VLE activities that were recommended but not obligatory. There were 20 students in the level of Null/Low PK (CP) and 6 in the Medium/High. As in the previous semester, the scope of work was Algorithmics.

Starting from a permanent improvement of the pedagogic design, during the practical classes, it was required to perform each exercise of the practical work guide by using pencil and paper and to check the result with the DFD application [17]. This practice was fulfilled with the presentation of the results (sometimes mistaken) of students on the blackboard together with the teaching staff. In the VLE a parameter of timing was added, which allowed the access to the questionnaire after the date of the practical classes. This change improved the comprehension of the exercises. The parameter of Unlimited Attempts was also modified to just two attempts with the objective of minimizing the responses by trial and error and to reinforce the previous practice. The other parameters were the same as in the first semester.

The results of the questionnaire indicated that 85% of the students with Null/Low PK reached the expected score, and the group of Medium/High PK 100%.

The follow up and development in the mid-term tests, when comparing to the students that did the self-evaluation tests in the VLE with the ones who did not, shows: 85% of the students with Null/Low PK that performed the questionnaires (17 students) got high marks in the item in both exams (overcoming the development of the previous semester) and all the students of Medium/High PK got the highest score in both tests (6 students). In the group that did not do the questionnaire, 35% of the students with Null/Low PK (6 students), resolved the item in both exams and again there was high absenteeism. In the Medium/High Level of PK, 25% reached the score to pass the item (1 student) [18, 19].

4   Discussion, New Advances and Conclusions

In the first instance, the results of the formative evaluation tests show a better development in the administered mid-term tests. In this way, the evaluation oriented to the learning as a guiding principle of the presented experience [11]. Lets us infer that it is effectively contributing to the significant learning by means of the adaptation of objectives, contents and activities. On the other hand, the adaptation supported in the predominant learning styles, allowed the developing of activities concordant with the instruction designs focused on the student.

The progressive improvements in the adaptation of questionnaires, arose based on the review process, and making the necessary adjustments. As an example, as regards the contents it was important to focus on the topic Algorithmics, taking into account its importance and the difficulties in the comprehension for students of the 1st year. From the perspective of the questionnaires design, the revision allowed the introduction of the variable of the PK level, adapting the tests to each level and applying restrictions to the access by means of the use of conditionals in Moodle per group and timing. The complementarity on site teaching increased the practice before accessing to the questionnaires and minimized random answers. In addition, the effective specific feedback that offers the tool Questionnaire, especially in incorrect responses, finished a didactic sequence that favored a better development.

We highlight especially the process of the students with Null/Low PK that showed an increase in the performance of the questionnaires resolution in the VLE and in the scores assigned to the item of domain in the mid-term exams. In this way, we can deduce that the students that started their learning process with little or no previous information about the topic could build new nets of knowledge that were meaningful in being successfully applied in the resolution of the proposed exercises.

In this respect, a positive relationship is inferred between the objective reached by the students and the personalization and adaptation procedures applied to the formative self-evaluation tests.

In the year 2019 the learning styles analysis was expanded, adding 5 more cohorts. Over a sample of 230 students belonging to the same subject, the results showed a notorious percentage of balanced styles in all dimensions, together with a trend to visual, sensorial and sequential styles. A slight tendency towards the reflective sample, was also observed without losing the balance in this dimension [20].

Table 1 show the students distribution, and Table 2 the total students by preference in each ILS dimension, 230 students (N), who answered the ILS questions, distributed in eight cohorts

Table 1. Students distribution

Year – Semester	Total students
2014 – 2nd	14
2015 – 2nd	25
2016 – 1st	24
2016 – 2nd	39
2017 – 1st	23
2018 – 1st	24
2018 –2nd	42
2019 – 1st	39
N	**230**

Table 2. Total students by preference in each ILS dimension - 8 cohorts

Pole	Strong	Moderate	Balanced	Moderate	Strong	Pole
Active	9	32	133	49	7	Reflexive
Sequential	8	56	146	18	2	Global
Visual	32	70	110	15	3	Verbal
Sensing	14	51	142	16	7	Intuitive
N: 230						

Although the processes of personalization and adaptation were performed considering the predominant learning styles and the previous knowledge, the further trend towards the balance in all the dimensions of the styles has lead to generate the deepening of the enquiry that has recently been presented in a new research project.

Following this line, the proposal pretends to advance in the enlargement of the processes of personalization and adaptation, designing personalized learning itineraries considering not only learning styles and previous knowledge, but also common mistakes detected by professors. In this way a better adequacy of the feedback and presentation of study materials is expected towards the objective of a better development in the learning process.

In order to do so, it was stated as general objectives to define and develop personalized learning itineraries, with study materials and activities with accurate feedback according to the learning and levels of previous knowledge and to explore the interaction of the student in the VLE as regards the search and selection of instructional materials related to the learning styles.

Although we understand that the variables that take place in learning do not use up in the ones here defined (it would be necessary to fill in the profiles as regards motivation and characteristics of students' personality, for example), the results obtained in this experience of adaptation seem to indicate that the way is promissory [19].

References

1. Klašnja-Milićević, A., Vesin, B., Ivanovic, M., Budimac, Z., Jain, L.: e-Learning Systems Intelligent Techniques for Personalization. Springer, Switzerland (2017). https://doi.org/10.1007/978-3-319-41163-7
2. Gu, Q., Sumner, T.: Support personalization in distributed e-learning systems through learner modeling. In: 2nd Information and Communication Technologies, ICTTA, vol. 1, pp. 610–615. IEEE, Damascus (2006). https://doi.org/10.1109/ictta.2006.1684441
3. Tian, F., Zheng, Q., Gong, Z., Du, J., Li, R.: Personalized learning strategies in an intelligent e-learning environment. In: 11th International Conference on Computer Supported Cooperative Work in Design, pp. 973–978. IEEE, Melbourne (2007). https://doi.org/10.1109/cscwd.2007.4281570
4. González, M., Benchoff, D., Huapaya, C., Remon, C.: Aprendizaje Adaptativo: Un Caso de Evaluación Personalizada. Revista Iberoamericana de Tecnología en Educación y Educación en Tecnología **19**, 65–72 (2017)
5. Czajkowski, K., Fitzgerald, S., Foster, I., Kesselman, C.: Grid information services for distributed resource sharing. In: 10th IEEE International Symposium on High Performance Distributed Computing, pp. 181–184. IEEE, San Francisco (2001). https://doi.org/10.1109/hpdc.2001.945188
6. Bray, B., McClaskey, K.: Personalization vs differentiation vs individualization. Technical report, Alberta Education (2010)
7. Moser, S., Zumbach, J.: Exploring the development and impact of learning styles: an empirical investigation based on explicit and implicit measures. Comput. Educ. **125**, 146–157 (2018). Elsevier
8. Watkins, C.: Meta-learning in classrooms. In: Scott, D., Hargreaves, E. (eds.) Sage Handbook of Learning, p. 321 (2015)
9. Soloman, B.A., Felder, R.: Index of learning styles questionnaire. NC State University. https://www.webtools.ncsu.edu/learningstyles/
10. Figueroa, N., et al.: Los estilos de aprendizaje y el desgranamiento universitario en Carreras de informática In: I Jornadas de Educación en Informática y TICs en Argentina, SEDICI, pp. 15–19 (2005)
11. Felder, R., Spurlin, J.: Applications, reliability, and validity of the index of learning styles. Int. J. Eng. Educ. **21**(1), 103–112 (2005)
12. Rodríguez, J.: Educación médica. Aprendizaje basado en problemas. Médica Panamericana, México, chap. 3, pp. 25–45 (2002)
13. Carretero, M.: Introducción a la Psicología Cognitiva. Buenos Aires, Argentina (1997)

14. Carless, D.: Learning-oriented assessment: conceptual bases and practical implications. Innov. Educ. Teach. Int. **44**(1), 57–66 (2007)
15. Remón, C., Benchoff, D., González, M., Huapaya, C.: Aplicación de la mejora continua de la calidad para analizar el rendimiento de un grupo de estudiantes de ingeniería. In: V Encuentro Regional SAMECO, Mar del Plata, Argentina (2017)
16. Huapaya, C., Gonzalez, M., Benchoff, E., Guccione, L., Lizarralde. F.: Estimación del Diagnóstico Cognitivo del Estudiante de Ingeniería y su mejora con pruebas adaptativas. In: X Congreso de Tecnología en Educación y Educación en Tecnología - TE&ET 2015, vol. 1, pp. 480–489. EUDENE, Corrientes (2015)
17. Introducción a la Programación Estructurada. https://sites.google.com/site/informaticaieen-sma/home/diagramas-de-flujo/dfd-1-0
18. Benchoff, D., González, M., Huapaya, C.: Personalization of tests for formative self-assessment. Revista Iberoamericana de Tecnologías del Aprendizaje **13**(2), 70–74. IEEE, Spain (2018). https://doi.org/10.1109/rita.2018.2831759
19. González, M., et al.: Avances en la Personalización y Adaptación de Pruebas en un Ambiente Virtual de Aprendizaje. In: XXIV Congreso Argentino de Ciencias de la Computación CACIC 2018, pp. 193–202. Tandil, Argentina (2019)
20. Benchoff, D., González, M.: Estilos de aprendizaje en estudiantes de Ingeniería Informática. In: 6° Congreso Nacional de Ingeniería Informática – Sistemas de Información. Mar del Plata, Argentina (2018)

Learning Objects. Case Studies

María Lucía Violini[1][(✉)] and Cecilia Verónica Sanz[1,2]

[1] National University of La Plata, La Plata, Buenos Aires, Argentina
{lviolini, csanz}@lidi.info.unlp.edu.ar
[2] Scientific Research Agency of the Province of Buenos Aires,
La Plata, Argentina

Abstract. In this article, we present a review on the topic of Learning Objects (LOs) based on case studies presented in the bibliography. We start by considering the origins of the term, various conceptualizations, and then focus on LO reutilization. The case studies selected are used to analyze aspects pertaining to LO creation and use in specific educational contexts. The results obtained can be used to consider issues such as reasons why educators choose to work with LOs, LO design methodologies (technological, pedagogical, hybrid), types of design scenarios (audiovisual, interactive, mixed), development tools (for assembling LO, generating contents, generating activities/self-evaluations, loading metadata), publication environments (LO repositories and Virtual Teaching and Learning Environments), and assessment processes (tests with students and educators). This review reveals a positive, progressing outlook as regards LO creation and their incorporation/use in educational contexts. There are also some aspects that would have to be considered in more detail in relation to LO reutilization that are good for analysis and coming up with new lines of action.

Keywords: Learning Objects · Digital Educational Materials · Case studies

1 Introduction

With the advent of web 2.0, educators became more involved in the production of their own Digital Educational Materials (DEMs) [1]. For a while now, DEMs have become a cornerstone of educational proposals mediated by Information and Communication Technologies. In this context, further research is carried out in relation to Learning Objects (LOs) [2].

So far, there is no consensus definition for the term Learning Object. The lack of conceptual clarity is apparent from the number of definitions and uses for LOs [3]. It is for this reason that our first step in this article is adopting a specific definition: "A learning object is a type of digital educational material that is characterized, from a pedagogical point of view, for its orientation towards a specific learning objective, and having at least the following: a series of contents that allow presenting the topic related to the objective, activities that allow students to put the contents presented into practice or consider related problems, and a self-evaluation that allows students to determine if they have understood the contents linked to the objective. From a technological standpoint, it is characterized for containing a set of standardized metadata used for search and retrieval operations, as well as for being integrated, using a standard-

P. Pesado and C. Aciti (Eds.): CACIC 2018, CCIS 995, pp. 62–73, 2019.
https://doi.org/10.1007/978-3-030-20787-8_5

compliant packing model, which allows the interaction with different technology environments" [4].

LOs are DEMs that can be used to facilitate learning a specific concept based off the specific objective they propose. They can also be added to lessons/topic units or form learning itineraries, under certain circumstances and with a given relationship between them, that help achieve educational goals that would not be possible in isolation [5]. LOs can be included both in education proposals that are carried out inside a classroom, as well as in distance education and hybrid ones, through their publication in Learning Object Repositories (LORs) or Virtual Teaching and Learning Environments (VTLEs) [6].

When educators decide to create LOs, they need to explore into design and development processes. To do this, there are methodologies aimed at guiding all tasks related to LO design, development and publication [7]. There are also multiple tools that help create these DEMs, some more specific than others [8].

This article is an extension on a previous publication [9] by the same authors. Our work revolves around studying a subset of selected cases that propose the creation of LOs and their subsequent use in specific educational contexts. The discussion presented here is aimed at considering the following aspects: main stages LOs go through, reasons why educators consider creating LOs, aspects related to issues linked to LOs, and LO reutilization. Additionally, we expand on the state-of-the-art by including a review on LOs that encompasses term origin and various conceptualizations, and focuses on LO reutilization (foundation of these DEMs). We also delve deeper into the issues discussed in each of the case studies. This more in-depth analysis helps move forward in our conclusions and set new lines for work in the future.

This paper is organized as follows: in Sect. 2, a review encompassing the origins and concept of the term Learning Object is presented, with emphasis on the reutilization feature that differentiates LOs from other DEMs. In Sect. 3, a subset of selected cases is introduced, case selection being based on a number of research questions and given criteria. Section 4 is used to discuss key aspects related to LO creation and use, based on the analysis carried out in Sect. 3. Finally, Sect. 5 details our conclusions and presents future lines of work.

2 Learning Objects

By the end of the '60s, Gerard [10] proposed an idea that turned out to be an early vision of the concept of LOs: *"with highly individualized instruction, curricular units can be of smaller sizes and combined with each other, the same as standard MECCANO[1] pieces, into a large variety of programs that are custom made for each student"*.

At the beginning of the '90s, Merrill [11] also touched on the concept of LO when he used the term *frames* to refer to objects that could represent knowledge and be combined with other objects to create a course.

---

[1] *MECCANO*: Children's game that consists of metal pieces with several holes in each that allow assembling them using nuts and bolts. http://www.meccano.com.

Hodgins [12] was the first person to use the term LO to name his group at *CedMa*[2]: "*Learning Architecture and Learning Objects*". This name was inspired by watching his son and daughter play with *LEGO*[3] blocks, which are small plastic blocks that can be assembled to create different shapes. He then established an analogy between *LEGO* blocks and LOs, considering the latter as the smallest possible content units that can be assembled and reused.

Later on, Wiley [13] expressed that the *LEGO* metaphor could limit how LOs are conceptualized. *LEGO* blocks are characterized by the following properties: (1) any block can be combined with any other block; (2) blocks can be assembled in any way; (3) blocks are so simple that even children can combine them. Wiley stated that implicitly assuming that LOs share these properties with *LEGO* adds unnecessary restrictions to what could potentially be done with them, and what LOs could potentially become. Wiley then recommended the atoms metaphor.

The atoms metaphor considers the atom as a small "object" that can be combined and re-combined to form large "objects". This would seem to capture the overall meaning conveyed by the *LEGO* metaphor. However, the atoms metaphor differs from the *LEGO* one in some key aspects: (1) not all atoms can be combined with any other atom; (2) atoms can only be assembled into certain structures, determined by their own internal structure; (3) some kind of training is required to assemble atoms.

According to Wiley [13], using the *LEGO* metaphor to combine LOs without any kind of *Instruction Theory* would likely result in larger structures that would not be useful. However, this would not be the case with the atoms metaphor, where the structure of the combination determines compatibility to be combined with other structures.

Since then, various concepts to define LOs were proposed. Most authors specialized in the field agree that LOs should be: digital in nature, with pedagogical intent, reusable, and capable of being assembled into larger structures. However, and even though research and development of LOs has been going on for years, there is no consensus that formally defines *what an LO is* and *what it is not*.

2.1 Learning Object Reutilization

The concept of LO, which has spread quickly without a specific universal definition, is aimed at providing high reusability levels. One of the founding ideas of LOs was that they should be DEMs represented by small, separate pieces that could be used and reused in various educational situations, and be combined with other pieces [14].

However, not having a single, formally accepted definition but rather a diversity of conceptualizations for what LOs are, negatively impacts LO interoperability and reutilization. The current controversy to establish which DEMs are LOs and which are not opens the road towards the creation of a variety of LOs with different interoperability levels that may be hard to reuse and assemble with each other.

---

[2] *CedMa (Computer Education Managers Association)*: https://www.cedma.org.

[3] *LEGO*: Children's game that allows building different objects by interlocking blocks, commonly referred to as "bricks". https://www.lego.com.

Reutilization is a key and distinctive feature in LOs compared to other types of DEMs [15]. To offer this feature, LOs have metadata, which are considered as their digital catalog card and provide the following information: LO contents, target audience, creation date, authors, technical and educational requirements and recommendations for use, copyright, and any applicable use or reproduction restrictions [16].

To make reutilization easier, online repositories index LOs and provide functionalities that are similar to those offered by search engines. These repositories allow collecting specific LOs that educators can add to their educational proposals without any changes or by adapting them based on their needs [17]. There are LO assembler systems and systems that recommend LOs based on objectives [18, 19].

In the following section, the core of this work is presented, namely, case studies of LO creation and use in specific educational contexts.

3   Case Studies

In this section, we discuss the case studies selected to answer a number of research questions related to LO creation and use. First, research questions are presented. Then, the case selection process used is described. Then, analysis criteria are defined. Finally, the results obtained after analyzing these cases of interest are discussed.

3.1   Research Questions

Our continued work on this topic [2, 4, 7, 8] has allowed us to come up with a number of research questions to guide the study of LOs and shed some light on various aspects that require deeper consideration. Below, the questions prepared to guide case studies are listed.

Q1.   What motivates educators to create and use LOs?
Q2.   What are the methodologies used by educators to design LOs?
Q3.   What types of design scenarios are used by educators?
Q4.   What are the tools used by educators to carry out LO development tasks?
Q5.   What are the technological environments used by educators to publish their LOs?
Q6.   What are the assessment processes used by educators on LOs?

3.2   Case Selection

Initially, a bibliography search was carried out to find cases describing the creation of LOs and their subsequent use in specific educational contexts. The period of time between 2000–2018 was considered. As regards language, articles published in English or Spanish were considered. Our search focused on the areas *Technology* and *Education* and was carried out on *ELSEVIER*[4], *IEEE Xplore Digital Library*[5], and *ACM*

---

[4] *ELSEVIER*: https://www.elsevier.com/.
[5] *IEEE Xplore Digital Library*: https://ieeexplore.ieee.org/.

Digital Library[6] and the following scientific journals: *IEEE Journal of Latin-American Learning Technologies (IEEE-RITA)* and *Interdisciplinary Journal of Knowledge and Learning Objects (IJKLO)*. Additionally, the following international conferences were considered: *Latin American Conference on Learning Technologies (LACLO)*, *International Conference on Engineering Education (ICEED)*, *International Conference on Advances in Mobile Computing & Multimedia (MoMM)*, *International Conference on Advanced Learning Technologies (ICALT)*, *International Conference on Technological Ecosystems for Enhancing Multiculturality (TEEM)*, and *Frontiers in Education Conference (FIE)*. The search string used was: *Learning Object/Objeto de Aprendizaje*. After the initial review, using titles and summaries to determine if they were relevant for our interests, 40 articles were selected to read in full. Then, a new selection process was carried out based on the following priorities.

Those cases where the concept of LO used was closest to the definition of LO adopted here were selected first. Thus, the first selection filter applied was that the LO being discussed should: (1) be a DEM with a specific learning objective; (2) present contents on the topic at hand; (3) propose, at least, one activity/self-evaluation that would allow students to use/self-evaluate the contents introduced by the LO.

Then, those cases that were explained in more detail, allowing to analyze most, or even all, the issues covered by the research questions, were selected. Therefore, the second selection filter applied was that the description of the case should make reference to educator motivation and LO design, development, publication and assessment.

Ultimately, a subset of 10 cases of interest was obtained as corpus for analysis. Table 1 lists all selected cases [20–29], specifying for each of them year of publication, authors, and related discipline.

Table 1. Selected cases: specifications.

Selected cases			
Case #	Year of publication	Authors	Discipline
1	2003	Chalk et al.	*Computer Science – Programming*
2	2005	Krauss and Ally	*Pharmacology – Pharmacokinetics*
3	2006	Reis et al.	*Computer Science – Computational Intelligence*
4	2009	Ummi et al.	*Engineering – Electronics*
5	2009	Matthews et al.	*Computer Science – Programming*
6	2012	Tuparov et al.	*Computer Science – Programming*
7	2014	Orozco et al.	*Mathematics – Geometry*
8	2015	Tiosso et al.	*Computer Architecture – Memory*
9	2017	Violini and Sanz	*Computer Science – Programming*
10	2018	Redmond et al.	*Nursing – Wound Care*

3.3 Criteria for Analysis

Analysis criteria were defined to make sure all research questions were considered. Table 2 lists these criteria, including for each of them: related research question, description, and goals.

---

[6] *ACM Digital Library*: https://dl.acm.org/.

Table 2. Analysis criteria: description and goals.

C1. Motivations	Related to *Q1*

Motivations that led educators to create and use the LO. These can be: (a) encourage active, autonomous learning; (b) motivating students; (c) integrating visual/interactive information; (d) producing reusable educational material.
- ✓ Identifying the main motivations for the creation and use of LOs.
- ✓ Establishing how often the reutilization feature of LOs is considered.

C2. Design Methodology	Related to *Q2*

Methodology used to design the LO, if a specific design methodology was followed. Methodologies are classified based on their approach: technological (technological aspects are prevalent; they are related to *software* development), pedagogical (pedagogical aspects are prevalent, they a re related to instructional design), or hybrid (combination of technological and pedagogical aspects) [7].
- ✓ Identifying the use of methodologies to guide LO design.
- ✓ Identifying the type of approach used for LO design.
- ✓ Considering how these issues affect LO creation.

C3. Types of Design Scenarios	Related to *Q3*

Types of scenarios included by the LO in its various parts. The following scenarios are considered: audiovisual (audio, images, video), interactive (they allow students to interact with the elements shown on the screen), and mixed.
- ✓ Identifying the different types of scenarios used.
- ✓ Establishing if both types of scenarios are combined.
- ✓ Considering how the advantages of each scenario are exploited.

C4. Development Tools	Related to *Q4*

Authoring tools used to implement the LO. The following tools are considered: LO assembly tools, content generation tools, tools to create activities/self-evaluations, tools to load metadata [8].
- ✓ Identifying the use of tools for the various development tasks.
- ✓ Identifying the use of tools that integrate design methodologies.
- ✓ Considering how the use of tools impacts educator work.

C5. Publication Environments	Related to *Q5*

Technological environments to which the LO has been or will be published. These can be: LORs or VTLEs.
- ✓ Identifying the publication of the LOs in interoperable environments.
- ✓ Identifying the type of environments used to publish the LOs.
- ✓ Considering the benefits offered by the publication of the LOs in these environments.

C6. Assessment Processes	Related to *Q6*

Assessment processes applied to the LO, if any, or processes that are planned for future application. This includes tests with the target audience for the LO (students) and experts (educators/researchers that specialize in the topic covered by the LO).
- ✓ Identifying if any assessment processes are applied to LOs.
- ✓ Identifying the tests that are carried out with students and educators.
- ✓ Considering if the results obtained with the tests have any impact on improvement plans for the LOs.

3.4 Cases of Interest - Analysis

Based on the criteria established, all the selected cases were studied. Table 3 details the results obtained for each criterion.

Table 3. Case analysis results.

Analysis criteria	Results obtained from studied cases
C1 *Motivations*	100% of the cases (cases 1–10) → mention the fact that educators want to take advantage of DEM languages potential, considering that LOs are a type of DEM. They present text information together with other resources: visual (static and moving images), auditory, interactive, and so forth
	60% of the cases (cases 2, 4–7, 9) → mention the fact that educators consider LOs as DEMs that can motivate students to learn. Educators believe that, due to the innovative nature and the interaction possibilities offered by LOs, they will help students find interest in the topic being discussed
	50% of the cases (cases 4–5, 8–10) → mention the fact that educators want to encourage student active participation in their own learning process. LOs have a specific learning objective and the following components: contents on the topic to be learned/taught, student activities related to those contents, and a self-evaluation that students use to test their knowledge. This allows students to work autonomously with self-contained DEMs that encourage them to learn
	40% of the cases (cases 2–4, 9) → mention the fact that the educators create LOs with the goal of generating DEMs that will be available for other educators and can be reused in other educational contexts
C2 *Design Methodology*	70% of the cases (cases 1–2, 4–5, 7, 9–10) → describe methodologies, theories and/or principles applied to LO design. Use of LO design methodologies, such as the hybrid approach *CROA Methodology*[a] [4] (case 9). Considering learning theories as framework for LO design (cases 2, 4–5, 7, 9–10), such as constructivist learning theories [30] (case 10), the *Significant Learning Theory* [31] (case 9), the *Cognitive Theory of Multimedia Learning* [32] (cases 5, 10), and the *Instructional Design Theory* [13] (case 5). Application of LO design principles based on *Software Engineering* (case 1)
	The remaining 30% of the cases → do not mention methodologies, theories or principles applied to LO design
C3 *Types of Design Scenarios*	100% of the cases (cases 1–10) → mention using audiovisual scenarios that include charts, images, animations, and videos. These scenarios were mainly used to present contents within the LOs
	100% of the cases (cases 1–10) → mention using interactive scenarios that allow solving activities, receiving feedback and checking solutions. In general, these scenarios were used for LO activities/self-evaluations

(continued)

Table 3. (*continued*)

Analysis criteria	Results obtained from studied cases
C4 *Development Tools*	60% of the cases (cases 2–4, 6–7, 9) → mention using development tools such as *Ardora*[b] to generate activities (case 9), *eXeLearning*[c] to assemble LOs and load metadata (cases 7, 9), and multimedia authoring *software* (case 4)
	The remaining 40% of the cases → do not mention using any tools for LO development
C5 *Publication Environments*	80% of the cases (cases 1, 3–4, 6–10) → refer to LO publication. This was done in VTLEs that comply with LO packing standards (cases 1, 6–7, 9), such as *Moodle*[d] (cases 6–7), or in LORs (cases 3–4, 8) such as *MERLOT*[e] (case 8). On the other hand, one of the cases (case 10) mentions that LOs will be available on the *Web* for a given period of time, but there is no mention to them being published to VTLEs/LORs
	The remaining 20% of the cases → do not mention LO publication
C6 *Assessment Processes*	80% of the cases (cases 1–2, 5–10) → mention testing their LOs with students using methods such as surveys (cases 2, 6), questionnaires before and after using the LOs (cases 5, 10), online assessment (cases 7–8, 10), usability tests (case 2), thinking-out-loud sessions (case 2), and interviews (cases 1, 5). Their goal was obtaining both technical and didactic feedback, as well as identifying potential use problems, such as navigation issues (case 2)
	The remaining 20% of the cases → do not mention student participation in LO testing
	50% of the cases (cases 2, 4, 7, 9–10) → mention testing their LOs with experts/educators using methods such as sample sessions (case 9), surveys (cases 2, 9), reviews (cases 2, 4, 10), peer assessment (case 9). Their goal was assessing LO contents and design and obtaining expert feedback for potential improvements
	The remaining 50% of the cases → do not mention expert/educator participation in LO testing

[a]*CROA Methodology*: http://croa.info.unlp.edu.ar/.
[b]*Ardora*: http://webardora.net/.
[c]*eXeLearning*: http://exelearning.net/.
[d]*Moodle*: https://moodle.org/.
[e]*MERLOT*: https://www.merlot.org/.

4 Discussion

The results obtained through these case studies are good to ponder over key issues related to LO creation and use. Below, each research question is discussed in the light of related analysis criteria.

- On *Q1* and *C1*: *Motivations*. Even though the reasons why educators create LOs and add them to their educational proposals are specific to each case, some shared aspects have been found. These can be summarized as follows: (a) encouraging active, autonomous participation of the students in their own learning process; (b) encouraging students to learn by offering innovative and dynamic DEMs; (c) offering students DEMs that are visually appealing and interactive to take advantage of the benefits of different languages; (d) creating DEMs that can be reused in other educational contexts. Reutilization is a core characteristic of LOs, but it is not the one that educators found most appealing for using LOs. Most of the cases that were reviewed made no reference to reusability as one of the reasons why the corresponding LOs were created.
- On *Q2* and *C2*: *Design Methodology*. The use of design methodologies specifically aimed at LOs is not very widespread among the cases that were reviewed. However, learning theories are widely considered when designing LOs. The hybrid approach is the preferred method when designing LOs. Design methodologies, hybrid ones in particular, help educators create LOs without disregarding technological or pedagogical aspects.
- On *Q3*: *Types of Design Scenarios*. The LOs used in the cases that were reviewed use both audiovisual and interactive scenarios. In general, both types of scenarios are combined. Audiovisual scenarios are found useful to present contents, since they do so through audio, image and video. Similarly, the features of interactive scenarios allow proposing activities for students to solve, and students can also check solutions and receive feedback. The fact that the features of the different types of scenarios can be exploited is considered to be positive. However, interactive scenarios could be used more thoroughly to explore contents.
- On *Q4* and *C4*: *Development Tools*. The most of the cases that were reviewed mention using tools for the various tasks pertaining to LO development, but no tools incorporating design methodologies are identified (this reinforces conclusions reached in previous articles [7, 8]). The availability of tools to implement the different parts of LOs is a great opportunity for educators interested in creating LOs. However, the use of any given tool requires educators to have some basic knowledge, and sometimes not so basic, about how to use the tool in question. If these tools require an advanced user level, those educators who are not too familiar with technology could have a hard time using them. Tools that can be used throughout the different stages of the LO creation process and take into account methodological steps guiding those processes are required.
- On *Q5* and *C5*: *Publication Environments*. In most of the cases that were reviewed, LOs are published to technological environments that meet packing standards. It was observed that LOs are mostly published to VTLEs when they are going to be used in specific educational contexts. However, when educators want to make their LOs available to the general educational community, they usually publish them to LORs. Educators seem to be aware that LOs should be published to interoperable environments to help locate and access them to allow others to reuse them. This is an aspect that should be considered in more detail for effective LO reutilization.

- On *Q6* and *C6*: *Assessment Processes*. In most of the cases that were reviewed, LOs go through some kind of assessment process. Tests with students and/or educators/experts are used. These tests are aimed at obtaining results/feedback/assessments that can be used to improve the LOs being developed. It should be noted that both educators and students have a positive opinion on the use of LOs in educational contexts.

5 Conclusions and Future Work

In this section, we discuss the conclusions drawn from the review carried out.

Since their inception, through the *MECCANO, LEGO*, and atoms metaphors first and the evolution of the concept with the contributions of various specialized authors thereon, LOs have been defined as reusable DEMs that can be assembled. To favor reutilization, LOs have metadata that identify and describe them, and LORs are used to index them and make them available to any interested parties that want to use them, adapt them or assemble them as needed.

Reutilization is one of the core features behind the concept of LOs, but there are issues that make its implementation difficult. The lack of a single definition of LO that is formally accepted hinders the creation of reusable LOs, since different concepts may be used to create them. For instance, LOs could have different granularities – one LO could encompass all contents for a given course whereas a second LO could include only one resource (such as an image). These differences create a barrier for LO reutilization and integration in specific learning itineraries.

Motivations shared by all educators when creating LOs and adding them to their educational proposals were found, such as encouraging active and autonomous learning, encouraging students to learn, incorporating visual and interactive information, and generating reusable educational material. Despite the fact that reutilization is one of the identifying features of LOs, it was observed that it is not the main motivation behind LO creation – only 40% of the cases that were reviewed mention it as motivation. Additionally, only 30% of the cases that were reviewed mention publishing their LOs to LORs. If a larger sample were analyzed and these trends were confirmed, they could officially become causes contributing to the lack of LO reutilization by educators.

As regards LO design and development stages, it was observed that the use of LO design methodologies is scarce. Improving on this aspect would undoubtedly help improve the quality of the LOs that are produced and promote their reusability. A significant integration of audiovisual and interactive scenarios to LO design was observed, which is favorable and allows exploiting hypermedia language. On the other hand, tools were used for the various development tasks involved in LO creation (60% of the cases that were reviewed), but such tools are not accompanied by methodologies that are specific for LO creation.

In relation to LO assessment, the application of tests before, during and/or after the use of LOs was found to be quite common; both students (80% of the cases that were reviewed) and educators (50% of the cases that were reviewed) are involved in these tests. In general, these results can be used as a starting point to achieve improvements in LOs.

There are positive aspects and barriers for the educational community that takes part in LO design and development. This review also helped consolidate the reasons to continue with the development of *MarCOA*, a *framework* proposed for LO creation [7] that is based on the *CROA Methodology* [4]. The functionality of this *framework* is aimed at meeting the main needs identified in relation to LO creation, use and reutilization. It proposes a hybrid methodology integrated into an authoring tool for the creation of LOs, so that guidance is offered to educators both for technological and pedagogical aspects throughout the creation process. It also allows considering reutilization as part of the design of LOs, helping educators create LOs that offer this feature.

References

1. Del Moral, M., Villalustre, L.: Didáctica universitaria en la era 20: competencias docentes en campus virtuales. RUSC. Univ. Knowl. Soc. J. **9**(1) (2012)
2. Sanz, C.: Los objetos de aprendizaje, un debate abierto y necesario. Bit & Byte (2015)
3. Polsani, P.: Use and abuse of reusable learning objects. J. Digit. Inf. **3**(4) (2006)
4. Sanz, C., Barranquero, F., Moralejo, L.: CROA: a learning object design and creation methodology to bridge the gap between educators and reusable educational material creation. In: EDULEARN16, pp. 4583–4592 (2016)
5. Prendes, M., Martínez, F., Gutiérrez, I.: Producción de material didáctico: los objetos de aprendizaje. Revista Iberoamericana de Educación a Distancia (RIED) **11**(1), 80–106 (2008)
6. Mora-Vicarioli, F.: Objetos de aprendizaje: Importancia de su uso en la educación virtual. Revista Electrónica Calidad en la Educación Superior **3**(1), 104–118 (2012)
7. Violini, L., Sanz, C., Pesado, P.: Propuesta de un Framework para la creación de Objetos de Aprendizaje. In: XXIII Congreso Argentino de Ciencias de la Computación, pp. 383–392. UNLP, Argentina (2017). ISBN 978-950-34-1539-9
8. Violini, L., Sanz, C.: Herramientas de Autor para la creación de Objetos de Aprendizaje. ESTADO DEL ARTE. In: XXII Congreso Argentino de Ciencias de la Computación, pp. 353–362. UNSL, Argentina (2016). ISBN 978-987-733-072-4
9. Violini, L., Sanz, C.: Diseño, desarrollo, publicación y evaluación de Objetos de Aprendizaje. Un estudio de casos. In: XXIV Congreso Argentino de Ciencias de la Computación, pp. 223–232. UNCPBA, Argentina (2018). ISBN 978-950-658-472-6
10. Gerard, R.: Shaping the mind: computers in education. Appl. Sci. Technol. Progr. 207–228 (1967)
11. Merrill, D., Li, Z., Jones, M.: Second generation instructional design (ID$_2$). Educ. Technol. **30**(2), 7–14 (1990)
12. Hodgins, W.: The future of learning objects. In: The Instructional Use of Learning Objects: Online Version (2000)
13. Wiley, D.: Connecting learning objects to instructional design theory: a definition, a metaphor, and a taxonomy. Instr. Use Learn. Objects **2830**(435), 1–35 (2000)
14. Allen, C., Mugisa, E.: Improving Learning object reuse through OOD: a theory of learning objects. J. Object Technol. **9**(6), 51–75 (2010)
15. Sicilia, M., García, E.: On the concepts of usability and reusability of learning objects. Int. Rev. Res. Open Distrib. Learn. **4**(2) (2003)

16. De La Torre, L., Dominguez, J.: Las TIC en el proceso de enseñanza aprendizaje a través de los objetos de aprendizaje. Revista Cubana de Informática Médica **4**(1), 83–92 (2012)
17. Gasparetti, F., De Medio, C., Limongelli, C., Sciarrone, F., Temperini, M.: Prerequisites between learning objects: automatic extraction based on a machine learning approach. Telemat. Inform. **35**(3), 595–610 (2018)
18. Sergis, S., Sampson, D.: Learning object recommendations for teachers based on elicited ICT competence profiles. IEEE Trans. Learn. Technol. **9**(1), 67–80 (2016)
19. Salehi, M., Pourzaferani, M., Razavi, S.: Hybrid attribute-based recommender system for learning material using genetic algorithm and a multidimensional information model. Egypt. Inform. J. **14**(1), 67–78 (2013)
20. Chalk, P., Bradley, C., Pickard, P.: Designing and evaluating learning objects for introductory programming education. In: ACM SIGCSE Bulletin, p. 240 (2003)
21. Krauss, F., Ally, M.: A study of the design and evaluation of a learning object and implications for content development. Interdisc. J. Knowl. Learn. Objects (IJKLO) **1**, 1–22 (2005)
22. Reis, F., et al.: A learning object on computational intelligence. In: Sixth International Conference on Advanced Learning Technologies (ICALT), p. 33. IEEE (2006)
23. Ummi, H., Aida, K., Azrita, A., Elia, H.: Development of learning object for engineering courses in UTeM. In: International Conference on Engineering Education (ICEED), pp. 19–195. IEEE (2009)
24. Matthews, R., Hin, H., Choo, K.: Multimedia learning object to build cognitive understanding in learning introductory programming. In: 7th international Conference on Advances in Mobile Computing and Multimedia (MoMM), pp. 396–400. ACM (2009)
25. Tuparov, G., Tuparova, D., Tsarnakova, A.: Using interactive simulation-based learning objects in introductory course of programming. Procedia-Soc. Behav. Sci. **46**, 2276–2280 (2012)
26. Orozco, C., Morales, E.: The eXeLearning and GeoGebra integration for teaching geometrics definitions and vectors representations through learning objects. In: Second International Conference on Technological Ecosystems for Enhancing Multiculturality (TEEM), p. 639–645. ACM (2014)
27. Tiosso, F., Bruschi, S., Souza, P., Barbosa, E., de Andrade, C.: Amnesia: a learning object for memory hierarchy teaching. In: Frontiers in Education Conference (FIE), pp. 1–7. IEEE (2015)
28. Violini, L., Sanz, C.: Learning objects: how to insert an element into a vector? In: Twelfth Latin American Conference on Learning Technologies (LACLO), pp. 1–4. IEEE (2017). ISBN 978-1-5386-2376-3
29. Redmond, C., et al.: Using reusable learning objects (RLOs) in wound care education: undergraduate student nurse's evaluation of their learning gain. Nurse Educ. Today **60**, 3–10 (2018)
30. Bannan-Ritland, B., Dabbagh, N., Murphy, K.: Learning object systems as constructivist learning environments: related assumptions, theories and applications. In: Wiley, D.A. (ed.) The Instructional Use of Learning Objects (2000)
31. Ausubel, D.: Teoría del aprendizaje significativo. Fascículos de CEIF **1**, 1–10 (1983)
32. Mayer, R.: Multimedia Learning. Cambridge University Press, Cambridge (2009)

A Nomadic Testbed for Teaching Computer Architecture

Pablo D. Godoy[1,2,3(✉)], Carlos G. García Garino[1,2], and Ricardo L. Cayssials[4]

[1] ITIC, Universidad Nacional de Cuyo, Mendoza, Argentina
`pablo.godoy@ingenieria.uncuyo.edu.ar`
[2] Facultad de Ingeniería, Universidad Nacional de Cuyo, Mendoza, Argentina
[3] FCEN, Universidad Nacional de Cuyo, Mendoza, Argentina
[4] Universidad Tecnológica Nacional - FRBB, Bahía Blanca, Buenos Aires, Argentina

Abstract. A nomadic laboratory or testbed, based on Raspberry Pi 3 computers and Arduino microcontrollers, has been developed in order to teach subjects related to computer architecture. The testbed can be transported to the classroom. Students can access it through the available network, which can be a wireless LAN, wired LAN o a custom network. Students can access without constraints to the platforms, therefore there are a wide range of possible experiments. This laboratory was used during 2017 for practical works in the course Introduction to Technology, and during 2018 in two courses of Computers Architecture at Universidad Nacional of Cuyo and in a course of Wireless Networks at Universidad de Mendoza. Some of the experiments that are been carried out by students are: to explore and analyse the architecture of computers through Linux commands, write and run programs on different programing languages, input and output operations through memory mapped addressing and isolated addressing, write interrupt service routines in order to service interrupts, multithreading programing, explore memory maps, CPU features, etc. This paper describes the testbed architecture, experiments performed by students in the mentioned subjects, present the students feedback, and describes the possible methods in order to integrate it to a remote laboratory.

Keywords: Nomadic testbeds · Teaching platform ·
Computer architecture

1 Introduction

Computer architecture is a central subject in careers such as engineering or bachelor degrees in computer, information systems, electronics, information and communication technology, etc. Laboratory experiences and practical activities about computer architecture usually implies to recognize all components, their functions and features in different computer systems, such as the processors, data memories, data buses, bridges, etc., to employ operating system tools to visualize and analyze the processors workload, memory usage, peripheral status,

P. Pesado and C. Aciti (Eds.): CACIC 2018, CCIS 995, pp. 74–87, 2019.
https://doi.org/10.1007/978-3-030-20787-8_6

etc., and to build programs to perform input/output operations, multithreading task over superscalar processors or multiple core processors, etc. In order to perform laboratory experiences and practical activities, students need to access to different kind of computers, in order to understand and compare different computer architectures. As a result, it is very useful to build platforms to enable students carrying out practical works and laboratory experiences.

University computer laboratories usually have computers based on x86 processors (Intel, AMD, etc.). This limits the kinds of architectures over which students carry out experiments. As a result, it is useful to deploy platforms and facilities with different architectures, for example: ARM, in order to give students more options about different computer architectures for performing experiments. In the literature several experimental platforms have been proposed, with educational and scientific purposes [1–4].

Horneber and Hergenröder [2] distinguish between two kinds experimentation platforms or testbeds, nomadic testbeds and remote testbeds. Nomadic testbed can be completely or partly movable to the place where the experiments will be performed. The main advantage of nomadic testbeds for teaching purposes is that students can put hands on the equipments. But the main disadvantage is the limited time for performing the experiments. Remote testbeds can be accessed remotely through Internet. The advantage of remote testbeds is that they can be accessed all time, but the main disadvantage is that students can not put hands on the equipments under test. Our platform can be entirely transported to the classroom in order to students carry out experiments. But also can be remotely accessed by SSH protocol. Therefore, our platform have features of both kind of experimental platforms.

However, until today our platform only has been used as a nomadic testbed. As a result, we classify our platform as a nomadic testbed for teaching purposes, with capacity to be transformed in a remote and nomadic testbed. The main contributions of this papers are two:

- The proposed architecture to build a nomadic experimental platform to perform experiments related with computer architecture based on ARM processors.
- The proposed experiments for putting in practice theoretical knowledges about computer architectures, that students acquire during theoretical classes.

This paper is an extended version of the paper presented in the 24rd Argentina Congress on Computer Science, CACIC 2018, held in Tandil, Argentina, in October 2018 [5]. Regard to the original paper, this extended version adds:

- More details about the performed experiments, results and feedbacks obtained from students.
- Results produced by the use of the nomadic laboratory in two additional courses that were not reported in the original paper: "Computer Architecture" of the Networks and Telecommunication career at the University Technological Institute (ITU) in Universidad Nacional de Cuyo, and "Wireless Networks" of the Master in Teleinformatics career at the Mendoza University.

This extended version of the paper presents all needed information in order to reproduce the teaching activities described bellow, so that readers will be able to reproduce these teaching experiments in their classes.

2   Remote Laboratory Architecture

2.1   Equipment

The laboratory are formed by nodes. The central part of the nodes are Raspberry Pi 3 computers [6]. The election of this computer is due to they have processor of four cores, which enables multicore and multithreading experiments. These kinds of experiments are needed in the last part of the subject *Computer Architecture*, in order to students can write programs over parallel architectures. On the other hand, computer laboratories for teaching purposes usually are built with PC computers with x86 processors. One objective of our proposed testbed is to use ARM processors, in order to extend the architecture types over which students carry out practical works. In addition, the small size of these computers are a very important feature due to the laboratory must be transported. An auxiliary board with leds and buttons is attached to the Raspberry Pi 3 computer. The leds and buttons are connected to the general purpose input/output pins of the Raspberry Pi 3, to enable performing input and output experiments.

In addition, an Arduino UNO board [4,7] is attached to each Raspberry Pi 3 computer, for enabling experiments over a simpler computer and over other kind of peripheral, like analogical to digital converters, etc. An auxiliary board with leds and buttons is attached to the Arduino board. The leds and buttons are connected to the general purpose input/output pins of the Arduino, to enable performing input and output experiments. The Arduino Integrated Development Environment (IDE) is installed on the Raspberry Pi 3 computer. Both computers are attached by a USB cable. The equipment is completed by:

- The teacher computer: that enables monitoring the students activities through SSH or VNC protocols.
- An access point: that enables wireless access to the Raspberries.
- Ethernet cables: that enable wired access to the Raspberries.

The kind of access is selected in function of the infrastructure and network available in the classroom. The Fig. 1 shows a block diagram of a node.

2.2   Access to the Equipment Under Test

The access to the equipment under test is through SSH or VNC protocols. In some experiments students need to consult configuration files or run Linux commands. To other experiments, students need to write and run programs. To almost all activities, both SSH and VNC can be used equally. The VNC protocol is mandatory only to employ the tools provided by the Raspberry Pi operating system. Both tools, SSH and VNC, have been used in several testbeds presented

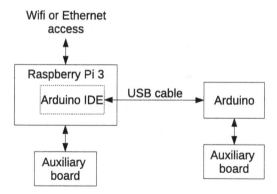

Fig. 1. Node block diagram

in the bibliography, for example: [8,9]. The experiences carried out during 2017 and 2018 shown that students prefer VNC, maybe due to students prefers to interact through a graphical user interface (GUI) proper of desktop operanting systems. As a result, students are encouraged to use both: SSH and VNC, in order to acquire experience in the use of a wider range of tools. In order to access to the equipment, three methods are provided:

- Through Ethernet network.
- Through Wifi Network.
- Through a cloud services provider accessible through Internet.

The first method can be used if there is an Ethernet network deployed in the classroom. The second method, through Wifi, is always available due to the platform has a Wifi access point as a part of its equipments, and each Raspberry Pi 3 computer can be used as an access points for deploying a wireless network. The access through a cloud platform was implemented using the services of Remote-IoT [10]. Through this service, a computer can be accessed remotely through Internet, via SSH and VNC protocols. The access through a cloud platform will be investigated and analyzed in greater details in future works. The three methods were used during 2017 and 2018, in the courses of *Computers Architecture*, *Introduction to Technology* and *Wireless Networks* with successful results.

2.3 Deployment of the Laboratory in a Typical Experiment

Each node has two interfaces: an Ethernet interface and a Wifi interface, as it is shown in Fig. 2. The Ethernet interfaces are configured with 192.168.0.x addresses, with x between 0 and 255. The Wifi interfaces are configured with 192.168.1.x addresses, with x between 0 and 255. In the classroom, the nomadic laboratory can be deployed in three different methods: (i) using the available Ethernet network, (ii) deploying a Wifi network, (iii) through Internet using cloud computer services, as it is described follow:

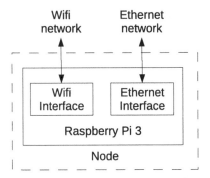

Fig. 2. Node interfaces

Deployment Through the Available Ethernet in the Classroom. If there
is an Ethernet network available in the classroom that enables to add new computers, the same can be used by to deploy the nomadic laboratory. To this
purpose, the IP addresses of the Ethernet interfaces of the nodes must be modified in order to use the available IP addresses of the Ethernet network. In order
to configure Ethernet interfaces, the wireless interfaces of the nodes are used.
This is the preferred method to deploy the laboratory, because the nodes are
integrated to another network. As a result, students can perform experiments
over the ARM computers of the nomadic laboratory and also over the classroom
computers, which are usually of x86 architecture.

Deployment Through a Wireless Network. If an Ethernet network is not
available in the classroom, or the users prefer it, a wireless network can be used to
deploy the nomadic laboratory. In this case, the Raspberry Pi wireless interface
have to be used. Two options are possible:

– Take advantage of a wireless network available in the classroom.
– To deploy a new wireless network.

In the first case, access permission to the wireless network is needed, and the
node IP addresses have to be configured, according the available IP addresses
of the wireless network. In the second case, an access point is needed. For this
reason, the nomadic laboratory has an access point as part of its equipment. In
the other hand, the nodes IP addresses can be configured without constraints,
for example, the preconfigured nodes IP addresses can be used.

Deployment Through Cloud Computing Services. This is not an example
of nomadic use, but is a remote access example. In this case, a cloud computing
service provider is needed. This cloud computing service provider have to enable
to connect computers to the cloud and have to allow access to these computers
through SSH or VNC protocols. Therefore, users can access in the same way that
in situ experiments, but remotely. The disadvantage is that users can not put

hands on the equipment, consequently, these kind of experiments would have to be complemented with classroom experiments, which are possible through the nomadic function of the laboratory.

3   Performed Experiments

In this section, some experiments carry out by students during 2017 and 2018 over the presented laboratory are described.

3.1   Architecture Analysis

In these experiments, students analyze the architecture of a computer through Linux commands. The objective is that students learn how to explore the hardware of a computer through the operating system. In order to perform this activity, students need knowledge of computer components, processors, memory, bridges, input/output devices, ports and buses.

Even though there are a lot of commands and methods to explore the hardware of a computer, for this practical work a list of proposed Linux commands have been selected. The commands employed were:

- lshw (HardWare LiSter for Linux): tool to show information about the hardware configuration of the computer. The information shown by lshw includes: (a) memory configuration, (b) CPU features and speed, (c) cache memory configuration, (d) type of buses and speeds, (e) bridges between buses, (f) massive storage devices, (g) different peripheral, etc.
- lspci: shows information about PCI buses and devices attached to these buses.
- free: shows information about memory, used and free physical and swap memory, and memory used as buffers.
- uname: displays information about the operating system.
- df: shows information about the hard disk (option used: -h).
- ifconfig: displays information about the network interfaces.

These commands and most of their options and output formats have been selected for performing this practical activity (see [10] for detailed information about these commands and their options). The activity carried out by the students consisted in:

- Execute these commands.
- Analyze the information produced.
- Draw a block diagram of the computer architecture and specify their characteristics.

The last part of the practical work, to draw a block diagram of the computer architecture, was a difficult activity for students, it required the aid of the teachers.

3.2   Input-Output Operations

The objectives of this activity are:

– Distinguish between the two addressing methods of input and output devices: memory mapped and isolated addressing [11].
– Get experience in writing programs with input and output operations.

The practical work consists of switching off and on leds and to read the state of input pins through two methods:

– Memory mapped I/O devices
– Isolated I/O devices

For Arduino computers, students can use both methods, and for Raspberry Pi 3 computer, only memory mapped access is available. In order to see the differences between these two methods, students must program the processors in assembler language, since a high level language hides these details for programmers. The students write code segment in assembly language embedded in C, C++ or Python language (known languages for students).

   For Raspberry Pi 3 computers, students have to write a program in C o Python language, and to write and read the files located in the /sys/class/gpio folder of Raspbian operating system [6]. For Arduino computers, students have to write input and output routines in assembler language, using the AVR Instruction Set [12]. These input and output routines are embedded in C language. The Table 1 shows and example of an output operation performed through the two methods: memory mapped I/O and isolated I/O. In the memory mapped I/O, the port B is mapped in the 0x25 address, and for the isolated I/O method, the port B is accessed though the 0x05 address.

Table 1. Output routine examples written in AVR assembler language

Memory mapped I/O	Isolated I/O
lds r17, 0x25	in r17, 0x05
ori r17, 0b00100000	ori r17, 0b00010000
sts 0x25, r17	out 0x05, r17

3.3   Writing of Interrupt Service Routines

Writing of Interrupt Service Routines in Arduino UNO. The practical activities consist of writing service routines to attend interrupts caused by signals detected in input pins. For this purpose, students are provided with a guide about Arduino IDE programing (obtained from [7]) and the instruction set of the ATmega328P processor [12], that is the processor used by the Arduino UNO platform. In addition, a pre-written code that include the scheme of an

Arduino program in C language and the code to embed assembler instructions are provided.

Students write service routines for the two interrupt sources of the Arduino Uno platform, INT.0 for the pin 2 and INT.1 for the pin 3. These pins are activated by buttons. These service routines inform when an interrupt is detected. Service routine of the pin 0 turn on leds in a sequence, and the service routine of the pin 1 turn on leds in a different sequence. After, students have to push the buttons in order to find out what interrupt source has higher priority and if the Arduino UNO enable nested interrupts. Students can conclude that:

- While an interrupt is been attended running its service routine, the interrupts are disabled. Therefore, Arduino UNO does not allow interrupt nesting.
- If the two interrupts are triggered at the same time, interrupt INT.0 (pin 2) always is attended first. In order to activate both interrupts at the same time, both pins must be attached to the same button.
- If both interruptions are triggered while global interruptions are disabled, then, when global interrupts enable, always interrupt INT.0 (pin 2) is going to be attended first, although interrupt INT.1 (pin 3) had been triggered first.

Writing of Interrupt Service Routines in Raspberry Pi 3. A similar activity is carry out over Raspberry Pi 3 platform. Two differences with Arduino UNO activity are proposed to students:

- Write programs using Python language and the RPi.GPIO library [13] for handling interruptions.
- Use the configuration files of the Linux file system in order to control the hardware instead of assembly language.

These changes have the purpose of give new knowledge to students. Python language is chosen in order to motivate students to use several programming languages. Similar to the previous activity, students write service routines for two interrupt sources of the Raspberry Pi 3 platform. These interrupts are triggered by signals over different input pins. These service routines inform when an interrupt is detected. After, students carry out a set of actions to analyze the interruption priorities. In addition, students can analyze interrupts statistics through the */proc/interrupts* Linux file.

3.4   Multithreading Programing

The objective of this activity is to show to students the speed-up that can be achieved in some task using multithreading programing. For this activity, Raspberry Pi 3 computers were used due to they have processors with four cores. Because students at this points of theirs career have reduced knowledge of programming, this activity was performed using C++ language, due to it enables to write multithreading programs in an easy way. Other options (like Python, Java or C) require to use classes and objects, and students still does not have knowledge about these topics. The activity consists of writing a program that uses a 200x200 matrix of float point variables, and several subroutines that perform the following tasks:

- Modify a randomly chosen elements of the matrix with a random value every time that this function is called.
- Calculate the root mean square value of all elements of the matrix.
- Obtain the highest value inside the matrix.
- Find the row whose sum of their elements has the highest value.

After verify the proper execution of their programs, students verify some statistic of execution through Linux commands, like number of threads, cores usage, execution speed of every function, etc. Some Linux commands and tools used in this activity are:

- top: shows a list of process in execution state, with some statistic. In this exercise students have to verify processor and memory usage,
- content of the file */proc/process PID/status*, that show information of the process. In this exercise is the special interest the parameter *Threads*, that shows the number of threads of the process.

Then, students are instructed to divide their programs in several threads using the functions provided by C++ language. For simplicity, students are suggested to execute every subroutine in a different thread. After verify the proper functioning of their programs, students verify again the above mentioned execution statistics, and compare against the prior values. Students can see how the parallel execution of their functions increases the processor usage and the speed of every function. Some results obtained by students are:

- Without threads the usage percentage of one processor is almost 100%, and for the other processors is very low (around 10%), since only one processor run the process. With threads, the usage percentage of all processor is around 60%, since the threads of the process are allocated to the four processors.
- The throughput of the tasks described above increases around four times.
- The total percentage of use of the processor (included the four cores) increase from around 25% (without threads) to around 60% (with threads).

Some students, for their own initiative, went beyond what was requested them and divided their programs in more threads (a group divided its program in 64 threads), and a competition for achieve a higher number of threads was generated between students. Students obtained higher and lower speed-ups. This result allowed showing to students that the parallelization must be performed in an efficient way (students will acquire knowledge about efficient parallelization and execution of tasks in later subjects of their career).

3.5   Interference in Wireless Networks

The objective of these experiments is to show the effect of interference on wireless networks (IEEE 802.11). For this purpose, the Raspberries Pi 3 computers were used as wireless access points of IEEE 802.11 wireless networks on infrastructure mode. Wireless access points based on Raspberry Pi 3 computers are chosen due to they enable to configure a wider range of parameters than commercial wireless access points, like the inter-frame time for different kind of data. Information about how configuring a Raspberry Pi 3 as an access point can be found in the web site of the Raspberry Pi Foundation [6].

The experiments performed by students consist of measuring the following parameters:

- Data rate while a large size file is transferred.
- Latency for a ping command during the transference.

These parameters were measured under the following conditions:

- Three wireless access points in different wireless channels.
- Three wireless access points in the same wireless channel with time inter-frame values similar to commercials wireless access points.
- Three wireless access points in the same wireless channel with time inter-frame values modified a their minimum value [14].

In order to perform the last modification, students have to modify the parameters "wmm_ac_xx_aifs" in the file /etc/hostapd/hostapd.conf.

The measurements were performed while three users were transferring big size files between the wireless access points to their computers through SSH protocol, being connected every user to a different wireless access point. That is, three different wireless networks sharing the same physical space. The values of the above mentioned parameters were obtained through the values displayed by the ping and SCP (secure copy protocol) commands.

Students can see how the channel occupation affect the individual data rate and latency. The methodology of these experiments was obtained of a similar experiment, carried out with scientific purposes, using a wireless sensor network [15].

4   Answer to an Anonymous Survey About the Use of the Testbed

Eighteen students that took the course "Technology Introduction" of the Computer Science career at Universidad Nacional de Cuyo in the year 2017, were invited to answer an anonymous survey about the use of the platform. The questions of the survey and the students answers were:

1. Was the proposed platform useful in your process of acquiring new knowledge?
   Answers:
   (a) It was not useful: 0%
   (b) It was useful: 20%
   (c) It was very useful: 80%.

2. Were the experiments interesting and amused?
   Answers:
   (a) The experiments were boring and no interesting: 0%
   (b) The experiments were interesting and amused: 10%
   (c) The experiments were very interesting and amused: 90%.
3. Were the experiments easily to perform and could you understand the theoretical concepts behind each activity?
   Answers:
   (a) The experiments were complicated and I could not understand the concepts: 0%
   (b) The experiments were easy to follow and I could understand the concepts: 20%
   (c) The experiments were easy to follow and I could understand very well the concepts: 80%.

In addition, student were invited to make suggestions and comments. Some of these suggestions and comments (literally transcribed) were:

- *"It was very amused and motivating"*.
- *"It was a very good experience"*.
- *"It would be good to have more time to work with the platform"*.

In addition, students that took the course "Computer Architecture" of the Computer Science career at Universidad Nacional de Cuyo in the year 2018, must answer an anonymous survey about the performance of teachers and the course. This survey does not include any question about the platform presented in this paper, but students mention it in their answer. Some of the students answer to the question *"What did you find most positive and worth repeating?"* were:

- *"The projects with Arduinos"*.
- *"I really like the exercises with Raspberry Pi and remote connections"*.
- *"The exercises with Raspberries and Arduinos"*.

Surveys to students of the courses "Computer Architecture" of the Networks and Telecommunication career at the University Technological Institute (ITU) in Universidad Nacional de Cuyo, and "Wireless Networks" of the Master in Teleinformatics career at the Mendoza University, both in the year 2018 are pending. But in both courses students shown a positive reception.

5   Future Work

Remote laboratories, also known as remote testbeds, are platforms that allow remote access to different types of equipments, devices, laboratories, etc. through a LAN networks or Internet. They are complex systems that include a large number of components with functions such as: access control, monitoring of activities, information storage, etc. They may be aimed at scientific research, application development, training, teaching, etc. [3, 16, 17].

Cloud computing is a model for allowing on demand and ubiquitous access to a configurable, virtualized and shared computational resources set (for example networks, servers, storage, applications and services), that can be quickly provided and released with minimal management effort and interaction with the cloud services provider. These resources are offered by cloud computing services providers to external customers through Internet as web services, based on negotiated agreements between the service provider and customers [18].

The immediate future work will be to integrate the proposed testbed to a cloud computing platform, similar to [19,20]. The objective of this integration is to provide access to the testbed all time through Internet, overcoming the time limitation for accessing the nomadic testbed mentioned by students.

In addition, the laboratory is going to be used in courses of computer networks and distributed architectures in 2019.

6 Conclusions

The experiments performed by students during 2017 and 2018 show the versatility of the proposed platform for performing different kind of experiments, including:

- Analyze the internal architecture of different computers.
- Perform input and output operations and to write interruption service routines.
- Basic parallelization of tasks.
- Analysis of wireless networks behavior.

During the experiments it can be noted that students adopted very well the proposed educational testbed, and they wanted to exploit it adding activities different to the proposed ones. In addition, the feedback obtained from students through an anonymous survey was very positive. This shows the motivation of students to work with new and different technology. For this reason, it is needed to increase the number of nodes of the platform and to add a mechanism that enable remote access to the platform. In this way, students would be able to access the platform from their homes.

Acknowledgment. The authors acknowledge the financial support received from the *Universidad* Nacional de Cuyo through the project *B041 "Implementación de laboratorios remotos basados en cloud computing"*. Also, authors acknowledge to the professors *Lucas Iacono* and *Osvaldo Marianetti*, professors of *Introduction to Technology* and *Computer Architecture* respectively, at *Universidad Nacional de Cuyo*, for allow us to use our platform on their courses. In addition, authors acknowledge to the University Technological Institute (ITU) in Universidad Nacional de Cuyo, and to the Mendoza University, for allowing us to use our platform in the courses mentioned in this paper.

References

1. Steyn, L.P., Hancke, G.P.: A survey of wireless sensor network testbeds. In: IEEE Africon 2011, pp. 1–6, September 2011
2. Horneber, J., Hergenröder, A.: A survey on testbeds and experimentation environments for wireless sensor networks. IEEE Commun. Surv. Tutor. **16**(4), 1820–1838 (2014)
3. Orduña, P., Gómez-Goiri, A., Rodriguez-Gil, L., Diego, J., de Ipiña, D.L., Garcia-Zubia, J.: wCloud: automatic generation of weblab-deusto deployments in the cloud. In: Proceedings of 2015 12th International Conference on Remote Engineering and Virtual Instrumentation (REV), pp. 223–229, February 2015
4. Mostefaoui, H., Benachenhou, A., Benattia, A.A.: Design of a low cost remote electronic laboratory suitable for low bandwidth connection. Comput. Appl. Eng. Educ. **25**(3), 480–488 (2017). https://onlinelibrary.wiley.com/doi/abs/10.1002/cae.21815
5. Godoy, P.D., García Garino, C.G., Cayssials, R.L.: A nomadic testbed for teaching computer architecture. In: XVII Workshop Tecnología Informática Aplicada en Educación (WTIAE), XXIV Argentina Congress on Computer Science, (CACIC) (2018)
6. Raspberry Pi Foundation website: Raspberry pi 3 single-board computer (2018). https://www.raspberrypi.org/. Accessed 2018
7. Arduino s.r.l: Arduino Uno rev3 documentation (2018). https://www.arduino.cc/. Accessed 2018
8. Kabiri, M.N., Wannous, M.: An experimental evaluation of a cloud-based virtual computer laboratory using Openstack. In: 2017 6th IIAI International Congress on Advanced Applied Informatics (IIAI-AAI), pp. 667–672, July 2018. https://doi.ieeecomputersociety.org/10.1109/IIAI-AAI.2017.94
9. Gerhard, T., Schwerdel, D., Müller, P.: A networkless data exchange and control mechanism for virtual testbed devices. In: Leung, V.C.M., Chen, M., Wan, J., Zhang, Y. (eds.) TridentCom 2014. LNICST, vol. 137, pp. 14–22. Springer, Cham (2014). https://doi.org/10.1007/978-3-319-13326-3_2
10. Remote-IoT: Remote-IoT website (2018). https://remote-iot.com/web/index.htm. Accessed 2018
11. Stallings, W.: Computer Organization and Architecture Designing for Performance, 9th edn. Pearson, London (2013)
12. Microchip Technology Inc.: DS40001984A: Complete Datasheet of the ATmega-328/P (2018). https://www.microchip.com. Accessed 2018
13. Python Software Foundation: RPi.GPIO Project (2018). https://pypi.org/project/RPi.GPIO/. Accessed 2018
14. IEEE Institute: IEEE std 802.15.4-2003, pp. 1–670 (2003). Accessed 2015
15. Godoy, P.D., Cayssials, R.L., García Garino, C.G.: Communication channel occupation and congestion in wireless sensor networks. Comput. Electr. Eng. **72**, 846–858 (2018). http://www.sciencedirect.com/science/article/pii/S0045790617300782
16. Godoy, P.D., Cayssials, R., García Garino, C.: A WSN testbed for teaching purposes. IEEE Lat. Am. Trans. **14**(7), 3351–3357 (2016)
17. Waldrop, M.: Campus 2.0. Nature **495**(7440), 160–163 (2013)
18. Buyya, R., Yeo, C.S., Venugopal, S., Broberg, J., Brandic, I.: Cloud computing and emerging IT platforms: vision, hype, and reality for delivering computing as the 5th utility. Futur. Gener. Comput. Syst. **25**(6), 599–616 (2009)

19. Godoy, P., Cayssials, R., García Garino, C.: A cloud based WSN remote laboratory for user training. In: Morón, U. (ed.) Proceedings of TE&ET (Technology in Education and Education in Technology) (2016)
20. Godoy, P., Cayssials, R., García Garino, C.: Laboratorio remoto para la formación de usuarios basado en el cloud. Revista Iberoamericana de Educación en Tecnología y Tecnología en Educación **18**, 7–18 (2016)

Graphic Computation, Images and Visualization

Evaluating an End-to-End Process for Herpetological Heritage Digital Preservation

Nicolás Jofré, Graciela Rodríguez($^{\boxtimes}$), Yoselie Alvarado, Jacqueline Fernandez, and Roberto Guerrero

Laboratorio de Computación Gráfica (LCG), Universidad Nacional de San Luis, Ejército de los Andes 950, San Luis, Argentina
gbrodriguez@unsl.edu.ar

Abstract. Documentation of institutional biological collections are essential for scientific studies and conservation of the biodiversity of a region. In particular, preserved specimens require the development of a short- and long-term plan to prevent damage.

In this context, the 3D digitisation of this type of documentation provides innovative mechanisms to safeguard the valuable information provided by the collections and at the same time prevent any possible loss of information. At the moment, the potential of laser scanning in model reconstruction is well-known, but developed works using this method for 3D construction reveal a lack of reliable, precise and flexible solutions. Furthermore, visualisation of results is often very useless and does not go beyond web-based applications.

This work presents an analysis of 3D modelling using two digitisation techniques: laser scanning and photogrammetry; combined with real time VR and AR visualizations and 3D printing. Subsequently, in accordance with the processes carried out, qualitative and quantitative evaluations of the results obtained are accomplished.

Keywords: Reality Computing · Digital photogrammetry ·
3D scanning · Virtual Reality (VR) · Augmented Reality (AR) ·
3D printing

1 Introduction

Generally, digitisation has been identified as one of the major trends changing society and business in the near and long term future, breaking down industry barriers and creating opportunities for new applications [1,2].

Particularly, three-dimensional digital models have become relevant in many applications such as inspection, navigation, object identification, visualisation and animation [3–5]. It can be said that the most important use it has been given in the last years is cultural heritage digital archiving thorough different motivations: documentation in case of loss or damage, virtual tourism and museum, educational resources, interaction without risk of damage, and so forth [6].

© Springer Nature Switzerland AG 2019
P. Pesado and C. Aciti (Eds.): CACIC 2018, CCIS 995, pp. 91–108, 2019.
https://doi.org/10.1007/978-3-030-20787-8_7

In this context, nowadays there are institutional biological collections which are specialised repositories of strong scientific matrix, being essential for scientific studies on the biodiversity of the region and its conservation [7,8]. These collections are very useful for students, professors, researchers and other professionals, turning them into centres of scientific and social studies. Consequently, these collections are usually digitised. Nevertheless, similarity among digital collections with real collections will depend essentially on the used technique [9,10].

At present, in computer graphics, capturing geometric models is a result of the use of *laser triangulation* and/or *image processing* [11,12]. Particularly, 3D reconstruction from images has undergone a revolution in the last few years [12–14]. Computer vision techniques use photographs from data set collection to rapidly build detailed 3D models. The results are promising because the obtained models are beginning to challenge the precision of laser-based reconstructions [15].

Furthermore, the fast popularisation of sophisticated human-computer interaction devices has brought unrivalled convenience and entertainment experience in human life [16]. Thanks to technologies such as *Virtual Reality* (VR) and *Augmented Reality* (AR), the user has the ability to manipulate the perception to such an extent that can enter to another type of "reality" [17]. VR allows the creation of interaction's environments that facilitate new contexts of exchange and communication of information. Currently, VR applications consist in user immersion into a computer-generated environment, resulting in a natural idea to improve the impression of living in a simulated reality. On the other hand, an AR system can overlay computer-generated contents on views of the physical scene, augmenting a user's perception and cognition of the world. Development of AR technology with precise information augmentation in real-time is a foreseeable reality that can be used in almost any domain. Over the past decade, AR has undergone a transition from desktop to mobile computing [18].

3D digitisation have promoted not only the mentioned technologies but also 3D printing technology. 3D printing technology was a change in the industrial/manufacturing field and in the way of human life. Basically, the printing process is defined as the process of joining materials to make objects from 3D model data. In recent times, many educational research have begun to use this technology like a learning tool [19].

This work explains the set of processes developed for the preservation and use of a representative set of type herpetological specimens through digital techniques. The specimens were processed into a three-dimensional textured model that can be used in VR and AR environments and 3D printing, allowing for multiple educational and research purposes.

2   Context

This effort aims to preserve and enrich the collections of the *Unidad de Herpetología* at the *Universidad Nacional de San Luis*, due to the fact that it is a space that concentrates specimens of the type series and typical sites, bibliographic material of difficult achievement, as well as a vast photographic record, which represents and protects a large part of the herpetological heritage of the Argentinian Central and Patagonian Regions.

It is common for samples of preserved specimens to suffer deterioration that can sometimes affect their functionality, the most common wear and tear is due to the passage of time and the handling of users.

With the aim of protecting and conserving the heritage of the *Unidad de Herpetología*, this work consisted of generating digital replicas of a representative set of type specimens, thus achieving the corresponding 3D models of the real samples. These 3D models are intended to be used for the creation of a structured and organised digital collection of the preserved specimens, developed according to a predefined conceptual scheme, in order to expand the didactic-scientific potential of these resources. In addition, digitisation will improve the professional and educational transfer capacity of the *Unidad de Herpetología*, given the valuable and specific educational contribution that the collections can offer [20].

The virtual interaction with the documented specimens on the computer (e.g. deliberate cross sections; changing perspectives) allows for a more detailed understanding from it. These computer-based 3D representations of reality also offer various possibilities for reproducing models for publication and presentation purposes. A comprehensive 3D process chain can also result in animations, games and elaborate computer applications [21, 22].

3   Digitising

Today a large number of remote sensing sensors and data are available for mapping purposes and digital recording of visual Cultural Heritage. Generally optical recording sensors are divided in passive and active systems. Passive sensors deliver image data which are then processed with some mathematical formulations to infer 3D information from the 2D image measurements. On the other hand, active sensors can provide data directly from 3D information or ranges [23].

This work was developed by researchers from the *Laboratorio de Computación Gráfica* at the *Universidad de San Luis*, which has the necessary equipment to work with both sensor systems.

At first, to obtain the digital models corresponding to the herpetological specimens, the process chain was started using optical recording sensors based on active systems because this method was recommended for beginners in digitisation.

3.1   Active Sensors Systems: Laser Scanning

These systems use laser scanning technology that analyses and captures the geometry and colors of physical objects to transform them into digital 3D models [24]. In this instance, the *NextEngine* 3D laser scanner was used and the following steps were established:

1. **Object Positioning:** In this case, *ScanStudio*, the *NextEngine* scanner software, was employed. The scanner has a rotating platform dedicated to holding the objects to be scanned. Different orientations of the specimens were analyzed, obtaining the best result by vertically aligning the spine.
2. **Object and Turntable Setup:** Before starting the scanning process, the area to be scanned is selected to limit the amount of foreign information registered by the scanner. Then, it is rotated 360° to the object, stopping momentarily to analyze the surface of the object using triangulation techniques by infrared light. As a result of this process, the quality of a model is directly related to the amount of analysis (stops; 32 in this case) carried on the object.
3. **Model and Texture Scanning:** Each surface analysis is accompanied by an object's snapshot, which is associated with the digitized model. Different resolutions were considered and the highest resolution of those offered by the tool was selected (2.048 × 1.536 pixels).
4. **Model Verification and Correction:** Once the digitized model was obtained, it is necessary to check it. Digitisation failure are displayed by incomplete or incorrect parts, and manual corrections had to be made. For this issue, the *Blender 3D* modelling tool was used. In reptile specimens the areas most prone to problems are claws and tail.

The 3D models resulting from this digitisation methodology were analysed by the *Unidad de Herpetología* people without obtaining their approval. The reason was the poor detail obtained from both the 3D model and the texture, specifically, the appreciation of each specimen scale at the lumbar and ventral area, the reproductive region and the head area. Therefore, a more professional method of obtaining realistic digital models was needed.

3.2 Passive Sensors Systems: Photogrammetry

There is a technique based on passive sensor systems known as *Digital Photogrammetry*. It is based on image data processing and can deliver accurate, metric and detailed 3D information at any scale of application with estimates of accuracy and reliability of unknown parameters from a set of images [25].

Objects well suited for this technique should have amorphous geometries, structured surfaces, many edges, many corresponding image points and an inhomogeneous colouring, characteristics of typical objects in herpetology and preservation of specimens.

Currently, there are tools dedicated to digital photogrammetry such as *ReCap*, *Agisoft* and *Regard 3D*, which require high performance computers for the large amount of calculations that this methodology requires. According with these tools, the following stages of the digitization process can be set:

1. **Data acquisition:** Ideally, images of the specimen should cover each region in order to achieve a complete 3D reconstruction. In this work, a *Nikon D3400* camera with a resolution of 3.872 × 2.592 pixels was used to capture specimen

images (over 100 captures per specimen). Climate is a key factor, because it directly influences the light received by the objects and the texture of the digitised model. Therefore, a cloudy weather is recommended where light rays are distributed evenly. For this reason, the main setting on the camera is light sensitivity (ISO).

2. **Data processing:** The processing of image data consist of image matching algorithms which identify homologous points between images by correlating grey level variations and contrast within a template window. This step achieves the alignment of the photos and the generation of a cloud of dense points representing the outer skin of the object. In this stage it must be adjusted, among other variables, the number of points that will be searched in other captures (set 60.000 points) and the number of points of links between different captures (set 4.000 points).

3. **3D model generation:** This stage reconstructs a 3D polygonal mesh representing the object surface based on the dense or sparse point cloud. Generally there are two algorithmic methods available that can be applied to 3D mesh generation: for planar type surfaces or for any kind of object. Due to the specimens are complex objects and it is desired to obtain high quality meshes, it was specified that the final models are conformed by at least 50.000 polygons.

4. **Texturing:** After geometry is reconstructed, it can be textured. Different texturing modes determines how the object texture will be packed in the texture atlas. Because it is important to record small details, such as specimen scales, it was necessary to obtain high resolution texture images (4.096 × 4.096 pixels).

5. **Model Verification and Correction:** In this case, it was necessary to reconstruct some small parts of the specimens (claws) using *Blender 3D*.

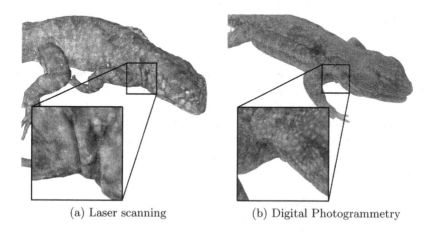

(a) Laser scanning   (b) Digital Photogrammetry

Fig. 1. Texture detail.

Figure 1 shows the texture returned by the digitization methodologies tested. Once again, the new resulting 3D models were analysed by the herpetology unit people and in this time, with a positive feedback. The main reason for the improvement of the 3D models is the possibility of selecting certain areas of the specimens to maximize the detail of the resulting model.

On the other way, the *Unidad de Herpetología* people expressed the need to show each 3D specimen model to users for analysis and study.

4   3D Models Implementations Approaches

Once an object has been digitised, in this case a specimen, the computer uses are almost endless. It can be displayed as a two-dimensional image through a process called *3D rendering* or used in a computer simulation. Accordingly, display methods are classified into those that perform real-time processing and those that do not.

Consequently, since the 3D modelling process was performed from real objects which is usually called *Reality Capture*, this work use this in combination with 3D printing to create an end-to-end process known as *Reality Computing*. In this process the virtual model allows the physical recreation of the real object using 3D printing devices [26].

In accordance with the above, the following subsections describe the developments in both visualisation and 3D printing in which the 3D models obtained were included.

4.1   Visualization

The *Laboratorio de Computación Gráfica* works with different real-time visualization technologies such as virtual reality and augmented reality, among others. These technologies were proposed as a solution for the appreciation of digitized specimens to users [27].

Immersive Virtual Reality. It is known Virtual-reality-enhanced interactive learning environments are increasingly common. VR brings together a mixture of virtual and real-life scenarios for a wide range of potential possibilities in teaching and learning. Particularly, the *Laboratorio de Computación Gráfica* of *Universidad Nacional de San Luis* owns a Cave-like multi-VRmedia System which comprises the hardware and software necessary to gather the information obtained during the interaction between the user and the system: via a motion sensing device, sound system, microphone, screen/projection surfaces and projectors, among others.

This system provides the necessary structure for attributes definition, rendering and collaborative multi-visualizations, as well as the needed interactive resources. Therefore, as an innovative and interesting way where users can interact and observe the different digitised specimens, a scenario, set up with ambient sound, inanimate objects (trees, plants, ground) and animated objects (specimens) was modelled and rendered. The specimens on stage are dynamic objects which are controlled by an avatar (representing the user). The user can control (e.g. rotate) the virtual replica of the specimen by using a keyboard, mouse and motion detection devices. In this way, the user will be able to observe it in more detail and from various angles (See Fig. 2a).

Augmented Reality. Many students and general audience of San Luis province don't know about biodiversity of the region and its conservation. Thus, a interesting way of diffusion of specimens' biodiversity located in San Luis is trough mobile applications, which are highly popularised.

As was mentioned, an AR system allows overlay computer-generated contents on views of the physical scene. In this case, an AR mobile application was implemented where image-based tracking uses 2D targets denominated *markers*. The goal is to stimulate learning interests in a less complex way when compared to other traditional teaching methods (books, web sites, among others).

The application consisted of 3D visualisation of native reptiles and amphibians so that people can understand and observe the skin texture, the traits and the structure. The user must use the camera of mobile device to identify visual specific markers (one marker per specimen), to showcase an overlay only when a marker is sensed by the device (See Fig. 2b).

Once the marker is recognised, a 3D virtual version of the corresponding specimen is displayed on the screen. In such a way, the user will observe it in more detail and from various angles and by rotating the marker would rotate the virtual replication as well.

(a) Immersive Virtual Reality System   (b) Augmented Reality System

Fig. 2. Visualization systems

4.2 3D Printing

The end-to-end process from *Reality Computing* ends with 3D printing. Once a suitable 3D model is created, it can quickly be produced by a 3D print.

3D printing is a form of additive manufacturing technology where a three dimensional object is created by laying down or build from successive layers of material. 3D printing is a great way to create objects because you can create objects that you couldn't make otherwise without having complex expensive molds created or by having the objects made with multiple parts.

A 3D printed herpetological specimen can be edited by simply editing the 3D model; in such manner, for example, it is possible to scale a reptile or modify its original pose.

A type of filament called Acrylonitrile Butadiene Styrene (ABS), was used for printing reptile models. According to the characteristics of each model, printing tests and modifications were made to the models in order to achieve prints without the need to use supports on the parts. It is because the supports must be cut increasing the chances of damaging the printed specimen.

Figure 3 shows a real specimen and its printing.

(a) Real Specimen   (b) Printed Specimen

Fig. 3. Reality Computing

5   Evaluation and Discussion

The main objective of the evaluations was to determine whether the set of processes carried out could be effective or not in preserving, archiving and reproducing herpetological heritage. The results of the digitalization and printing will be analyzed as a whole, because their evaluations will try to measure the quality of replication with respect to the real specimen. Finally, for Virtual Reality and Augmented Reality applications, user based tests will be carried out.

5.1   Digitising and 3D Printing

In order to evaluate the results obtained during the digitisation and printing of herpetological specimens, two types of studies had been stablished: *qualitative* and *quantitative* study.

Qualitative Study. This study considers the subjective point of view of the users.

Participants. During the qualitative experiment, a group of 30 users was considered, including students and teachers of natural sciences. Most participants were provided by the *Unidad de Herpetología* in such a way that it was possible to assure that validation process was carried out by the right end-users.

Performance Measures. Within each application, there are numerous criteria that may be used in evaluating digitising and printing processes. However, according to user experience studies, the following are the most common and most important:

- *Portability:* ability to be transported to remote sites, transport requirements, care and other factors.
- *Maintenance:* number of activities carried out for the preservation of the optimal state of a given sample to prevent its degradation.
- *Field operability:* restrictions in relation to field work.
- *Robustness:* ability to withstand weather conditions, the passage of time and other adverse effects.
- *Cost of use:* the use of the resource has a direct impact on its current state.

Experiment Procedures. The experiment consisted of participants carrying out an analysis based on the use of 10 representative set of type herpetological specimens. Each sample was available in its real, digital and printed version in order to establish a value for each performance measure. Each user was previously instructed on the meaning of the performance measures and their possible rate values. Values were defined in a range of $[0, 100]$ percent, where 0% means that the sample did not comply at all with the performance measurement and 100% means that it complied fully with it. This procedure allowed a subjective (user) comparison of a real specimen and its digital and printed versions.

Experiment Results. Table 1 shows an average of the recorded percentages of tests performed by users using sets of samples made up of a specimen in its real, digital and printed versions.

For *Portability*, users considered that the real specimen is the most difficult to transport; otherwise, the digital sample appears to be simpler to send to other geographic sites. According to the users' analysis, for *Maintenance* the best option turns out to be the digital model. Due to the fact that the digital sample is not a materialization it is to be expected that its transport and its maintenance are almost lacking. When users were consulted about the *Field operability*, the printed version was the winner. On the other hand, for *Robustness*, the highest percentage is presented in the digital model at the same time that there is a wide difference with the real specimen, which highlights an important disadvantage of the real sample. Finally, the *Cost of use* indicates that the highest cost is found when using the real sample, this cost decreases with the printed version to fall considerably in the digital model.

These results indicate that both digital and printed replicas appear to be a good option when preserving species for study and dissemination.

Table 1. Experiment with performance measures

Averages of performance measures			
Parameters	Real specimen	3D digital	3D printed
Portability	24%	96%	87%
Maintenance	89%	23%	46%
Field operability	34%	82%	94%
Robustness	17%	96%	63%
Cost of use	93%	8%	59%

Quantitative Study. This study performs a more technical analysis of digital and printed samples.

Samples. This analysis is based on the use of 10 type-specimens samples. Each sample was arranged in its real, digital, and printed version with the purpose of evaluating the capacity of digital reproduction of a specific herpetological specimen.

Performance Measures. For *Unidad de Herpetología* people, the phenotype of the specimens, i.e. their visible characteristics, identify each herpetological individual. Fortunately, 3d digitization gets both morphological and texture information. On the other hand, current 3d printing can recreate the main dimensions of the specimens but can not recreate the textures.

Knowing this, areas (head, body and tail) that can be achieved in a complete way both by 3d digitization and 3d printing were compared. In accordance, 5 dimensions to be analyzed were established (Fig. 4).

Experiment Procedures. Considering the dimensions mentioned by the *Unidad de Herpetología* people, it was decided to analyze a subset of the set of printed specimens. This subset was constituted by specimens with particular characteristics, with the objective of analyzing the greatest number of sizes and appearances.

Dimensions of 10 real specimen were recorded (units in millimetres) for comparison with the corresponding digital and real specimen. This comparison will be made by calculating in millimeters the difference between real and digital dimension for each part of the specimen.

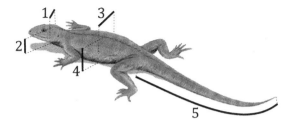

Fig. 4. Dimensions considered: 1 Head width, 2 Head height, 3 Body width, 4 Body height and 5 Tail length.

Experiment Results. The data obtained from the experiment are shown in the Table 2a and b. Averages were also added for each sector to assist in the interpretation of the information.

Table 2. Dimensional differences.

(a) Real specimen/Digitized specimen

Differences in millimetres					
scientific name	dim 1	dim 2	dim 3	dim 4	dim 5
Cnemidophorus abalosi	2	2	3	2	11
Liolaemus anomalus	5	1	2	4	8
Liolaemus ditadai	4	1	0	5	6
Liolaemus famatinae	0	0	1	2	11
Liolaemus gallardoi	1	2	1	3	9
Atelognathus salai	1	1	1	2	9
Odontophrynus lavillai	3	4	2	7	5
Phymaturus mallimaccii	2	1	1	1	7
Phymaturus sp.	0	4	4	1	10
Pristidactylus nigroingulus	4	2	4	5	7
Average	2.2	1.8	1.9	3.2	8.3

(b) Real specimen/Printed specimen

Differences in millimetres					
scientific name	dim 1	dim 2	dim 3	dim 4	dim 5
Cnemidophorus abalosi	3	7	6	9	25
Liolaemus anomalus	7	2	8	7	11
Liolaemus ditadai	4	3	3	6	13
Liolaemus famatinae	2	4	5	5	19
Liolaemus gallardoi	2	3	2	6	15
Atelognathus salai	3	2	3	4	22
Odontophrynus lavillai	4	5	4	9	15
Phymaturus mallimaccii	8	9	5	4	21
Phymaturus sp.	2	6	8	4	16
Pristidactylus nigroingulus	5	4	6	7	14
Average	4.0	4.5	5.0	6.1	17.1

A smaller average indicates that dimension of the real specimen was correctly achieved in the digitized or printed specimen. On the other hand, a bigger average indicates that the digitized or printed specimen had noticeable differences from the real specimen.

As expected, digital models show low error averages compared to printed models. This is because digital models only suffered the digitization process, while printed models suffered the digitization and 3d printing processes.

A better compression of the data distribution is possible with box and whiskers graphs corresponding to the comparison between real and digitized specimens (Fig. 5a), and on the other hand, real and printed specimens (Fig. 5b).

Box and whiskers graphs allow to see the dispersion and symmetry of the data. The line that divides the box represents the value of the median. The median divides the box into two parts showing the dispersion belonging to 25% of the data for each side of the median. Finally, whiskers show the range between the minimum and maximum values.

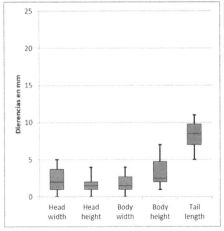 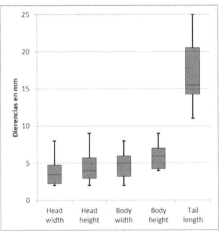

(a) Real specimen/Digitized specimen   (b) Real specimen/Printed specimen

Fig. 5. Real specimen versus processed specimen errors distribution.

For this evaluation, the graphs allow to quickly distinguish two types of behavior from the values that represent the error with relation to the measurements of the real specimen. In Fig. 5a, the error related to the head and the body varies about 0 mm to 7 mm. However, the tail length error varies notably between 5 mm and 11 mm. In Fig. 5b, the error related to the head and body increases approximately between 4 mm and 9 mm. And finally, the tail length error increases between 11 mm and 25 mm.

The last error may be caused by the digitization and printing processes. During the digitization processes (Photogrammetry), 3D model generation reconstructs a 3D polygonal mesh representing the object surface based on the dense or sparse point cloud. This point cloud depends on the quality of the images collected in the data acquisition. On the other hand, during printing processes, the 3d printer used was configured to deposit the material at a height of 0.2 mm per layer and 0.4 mm in thickness. While this configuration provides short print times, it makes it difficult to print the thin and small parts of the model, such as claws and the tail.

5.2   Visualization: VR and AR

As it was mentioned, Virtual reality and augmented reality were used as a media for the visualisation of digitized specimens by users. Then a VR system usability evaluation and AR system usability evaluation were performed.

Qualitative VR System Evaluation. The methodology used for a pedagogical validation of the educational VR system was the one developed by Abreu [28,29]. This work is usually used when the didactic point of view of an educational material needs to be evaluated.

Participants. In order to simulate a class, students groups have been able to use the VR system supervised by a teacher of Natural Sciences. Participants involved in this evaluation are the same as those who collaborated in the previous digitalisation and 3D printing evaluations.

Performance Measures. The Abreu's methodology consists of three groups of criteria to be evaluated: general usability, didactic usability and usability of distance learning websites. For this work purposes, only the group of didactic usability was used, where the evaluated criteria are: *Control of the student, Student activity, Collaborative/ cooperative learning, Orientation to Objectives, Applicability, Value Added, Motivation, Evaluation of previous knowledge, Flexibility* and *Feedback*.

Experiment Procedures. After the experience, twenty students were asked to fill out a questionnaire about their experience while using the VR system. The questionnaire included questions about knowledge, emotions and attitudes as follows:

1 When I use the system I feel that I have control over the tool and not the other way around (*Control of the student*).
2 When I work with the system, I can abstract myself so much that I loose track of time (*Student activity*).
3 The system allows me to interact with other students (*Cooperative learning*).
4 The system itself shows why it is important to learn how to use it (*Orientation to objectives*).
5 The system fits into the my (student) abilities (*Applicability*).
6 The images in the system help to learn (*Value Added*).
7 I want to learn as much as I can from the system (*Motivation*).
8 I can use my previous knowledge when I use the system (*Evaluation Knowledge*).
9 The system allows the development of consecutive tasks (*Flexibility*).
10 The system sends me a motivational feedback (*Feedback*).

Questions have response alternatives of "Agree", "Partially agree", "Undecided", "Partially disagree" and "Disagree" and are scored from 1 to 5, meaning the following: (5) Agree, (4) Partially agree, (3) Undecided, (2) Partially disagree and (1) Disagree.

Experiment Results. To be able to make an evaluation, it is necessary to make a survey applying the selected methodology. This survey is based on the methodology criteria for didactic usability, which has 10 questions. Results of the survey are shown in Table 3 where the criterion column represents the evaluated criterion and the next column represents the average score obtained with each question (first column).

Table 3. Didactic usability test of VR system.

Averages of performance measures		
Question	Criterion	Average
1	Control of the student	4.33
2	Student activity	3.86
3	Cooperative learning	4.61
4	Orientation to objectives	4.10
5	Applicability	4.89
6	Motivation	4.73
7	Value Added	4.03
8	Evaluation Knowledge	3.93
9	Flexibility	4.50
10	Feedback	4.38

Results show high values in score, meaning a general acceptance to the criteria of didactic usability and validating the didactic value of this software.

Qualitative AR System Test. This test is based on the reinterpretation, for an AR context, of the heuristics set proposed by Nielsen in the [30].

Participants. A number of twenty users were evaluated in this test. All of them had already participated in the previous VR test, and have experience with smartphones (but limited experience with AR applications in smartphones).

Performance Measures. The AR heuristics chosen of [30] were: *Satisfaction, Visibility of system status, Match between system and the real world, Recognition rather than recall, Visibility of system status* and *User control and freedom*.

Experiment Procedures. The task to be performed by the user is quite simply, just to run the AR application using certain markers. After that, participants had to answer a set of questions associated to the mentioned heuristics:

1 Is the number of virtual objects in the scene appropriate? (*Satisfaction*).
2 Are you satisfied with the freedom to move around during interactions? (*Satisfaction*).
3 Is the loading time of virtual objects in the scene satisfactory? (*Visibility of system status*).
4 Are the virtual objects merged correctly with the real world (position, texture, scale)? (*Match between system and the real world*).
5 Is the virtual object animation coherent with the real world? (*Match between system and the real world*).

6 Is it easy to stand the marker in an appropriate position and orientation to be detected by the camera/sensor? (*Recognition rather than recall*).

7 Is it possible to execute "redo" or "undo" easily? (i.e., return to a previous state without the virtual object) (*User control and freedom*).

8 Does the application achieve the goal? (*User control and freedom*).

Questions have the same response alternatives used in VR system test: "Agree", "Partially agree", "Undecided", "Partially disagree" and "Disagree", and are scored from 1 to 5, meaning the following: (5) Agree, (4) Partially agree, (3) Undecided, (2) Partially disagree and (1) Disagree.

Experiment Results. As in the VR system test section, to be able to make an evaluation, it is necessary to make a survey applying the selected methodology. This survey is based on the methodology heuristics, which has 8 questions. Results of the AR survey are shown in Table 4 where the heuristic column represents the evaluated heuristic and the next column represents the average score obtained with each question (first column).

Table 4. Usability test of AR system.

Averages of performance measures		
Question	Heuristic	Average
1	Satisfaction	4.02
2	Satisfaction	4.65
3	Visibility of system status	5.00
4	Match between system and the real world	4.13
5	Match between system and the real world	3.66
6	Recognition rather than recall	4.37
7	User control and freedom	2.86
8	User control and freedom	3.24

Scores show good values for the 90% of the heuristics with a particular low value for "User control and freedom" heuristic. According to the students, this last statement is due to the fact that the application graphics interface should better guide the interaction.

6   Conclusions and Future Works

This paper describes an approach to digitising herpetological specimens. The digitising process allows to built a 3D model from a real object. Because different ways lead to a 3D model for the development of this work, more than one technique was tested.

At the beginning, this work consisted in the survey of a representative set of type specimens, which were digitised through the *Laser Scanning Method* in order to achieve a three-dimensional textured model of each one. According with the *Unidad de Herpetología* feedback these models and theirs characteristics were not suited to the needs, interests and preferences, herpetologically speaking. Then, the *Photogrammetry Method* was carried out which allowed obtaining models with a higher resolution; which in turn were considered as more accurate replicas and according to the needs of the *Unidad de Herpetología*.

In order to the digitised models to be visualised, two applications were developed: an *Augmented Reality* application that allows the visualisation of the specimens in an attractive way and from any mobile device; and an *Immersive Virtual Reality* application that achieves a more personalised and detailed use of the digitised samples. In addition, the *3D prints* allowed to obtain tangible replicas of the herpetological specimens in which it is possible to appreciate the non-textured characteristics of a specimen.

The results obtained in the different stages were evaluated and analyzed: the digital specimen (Digitalization: photogrammetry), the printed specimen (3D printing) and the visualized specimen (VR and AR Visualization). In order to evaluate the fidelity of the copies of the specimen (digital and printed), information was collected and compared with respect to the real specimen considering several quantitative and qualitative parameters. On the other hand, the VR and AR applications were subjected to usability tests (qualitative evaluation). Both types of evaluation returned favorable results and pointed out some existing defects in digital and printed specimens, which have although not great importance for the *Unidad de Herpetología*.

Given the interdisciplinarity of the work carried out, the technologies used for its implementation and the unique characteristics of the collections, the process generated is, in itself, unique and innovative, and its result is a trigger for a wide range of scientific and educational activities. The obtained 3D photorealistic models offer new possibilities for the daily practice of herpetology, protection and conservation of specimens. As well as being objective 3D documentations, they achieve a reliable conservation of the herpetological heritage.

Future works will include: to reproduce the process with all the specimens of the *Unidad de Herpetología*; to build a 3D digital library of the *Unidad de Herpetología*, which can be accessed online; to incorporate animations to give more realism to the models; to automate the process related to the capture of photographic samples, with the necessary equipment, as a rotating base, light-box photo studio, among others; to address digitalisation and printing defects.

References

1. Degryse, C.: Digitalisation of the economy and its impact on labour markets. In: Working Paper 2016.02. European Trade Union Institute, Brussels (2016)
2. Bouwman, H., de Reuver, M., Nikou, S.: The impact of Digitalization on business models: how IT artefacts, social media, and big data force firms to innovate their business model. Technical report (2017)

3. Hoyek, N., Collet, C., Di Rienzo, F., De Almeida, M., Guillot, A.: Effectiveness of three-dimensional digital animation in teaching human anatomy in an authentic classroom context. Anat. Sci. Educ. **7**, 11 (2014)
4. Malik, H.H., et al.: Three-dimensional printing in surgery: a review of current surgical applications. J. Surg. Res. **199**(2), 512–522 (2015)
5. Santos, P., Ritz, M., Fuhrmann, C., Fellner, D.: 3D mass digitization: a milestone for archeological documentation. Virtual Archaeol. Rev. **8**(16), 1–11 (2017)
6. Lercari, N., Shulze, J., Wendrich, W., Porter, B., Burton, M., Levy, T.E.: 3-D digital preservation of at-risk global cultural heritage. In: Catalano, C., De Luca, L. (eds.) Eurographics Workshop on Graphics and Cultural Heritage. The Eurographics Association (2016)
7. Lavoie, C.: Biological collections in an ever changing world: herbaria as tools for biogeographical and environmental studies. Perspect. Plant Ecol. Evol. Syst. **15**(1), 68–76 (2013)
8. Bakk, D., Urban, R.: Scientific and social value of biological collections, pp. 6–9, August 2014
9. Beaman, R.S., Cellinese, N.: Mass digitization of scientific collections: new opportunities to transform the use of biological specimens and underwrite biodiversity science. Biol. Rev. **209**, 7–17 (2012)
10. Keaveney, S., Keogh, C., Gutierrez-Heredia, L., Reynaud, E.G.: Applications for advanced 3D imaging, modelling, and printing techniques for the biological sciences. In: 2016 22nd International Conference on Virtual System Multimedia (VSMM), pp. 1–8, October 2016
11. Nex, F., Remondino, F.: UAV for 3D mapping applications: a review. p. 6, March 2014
12. Moussa, W.: Integration of digital photogrammetry and terrestrial laser scanning for cultural heritage data recording, January 2014
13. Shashi, M., Jain, K.: Use of photogrammetry in 3D modeling and visualization of buildings. p. 2, January 2007
14. Shahbazi, M., Sohn, G., Théau, J., Menard, P.: Development and evaluation of a UAV-photogrammetry system for precise 3D environmental modeling. Sensors **15**, 27493–27524 (2015)
15. Ippolito, A., Cigola, M.: Handbook of Research on Emerging Technologies for Digital Preservation and Information Modeling, 2017
16. Vajak, D., Livada, C.: Combining photogrammetry, 3D modeling and real time information gathering for highly immersive VR experience. In: 2017 Zooming Innovation in Consumer Electronics International Conference (ZINC), pp. 82–85, May 2017
17. Aukstakalnis, S.: Practical Augmented Reality: A Guide to the Technologies, Applications, and Human Factors for AR and VR. Usability Series. Addison-Wesley, Boston (2016)
18. Chen, P., Liu, X., Cheng, W., Huang, R.: A review of using augmented reality in education from 2011 to 2016. In: Chen, N.-S., Sampson, D.G. (eds.) Innovations in Smart Learning. LNET, pp. 13–18. Springer, Singapore (2017). https://doi.org/10.1007/978-981-10-2419-1_2
19. Ford, S., Minshall, T.: 3D printing in teaching and education: a review of where and how it is used, October 2017
20. Espeche, B., Alvarado, Y., Rodríguez, G., Jofré, N., Jofré, M., Guerrero, R.: Repositorio virtual de ejemplares - Unidad de Herpetología - UNSL, Argentina, In: XVIII Congreso Argentino de Herpetología (2017)

21. Yastikli, N.: Documentation of cultural heritage using digital photogrammetry and laser scanning. J. Cult. Herit. **8**(4), 423–427 (2007)
22. Behm, J., Waite, B.R., Hsieh, S.T., Helmus, M.R.: Benefits and limitations of three-dimensional printing technology for ecological research. bioRxiv (2018)
23. Sansoni, G., Trebeschi, M., Docchio, F.: State-of-the-art and applications of 3D imaging sensors in industry, cultural heritage, medicine, and criminal investigation. Sensors **9**(1), 568–601 (2009)
24. Kuzminsky, S.C., Gardiner, M.S.: Three-dimensional laser scanning: potential uses for museum conservation and scientific research. J. Archaeol. Sci. **39**(8), 2744–2751 (2012)
25. Schenk, T.F.: Fotogrametría digital (2002)
26. Deutsch, R.: Convergence: The Redesign of Design. AD Smart. Wiley, Hoboken (2017)
27. Aciti, C., Pesado, P.: XXIV Congreso Argentino de Ciencias de la Computación-CACIC 2018. Universidad Nacional del Centro de la Provincia de Buenos Aires (2018)
28. d Abreu, A.: Avaliação de usabilidade em softwares educativos. Master's thesis, Universidade Estadual do Ceará, Brasil (2010)
29. Becerra, D.A.I., et al.: Evaluation of a gamified 3D virtual reality system to enhance the understanding of movement in physics. In: CSEDU (2017)
30. Guimarães, M.d.P., Martins, V.F.: A checklist to evaluate augmented reality applications. In: 2014 XVI Symposium on Virtual and Augmented Reality, pp. 45–52, May 2014

Color Image Enhancement Using a Multiscale Morphological Approach

Raul Mendez[1], Rodolfo Cardozo[1], José Luis Vázquez Noguera[1(✉)],
Horacio Legal-Ayala[1], Julio César Mello Román[1], Sebastian Grillo[2],
and Miguel García-Torres[3]

[1] Facultad Politécnica, Universidad Nacional de Asunción, San Lorenzo, Paraguay
aramfara@gmail.com, rkrdozo@gmail.com,
{jlvazquez,hlegal,juliomello}@pol.una.py
[2] Universidad Autónoma de Asunción, Asunción, Paraguay
sgrillo@uaa.edu.py
[3] Division of Computer Science, Universidad Pablo de Olavide, 41013 Seville, Spain
mgarciat@upo.es

Abstract. Color image enhancement has been widely applied in a variety of applications from different scientific areas. On the other hand, mathematical morphology is a theory that deals with describing shapes using sets and, therefore, it provides a number of useful tools for image enhancement. Despite its utility, one of the challenges of this theory, when applied to color images, is to determine an order between the components of the image. Color images are represented by multidimensional data structures, which implies that there is no natural order between their components. In this work we propose an image enhancement method for color images that uses the extension of the multiscale mathematical morphology with different color spaces and ordering methods. The experiments carried out show that the proposed method generates competitive results using different ordering methods in terms of both local and global contrast, as well as the color quality of the image.

Keywords: Image enhancement · Color images · Color spaces · Multiscale mathematical morphology · Ordering methods

1 Introduction

Digital image processing and analysis consists of a set of methods and techniques applicable to digital images in order to obtain relevant information from them. Contrast is often defined as the difference in mean luminance between an object and its surroundings [1]. The higher the contrast, the better one can observe the difference between background and object. High contrast images usually have a stretched histogram. Contrast enhancement, makes the images more suitable for human visual perception and subsequent digital processing. Contrast

© Springer Nature Switzerland AG 2019
P. Pesado and C. Aciti (Eds.): CACIC 2018, CCIS 995, pp. 109–123, 2019.
https://doi.org/10.1007/978-3-030-20787-8_8

enhancement is important for its applications in different areas of science, such as medicine [2–5], engineering [6,7] and geoscience [8–10].

In the literature there are different types of algorithms that improve the contrast of an image. Histogram based algorithms [11–14] are widely used and are efficient at improving bright image areas. Fuzzy logic based algorithms are used in noise images. Fuzzy logic is a suitable tool for improving multispectral images or images in general [8,15]. Algorithms in the frequency domain work well in many cases for medical imaging [16–18].

Color images allow to obtain more quantity and quality of information. This allows its use in different practical applications for various research areas [19]. Color spaces are models of reference that describe the way in which colors are organized and represented [20]. Some of the most popular color spaces are RGB, L*a*b*, HLS, HSI, HSV, CMYK. To enhance the contrast of color images, a single component of the image is usually used (commonly the component of the luminosity or intensity of the image). The use of a simple color component causes the loss of valuable information about the colors of the image.

In mathematical morphology one of the most popular operations is the top-hat transform [21–23]. Enhancing the image by top-hat transform consists of adding the bright areas and subtracting the dark areas from the original image [24,25]. Multiscale top-hat transform is extensively utilized to enhance grayscale images [26,27]. Multiscale mathematical morphology is useful in many applications, such as the study of the retinal image [28], ultrasound imaging enhancement [29], infrared thermal imaging enhancement [30], fusion of infrared and visible images [31,32] or detection of small objects in infrared images [33].

Any operation in mathematical morphology requires the comparison of the pixels of the images. In grayscale images pixels comparison is an almost trivial process, since pixel values have a natural order. In color images, on the other hand, the comparison between pixels implies an extra effort because it requires the comparison of multidimensional data structures from which the pixels of a color image are conformed. In order to perform such comparison it is necessary to stablish an ordering strategy. Many ordering methods have been proposed in previous works as, for example, the lexicographical ordering [34], and its variants [19]. Other methods used in this work are: the Euclidean distance in spaces RGB and L*a*b* [19], bit mixing [35], and an ordering that uses image histogram based information [36].

In this work, we propose the extension of a method based on multiscale mathematical morphology to improve the contrast of color images [37]. In order to achieve this extension it is necessary: analyse and evaluate the improvement of the local and global contrast, as well as the enhancement of the color of the image using different ordering methods.

The rest of the paper is organized as follows. Section 2 introduces the theoretical foundations. Then, in Sect. 3, the proposed method is described. Section 4 presents the experiments conducted for testing the proposed method. Finally, the conclusions are in Sect. 5.

2   Theoretical Foundations

An RGB digital image can be represented as a function $f : \mathbb{Z}^2 \longrightarrow \mathbb{Z}^3$, where each pixel in the position $(r, c) \in \mathbb{Z}^2$ is represented by a multidimensional data structure. In the RGB color space the colors are formed from three independent image planes $C = \{R, G, B\}$, each plane can be treated as a grayscale image corresponding to a primary color red, green, and blue.

The color space is a system that allows the specification, organization and combination of colors to be used for the processing of digital images [20]. There is a wide variety of color spaces among which we can mention the color space HSI [38], the color space L*a*b* [39] and the color space RGB (Red, Gren, Blue) that represents a color through positive quantities of red, green and blue [19].

Mathematical morphology is an area of digital image processing and is based on set theory, algebraic and geometric principles [19].

The basic operations of mathematical morphology are erosion and dilatation [19]. The erosion operation $\varepsilon_B(f)$ is obtained as a result of computing the lowest value within a window B called structuring element. The dilatation operation $\delta_B(f)$, in contrast, is obtained from the highest value element within the domain of the structuring element δ_B. Both operations are defined as follows:

$$\varepsilon_B(f)(r, c) = \min\{f(r + d, c + l)|(d, l) \in B\}. \tag{1}$$

$$\delta_B(f)(r, c) = \max\{f(r - d, c - l)|(d, l) \in B\}. \tag{2}$$

There exist many other operations such as opening and closing, which are obtained by combining the basic operations in different ways. The morphological opening of an image f by a structuring element B is denoted as $f \circ B$ and is defined as the erosion of f by B, followed by dilatation by the same structuring element.

$$f \circ B(f) = \delta_B(\varepsilon_B(f))(r, c). \tag{3}$$

The closing of an image f by a structuring element B is denoted by $f \bullet B$ and is defined as the dilatation of f by B, followed by erosion by the same structuring element.

$$f \bullet B(f)(r, c) = \varepsilon_B(\delta_B(f))(r, c). \tag{4}$$

The Top-Hat transform is a contrast enhancement technique that uses mathematical morphology operations combining opening and closing operations [4, 40]. There are two types of top-hat transforms: the White Top-Hat (WTH) and the Black Top-Hat (BTH).

WTH transform is used to highlight bright image regions that are smaller than the structuring element. It is obtained by subtracting the opening $(f \circ B)$ to the original image f:

$$WTH_B(f)(r, c) = f(r, c) - f \circ B(f)(r, c). \tag{5}$$

The other transform, BTH, is used to extract dark regions that are smaller than the structuring element. The BTH transform is obtained by subtracting the original image f to the closing operation $(f \bullet B)$. That is:

$$BTH_B(f)(r,c) = f \bullet B(f)(r,c) - f(r,c). \tag{6}$$

3 Proposal

Multiscale mathematical morphology is a generalization of mathematical morphology where a scalable structuring element is used.

3.1 Multiscale Mathematical Morphology

A scalable structuring element is obtained by means of a structuring element B and an integer value n which represents the scale factor [23,24,40]. The value nB is obtained by dilating B recursively on itself $n-1$ times, as long as B is convex.

The morphological operations of erosion, dilatation and their combinations opening, closing are used with the scalable structuring element for grayscale images f. The multiscale top-hat transform is a strategy of contrast enhancement using multiscale erosion, dilatation, opening and closing operations [23,24,40].

The proposed color image enhancement strategy includes the use of the multiscale top-hat transform for grayscale images the strategy mentioned in [24] whose practical application extends for digital color images. The proposed contrast enhancement strategy for color images is represented as follows:

$$\tilde{f}_v(r,c) = f_v(r,c) + 0.5 \sum_{n=1}^{m} WTH_{nB}(f_v)(r,c) - 0.5 \sum_{n=1}^{m} BTH_{nB}(f_v)(r,c), \tag{7}$$

where, $\tilde{f}_v$ represents the result of the improvement applied to the color image f_v. The operations are performed n times with a scalable B structuring element. The 0.5 constant prevents gray levels overflow in the pixels of the image.

3.2 Ordering Strategies

In this section, different ordering strategies are described, among which we can mention and classify as dependent or independent of the image histogram information.

Histogram Independent Ordering

- **Lexicographical ordering:** It is based on the attribution of priorities to the components of the vector so that some components are more important than others when comparing and defining the order [41]. There are variants, such as the α-lexicographical ordering, where the number of times the order is decided by the first component of the vector is reduced by adding a value α to the first component of the vector [19]. The α-module lexicographical ordering reduces the number of times the order is decided by the first component of the vector making an integer division between the first component of the vector and a constant value α [19]. The lexicographical ordering has variants with different color spaces, for example, HSI lexicographical ordering, where the vectors are represented as coordinates of HSI space and the order is established by the priorities $I \to S \to H$.

- **Euclidean distance (ED):** This ordering strategy computes the distance to a reference pixel, which is usually the origin, when so the distance is equivalent to the vector $\|v\|$ norm. This ordering strategy has variants with color spaces, such as the RGB space and L*a*b* as mentioned in [19].
- **Bit mixing (BM):** This strategy uses a reduction technique where the transformation of each vector is defined as the integer value obtained from interlacing the bits representing the intensities of each component of the vector [35].

Histogram-Dependent Ordering

- **Ordering using histogram information:** Noguera et al. [36] propose a ordering strategy using histogram information. For this, the reduction of the color C is carried out by means of the transformation function T. This transformation $(T(C))$ is achieved by means of the inner product between the color C and a weight vector $w = (w_1, w_2, w_3)$:

$$T(C) = \sum_{k=1}^{3}(w_k \cdot C_k) \tag{8}$$

where k is the index of the component and $w_k \in \mathbb{R}$ is a weight extracted from the k component of the image.

The colors C_x and C_y, with $C_x \neq C_y$, can have the same transformation, that is $T(C_x) = T(C_y)$, that is why the $T(C)$ transformation is used as the first component of the lexicographical ordering. The ordering method is based on the calculation of weights w which is carried out by means of a function ϕ applied to the histogram of the image where subdivisions of the image are also performed in regions called domains or windows.

- **Weight Calculation:** The function ϕ applied to the histogram of each component k of the image f_v for the calculation of the weights w_k.

The weights used can be, the average ($MEAN$) of grey intensity levels, the minimum (MIN) which is the lowest level of intensity, the maximum (MAX) which represents the highest level of intensity, the minimum mode ($MO1$) which is the lowest level of intensity that repeats the most, the maximum mode ($MO2$) that is the highest level of intensity that repeats the most, the variance (VAR) that represents the variance of the levels of intensity, all of these for a given domain D. The weights obtained from the metrics mentioned previously are obtained by dividing the image into windows or domains, in such a way to obtain local information from a given region of the image.

– **Division of the Image into Windows:** Image f is divided into sub-regions $W_1, W_2, \ldots, W_s$ as mentioned in [36]. The sub-regions W_s allow you to define areas to obtain local image characteristics. Let B be a structuring element, the domain D corresponding to the structuring element B centered on (r, c) is defined as the set of sub-regions $W_{\{1,2,\ldots,s\}}$, which intersect some pixel of B. Each domain D is processed independently to obtain the particular or local characteristics associated with each domain.

4   Experimental Results

In this section, experimental results for color images are presented, in addition to the contrast enhancement metrics used to measure the quality of the resulting image. For the experiments, 100 images from public database were used. The size of the color images are 481×321 and 321×481 [42].

Quantification of contrast enhancement is difficult; there is no specific way to measure the performance of the enhancement algorithm [1,43]. The metrics used to validate the image enhancement method, based on multiscale mathematical morphology, for color images are: Variance (VAR); Contrast Improvement Ratio (CIR) [1], a measure of contrast enhancement for a given region of the image; and Color Enhancement Factor (CEF) [44], that measures the perception of the color quality of an image.

4.1   Assessment Metrics

Variance (VAR) is used to quantify the overall contrast of grayscale images, and it is defined as:

$$VAR(f) = \sum_{j=0}^{L-1} (j - \mu_f)^2 \times P(j), \tag{9}$$

where μ_f is the average intensity of the grayscale image f and $P(j)$ is the probability of occurrence of intensity level j in the image f for L gray levels. For its application in color images, it is done by averaging the VAR of the RGB components of the image, that is to say:

$$VAR(f_v) = \frac{VAR_R(f_v) + VAR_G(f_v) + VAR_B(f_v)}{3}, \tag{10}$$

where f_v represents a color image.

Local contrast is defined as the subtraction of the average values in two rectangular windows centered on a pixel. Specifically, the local contrast $w(u,v)$ is defined as:

$$w(u,v) = \frac{|\rho - \iota|}{|\rho + \iota|}, \tag{11}$$

where ρ and ι are the values of the gray levels of the central pixel and the average of the neighbors within a 3×3 window.

CIR, which is the relation between the enhanced image f_E and the original image f within the region of interest Ω, is defined as follows [1]:

$$CIR(f, f_E) = \frac{\sum_{(u,v)\in\Omega} |\omega(u, v) - \tilde{\omega}(u, v)|^2}{\sum_{(u,v)\in\Omega} \omega(u, v)^2}, \tag{12}$$

where ω and $\tilde{\omega}$ are the local contrast values of the original and enhanced images, respectively. In our experiments, we assume that Ω is the whole image. *CIR* was adopted to assess the local contrast enhancement of grayscale images. For its application in color images, it is done by averaging the CIR of the RGB components of the image, that is to say:

$$CIR(f_v, \tilde{f}_v) = \frac{CIR_R(f_v, \tilde{f}_v) + CIR_G(f_v, \tilde{f}_v) + CIR_B(f_v, \tilde{f}_v)}{3}, \tag{13}$$

where, $\tilde{f}_v$ represents the result of the improvement applied to the color image f_v.

The metric used to evaluate the overall color improvement of an image is called the *Color Enhancement Factor (CEF)*. This metric quantifies the level of colorfulness enhancement of an image as mentioned in [45], applied to the image f; is based on the mean and standard deviation of two axes of a simple opposite color representation with $\gamma = f_1 - f_2$ and $\beta = \frac{1}{2}(f_1 + f_2) - f_3$, where f_1 represents the R component, f_2 represents the G component and f_3 represents the B component of the RGB color space. Equation 14 represents the color level of the image f as follows:

$$CM(f) = \sqrt{\sigma_\gamma^2 + \sigma_\beta^2} + 0.3\sqrt{\mu_\gamma^2 + \mu_\beta^2}, \tag{14}$$

where σ_γ and σ_β correspond to the standard deviation of γ and β respectively. Similarly, μ_γ and μ_β correspond to the average respectively. Then, *CEF* is calculated by the ratio between the values of the $CM(\tilde{f}_v)$ and $CM(f_v)$:

$$CEF(f_v, \tilde{f}_v) = \frac{CM(\tilde{f}_v)}{CM(f_v)}, \tag{15}$$

where $CM(\tilde{f}_v)$ represents the result of applying Eq. 14 to the image $\tilde{f}_v$ with contrast enhancement and $CM(f_v)$ represents the result of applying Eq. 14 to the original color image $\tilde{f}_v$. If the ratio result is more than 1, then the metric of Eq. 15 indicates an enhancement of the colorfulness of the image.

4.2   Results

The ordering methods were classified in 2 large groups: the histogram independent orderings and the orderings using histogram information. Table 1 shows the histogram independent orderings. Table 2 shows the orderings using histogram information.

Table 1. Histogram independent ordering

Method	Abbreviation
Bit mixing [35]	BM
Lexicographical ordering [19]	LEX
α-lexicographical ordering [19]	$ALEX$
Euclidean distance in L*a*b [19]	$DLAB$
α-module lexicographical [46]	$AMLEX$
HSI lexicographical ordering [47]	$HLEX$
Euclidean distance in RGB [19]	ED

Table 2. Histogram-dependent ordering

Method	Abbreviation
Minimum	MIN
Minimum mode	$MO1$
Maximum mode	$MO2$
Mean	$MEAN$
Variance	VAR
Maximum	MAX

As a reference, a WX suffix is added for ordering dependent on histogram information, where X represents the number of windows into which the image was divided. If $X = 0$, the domain is the structuring element B; if $X = 1$, the domain is the whole image; if $X = 9$, the image was divided into 9 sub-regions of size 3×3 and so on.

Global Contrast Enhancement (VAR): The objective of this metric is to evaluate the global contrast enhancement of the color image. The best results are shown (on average) for each of the iterations.

Table 3 shows the top 10 average results for the 100 images of the VAR metric. We can see that the ordering BM performs better in all iterations, then follow the ordering MIN, $MO1$ and $MO2$.

In general, all ordering show good results on average according to the VAR metric, which seeks to measure the global stretch of the histogram of the color image. Ordering is important in all cases, as well as the configuration of windows that are used for histogram-dependent ordering methods. In this experiment the BM method generates better results on average for all iterations; it is followed by histogram-dependent orderings, where the domain of the structuring element is better than the division by windows. An image of the database is shown in Fig. 1.

Table 3. VAR average of best results (Top 10)

Methods	m = 2	m = 3	m = 4	m = 5	m = 6	m = 7
BM	**3316.576**	**3864.611**	**4665.250**	**5697.019**	**6806.257**	**7904.776**
MINW49	3258.434	3796.188	4578.353	5587.750	6678.743	**7759.869**
MINW25	3258.442	3796.102	4578.500	5587.919	**6678.947**	7759.401
MINW0	**3258.952**	**3797.176**	**4579.518**	**5588.219**	6678.795	7757.443
MINW1	**3258.627**	**3797.238**	**4579.773**	**5588.741**	**6678.826**	7755.024
MINW9	3258.531	3796.315	4578.349	5587.758	6675.713	7754.924
MO1W9	3259.042	3797.097	4577.706	5583.205	6667.705	7738.447
MO2W9	3259.058	3797.106	4577.740	5583.222	6667.388	7738.182
MO2W1	3258.906	3796.771	4577.421	5581.397	6667.439	7737.405
MO1W1	3258.901	3796.770	4577.417	5581.367	6667.399	7737.398

Fig. 1. Original image taken from the database [42].

In the Fig. 2 it can be seen how the histogram of the image is more stretched in the 5th iteration (m = 5).

Local Contrast Enhancement (CIR): The objective of this metric is to evaluate the local contrast enhancement of the color image. Table 4 shows the top 10 average results for the 100 images of the CIR metric. Among the top ten, there are the methods $MEAN$, $MO1$, $MO2$ and MAX (all are histogram-dependent ordering methods).

Color Enhancement (CEF): This metric evaluates the improvement of the color of the images. In the Fig. 3 it can be seen that the improvement of color are increasingly noticeable as the iterations increase (m).

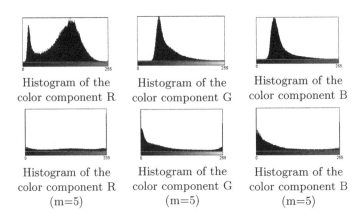

Fig. 2. Histogram of each component of the RGB image. (Color figure online)

Table 4. CIR average of best results (Top 10)

Methods	m = 2	m = 3	m = 4	m = 5	m = 6	m = 7
MEANW0	0.6148	3.2564	8.9259	17.7897	28.2444	**37.8354**
MO1W0	**0.6171**	**3.2668**	**8.9516**	**17.8376**	**28.2935**	37.8182
MEANW49	0.6146	3.2559	8.9183	17.7590	28.1968	**37.8176**
MO2W0	**0.6173**	**3.2665**	8.9496	**17.8276**	**28.2870**	37.8156
MEANW9	0.6146	3.2566	8.9204	17.7630	28.1920	37.8087
MEANW25	0.6147	3.2565	8.9207	17.7612	28.1963	37.8080
MAXW0	0.6157	3.2579	8.9221	17.7478	28.1703	37.8031
MEANW1	0.6146	3.2582	8.9264	17.7728	28.2002	37.7993
MO1W25	**0.6169**	**3.2692**	**8.9566**	17.8201	**28.2535**	37.7957
MO1W49	0.6168	3.2680	**8.9524**	**17.8211**	28.2504	37.7956

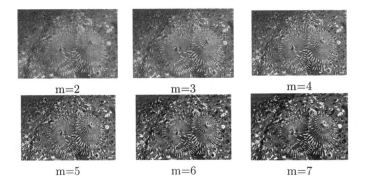

Fig. 3. Improved color image as the number of iterations increases

Table 5 shows the top ten results of the CEF metric. Among the top ten, there are the methods MIN, $MO1$ and $MO2$ (all are histogram-dependent ordering methods).

Table 5. CEF average of best results (Top 10)

Methods	m = 2	m = 3	m = 4	m = 5	m = 6	m = 7
MINW1	**1.013045**	**1.051822**	**1.124872**	**1.231890**	**1.368238**	**1.529108**
MO1W1	**1.009614**	**1.040297**	**1.105122**	**1.206343**	**1.341457**	**1.504726**
MO2W1	**1.009619**	**1.040295**	**1.105109**	**1.206350**	**1.341461**	**1.504693**
MO1W9	1.009181	1.039318	1.102214	1.202283	1.334507	1.499447
MO2W9	1.009194	1.039327	1.102255	1.202257	1.334250	1.499198
MINW9	1.009470	1.040141	1.104012	1.203391	1.334754	1.496082
MO1W25	1.009264	1.039142	1.101910	1.201898	1.333040	1.494616
MO2W25	1.009269	1.039118	1.101847	1.201633	1.332722	1.494025
MINW25	1.008607	1.037187	1.099015	1.196997	1.328103	1.490025
MINW49	1.008336	1.036289	1.096778	1.194335	1.325822	1.489206

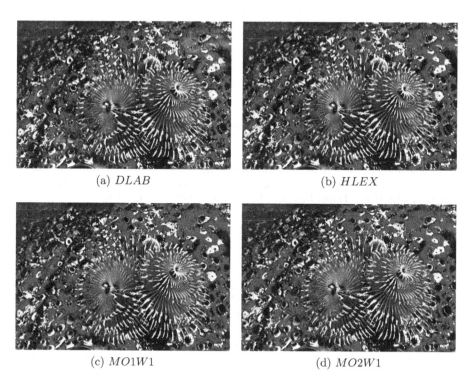

(a) $DLAB$ (b) $HLEX$

(c) $MO1W1$ (d) $MO2W1$

Fig. 4. Visual results obtained applying the multiscale morphology method using different ordering methods

In the Fig. 4 it is possible to see the visual results obtained applying the multiscale morphology method using different ordering methods. The histogram-dependent ordering methods ($MO1$ and $MO2$) generate greater improvements compared to the other methods.

5   Conclusions

In this work we present an extension of the multiscale contrast enhancement method to the color images. The proposed method uses different types of ordering methods.

The bit mixing (BM) obtained the best results in global contrast enhancement (measured by variance). Among all the ordering methods considered in this work, the histogram information-dependent based ordering is the one that achieves better results in terms of local contrast and color enhancement. Specifically, when mode ($MO1$ and $MO2$) is used as histogram information, satisfactory results are obtained in all evaluated metrics.

Improvements in global, local and color contrast are quite noticeable by applying the multiscale morphology method as the number of iterations increases.

A proposal for future work is the comparison of the multiscale image enhancement method, using the multiscale top-hat transform operation with other state of the art methods. In this respect, other multiscale methods could be extended.

References

1. Wang, Y.P., Wu, Q., Castleman, K.R., Xiong, Z.: Chromosome image enhancement using multiscale differential operators. IEEE Trans. Med. Imaging **22**(5), 685–693 (2003)
2. Mencattini, A., Salmeri, M., Lojacono, R., Frigerio, M., Caselli, F.: Mammographic images enhancement and denoising for breast cancer detection using dyadic wavelet processing. IEEE Trans. Instrum. Meas. **57**(7), 1422–1430 (2008)
3. Boccignone, G., Picariello, A.: Multiscale contrast enhancement of medical images. In: 1997 IEEE International Conference on Acoustics, Speech, and Signal Processing, vol. 4, pp. 2789–2792. IEEE (1997)
4. Stojić, T., Reljin, I., Reljin, B.: Local contrast enhancement in digital mammography by using mathematical morphology. In: International Symposium on Signals, Circuits and Systems, ISSCS 2005, vol. 2, pp. 609–612. IEEE (2005)
5. Angelelli, P., Nylund, K., Gilja, O.H., Hauser, H.: Interactive visual analysis of contrast-enhanced ultrasound data based on small neighborhood statistics. Comput. Graph. **35**(2), 218–226 (2011)
6. Yang, G.Z., Hansell, D.M.: CT image enhancement with wavelet analysis for the detection of small airways disease. IEEE Trans. Med. Imaging **16**(6), 953–961 (1997)
7. Truc, P.T., Khan, M.A., Lee, Y.K., Lee, S., Kim, T.S.: Vessel enhancement filter using directional filter bank. Comput. Vis. Image Underst. **113**(1), 101–112 (2009)

8. Yang, C., Lu, L., Lin, H., Guan, R., Shi, X., Liang, Y.: A fuzzy-statistics-based principal component analysis (FS-PCA) method for multispectral image enhancement and display. IEEE Trans. Geosci. Remote. Sens. **46**(11), 3937–3947 (2008)
9. Liao, B., Yin, P., Xiao, C.: Efficient image dehazing using boundary conditions and local contrast. Comput. Graph. **70**, 242–250 (2018)
10. Bai, X.: Microscopy mineral image enhancement through center operator construction. Appl. Opt. **54**(15), 4678–4688 (2015)
11. Wan, Y., Shi, D.: Joint exact histogram specification and image enhancement through the wavelet transform. IEEE Trans. Image Process. **16**(9), 2245–2250 (2007)
12. Garg, R., Mittal, B., Garg, S.: Histogram equalization techniques for image enhancement. Int. J. Electron. Commun. Technol **2**(1), 107–111 (2011)
13. Wong, C.Y., et al.: Histogram equalization and optimal profile compression based approach for colour image enhancement. J. Vis. Commun. Image Represent. **38**, 802–813 (2016)
14. Huang, J., Ma, Y., Zhang, Y., Fan, F.: Infrared image enhancement algorithm based on adaptive histogram segmentation. Appl. Opt. **56**(35), 9686–9697 (2017)
15. Choi, Y.S., Krishnapuram, R.: A robust approach to image enhancement based on fuzzy logic. IEEE Trans. Image Process. **6**(6), 808–825 (1997)
16. Greenspan, H., Anderson, C.H., Akber, S.: Image enhancement by nonlinear extrapolation in frequency space. IEEE Trans. Image Process. **9**(6), 1035–1048 (2000)
17. Agaian, S.S., Panetta, K., Grigoryan, A.M.: Transform-based image enhancement algorithms with performance measure. IEEE Trans. Image Process. **10**(3), 367–382 (2001)
18. Grigoryan, A.M., Agaian, S.S.: Transform-based image enhancement algorithms with performance measure. Adv. Imaging Electron. Phys. **130**, 165–242 (2004)
19. Ortiz Zamora, F.G.: Procesamiento morfológico de imágenes en color: aplicación a la reconstrucción geodésica (2002)
20. Joblove, G.H., Greenberg, D.: Color spaces for computer graphics. In: ACM SIGGRAPH Computer Graphics, vol. 12, pp. 20–25. ACM (1978)
21. Serra, J.: Image Analysis and Mathematical Morphology. Academic Press, Inc., Cambridge (1983)
22. De, I., Chanda, B., Chattopadhyay, B.: Enhancing effective depth-of-field by image fusion using mathematical morphology. Image Vis. Comput. **24**(12), 1278–1287 (2006)
23. Bai, X., Zhou, F., Xue, B.: Image enhancement using multi scale image features extracted by top-hat transform. Opt. Laser Technol. **44**(2), 328–336 (2012)
24. Mukhopadhyay, S., Chanda, B.: A multiscale morphological approach to local contrast enhancement. Signal Process. **80**(4), 685–696 (2000)
25. Soille, P.: Morphological Image Analysis: Principles and Applications. Springer, Heidelberg (2013). https://doi.org/10.1007/978-3-662-05088-0
26. Román, J.C.M., Ayala, H.L., Noguera, J.L.V.: Image color contrast enhancement using multiscale morphology. In: 4th Conference of Computational Interdisciplinary Science (2016)
27. Bai, X., Zhou, F., Xue, B.: Noise-suppressed image enhancement using multiscale top-hat selection transform through region extraction. Appl. Opt. **51**(3), 338–347 (2012)
28. Liao, M., Zhao, Y.Q., Wang, X.H., Dai, P.S.: Retinal vessel enhancement based on multi-scale top-hat transformation and histogram fitting stretching. Opt. Laser Technol. **58**, 56–62 (2014)

29. Peng, B., Wang, Y., Yang, X.: A multiscale morphological approach to local contrast enhancement for ultrasound images. In: 2010 International Conference on Computational and Information Sciences, pp. 1142–1145. IEEE (2010)

30. Román, J.C.M., Ayala, H.L., Noguera, J.L.V.: Top-hat transform for enhancement of aerial thermal images. In: 2017 30th SIBGRAPI Conference on Graphics, Patterns and Images (SIBGRAPI), pp. 277–284. IEEE (2017)

31. Zhao, J., Zhou, Q., Chen, Y., Feng, H., Xu, Z., Li, Q.: Fusion of visible and infrared images using saliency analysis and detail preserving based image decomposition. Infrared Phys. Technol. **56**, 93–99 (2013)

32. Bai, X., Zhou, F., Xue, B.: Fusion of infrared and visual images through region extraction by using multi scale center-surround top-hat transform. Opt. Express **19**(9), 8444–8457 (2011)

33. Ye, B., Peng, J.X.: Small target detection method based on morphology top-hat operator. J. Image Graph. **7**(7), 638–642 (2002)

34. Aptoula, E., Lefèvre, S.: A comparative study on multivariate mathematical morphology. Pattern Recognit. **40**(11), 2914–2929 (2007)

35. Chanussot, J., Lambert, P.: Bit mixing paradigm for multivalued morphological filters. In: 1997 Sixth International Conference on Image Processing and Its Applications, vol. 2, pp. 804–808. IET (1997)

36. Noguera, J.L.V., Ayala, H.L., Schaerer, C.E., Facon, J.: A color morphological ordering method based on additive and subtractive spaces. In: 2014 IEEE International Conference on Image Processing (ICIP), pp. 674–678. IEEE (2014)

37. Cardozo, R., Méndez, Á., Legal Ayala, H., Vázquez Noguera, J.L.: Mejora de imágenes a color utilizando un enfoque morfológico multiescala. In: XXIV Congreso Argentino de Ciencias de la Computación (La Plata, 2018) (2018)

38. Tobar, M.C., Platero, C., González, P.M., Asensio, G.: Mathematical morphology in the *HSI* colour space. In: Martí, J., Benedí, J.M., Mendonça, A.M., Serrat, J. (eds.) IbPRIA 2007. LNCS, vol. 4478, pp. 467–474. Springer, Heidelberg (2007). https://doi.org/10.1007/978-3-540-72849-8_59

39. Hanbury, A., Kandaswamy, U., Adjeroh, D.A.: Illumination-invariant morphological texture classification. In: Ronse, C., Najman, L., Decencière, E. (eds.) Mathematical Morphology: 40 Years On, vol. 30, pp. 377–386. Springer, Heidelberg (2005). https://doi.org/10.1007/1-4020-3443-1_34

40. Mello Román, J.C., Vázquez Noguera, J.L., Legal-Ayala, H., Pinto-Roa, D.P., Gomez-Guerrero, S., García Torres, M.: Entropy and contrast enhancement of infrared thermal images using the multiscale top-hat transform. Entropy **21**(3), 244 (2019)

41. Chanussot, J., Lambert, P.: Total ordering based on space filling curves for multivalued morphology. Comput. Imaging Vis. **12**, 51–58 (1998)

42. Arbelaez, P., Fowlkes, C., Martin, D.: The Berkeley segmentation dataset and benchmark (2007). http://www.eecs.berkeley.edu/Research/Projects/CS/vision/bsds

43. Gordon, R., Rangayyan, R.M.: Feature enhancement of film mammograms using fixed and adaptive neighborhoods. Appl. Opt. **23**(4), 560–564 (1984)

44. Hasler, D., Suesstrunk, S.E.: Measuring colorfulness in natural images. In: Human vision and electronic imaging VIII, vol. 5007, pp. 87–96. International Society for Optics and Photonics (2003)

45. Susstrunk, S.E., Winkler, S.: Color image quality on the internet. In: Internet Imaging V, vol. 5304, pp. 118–132. International Society for Optics and Photonics (2003)

46. Angulo, J., Serra, J.: Morphological coding of color images by vector connected filters. In: Proceedings of Seventh International Symposium on Signal Processing and Its Applications, vol. 1, pp. 69–72. IEEE (2003)
47. Ortiz, F., Torres, F., Gil, P.: Gaussian noise elimination in colour images by vector-connected filters. In: Proceedings of the 17th International Conference on Pattern Recognition, ICPR 2004, vol. 4, pp. 807–810. IEEE (2004)

An Approach to Automated Recognition of Pavement Deterioration Through Machine Learning

Rodrigo Huincalef[1(✉)], Guillermo Urrutia[1], Gabriel Ingravallo[1], and Diego C. Martínez[2]

[1] Departamento de Informática Trelew, Facultad de Ingeniería, Universidad Nacional de la Patagonia San Juan Bosco, Comodoro Rivadavia, Argentina
rhuincalef91@gmail.com, guilleurrutia10@gmail.com, gabrielingravallo@gmail.com
[2] Instituto de Ciencias e Ingeniería de la Computación, CONICET-UNS, Bahía Blanca, Argentina
dcm@cs.uns.edu.ar

Abstract. Roads are composed of various sorts of materials and with the constant use they expose different kinds of cracks or potholes. The aim of the current research is to present a novel automated classification method to be applied on these faults, which can be located on rigid pavement type. In order to collect proper representation of faults, a Kinect device was used, leading to three-dimensional point cloud structures. Images descriptors were used in order to establish the type of pothole and to get information regarding fault dimensions.

This work is an extension of a preliminary version published in the Argentine Congress of Computer Science CACIC 2018 [8]. We would like to thank the anonymous reviewers for their useful comments. In this article a deeper explanation of the techniques combining cloud descriptors and machine learning is included, with a detail of the results. Some extra figures were added.

1 Introduction

The pavement of a street or highway is a structure composed of a set of layers of materials processed on the ground, whose function is to distribute the load of vehicles to the subsoil and allow the constant transit. The structure of the pavement should provide a surface of acceptable quality for the circulation of vehicles, adequate slip resistance, a lower level of noise, a waterproof, structural strength and a long life cycle with low maintenance cost. However, cracks are usual due to several factors. A *fissure* is a long, narrow opening in a slab of material that can be a corner fissure, longitudinal (if it extends along a slab) or transversal (if it extends perpendicular to the overturning of the slab material).

P. Pesado and C. Aciti (Eds.): CACIC 2018, CCIS 995, pp. 124–140, 2019.
https://doi.org/10.1007/978-3-030-20787-8_9

The repair method for this type of failure consists of sealing joints and fissures, and repairing the entire thickness. On the other hand, a *pothole* is defined as a cavity, generally rounded due to the loss of the pavement on a part of the surface. The repair method for this type of failure depends on its deterioration, and is special for each case. In Fig. 1 both faults are shown.

Fig. 1. A pothole and a longitudinal fissure, common in roads.

Due to the constant degradation of the different types of faults, these must be detected and repaired as soon as possible. The task of registering defects and depressions in the pavement has always been crucial to adopt a precise strategy for the maintenance and repair of roadways. However, manual measurement is a costly task both in time and resources. In this work we present an automated, AI-based classification of pavement faults, mainly potholes and fissures, through machine learning techniques using proper, accessible 3D models. There are previous works that apply different technologies for this purpose [4–7, 9, 10, 12–16] but they require special devices and a good degree of important human intervention. Our interest is to formalize a process that is both accessible and cost-efficient. As a consequence, we implement an assistive application for the detection and classification of faults in the pavement, which will be useful for cost estimates. Our proposal make use of accessible domestic technologies, such as the 3D sensor of videogame consoles, to obtain a model of pavement fault that us appropriate for machine learning algorithms. A real implementation that offers an appropriate visualization and automatic geo-location of faults is also presented.

The work is organized as follows. Section 2 introduces the problem of road faults modelization. Section 2 explains the 3D sensors, the libraries to process the data obtained by these sensors, the management of point clouds, the descriptors that can be obtained from the analysis of these data and the machine learning technique used to generate the classification model. In Sect. 3 we describe a prototype application for a vehicle that is used to collect the data through the Kinect sensor. Finally, conclusions and future work are discussed.

2   Surface Recognition

As stated before, we are interested in the automated classification of faults. This requires the use of adequate data structures representing real potholes and fissures. Hence, surface recognition is the first part of the process towards intelligent evaluation of faults. Ideally, the task of collecting data from real pavement should be also be automated, by using an autonomous vehicle. However, the construction of such a kind of vehicle is beyond the goals of our project. We are interested in the use of accessible hardware towards a practical solution for city governments and contractors.

In order to classify depressions then it is mandatory to get a proper mathematical model using some surface measure device. Here 3D sensors are used to analyse real world objects or environments and obtain their relevant physical properties, such as colors or shape, which later can be used to produce three-dimensional digital models. There are diverse, expensive sensors that may be used to attain this purpose, but we are interested in the use of domestic, accessible resources. Hence, we use a Kinect Microsoft sensor that has the capability of generate Range Images, that keeps information regarding distance of each image pixel to the device capture point. We have used this device to record faults in a moving vehicle. The device should be mounted as shown in Fig. 2, although that structure was not built during this research project.

The scanning process must produce 3D model representations. We use *point cloud structures*, which are point sets on a coordinate systems (optionally with RGB point information), being the most frequently used the Cartesian three-dimensional system (X,Y,Z). These representations can be rendered, inspectioned and converted to polygonal or triangular meshes.

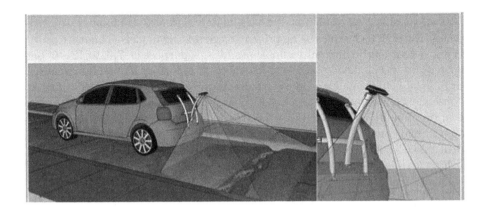

Fig. 2. The Kinect device can be easily installed on a vehicle.

There are several drivers and libraries (OpenNI, Freenect, OpenKinect, Point Cloud Library) that allow users to interact with the Microsoft Kinect sensor.

Point Cloud Library (PCL) [1] is an independent, open-source, multiplatform (also available in Windows, Linux, MacOS and AndroidOS), C++-written solution for sensing, geometrical point cloud processing and storing in 2D or 3D dimensions. The library PCL offers different standalone modules with algorithms that may be combined into a pipeline to spot several types of objects. These algorithms are meant to be applied on a wide range of tasks which is important for a correct object detection, for instance outliers filtering (filter point with values out of a certain range), point cloud reading, storing, format conversion, decomposition (in order to perform searches) and concatenation, perform segmentation on specific parts of a complete point cloud capture, keypoint extraction and geometric descriptors computation with the aim of identifying distinct sorts of objects. In Fig. 3 a point cloud of a real pavement fault is shown.

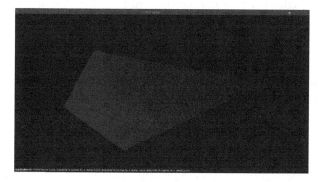

Fig. 3. Point cloud visualized with pcl_viewer tool from PCL. Full point cloud points are depicted with violet whereas points from a pavement depression, which have been isolated with classifier application, are with ligthblue and blue. (Color figure online)

The process of obtaining a proper 3D model for automated classification is important and somehow difficult. Regarding the PCL pipeline for object recognition, it consists of a point cloud pre-processing phase with the goal of getting rid of noise. Then an object segmentation step is performed which allow us to obtain clusters which can be associated with potholes. Lasty, a descriptor generation phase is executed with the goal of getting information about the object geometry. PCL descriptors are divided in two classes: local and global. On the one hand, local descriptors describe surface geometry around a point without taking into account the complete geometry of the object the point belongs to. Hence when the local descriptors computation is performed, it is necessary to previously filter keypoints which belongs the object under study. Local descriptors applications include objects recognition and registration, which is a technique to detect whether common areas in several point clouds exists. On the other hand, global descriptors describe geometry of a whole point cluster which represents an object. Therefore if there is a need to generate this type of descriptor it would be compulsory to perform previously a pre-processing step in order to isolate the cluster from the point cloud. Applications of this type of descriptors are the object recognition and classification, position estimation and geometry surface analysis (type of object, shape, etc.).

The process of collecting samples took several days. Also, during this phase it was observed that some cracks does not possess significant depth to be measured by the Kinect device. Although this seems to be a drawback, those cracks are not of real interest for evaluation costs of repair (at least not for the moment, because faults tend to increase in size as time goes by). Due to this fact we decided to classify only those types of cracks which have enough depth to be isolated and described by descriptors which make use the of geometrical information regarding angles between normals of a surface. Because of this, descriptors were selected taking into account processing hardware capabilities and normal associated descriptor properties. These are the following:

– Global Radious-based Surface Descriptor (GRSD): This descriptor uses local Radius-based Surface Descriptor (RSD), based on geometric description of a surface based on neighboring points. It estimates the minimum and maximum curvature radius from angle-distance pairs. This method is easy to compute and exhibits a good description capability, leading mainly to the detection of points belonging to different surfaces. It generates sets of points or voxels, where every voxel has a width of 2.5 cm, then computing maximum and minimum radius between this points and its neighbors, labeling every voxel according to this value. Labels are *plane*, if $radius > 0.1$, a *cylinder* if not a plane and $radius\_max > 0.175$, a *border/corner* if not a cylinder an y $radius\_min < 0.015$, a *sphere* if not a border and $radius\_max - radius\_min < 0.05$ and a generic surface otherwise. After labelling every voxel, a complete global histogram is computed describing the relations between clusters, according to the intersections of every surface

– Ensamble Shape of Functions (ESF): This descriptor does not applies pre-processing, using a set of surface voxels instead, called *voxel grid*. It iterates through every point in the cloud, choosing three extra random points and computing D2, D2 ratio, D3 and A3, each one generating histograms describing the geometric relation between these points. It leads to 10 sub-histograms consisting of 64 divisions.

The outcome of these complex processes is a data structure properly representing relevant pavement faults. In Fig. 4 a screenshot of the application is shown, with a pavement crack as a cloud of points. There is, however, the need of determining whether these faults are either potholes or fissures, as they require different treatments. In the following section we discuss the use of machine learning techniques to help this task.

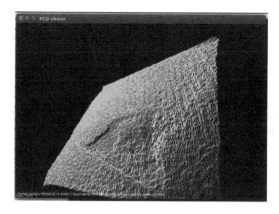

Fig. 4. Screenshot of the application showing a pavement crack.

3   SVM

Support Vector Machine [2] is a technique used for supervised learning [3,11] to solve classification and regression problems based on hyperplanes. In this method the p features associated with a certain amount of training samples are arranged in a *p-dimensional* (being each sample a p dimensional vector) where each feature represents the coordinates with regard to one specific sample. In this way the SVM model generation is based on computing, testing and selecting from several hyperplanes which separate input data in order to get the best. Thus, SVMs allow researchers to divide data in sets with linear hyperplanes. Nonetheless, there are situations in which input data cannot be linearly divided, causing an unsatisfactory performance. The solution offered by SVMs to this problem is the use of kernel decision functions which convert the feature input data space to a higher dimension space being these quadratic, cubic, polynomial or higher dimensions space with the goal of achieving the finding of a brand-new hyperplane that separate samples with a better precision. Therefore there are a diverse range of kernels employed to attain this objective, mainly Linear, RBF and Polynomial.

As a result of SVM being a classification binary algorithm, various techniques have been developed to attain multiclass classification which allow researchers to assign samples among two or more classes. Two of these methods are:

- One versus One (One-vs-One, OvO): Given N classes this algorithm perform the $N(N-1)/2$ binary classifiers training getting each for every class combination using the training dataset. Then during the prediction phase a voting scheme where every classifier gives a result for the same input data sample. Hence the class which has a greater amount of positive votes it is the result of the prediction process.
- One versus Rest (One-vs-Rest, OvR, OvA): Given N classes N classifiers are trained using the full training dataset, choosing as positive those classes

that belong to the classificator whilst the others are chosen as negatives. Accordingly, by receiving an input sample every classifier generate a decimal value which is a confidence score that indicates the probability of that sample of belonging to that type of element. Consequently the class with the highest score is considered the class in which the element is assigned.

In our current research project, an SVM implementation using C++ programming language was implemented for constructing the classification model (converting the data point cloud samples into SVM compatible format). Throughout this process, it was necessary to assign a class to every type of sample (crack or pothole) using OvO technique and testing the same dataset with Linear and RBF kernel.

3.1   Building a Classification Model

The process of construction of the classification model consisted in the following steps:

(I) Pavement surface samples collection: During this step an estimated amount of 1000 samples were captured using the Kinect sensor, which sensed different pavement streets in the cities of Trelew, Rawson, Playa Union and Gaiman in the Province of Chubut, Argentina. The recollection phase was performed when there was almost no sunlight reflecting the pavement faults. This is the best moment to capture data, not only for technical reasons (the sensor works better) but for practical reasons: traffic is low a couple of hours after office time.

Fig. 5. PCL RANSAC algorithm example. A set of points is shown with outliers that will be filtered with RANSAC using the plane geometric model. Blue points are those which can be fitted to the plane RANSAC model whereas red points belong to a real crack sample. (Color figure online)

(II) Samples pre-processing phase: The main target of this phase is the preparation of the raw samples in order to improve quality. Several PCL algorithms for discarding noise were studied. Consequently they were tested against several samples. Next, the amount of point cloud points was reduced because of the hardware limitations and high samples quantity. Thus, *Voxel Grid downsampling* technique was employed which makes use of voxels (set of points which are the minimum tridimensional unit such as a pixel is the smallest bidimensional unit) which compose the 3D grid of a tridimensional object. Voxel Grid algorithm allows the reduction of elements in the cloud, by performing a division in voxels and using the center of the voxel as a representative point.

Finally, it was necessary to obtain geometric properties in order to describe with higher precision the sensed pavement surface. Here, PCL normal computation algorithms were employed.

(III) Sample segmentation: Algorithms for PCL segmentation were analyzed employing the samples previously captured with the aim of isolating point cloud clusters which belong to the depressions on the pavement and the rest of the street. As a consequence, Planar and Euclidean Segmentation algorithms were selected and concatenated in the instructions pipeline.

Euclidean Segmentation iterates on every point of the cloud, computing euclidean distance between the point and its neighbours. If this distance is less than a threshold, then both points belong to the same cluster. This process continues with unvisited points and finishes when all of the clusters are defined. RANSAC (Random Sample Consensus) is a sampling algorithm that, given a set of data as input, it estimates the parameters needed to fit a particular model with an acceptable error threshold. It identifies points that are potentially suitable for the model (inliers) and those who are not (outliers). The main steps are:

(a) Random points are selected, and training occurs using this subset of points according to the specified model.

(b) Next, the algorithm verifies whether in the original cloud some points are consistent with the model and its previously estimated parameters using a *loss function*. Points that are characterized as non-consistent with the model are considered *outliers*. Consistent points are considered *inliers* and they conform the *consensus set*.

(c) Repeats from step (a).

Thus, RANSAC repeats until enough inliers are determined for a reliable estimation. This algorithm is robust and efficient in estimation, even with data suffering levels of noise, but there is no time limit for the computation. If this is a constraint then the quality of the solution may be low. In Fig. 5, an example of the analysis of a fissure is depicted, with the points related to the fissure clearly highlighted.

(IV) Curvatures computing: A deeper comprehension of fault dimension is obtained. The average curvature for clusters isolated earlier, which are thought to be part of a pavement depression, were computed so that allowed us to get curvatures minimum and maximum ranges, which let us get rid of those segments whose average curvature level was out of these ranges. PCL includes an algorithm called Principal Curvatures Estimation (PCE) to compute minimal and maximal curvatures in every point, by the use of eigenvectors and eigenvalues on a set of points and normals. This helped to improve the classifier application ability to filter or keep clusters based on alike geometry surface depressions.

(V) Feature building: Lastly, diverse PCL surface description methods were studied and compared with regard to the size in bytes for each sample and amount of samples to be processed, histogram shape associated with different types of samples and sort of descriptor (local or global). Later it was investigated whether PCL offered machine learning models support combined with descriptors. Due to the fact the library had machine learning SVM support (making use of libsvm tool) this method was chosen for the classification application and each one of the point cloud samples were converted to libsvm compatible format.

After faults were detected by the sensor and raw data was obtained, a complex process of data preparation is triggered. Although it was an integral part of the project, it is not, however, the intention of this paper to describe the process in detail, other than the stages mentioned above. In the following section we address the automatic classification of faults.

4   Automatic Classification

We started determining the amount of samples to be used for every step. We gathered 1000 samples of potholes and fissures, and we have decided to use 76% for training and 24% for testing. Then a Cropping Pipeline was applied in order to clean samples towards classification, isolating features related to the pavement cracks. To compute features of potholes and fissures, the focus was put in PCL descriptors using histograms with adequate dimensions in order to avoid excessive processing time.

Once every training sample was ready, classification process was initiated. FPH descriptors were generated from the sample set to be used by SVM, using potholes as positive samples and fissures as negative samples, in order to get a classification only about these to kind of pavement cracks. We tried with different sets of training samples: potholes, fissures and mixed (7 potholes and 28 non-pothole cracks). This test was not good, failing to recognize the potholes in the sets. After that, we have applied the same test for GRSD descriptor, with a much worst accuracy. We did not get better results after escalating features in the same dataset. Since the descriptors of the samples were not exhibiting significant differences, a graphical comparison was made between samples of the same set of training leading to the conclusion that GRSD was more notorious in the difference between cracks. Accuracy was much better after using training only with this descriptor and focusing on the detection of potholes from planes.

Since two different classifications are needed for every type of sample It was mandatory to perform a curvature value analysis using the PCL Principal Curvatures Estimation algorithm, which makes use of the minimum and maximum average values for each sample, with the aim of finding a parameter that could be used along with the GRSD descriptor to attain the clear division of different types of faults with just one classifier. Thus It was observed that the average curvature range for cracks was a subset of the potholes average curvature range so that they tend to had higher curvature values. Because of this It was decided to include the curvature value in the segmentation process and isolate only those samples whose average curvature was similar to a pothole or crack.

Afterwards average minimum and maximum curvature values for each sample were added to the GRSD descriptor and a multiclass SVM was trained. The training process began with the division of the samples into three classes: Potholes, Cracks and Planes (merely used for this experiment). Next the final training set was set up with potholes, cracks and planes isolated which had similar GRSD histograms (employing a RBF Kernel with $gamma = 0.0008$ and $cost = 1$) which lead to obtain a 55% precision value with a training subset from the complete set. Nonetheless only potholes and planes were able to be classified since the trained model could not distinguish cracks from potholes. As the precision value with GRSD was really low a FPFH descriptor test was carried out together with curvature faults value getting a 56,47% precision result, which did not improve considerably the classifier score.

Due to the low precision results, we decided to use Ensemble Shape of Functions (ESF) with the multiclass SVM and the previous training dataset. Nevertheless only a 54.4444% precision score was achieved since the classifier could only classify cracks and potholes as not being planes but not distinguishing potholes from cracks.

In another test, we computed and analyzed the volume and area of every training sample. By adding these characteristics to the GRSD descriptor we applied SVM with linear kernel obtaining a precision of 52.94% with the testing set of potholes and fissures, without planes. We also added some attributes related to the size of these cracks, such as height, width, depth and volume. Thus, we applied GRSD enriched with this information, distinguishing fissures when $|height - width| > 40$. Then, samples where re-classified according to this criterion, obtaining the following results:

- By adding height, width and depth, the GRSD descriptor improved accuracy reaching 79.8%.
- By considering the difference of width and height the GRSD descriptor improved accuracy reaching 100%.
- By adding volume and depth, the accuracy was reduced to 75%.
- By adding difference of weight and width, and testing only with GRSD, the accuracy was of 75% (kernel Linear) y 87.5% (kernel RBF) (with cost -c 2 and gamma -g 0.00000002).

Hence, since some samples in the dataset of training exhibit a similar ratio between heigth and width, a reclassification of cracks was made. After testing again with SVM using the GRSD descriptor and the difference between height and width, we obtained a precision of 87.5% with RBF kernel and a 100% with lineal kernel. Because the accuracy increased when reclassifying the training dataset, the same procedure was applied for the complete testing dataset. Since the calculated width and height are based on maximum and minimum values provided by the Oriented Bounding Box mechanism of PCL in the X-Y axes, which is adjusted and oriented to the size of the sample, those samples that contained outliers that introduced noise in the calculation of this difference were eliminated. From a total of 1000 samples, 806 samples were eliminated (753 for training and 53 for testing). When analyzing the statistics of dimensions of the training failure dataset, a limit of difference between height and width was selected to divide them according to the type (crack or fissure) of 0.49, since the cracks contained a length considerably greater than the thickness, a situation that is not present in potholes.

Types of samples	Kernel Linear			Kernel RBF		
	Precision	Recall	F1-Score	Precision	Recall	F1-Score
Potholes	1.0	1.0	1.0	0.0	0.0	0.0
Cracks	1.0	1.0	1.0	0.17	1.0	0.29
avg/total	1.0	1.0	1.0	0.03	0.17	0.05

Fig. 6. ESF descriptor metrics with Linear and RBF Kernel.

When running again the tests with training and testing dataset divided by this limit, 89% accuracy was obtained with Linear kernel and 71% with RBF kernel (with gamma 0.0000002 and cost C 1500) using a cross validation of 5 iterations with GRSD. Again, we proceeded to experiment with the difference between height and width, changing only the descriptor with ESF and FPFH, obtaining the following results for the same parameters and the same number of iterations.

– With FPFH, a 63% for lineal kernel and 60% RBF kernel.
– With ESF, a 98% for lineal kernel y 54% RBF kernel.

Finally, a comparison was made of the classification metrics regarding the different descriptors for the original division of samples (53 in total), in order to contrast the classification effectiveness of these and to verify the superiority of ESF with respect to the rest.

Types of samples	Kernel Linear			Kernel RBF		
	Precision	Recall	F1-Score	Precision	Recall	F1-Score
Potholes	0.83	1	0.91	0.00	0.00	0.00
Cracks	0.23	0.78	0.36	0.17	1.00	0.29
avg/total	0.80	0.53	0.58	0.03	0.17	0.05

Fig. 7. GRSD descriptor metrics with Linear and RBF Kernel.

To do this, F1-Score and Recall values were calculated for both classes and the confusion matrix to show the number of elements effectively assigned to each class. The values of F1-Score and Recall for the partition of the initial dataset, with the linear and RBF kernels, can be seen in Figs. 6, 7 and 8.

	Kernel Linear			Kernel RBF		
Types of samples	Precision	Recall	F1-Score	Precision	Recall	F1-Score
Potholes	0.91	0.48	0.63	1	0.09	0.17
Cracks	0.23	0.78	0.36	0.18	1.00	0.31
avg/total	0.80	0.53	0.58	0.86	0.25	0.19

Fig. 8. FPFH descriptor metrics with Linear and RBF Kernel.

The confusion matrix for FPFH, ESF and GRSD are shown in Figs. 9a and b and in Fig. 11 with the initial data partition.

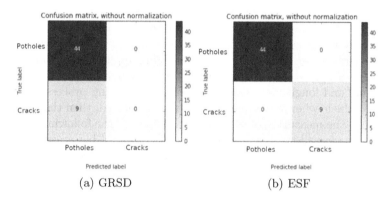

(a) GRSD   (b) ESF

Fig. 9. GRSD and ESF descriptor SVM confusion matrix.

Type of descriptor	ESF		GRSD		FPFH	
Type of classification	ESF	DummyESF	GRSD	DummyGRSD	FPFH	DummyFPFH
Precision	0.98	0.45	0.89	0.516	0.63	0.494

Fig. 10. ESF, GRSD and FPFH descriptor Precision tests vs Dummy Precision tests.

Finally, a comparison (shown in Fig. 10) was made of the average precision of the k-folding of each of the methods with the precision provided by a Dummy classifier, verifying that the classification efficiency of the classifier (with linear kernel) exceeds that of a random classifier:

In the following section we describe the use of a vehicle in the collecting samples stage, as shown in Fig. 2, and the embedded system for registering faults and their position by geo-localization.

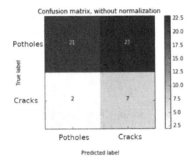

Fig. 11. FPFH descriptor SVM confusion matrix.

5 Application for a Vehicle Prototype

Ideally the sensing prototype device consists of a vehicle with a shell fixed in its back part, as it is seen in Fig. 2, which allows the operators to hold the device from an appropriate high and take samples directly from above the pavement surface. The sensor is connected to an electrical supply device as well as a notebook in which the pavement depression measuring application is running. This application is set up to work with a GPS device that provides the fault location (latitude and longitude). Thus the pothole measuring process workflow is to stop the vehicle when a pavement depression is spotted, then the application user performs the measuring of it and the car moves to the following one and so forth. This process allows the sensing and registration of big areas of a city in acceptable time. The application main architecture is composed of the following software modules:

- Kinect Device: we use the Microsoft Kinect sensor to get frames of video with depth information. These frames are requested continuously and they are rendered in real time within the application. Two visualizations are applied: one with real color and the other with colors associated with the depth between the pavement and the sensor. The first one is used when the daylight is good, and not directly applied on the pavement crack since solar light interferes with infra-red rays from the Kinect. The second one is used when it is mostly dark.
- Geofencing: This module is part of the application and it computes coordinates for geographic localization of the pavement crack, using a GPS device. Two modes are used: real-gps with real coordinates and fake-gps for places when the GPS signal is low (for instance, narrow alleys or inside an hangar).
- APIClient: This module implement the exchange of data between the web application and the capture application.
- Client Application: This application manages the capture of pavement cracks, interacting with the Geofencing module.

The general scheme of the application is shown in Fig. 13.

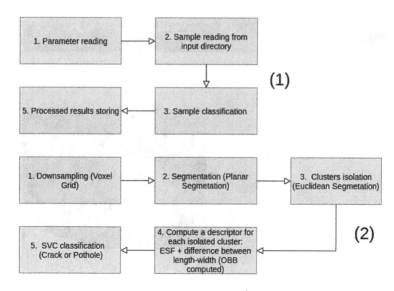

Fig. 12. (1) Classification application (2) Cropping pipeline.

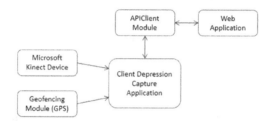

Fig. 13. General software modules from fault-capturing application.

5.1   Pothole Classification Application

The pothole classification application is developed in C++ and its operation consists in reading configuration parameters from a .json file which holds information regarding the built model and also a database file that keeps a previous processed samples log.

Thus the general workflow starts reading input point cloud files (from a earlier setted up directory) and applying the sample cropping pipeline in order to get possible pavement depressions clusters. Then for each one build the custom descriptor and use the previously trained machine learning model, which is read from hard disk drive, to get the pavement depression type. As a result, every isolated cluster are stored in point cloud format in an output directory together with their computed width, length and depth. This process is depicted in Fig. 12. In Fig. 14 a screenshot of the application is shown.

Fig. 14. Pavement depression measuring application interface (Left: RGB video view. Right: Night vision view.). (Color figure online)

6   Conclusions and Future Work

In this work we have described a system for the collection and intelligent classification of potholes and cracks in pavement surfaces, using a low-cost commercial device along with the open-source PCL algorithms connected in an easily configurable pipeline. Moreover the estimated properties related to the pavement depression (width, length, depth), which may be useful for performing a material budget estimation in the repairing process, were successfully computed and stored for each isolated cluster. The system successfully classified collected data as potholes or cracks with a proper accuracy.

There exists other proposals on pavement depressions detection and analysis, which encompass researching and image processing with 3D videos and images, the following investigations have been made [4,9,12,13,16]. Alternatively, studies have been performed utilizing vibration devices such as accelerometers in [5–7,14]. Otherwise, studies in which the main focus is on specific road potholes features with aim of getting to process three-dimensional points coordinates as it is seen on [10,15]. However none of them uses domestic devices nor classification algorithms based on machine learning. The use of automated learning is interesting since pavement faults tend to observe similar qualities within a city, as a consequence of climatic variations, used materials and quality of human work.

Future work has several directions. A continuous capture is desirable since it will make possible to avoid stopping the car. This requires a proper adaptation of dynamic gathering of data, since it demands real-time algorithms for point–cloud noise reduction. We are also interested in the estimation of materials and costs of repairing pavement faults. Since there is a 3D model of every fault a close, reliable estimation can be produced. This can be done after processing a whole street or neighborhood, hence helping to anticipate financial requirements and proper planning for e-governance. Even more, after long periods of time historic data can be mined to eventually detect areas that require special solutions other than normal patches to pavement. Finally, the addition of more than one type of sensor can be helpful to allow classification of faults which does not have enough depth to be fully captured by one sensing device.

References

1. Point cloud library (PCL). https://www.pointclouds.org
2. Scikit learn (support vector machines). http://scikit-learn.org/stable/modules/svm.html
3. Brink, H., Richards, J.W., Fetherolf, M.: Real-World Machine Learning. Manning Publications, Greenwich (2017)
4. Buza, E., Omanovic, S., Huseinovic, A.: Pothole detection with image processing and spectral clustering. In: Recent Advances in Computer Science and Networking, pp. 48–53. WSEAS (2013)
5. Casas-Avellaneda, D., López-Parra, J.: Detection and localization of potholes in roadways using smartphones. DYNA Mag. **83**, 156–162 (2016)
6. Chen, K., Lu, M., Fan, X.: Road condition monitoring using on-board three-axis acelerometer. In: 6th International ICST Conference on Communications and Networking in China. IEEE (2011)
7. Eriksson, G., Hull, N., Madden, B.: The pothole patrol: using a mobile sensor network for road surface monitoring. In: MobiSys (2008)
8. Huincalef, R., Urrutia, G., Ingravallo, G., Martínez,D.: Recognition of surface irregularities on roads: a machine learning approach on 3D models. In: XXIV Congreso Argentino de Ciencias de la Computación, pp. 401–411. Red de Universidades con Carreras en Informática (RedUNCI) (2018). ISBN 978-950-658-472-6
9. Korch, B.: Pothole detection in asphalt pavement images. Adv. Eng. Inform. **25-3**, 507–515 (2011). Elsevier
10. Mathavan, S., Rahman, M., Kamal, K., Usman, S., Moazzam, I.: Metrology and visualization of potholes using the Microsoft Kinect sensor. In: 16th International IEEE Annual Conference on Intelligent Transportation Systems (2013)
11. Mitchell, T.M.: Machine Learning. McGraw-Hill, New York (1997)
12. Nieber, S., Brooysen, M., Kroon, R.: Detection potholes using simple processing techniques and real-world footage. In: Proceedings of the 34th Southern African Transport Conference (2015)
13. Ryu, S.K., Kim, T., Kim, Y.R.: Image-based pothole detection system for its service and road management system. In: Mathematical Problems in Engineering, pp. 1–10 (2015)
14. Tecimer, A., Taysi, Z., Yavuz, A., Yavuz, M.K.: Assessment of vehicular transportation quality via smartphones. Turk. J. Electr. Eng. Comput. Sci. **23**, 2161–2170 (2013)

15. Xie, S.: 3D pavement surface reconstruction and cracking recognition using Kinect-based solution. Technical report, University of New Mexico (2015)
16. Yamaguchi, T., Nakamura, S., Saegusa, R., Hashimoto, S.: Image-based crack detection for real concrete surfaces. IEEE Trans. Electr. Electron. Eng. **3**, 128–135 (2008). Wiley Interscience

Software Engineering

White-Box Testing Framework for Object-Oriented Programming. An Approach Based on Message Sequence Specification and Aspect Oriented Programming

Martín L. Larrea[✉], Juan Ignacio Rodríguez Silva, Matías N. Selzer, and Dana K. Urribarri

Departamento de Ciencias e Ingeniería de la Computación,
Instituto de Ciencias e Ingeniería de la Computación (UNS-CONICET),
Laboratorio de I+D en Visualización y Computación Gráfica,
(UNS-CIC Prov. de Buenos Aires), Universidad Nacional del Sur (DCIC-UNS),
Bahía Blanca, Argentina
{mll,matias.selzer,dku}@cs.uns.edu.ar, nachorodriguez12@hotmail.com

Abstract. The quality of software has become one of the most important factor in determining the success of products or enterprises. This paper presents a white-box testing framework for Object-Oriented Programming based on Message Sequence Specification and Aspect Oriented Programming. In the context of an Object-Oriented program, our framework can be used to test the correct order in which the methods of a class are invoked.

Keywords: Software verification & validation · White-box testing · Object-Oriented Programming · Message Sequence Specification · Aspect-Oriented Programming

1 Introduction

Verification and Validation (V&V) is the process of checking that a software system meets its specifications and fulfills its intended purpose. The software engineering community has acknowledged the importance of the V&V process to ensure the quality of its software products. The V&V process, also known as software testing or just testing, consist of V&V techniques. There are many different V&V techniques which are applicable at different stages of the development lifecycle. The two main categories of testing techniques are white-box and black-box. In the first one, the testing is driven by the knowledge and information provided by the implementation or source code. While in the second one, the specification of the software, module, or function is used to test the object under review.

P. Pesado and C. Aciti (Eds.): CACIC 2018, CCIS 995, pp. 143–156, 2019.
https://doi.org/10.1007/978-3-030-20787-8_10

In 1994, Kirani and Tsai [1] presented a technique called Message Sequence Specification (MSS) that, in the context of an object-oriented program, describes the correct order in which the methods of a class should be invoked. The method-sequence specification associated with an object specifies all sequences of messages that the object can receive while still providing correct behavior. Daniels and Tsai [2] used the idea of MSS as a testing tool but without implementing a framework to support this technique.

In an earlier publication, we published a framework for testing object-oriented programs based on MSS [3]. Our framework could be used to test the correct order in which the methods of a class are invoked. The framework was implemented using Aspect-Oriented Programming (AOP). AOP provides transparent testing, i.e., the source code can be tested without additional modifications and while the software is running. Since this first version of the framework was limited to test only one instance of a class, it was suitable only for usages where the singleton pattern was appropriate. It could also be used to test the behavior of GUI elements. In this paper, we present a new version of the framework, one that can test multiple instances of a class using MSS. We also update the previous work with new references and expand our case study section.

The rest of the paper is structured as follows. Section 2.1 provides background information about V&V, concepts of MSS in the software development process, and AOP, which constitutes our framework's core. The framework's first implementation [3] is presented next, followed by the new proposed framework and how it differs from the one presented previously. We later introduce two examples of the framework's use. Finally, we conclude with a brief discussion on the limitations and advantages of our approach and the future work.

2   Background

2.1   Verification & Validation

Software testing is involved in every stage of software life cycle, however, how the test is performed and what is tested at each stage is different, as well as the nature and goals of what is being tested. Jorgensen [4] describes 8 types of testing in the life cycle: Unit testing is a code-based testing performed by developers to test each individual unit separately. The Unit testing can be used for small units of code, generally no larger than a class. Integration testing validates that two or more units work together properly, and focuses on the interfaces specified in the low-level design. System testing reveals that the system works end-to-end in a production-like location to provide the business functions specified in the high-level design. Acceptance testing is conducted by business owners; the purpose of acceptance testing is to test whether the system complies with the business requirements. Regression Testing is the testing of software after changes have been made to ensure that those changes did not introduce any new errors into the system. Functional Testing is done for a finished application to verify that the system provides all the required behavior.

In the context of V&V, black-box testing is often used for validation (i.e. are we building the right software?) and white-box testing is often used for verification (i.e. are we building the software right?). In black-box testing, the test cases are based on the information from the specification. The software testers do not consider the internal source code of the test object. The focus of these tests is solely on the outputs generated in response to selected inputs and execution conditions. The software tester sees the software as a black box, where information is input to the box, and the box sends something back out. This can be done purely based on the requirement-specification knowledge; the tester, who knows in advance the expected outcome of the black box, tests the software to guarantee that the actual result complies with the expected one.

On the other hand, in white-box testing, also called structural testing, the test cases are based on the information derived from the source code. White-box testing is concern with the internal mechanism of a system, mainly focusing on the program's control and data flows. White-box and black-box testing are considered a complement to each other. In order to test software correctly, it is essential to generate test cases from both the specification and the source code. This means that we must use white-box and black-box techniques on the software under development.

Both white-box and black-box test techniques must describe a test model and at least one coverage criteria. Test models describe how to generate test cases, and can be a graph, a table or a set of numbers. Coverage criteria, on the other hand, are usually boolean conditions to steer and stop the test generation process [5]. In the literature, coverage criteria are widely accepted for assessing the quality of a test [6].

The same testing technique that we classified as white or black box can be arranged as static or dynamic techniques. Static testing are those techniques in which the code is not executed. In this case, the code can be analyzed manually or by a set of tools. This type of testing checks the code, requirement documents, and design documents. Dynamic testing is done when the code is executed. Dynamic testing is performed when the code being executed is input with a value, and the result or the output of the code is checked and compared with the expected output.

2.2 Message Sequence Specification

In 1994, Kirani and Tsai [1] presented a technique called Message Sequence Specification (MSS) that, in the context of an object-oriented program, describes the correct order in which the methods of a class should be invoked by its clients. The method sequence specification associated with an object specifies all sequences of messages that the object can receive while still providing correct behavior.

Their strategy used regular expressions to model the constraints over the correct order of the invocation of the methods, i.e. the regular expression is the test model. Method names were used as the alphabet of the expression which was then used to statically verify the program's implementation for improper method sequences. A runtime verification system identifies incorrect method invocations by checking for sequence consistency with respect to the sequencing constraints.

According to Kirani's specification, if a class C has a method M_1, this is noted as C_{M_1}. Sequence relationships between two methods were classified into three categories, sequential, optional, and repeated. If the method M_1 of C should be invoked before the method M_2 of the same class, then this relationship is sequential and is represented as

$$C_{M_1} \bullet C_{M_2} \tag{1}$$

If one, and only one of the methods M_1 and M_2 can be invoked, then this relationship is optional and is represented as

$$C_{M_1} | C_{M_2} \tag{2}$$

Finally, if the method M_1 can be invoked many times in a row then this is a repeated relationship and is represented as

$$(C_{M_1})^* \tag{3}$$

For example, if a class X has three methods called *create*, *process*, and *close*, a possible sequencing constraint based on MSS could look like

$$X_{create} \bullet (X_{process})^* \bullet X_{close} \tag{4}$$

If class X is part of a larger system S, then we could statically check the source code of S to see if all calls to X's methods follow the defined expression. If a static analysis is not enough, we could implement a runtime verification system that tracks all calls to X's methods and checks dynamically the sequence of calls against its regular expression.

This technique can also be used to test the robustness of a system. Continuing with the class X as an example, we can use the defined regular expression to create method sequences that are not a derivation from it, i.e. incorrect sequences methods. These new sequences can be used to test how the class handles a misuse. For example, how does the class X respond to the following sequence of calls?:

$$X_{create} \bullet X_{close} X_{process} \tag{5}$$

Daniels and Tsai [2] extended the work of Kirani et al. [1] by testing with sequences that were both generated by the expression and not. Also in 1999, Tsai et al. [7] presented a work where MSS was used to create template scenarios than later were used to create test cases. In 2003, Tsai [8] used MSS as a verification mechanism to the UDDI servers in the context of Web Services. In 2014, a Java-based tool for monitoring sequences of method calls was introduced [9], it had similar objectives as our work but they used annotations instead of AOP. We introduced MSS as an approach for testing visualizations interactions [10] in 2018; and finally, Turner [11] used sequence specification for testing GUI in 2019.

2.3   Aspect Oriented Programming

Aspect Oriented Programming [12] (AOP) is a programming paradigm designed to increase modularity, based on the separation of cross-cutting concerns. With AOP "pointcut" specifications, the already implemented software can incorporate additional behavior without changing the source code. A pointcut declares a specification, for instance, "log all function calls when the function's name begins with *set*". Hence, behaviors that are not central to the business logic (such as logging or testing) can be added to a program without cluttering the code.

AOP entails breaking down program logic into distinct parts (so-called concerns). Nearly all programming paradigms support some level of grouping and encapsulation of concerns into separate, independent entities by providing abstractions (e.g., functions, procedures, modules, classes, methods) that can be used for implementing, abstracting and composing these concerns. Some concerns cut across multiple abstractions in a program, and defy these forms of implementation. These concerns are called cross-cutting concerns or horizontal concerns. Logging is an example of a crosscutting concern because a logging strategy necessarily affects every logged part of the system. Logging thereby cross-cuts all logged classes and methods.

See for example Listing 1.1, a simple Java class for a bank account. If we need to log all the events in the account one way to do it is as the listing shows. The main disadvantages of this approach are that we are mixing the logic of the bank account class with the requirement of logging its events. By using AspectJ, an implementation of AOP for Java, we can create an aspect, as in Listing 1.3 while the bank account class remains simpler 1.2. With these two classes, every time there is a call to *deposit* or *withdraw* the JRE will execute the methods in the AspectJ aspect.

Listing 1.1. Classic example

```
public class Account {
    protected int amount;

    public Account() {
        this.amount = 0; }

    public void deposit( int _amount ) {
        this.amount += _amount;
        Log.put("deposit for " + _amount); }

    public void withdraw( int _amount ) {
        this.amount -= _amount;
        Log.put("withdraw for " + _amount); }
}
```

Listing 1.2. Clear code

```
public class Account {
    protected int amount;

    public Account() {
        this.amount = 0; }

    public void deposit( int _amount ) {
        this.amount += _amount; }

    public void withdraw( int _amount ) {
        this.amount -= _amount; }
}
```

Listing 1.3. AspectJ code

```
public aspect AspectLogic {
    before(int _amount):
        call(void Account.deposit(int)) && args(_amount) {
            Log.put("deposit for " + _amount);
        }

    before(int _amount):
        call(void Account.withdraw(int)) && args(_amount) {
            Log.put("withdraw for " + _amount);
        }
}
```

By using AspectJ we can add new behavior to a source code without the need to change the code itself. This is a very appealing feature in the context of software verification and validation. More information about AOP can be found in [12].

3 Our Testing Framework

Our goal in this work is to present a testing framework for object-oriented source code based on MSS using AOP. AOP allows us to create test cases without the need to modify the source code, and those test cases can run automatically with each run of the program under test. The use of MSS allows the developer of a class to describe a regular expression that represents the correct behavior of such class. The framework takes each of these expressions, runs the program and checks that the methods are used according to the developer specification. We wanted to provide an easy to use framework, with an easy to read and understand representation for the correct usage of the methods. Particularly, the framework was designed to be used by any developer, without needing a testing specialist.

The first thing the developer must do to use the framework is to create the regular expression associated with the class under test. This regular expression must specify the correct behavior or order in which the methods of the class should be called. In order to express this in a simple way, the developer must use simple symbols (i.e. characters) to represent each method. This means that the actual names of the methods are not used in the expression. But, to be able to interpret it at some point the developer must create a map between the actual methods' names and their corresponding symbol. The regular expression and the map between methods and symbols are set in the *TestingSetup.java* class. The framework consists of two main components, an aspect, and a java class. The aspect is named *TestingCore.aj* and it contains the implementation of the framework's logic.

Listing 1.4 shows an example with a more complex Account class. In this case, the correct order to use the Account is: first, the account must be created and then it must be verified. The first money movement in the account must be a deposit. After that, we can deposit or withdraw money. Once the account is closed, no more operations are allowed.

Listing 1.4. Classic example

```
public class Account {
    protected int amount;
    protected boolean verify;

    public Account() {
        this.amount = 0;
        this.verify = false; }

    public void verify() {
        this.verify = true; }

    public void deposit( int _amount ) {
        if (this.isVerify())
            this.amount += _amount; }

    public void withdraw( int _amount ) {
        if (this.isVerify())
            this.amount -= _amount; }

    public void close() {
        this.amount = 0;
        this.verify = false; }

    public boolean isVerify() {
        return this.verify; }
}
```

Based on MSS, the regular expression for the correct use of this class is as follows:

$$create \bullet verify \bullet deposit \bullet (deposit|withdraw)^* \bullet close \qquad (6)$$

or as a simpler expression:

$$c \bullet v \bullet d \bullet (d|w)^* \bullet x. \qquad (7)$$

Instead of using the actual methods' names, a set of corresponding symbols are used to enhance the readability of the regular expression. For this reason, the framework allows the developer to map such methods' names to character symbols. After that, the developer is able to input the regular expression for the class being tested. Listing 1.5 shows the configuration of the *TestingSetup.java* class for the actual example. With these two steps completed, the framework checks at runtime that the methods of the Account class are being called in the correct order.

Listing 1.5. Class TestingSetup

```
//Specification of the test class
TestingCore.targetClass = Account.class.toString();

//Definition of the methods and their
// corresponding symbols
TestingCore.mapObjectsToCallSequence = new HashMap<>();
TestingCore.mapMethodsToSymbols =
    new HashMap<String, String>();
TestingCore.mapMethodsToSymbols.
    put("main.Account.<init>", "c");
TestingCore.mapMethodsToSymbols.
    put("main.Account.verify", "v");
TestingCore.mapMethodsToSymbols.
    put("main.Account.deposit", "d");
TestingCore.mapMethodsToSymbols.
    put("main.Account.withdraw", "w");
TestingCore.mapMethodsToSymbols.
    put("main.Account.close", "x");

//Definition of the regular expression
TestingCore.regularExpression =
    Pattern.compile("cvd(d|w)*x");

//Initializing the regular expressions controller
TestingCore.matcher =
    TestingCore.regularExpression.matcher("");
```

If a method call does not match the regular expression, the framework aborts the execution of the program. The hashcode of the object causing the error, the regular expression, the sequence of called methods, and the name of last called method are issued via the standard output for the developer to understand the error.

Listing 1.6 shows an invalid use of the methods in the Account class; particularly the *a1.verify()* line at the end of the program does not comply with the regular expression provided for the Account class. In this case, the framework issues the message shown in Listing 1.7 and aborts the program.

Listing 1.6. Invalid used of class Account

```
public static void main(String[] args) {
    Account a1 = new Account();
    a1.verify();
    a1.deposit(1000);
    a1.deposit(4000);
    a1.withdraw(3000);
    a1.verify();
    a1.close(); }
```

Listing 1.7. Error message by the framework

```
--------------------------------
---        ERROR FOUND        ---
--------------------------------
Object Code: 507084503
Method Executed: main.Account.verify
Regular Expression: cvd(d|w)*x
Execution Sequence: cvddwv
--------------------------------
-----  SYSTEM ABORTING...  -----
--------------------------------
```

The next section shows the framework usefulness in a real-life situation. By using this framework, we found two errors in an application developed in our research group.

4 Case Study. Rock.AR, a Software Solution for Point Counting

Point counting is the standard method to establish the modal proportion of minerals in coarse-grained igneous, metamorphic, and sedimentary rock samples. This requires to make observations to be made at regular positions on the sample, namely grid intersections. For each position, the domain expert decides which mineral corresponds to the respective grid point and its local neighborhood. By counting the number of points found for each mineral, it is possible to calculate the percentage that each value represent of the total counted points. These percentages represent the approximate relative proportions of the minerals in a rock, which is a 2D section of a 3D sample.

Rock.AR [13] is a visualization tool with a user-friendly interface that provides a semiautomatic point-counting method. It increases the efficiency of the point-counting task by reducing the user cognitive workload. This tool automates the creation of the grid used to define the point positions. The grid is overlaid on a sample image and allows to identify and count minerals at the intersections of the grid lines. This method significantly reduces the time required to conduct point counting, it does not require an expensive ad hoc device to perform the job, and it improves the consistency of counts.

4.1   First Detected Bug

The main class of this application contains three important methods:

- LoadSample() loads the rock thin section sample.
- AddNewRockType() links a type of mineral with the selected cell in the grid.
- MoveSelectedCell() selects a cell in the grid.

First, at least one sample must be loaded. Then, before linking a mineral type to a cell, a point (also known as a cell) must be selected.

The following regular expression can be defined:

$$(LoadSample \bullet LoadSample^* \bullet$$
$$(MoveSelectedCell \bullet MoveSelectedCell^* \bullet AddNewRockType^*)^*)^* \quad (8)$$

or in a simpler way:

$$(l \bullet l^* \bullet (m \bullet m^* \bullet a^*)^*)^* \quad (9)$$

Listing 1.8. Class TestingSetup for Rock.AR

```
//Specification of the test class
TestingCore.targetClass = ViMuGenMain2.class.toString();

//Definition of the methods and their
// corresponding symbols
TestingCore.mapObjectsToCallSequence = new HashMap<>();
TestingCore.mapMethodsToSymbols =
    new HashMap<String, String>();
TestingCore.mapMethodsToSymbols.
    put("ar.edu.uns.cs.vyglab.vimuge.main.
ViMuGenMain2.LoadSample", "l");
TestingCore.mapMethodsToSymbols.
    put("ar.edu.uns.cs.vyglab.vimuge.main.
ViMuGenMain2.MoveSelectedCell", "m");
TestingCore.mapMethodsToSymbols.
    put("ar.edu.uns.cs.vyglab.vimuge.main.
ViMuGenMain2.AddNewRockType", "a");

//Definition of the regular expression
TestingCore.regularExpression =
```

```
Pattern.compile("ll*(mm*a*)*)*");

//Initializing the regular expressions controller
TestingCore.matcher =
    TestingCore.regularExpression.matcher("");
```

A particularity of this regular expression is that, between loading a sample and adding a new rock type, at least one cell must be selected. We created this regular expression and input it into the framework as shown in Listing 1.8. After defining and providing this expression to the framework we used Rock.AR several times. After running the program several times, the test framework detected an error and output the sequence of calls that did not comply with the regular expression. The sequence was:

$$l \bullet m \bullet m \bullet a \bullet l \bullet l \bullet a \qquad (10)$$

The last three symbols in the sequence indicated that the application allowed calling AddNewRockType() right after LoadSample(), i.e. without calling MoveSelectedCell() in between. This calling sequence was not allowed in the regular expression. With this information we discovered that, when the user loaded a second sample, two variables were not re-initialized, causing this incorrect behavior. Before using our framework, there was no evidence of this error. The application did not generate any exception since the program was using old values for those not re-initialized variables.

4.2   Second Detected Bug

In order to help the domain expert to visualize the grid intersection, a colored grid is drawn on top of the mineral image. Each intersection is represented in the implementation by an instance of the class *SampleCell*. Usually, a mineral image requires around 1250 cells. The *SampleCell* class offers methods to set and get the dimensions of the cell and the mineral type. However, once the dimensions are set, they can not be changed. This is because the size of each cell is calculated by a math equation and it can not be set by the user. Since the mineral type of each cell depends on the user's subjective appreciation, it can be defined more than once. This behavior is defined in the following regular expression:

$$CreateSampleCell \bullet (setDimension \bullet setRockType|$$
$$setRockType \bullet setDimension) \bullet (setRockType|getRockType|$$
$$getDimension)^* (11)$$

or in a simpler way:

$$x \bullet (d \bullet r|r \bullet d) \bullet (r|w|e)^* \qquad (12)$$

As described in this expression, after the creation of the sample cell, both the dimension and mineral type must be set but in no particular order. After that, the mineral type can be set and get as many times as necessary. The dimension, however, can only be retrieve. Listing 1.9 shows how the class *TestingSetup* was modified.

Listing 1.9. Class TestingSetup for Rock.AR

```
//Specification of the test class
TestingCore.targetClass = SampleCell.class.toString();

//Definition of the methods and their
// corresponding symbols
TestingCore.mapObjectsToCallSequence = new HashMap<>();
TestingCore.mapMethodsToSymbols =
    new HashMap<String, String>();
TestingCore.mapMethodsToSymbols.
    put("ar.edu.uns.cs.vyglab.vimuge.data.
SampleCell.<init>", "x");
TestingCore.mapMethodsToSymbols.
    put("ar.edu.uns.cs.vyglab.vimuge.data.
SampleCell.SetDimension", "d");
TestingCore.mapMethodsToSymbols.
    put("ar.edu.uns.cs.vyglab.vimuge.data.
SampleCell.GetDimension", "e");
TestingCore.mapMethodsToSymbols.
    put("ar.edu.uns.cs.vyglab.vimuge.data.
SampleCell.SetRockType", "r");
TestingCore.mapMethodsToSymbols.
    put("ar.edu.uns.cs.vyglab.vimuge.data.
SampleCell.GetRockType", "w");

//Definition of the regular expression
TestingCore.regularExpression =
    Pattern.compile("x(dr|rd)(wer)*");

//Initializing the regular expressions controller
TestingCore.matcher =
    TestingCore.regularExpression.matcher("");
```

As in the previous study case, we ran Rock.AR several times to test the last regular expression. The framework detected an error and output the message shown in Listing 1.10. By inspecting the execution sequence we could see that a mineral type was retrieved from a sample cell without being previously set. This error occurred every time the user loaded a previously saved work.

When users saved their work, Rock.AR saved to a file only the sample cells with a mineral type assigned. All sample cell (with or without a mineral type assigned) are stored in an array, and the system keeps a second array to index those sample cell with an assigned mineral. When the work is saved to a file, the application goes through this last array and retrieves those cells with an assigned mineral. The method responsible for this operation had an error in a boolean condition: instead of iterate until $amount - 1$, it went until $amount$. This did not produce a runtime error because we keep the array as large as possible so, under certain conditions, $array[amount]$ was an actual sample cell. The problem was that this cell did not have an assigned mineral, so a value was obtained without first assigning it.

Listing 1.10. Error message by the framework on Rock.AR

```
--------------------------------
---        ERROR FOUND        ---
--------------------------------
Object Code: 1061804750
Method Executed: ar.edu.uns.cs.vyglab.vimuge.data.
SampleCell.GetRockType
Regular Expression: x(dr|rd)(wer)*
Execution Sequence: xdw
--------------------------------
-----   SYSTEM ABORTING...  -----
--------------------------------
```

The framework is available for downloading[1]. The source code is available and licensed under a Creative Commons Attribution-ShareAlike 4.0 International License.

5   Conclusions and Future Work

In a world where technology is part of everyone's life, software is a crucial element. The quality of software has become one of the most important factors and developers need tools to assist them in their work in order to achieve such high quality. In this work, we present a framework for white-box testing. Our framework combines MSS with Aspect Oriented Programming in order to create a tool that tests the correct order in which methods in a class are being called.

As we stated earlier, our goal was to create an easy to use framework for the developers to test source code without any modification of the code under review. The goal of this framework is to find those vulnerabilities that allow the expected execution order of the methods of a class to be broken. As it was shown in the case studies, the framework helps to detect errors that otherwise would be difficult to find. Future work will consider a more expressive framework. For the moment, the framework can only test the order in which methods of a class are being called. However, the actual values of the parameters of a method or the inner state of the instance can also be relevant in the execution order. For example, a class could require a method x to be called after method y if the value of a particular attribute is equal to 0.

---

[1] http://cs.uns.edu.ar/~mll/lapaz/.

At the moment, the framework can only test multiple instances of the same class. We will consider extending the framework to test multiple classes at the same time and the order between methods of different classes.

Finally, whenever an error is found, the framework aborts the execution of the program. A future improvement will allow the developer to specify for each particular error if the execution should continue or be aborted.

Acknowledgment. This work was partially supported by the following research projects: PGI 24/N037 and PGI 24/ZN29 from the Secretaría General de Ciencia y Tecnología, Universidad Nacional del Sur, Argentina.

References

1. Kirani, S., Tsai, W.T.: Specification and verification of object-oriented programs. Computer Science Department, University of Minnesota, Technical report (1994)
2. Daniels, F., Tai, K.: Measuring the effectiveness of method test sequences derived from sequencing constraints. In: Proceedings of Technology of Object-Oriented Languages and Systems-TOOLS 30 (Cat. No. PR00278), pp. 74–83. IEEE (1999). https://doi.org/10.1109/TOOLS.1999.787537
3. Silva, J.I.R., Larrea, M.: White-box testing framework for object-oriented programming based on message sequence specification. In: XXIV Congreso Argentino de Ciencias de la Computación (Tandil 2018), pp. 532–541 (2018)
4. Jorgensen, P.C.: Software Testing: A Craftsman's Approach. Auerbach Publications (2013). https://doi.org/10.1201/9781439889503
5. Weißleder, S.: Test models and coverage criteria for automatic model-based test generation with UML state machines. Ph.D. thesis, Humboldt University of Berlin (2010)
6. Friske, M., Schlingloff, B.H., Weißleder, S.: Composition of model-based test coverage criteria. In: MBEES, pp. 87–94 (2008)
7. Tsai, W.T., Tu, Y., Shao, W., Ebner, E.: Testing extensible design patterns in object-oriented frameworks through scenario templates. In: Proceedings of the Twenty-Third Annual International Computer Software and Applications Conference (Cat. No. 99CB37032), pp. 166–171. IEEE (1999). https://doi.org/10.1109/CMPSAC.1999.812695
8. Tsai, W.T., Paul, R., Cao, Z., Yu, L., Saimi, A.: Verification of web services using an enhanced UDDI server. In: Proceedings of the Eighth International Workshop on Object-Oriented Real-Time Dependable Systems (WORDS 2003), pp. 131–138. IEEE (2003). https://doi.org/10.1109/WORDS.2003.1218075
9. Nobakht, B., de Boer, F.S., Bonsangue, M.M., de Gouw, S., Jaghoori, M.M.: Monitoring method call sequences using annotations. Comput. Imaging Vis. **94**, 362–378 (2014). https://doi.org/10.1016/j.scico.2013.11.030
10. Larrea, M.L.: Black-box testing technique for information visualization. Sequencing constraints with low-level interactions. J. Comput. Sci. Technol. **17**, 37–48 (2017)
11. Turner, J.D.: Supporting interactive system testing with interaction sequences. Ph.D. thesis, The University of Waikato (2019)
12. Laddad, R.: AspectJ in Action: Practical Aspect-Oriented Programming. Manning Publications Co., Greenwich (2003)
13. Larrea, M.L., Castro, S.M., Bjerg, E.A.: A software solution for point counting. Petrographic thin section analysis as a case study. Arab. J. Geosci. **7**(8), 2981–2989 (2014). https://doi.org/10.1007/s12517-013-1032-0

Proposal for a Model of a Computer Systems Implantation Process (MoProIMP)

Marisa Panizzi[1,2(✉)], Rodolfo Bertone[3], and Alejandro Hossian[4]

[1] PhD Program in Computing Sciences, School of Computing,
Universidad Nacional de La Plata, La Plata, Argentina
marisapanizzi@outlook.com
[2] Engineering Department of Information Systems,
Universidad Tecnológica Nacional, Facultad Regional Buenos Aires,
Medrano 951 (C1179AAQ), Buenos Aires, Argentina
[3] Institute of Computing Research LIDI, School of Computing, UNLP – CIC,
La Plata, Argentina
pbertone@lidi.info.unlp.edu.ar
[4] Research Group of Intelligent Systems Applications in Engineering,
Universidad Tecnológica Nacional – Facultad Regional Neuquén,
Av. Pedro Rotter S/N Barrio Uno, (8318), Neuquén, Argentina
alejandrohossian@yahoo.com.ar

Abstract. From the analysis of software development methodologies, it was observed that many of them do not contemplate the process of system implantation or, if they do, they do not develop or manage them in a comprehensive manner.

As an answer to the identified gaps, MoProIMP, a model that allows to systematize the process of software implantation, is proposed. This model can be used together with the development methodology of the software producer organization.

MoProIMP identifies phases, activities, tasks (inputs and outputs) and existing dependencies in a software implantation, systematically managing each of them. Finally, a case study is presented as an initial validation to the proposed model.

Keywords: Software processes · Computing systems implantation ·
Process model · Customized development

1 Introduction

Computing systems implantation can be defined as a set of required activities and tasks that allow the transfer of the finished software product to its usage environment by the user community. [1].

The software engineering developed a set of methodologies and standards for the construction of computing systems. Some of them are included in the so called "traditional or robust" systems [2] and others are included in the group of the so called "agile" systems [2]. Despite the existing difference in scope between a methodology

© Springer Nature Switzerland AG 2019
P. Pesado and C. Aciti (Eds.): CACIC 2018, CCIS 995, pp. 157–170, 2019.
https://doi.org/10.1007/978-3-030-20787-8_11

[3], a standard [4, 5] or a method [6], in this article, the authors decided to give them an equal treatment based on how each support the implantation process.

Works [1] and [7] proposed a systematic review of a set of methodologies or standards of software with the aim to study the implantation process of computing systems.

The analysis of the reviewed methodologies and standards allowed to identify a series of deficiencies and/or gaps for the successful execution of the implantation process of computing systems. Due to the identified gaps, a computing systems **Impl**antation **Pro**cess **Mo**del called MoProIMP [12] is proposed. This process determines phases, activities, tasks representation techniques, and execution procedures for each task thus systematizing the implantation of software.

The following section presents a proposal for a solution which describes and explains the architecture of the proposed model. Subsequently, the first case study is presented followed by the conclusions and proposals for the process improvement.

2   IMPlantation Process Model (MoProIMP)

MoProIMP architecture displays its lifecycle model adopting 5 process groups. This derives from the PMIBOK [8]. These groups are: *Initiating, Planning, Execution, Monitoring and Controlling and Closing*. The reason for this choice is that the PMI-BOK is a widely recognized standard and of application in the software industry at a national level. The proposed model will name each of these processes *a phase*.

In order to apply the model to the software industry in Argentina and in a staged way, three levels of capabilities as proposed in the CMMI-DEV standard [9] were adopted. Such levels of capabilities are: *level 1 = Performed, level 2 = Managed and level 3 = Defined. Level 0 = Incomplete* has not been considered since it means that a process in the organization was either not performed or is partially performed. The three levels of capabilities considered were analyzed in a granularity level of the tasks proposed in the developed model. Levels of capability were chosen instead of levels of maturity because in the context of the Argentine industry, few companies have reached maturity levels 4 and 5, which would make it difficult to conduct the validation of the proposed model. The model adopts a group of tasks proposed in the methodology Metrica version 3 [10] because it is one of most comprehensive methodologies, making some adaptations for the argentine industry.

This work presents phases, activities and their goals, tasks (identifying links) and elements of dependence between them (elements of input and output).

Figure 1 shows phases, activities and interdependencies between the activities making up the proposed model. The SADT technique (Structured Analysis and Design Technique) [11] with some adaptations was used for the representation of the model.

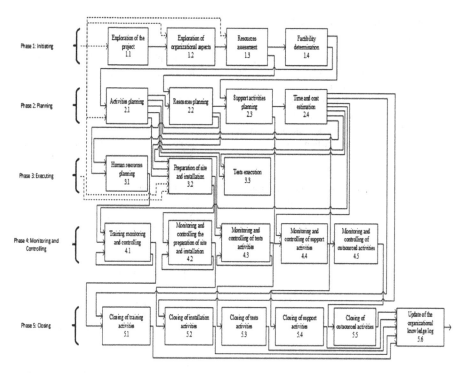

Fig. 1. Implantation Process (**MoProIMP**)

Phase 1: **Initiating,** it is composed of four activities: *Exploration of the Project,* aimed to conduct a study of the characteristics of the project and the documentation of the requirements determined for it; *Exploration of the organizational aspects,* aimed to identify the mechanisms of the documentation, the communication for the implantation in the organizational context and the management configuration; *Resources assessment* aimed to review the required resources to make the implantation and the *Factibility determination* aimed to identify risks and to define the factibility of the implantation. Table 1 shows **Phase 1: Initiating**, with the tasks for each activity, the level of capability determined for the task and the inputs and outputs of each task.

Phase 2: Planning, it is composed of four activities: *Activities planning* aimed to establish a set of activities that make up the implantation project considering the deliverables, the tests and the outsourced activities; *Resources planning* aimed to determine both the human and technological resources; *Support activities planning* aimed to identify the characteristics to be measured in the course of the implantation, the determination of the configuration management elements and to establish risk management; *Time and cost estimation* aimed to define time and cost for the development of the implantation activities. Table 2 shows **Phase 2: Planning** with the tasks of each activity, the level of capability for each task and the inputs and outputs of each task.

Table 1. Phase 1: Initiating, activities, tasks, level of capability, inputs and outputs.

Phase	Activities	Tasks	LC	Inputs	Outputs
1. Initiating	1.1	1.1.1. Review the project plan	2	Project plan	Situation report of the implantation
		1.1.2. Review the requirements document	2	Requirements document	
		1.1.3. Review the software product architecture	2	Software architecture document	
	1.2	1.2.1. Review the organization's documentation protocol	3	Documentation protocol	Situation report of the implantation
				Situation report of the implantation	
		1.2.2. Review the organization's communication protocol	3	Communication protocol	Situation report of the implantation
				Situation report of the implantation	
		1.2.3. Review the configuration management protocol	2	Configuration management	Situation report of the implantation
				Situation report of the implantation	
	1.3	1.3.1. Determine the organization's existing human resources	2	Situation report of the implantation	Internal human resources report
				List of users	Situation report of the implantation
				List of systems human resources (technicians)	
		1.3.2. Determine the organization's existing technological resources	2	Situation report of the implantation	Technological resources report
				Infrastructure document	Situation report of the implantation
	1.4	1.4.1. Identify risks	2	Situation report of the implantation	Risk analysis report
					Situation report of the implantation
		1.4.2. Conduct the factibility study	2	Situation report of the implantation	Factibility report
					Situation report of the implantation

Phase 3: Executing, it is composed of three activities: *Human resources training* aimed to design and implement the training course for the user community and the technical team; *Site and installation* preparation aimed to prepare the infrastructure, install the software product and upload data; *Tests execution* aimed to conduct installation environment tests, installation tests and the acceptance tests. Table 3 shows **Phase 3: Executing** with the tasks for each activity, the level of capability for each task and the inputs and outputs for each task.

Table 2. Phase 2: Planning, activities, tasks, level of capability, inputs and outputs.

Phase	Activities	Tasks	LC	Inputs	Outputs
2. Planning	2.1	2.1.1. Define activities related to the implantation	2	Project plan	Implantation plan
				Situation report of the implantation	Data upload document
					Installation guide
		2.1.2. Define deliverables milestones	2	Project plan	Implantation plan (with deliverables milestones)
				Implantation plan	
				Situation report of the implantation	
		2.1.3. Define verification and validation activities	2	Project plan	Implantation plan (with installation and acceptance tests)
				Situation report of the implantation	Tests document
				Implantation plan	
		2.1.4. Plan outsourced activities	2	Project plan	Implantation plan: outsourced activities
				Situation report of the implantation	Agreement with suppliers
				Implantation plan	
	2.2	2.2.1. Plan human resources	2	Situation report of the implantation	Required human resources report
				Internal human resources report	Implantation plan: resources allocation
				Implantation plan	
		2.2.2. Plan technological resources	2	Technological resources report	Required technological resources report
				Implantation plan	Implantation plan
		2.2.3. Plan human resources training	2	Required human resources	Implantation plan: technical team
				Implantation plan	Implantation plan: final users
				Situation report of the implantation	Implantation plan

(continued)

Table 2. (*continued*)

Phase	Activities	Tasks	LC	Inputs	Outputs
		2.2.4. Plan the installation environment adequacy of the technological resources	2	Situation report of the implantation	Implantation plan: Installation
				Software architecture diagram	Infrastructure diagram
				Implantation plan	Deployment diagram
	2.3	2.3.1. Determine the metrics to be used	2	Project plan	Metrics report
				Implantation plan	
				Situation report of the implantation	
		2.3.2. Determine the elements of the configuration management	2	Project plan	Report of configuration management elements
				Implantation plan	
				Situation report of the implantation	
		2.3.3. Plan risk management	3	Implantation plan	Implantation plan: risk management
				Risk analysis report	Implantation plan: risk mitigation
	2.4	2.4.1. Estimate time for the implantation activities	2	Implantation plan	Implantation plan: schedule
		2.4.2. Estimate costs for the implantation activities	2	Implantation plan: schedule	Implantation plan
					Estimated cost

Phase 4: Monitoring and Controlling, it is composed of five activities: *Training monitoring and controlling* aimed to monitor and control the training activities and to make the necessary adjustments; *Site and facilities preparation monitoring and controlling* aimed to monitor and adjust the activities related to the site and facilities preparation; *Tests activities monitoring and controlling* aimed to monitor and control the activities related to the tests and the necessary adjustments; *Support activities monitoring and controlling* aimed to monitor the configuration management, the metrics compliance and risks mitigation compliance if submitted; *Outsourced activities monitoring and controlling* aimed to monitor the activities carried out by the suppliers and the compliance with the established agreements. Table 4 shows **Phase 4: Monitoring and Controlling** displaying the tasks of each activity, the level of capability for the task, inputs and outputs of each task.

Table 3. Phase 3: Execution, activities, tasks, level of capability, inputs and outputs.

Phase	Activities	Tasks	LC	Inputs	Outputs
3. Executing	3.1	3.1.1. Design end users training course	1	Implantation plan: end users training	Training course material
					End users training report
		3.1.2. Design technicians training course	2	Implantation plan: technical team training	Training course material
					Technicians training report
		3.1.3. Train end users	1	Training course material	End users attendance report
				End users training report	
		3.1.4. Train technicians	2	Training course material	Technicians attendance report
				Technicians training report	
	3.2	3.2.1. Prepare installation site	1	Implantation plan: installation	Installation environment report
				Infrastructure diagram	
		3.2.2. Install software	1	Software architecture document	Software product installation
				Implantation plan: installation	
				Deployment diagram	
				Installation guide	
		3.2.3. Perform data upload	1	Dataset	Data upload report
				Data upload document Implantation	
				Implantation plan: installation	
	3.3	3.3.1. Perform implantation tests	2	Implantation plan: installation tests	Installation tests results report
				Tests document	
		3.3.2. Perform acceptance tests	2	Implantation plan: acceptance tests Tests document	Acceptance tests results report

Phase 5: Closing which consists of six activities: *Training activities closing*, aimed to record the formal closing of training activities; *Installation activities closing* aimed to record installation activities closing; *Tests activities closing*, aimed to record the formal closing of the installation tests and acceptance tests; *Support activities closing*, aimed to record the completion of support activities; *Outsourced activities closing*, aimed to record the results of the activities carried out by the suppliers and the degree of compliance with the established agreements; *Update of the organizational knowledge log*, aimed to record the project results to capitalize the knowledge of the organization. Table 5 shows **Phase 5: Closing** displaying the tasks of each activity, the level of capability determined for the task, the inputs and outputs of each task.

3 Study Case

A case study is presented to carry out an initial validation of the proposed model. The tasks corresponding to a capability level 2 = managed of each of the MoProIMP phases were considered because the organization is at an equivalent capability level. The case study corresponds to the implementation of a management system for advertising agencies in Latin America. The company in which the experimentation of the model was developed, is a multinational company that offers consulting services and is located in República Argentina. The management system is an ERP (Enterprise Resource Planning) and was customized for the management of advertising companies. It has the following modules: customers, suppliers, accounting, treasury, administration and parameters (module where master entities and the system configuration are created), expense reports and security. Possible scenarios for the implementation process include: (1) A new company in a new country (which implies the opening of a branch of the group of agencies in a new country which this leads to the configuration of all the tax aspects of the country), (2) A new company in an existing country (with experience regarding the tax aspects of the country) or (3) A new company in an existing installation (which involves the replication of an installation, using the same server of an existing branch without sharing the database). These different scenarios indicate different levels of complexity in the implementation process. The first scenario is the most complex and it is on which the proposed model was applied.

As a result of the evaluation of the application of the built model, a detailed technical report was generated. The main strengths and weaknesses that arose during the implementation of the management system of advertising agencies are summarized below.

In **Phase 1: Initiating,** the following are outstanding favorable points; the preparation of the *situation report of the implementation* that synthesizes all the key points for the process: scope of the project, implementation strategy, use of a wiki as a formal space to share documentation internally and with the client. Regarding human resources, the list of key users that are the client's users participating on behalf of the company in the design specifications and in the approval of the finished products delivered was reviewed. The user community was made up of thirty users. Those in charge of the implementation process were defined, the client's representatives and the consultant's work team, who are in a position to commit their respective organizations in the approval of the project, and in the negotiation of dates and scope thereof. The client was given the technological resources report with the required specifications for the implementation of the solution, which have been defined by the consultant. The client committed to acquire and install the basic hardware and software environment required to run the application, if the installation of the software product could not be performed using the equipment they owned The factibility of the implementation process was determined; the following possible risks were defined: (1) failures in the installation environment, (2) failures in the installation of the software product, (3) failures in the initial data upload and (4) failures in the training environment and the strategies to mitigate them. Given that the implementation scenario was a new company in a new country, it was decided to carry out a modular implementation, since there was

Table 4. Phase 4: Monitoring and Controlling, activities, tasks, level of capability, I/O.

Phase	Activities	Tasks	LC	Inputs	Outputs
4. Monitoring and Controlling	4.1	4.1.1. Monitor end users training	2	Implantation plan: end users training	Implantation plan: end users training
				End users attendance report	Corrective actions report
		4.1.2. Monitor technical team training	2	Implantation plan: technical team training	Implantation plan: technical team training
				Technical team attendance report	Corrective actions report (training)
	4.2	4.2.1. Monitor installation preparation	2	Implantation plan: installation	Installation environment report
				Installation environment report	Corrective actions report
		4.2.2. Control software installation	2	Implantation plan: installation	Implantation plan: installation
				Software product installation report	Software product installation report
					Corrective actions report
		4.2.4. Control data upload	2	Implantation plan: installation	Implantation plan: installation
				Data upload report	Data upload report
					Corrective actions report
	4.3	4.3.1. Control software installation tests	2	Tests document	Implantation plan: installation tests
				Implantation plan: installation	Corrective actions report
				Installation tests results report	Tests report
		4.3.2. Control acceptance tests	2	Tests document	Implantation plan: acceptance tests
				Implantation plan: acceptance tests	Corrective actions report
				Acceptance tests results report	Tests report
	4.4	4.3.1. Control configuration management	2	Implantation plan	Configuration management results report
				Configuration management elements report	
		4.3.2. Review metrics	2	Implantation plan	Metrics results report
				Metrics report	
		4.3.3. Review risks	3	Implantation plan: risk management	Risk review results report
				Implantation plan: risk mitigation plan	
	4.5	4.5.1. Monitor outsourced activities	2	Implantation plan: outsourced activities	Outsourced activities results report
					Implantation plan: outsourced activities
		4.5.2. Monitor agreement with suppliers	2	Implantation plan: outsourced activities	Suppliers agreement results report
				Agreement with suppliers	

Table 5. Phase 5: Closing, activities, tasks, level of capability, I/O.

Phase	Activities	Tasks	LC	Inputs	Outputs
5. Closing	5.1	5.1.1. Record completion of end users training	2	Corrective actions report	End users training completion
				Implantation plan: end users training	
		5.1.2. Record completion of technical team training	2	Corrective actions report (training)	Technical team training completion report
				Implantation plan: technical team training	
	5.2	5.2.1. Record completion of installation environment preparation	2	Implantation plan: installation	Installation environment report
				Installation environment report	
				Corrective actions report	
		5.2.2. Record completion of installation	2	Implantation plan: installation	Software product installation report
				Software product installation report	
				Corrective actions report	
		5.2.3. Record completion of data upload	2	Implantation plan: installation	Data upload report
				Data upload report	
				Corrective actions report	
	5.3	5.3.1. Record completion of installation tests activities	2	Implantation plan: installation tests//Tests report	Installation tests activities completion report
		5.3.2. Record completion of acceptance tests activities	2	Implantation plan: acceptance tests//Tests reports	Tests activities completion report
	5.4	5.4.1. Record completion of configuration management activities	2	Configuration management results report	Management activities completion report
				Implantation plan	
		5.4.2. Record completion of measurements activities	2	Implantation plan	Measurement activities completion report
				Metrics results report	
		5.4.3. Record completion of risk management	3	Risks review results report	Risk management report
	5.5	5.5.1. Record completion of outsourced activities	2	Outsourced activities results report`	Outsourced activities completion report
				Implantation plan: outsourced activities	
		5.5.2. Record completion of agreements with suppliers	2	Suppliers agreement results report	Suppliers agreement completion report

(*continued*)

Table 5. (*continued*)

Phase	Activities	Tasks	LC	Inputs	Outputs
	5.6	5.6.1. Update training activities results	3	End users training completion report	Learned lessons log: training results record
				Technical team training completion report	
		5.6.2. Update installation activities results	3	Installation environment report	Learned lessons log: installation record
				Software product installation report	
				Data upload report	
		5.6.3. Update verification tests results	3	Installation tests activities completion report	Learned lessons log: installation tests results record
		5.6.4. Update validation tests results	3	Acceptance tests activities completion report	Learned lessons log: Acceptance tests results record
		5.6.5. Update configuration management activities results	3	Configuration management activities completion report	Learned lessons log: configuration management results record
		5.6.6. Update measurements results	3	Measurement activities completion report	Learned lessons log: applied metrics results record
		5.6.7. Update risks results	3	Risk management report	Learned lessons log: risks results record
		5.6.8. Update outsourced activities results	3	Outsourced activities completion report	Learned lessons log: outsourced activities results record
		5.6.9. Update results of agreements with suppliers	3	Completion of agreements with suppliers report	Learned lessons log: outsourced activities results record

no previous existing system. The application of the model has been satisfactory, since all the tasks were carried out successfully. The only tasks that were not developed are those corresponding to level 3 = defined, given that the consultant has equivalent processes at level 2 = managed; this can be considered as an aspect for improvement not only for the process under study, but also in the rest of the processes of the organization.

In **Phase 2: Planning,** the plan of the implementation process was drawn up, in which tasks, their duration, delivery milestones and tests to be carried out (installation and acceptance) were considered. The client and the consultant responsibilities were also defined. From the analysis carried out for this project, it was decided to carry out the activities internally, without hiring suppliers. The team was formed by two analyst-trainers who will participate in the project from its inception, an implanter technician, an expert implanter and the project leader who is in charge of coordinating the implementation. In this instance, a key support user was defined who will be responsible for the maintenance once the implementation was considered completed. The specification of the infrastructure that the client must prepare for the installation environment was generated. The client's technical manager training, in charge of the future maintenance, and the user community training were planned. The user community training was developed in the client's facilities through half-day courses over two weeks. Cost and time were defined as metrics. The wiki was defined as a space for the storage of the artifacts versions: user manuals, documentation for the preparation of the installation environment, for installation, for data loading; and also the users of the Wiki with their corresponding security levels will be defined. The activities of the plan were scheduled. The cost in hours of the human resources required was calculated, the translation of hours to a monetary value is done by another area of the consultant.

As a result of phase 2, two weaknesses were found. First, the transfer of responsibility for the preparation of the installation environment to the client, without the supervision of the consultantant. This is a critical point when the software product installation is to be performed. Second, the scarce metrics used by the consultant in the processes.

In **Phase 3**: **Executing,** the training course material was developed, which was stored in the consultant's wiki. The two groups of users to be trained were identified. An instruction for data upload and parameterization of the system was developed to be used in the course, a procedure for the maintenance of the management system for the client was defined. The training was carried out at the client's facilities. The trainers helped verify the maintenance procedure. The system installation was performed. During the process, there were some inconveniences, which generated a remote consultation with the expert implementer of the consulting firm. Since it is a new system, the initial data upload was performed during the training course. The acceptance test was performed together with the user.

The preparation of the installation environment was made by the client and it was not adequately supervised by the consultant which became the biggest drawback in phase 3. The rest of the activities/tasks proposed by MoProIMP were developed satisfactorily.

In **Phase 4: Monitoring and Controlling,** the implementation coordinator monitored the tasks, systematically recording the monitoring of the activities. The training activities were according to the plan. Deviation and corrective actions proposed for the task of preparing the installation site were properly recorded. The tasks of installation, data upload to the ERP system and tests were developed according to the plan. It was noted that the wiki had been correctly managed as a versioned repository, given that the human resources of the consultant and the client are familiar with this type of work. The only inconvenience in this phase was a minimum delay in the time required. This delay (a few hours) could be corrected without affecting the tasks involved. The time indicator was satisfactorily fulfilled, however the hours/human resource indicator was diverted, given that the expert implanter provided additional assistance in the solution of the preparation of the installation environment.

In **Phase 5: Closing,** the formal closing of the training activities, site preparation, installation of the ERP system, data upload, tests, management of the artifacts versions and indicators used in the process was performed. A weakness found is the absence of an institutional space to share the practices carried out in this project to implement the ERP system.

4 Conclusions and Future Work

In this work the proposed model for the implementation of a management system for advertising agencies in Latin America was put into practice and used by a multinational company that offers consulting services as another business unit in the scope of the República Argentina.

The model has been applied at level of capability 2 (managed) defined in this proposal which allowed to confirm some weaknesses that continue to persist in the process of implementation in the national industry; among which we can mention specific metrics, risk management, institutional spaces to share knowledge, roles with specific competencies for the realization of the process.

MoProIMP has allowed to carry out the management of the implementation process since its phases architecture, activities, tasks and their dependencies contribute to make the model self-managed.

Future work includes: (a) the need to build input and output artifacts for each of the tasks of the model using the guidelines proposed by a standard and (b) to continue with the experimentation of the model in other argentine industry companies.

References

1. Panizzi, M., Bertone R., Hossian A.: Proceso de Implantación de Sistemas Informáticos – Identificación de vacancias en Metodologías Usuales. In: Libro de Actas de la V Conferencia Iberoamericana de Computación Aplicada CIACA 2017, pp. 207 –215. Vilamoura, Algarve, Portugal (2017). ISBN 978-989-8533-70-8
2. Carvajal Riola, J.: Metodologías Ágiles: Herramientas y modelo de desarrollo para aplicaciones JAVA EE como metodología empresarial. Tesis Final de Máster en Tecnologías de la Información – UPC, Barcelona (2008). https://upcommons.upc.edu/bitstream/handle/2099.1/5608/500%2015.pdf?sequence=1. Página vigente al 05 May 2018
3. Iglesias Fernández, C.: Definición de una Metodología para el desarrollo de sistemas Multiagente. Tesis Doctoral, Universidad Politécnica de Madrid, Madrid (1998). http://www.upv.es/sma/teoria/agentes/tesiscif.pdf. Página vigente al 08 May 2018
4. RAE, Diccionario de la Lengua Española, Real Academia Española. http://dle.rae.es/. Página vigente al 27 June 2017
5. IEEE 610. IEEE Standard Glossary of Software Engineering Terminology. IEEE Std 610.12-1990 (1990)
6. Maya, E.: Métodos y técnicas de investigación. Trillas, México (2014)
7. Panizzi, M., Hossian, A., García-Martínez, R.: Implantación de Sistemas: Estudio Comparativo e Identificación de Vacancias en Metodologías Usuales. In: Libro de Actas

del XXII Congreso Argentino de Ciencias de la Computación (CACIC 2017), pp. 546–555. Universidad Nacional de San Luis (2016). ISBN 978-987-733-072-4

8. A Guide to the Project Management Body of Knowledge. (PMIBOK® Guide), 5th edn. (2013). ISBN 978-1-935589-67-9. Project Manag. J. **44**(3), e1

9. CMMI® para Desarrollo, Versión 1.3 Mejora de los procesos para el desarrollo de mejores productos y servicios. Technical report, Editorial Universitaria Ramón Areces (2010)

10. PAe, Métrica versión.3. Portal de Administración Electrónica. Gobierno de España (2001)

11. Marca, D.A., McGowan, C.L.: SADT: Structured Analysis and Design Techniques. McGraw-Hill, New York (1988)

12. Panizzi, M., Hossian, A., Bertone, R.: Propuesta de un Modelo de Proceso de Implantación de Sistemas Informáticos (MoProIMP). In: XXIV Congreso Argentino de Ciencias de la Computación. UNCPBA, Argentina (2018). ISBN 978-950-658-472-6

Storage Space Use in Mobile Applications

Juan Fernández Sosa⬥, Pablo Thomas⬥, Lisandro Delía⬥,
Germán Cáseres⬥, Leonardo Corbalán$^{(\boxtimes)}$⬥, Fernando Tesone⬥,
and Verena Olsowy⬥

Computer Science Research Institute LIDI (III-LIDI),
School of Computer Science, National University of La Plata,
La Plata, Buenos Aires, Argentina
{jfernandez,pthomas,ldelia,gcaseres,corbalan,ftesone,
volsowy}@lidi.info.unlp.edu.ar

Abstract. The purpose of software development is meeting both functional and non-functional requirements. In mobile device applications, non-functional requirements are more relevant due to the restrictions inherent to these devices. One of these restrictions is the availability of limited storage space. Therefore, the size of a mobile application affects user preference for use. In this article, we assess how the choice of a mobile application development approach affects the final size of the application; we focus our analysis on text-, audio- and video-based applications and access to the camera in the device.

Keywords: Mobile devices · Multi-platform mobile applications ·
Native mobile applications · Application size

1 Introduction

Application development for mobile devices poses a number of challenges specific to this activity that were not present in traditional software development [1]. The diversity of platforms, programming languages and development tools, as well as device heterogeneity as regards computation power, storage and battery life, are just some of the issues that Software Engineers have to face.

In many cases, the success of an application for mobile devices depends on the popularity level it achieves. To maximize its presence in the market, an application benefits if it can be run on different platforms [2], or at least on the two main ones (98% of the market share). According to data gathered on February 2019, the universe of operating systems for mobile devices is led by Android (74.15%) and iOS (23.28%) platforms [2] which has been the case for the last two years. According to [3], Android has more than 70% of the market share since October 2016.

In recent years, various methodologies for developing mobile applications have been studied – the native approach and several multi-platform development approaches

Computer Science Research Institute LIDI (III-LIDI)—Partner Center of the Scientific Research Agency of the Province of Buenos Aires (CICPBA).

P. Pesado and C. Aciti (Eds.): CACIC 2018, CCIS 995, pp. 171–182, 2019.
https://doi.org/10.1007/978-3-030-20787-8_12

(web, hybrid, interpreted and cross-compilation). This classification is presented in [4]. The native approach consists in developing specific applications for each platform, with parallel development projects, using specific programming languages and tools for each platform. On the other hand, multi-platform approaches allow generating applications that can be run in more than one platform and produced within a single development project.

When choosing a development approach, costs and benefits should be considered. The potential impact on some issues that are relevant for the user of a mobile device must be analyzed. Battery life, computation power and storage space are non-functional requirements that significantly affect the decision of the end users to install or keep a mobile application in their smartphones.

In [5], the authors of this paper analyzed the advantages and disadvantages of the multi-platform development approaches mentioned above, from the point of view of the Software Engineer. The authors of [2] and [6] carried out, respectively, a comparative analysis of performance and battery consumption for native developments and various multi-platform approaches. This article focuses on storage space, thus completing a series of studies on the most significant non-functional requirements and their relation to the development approach used.

1.1 Storage Space

There is a lot of variation in storage space size among the different models of smartphones, this resource being critically scarce in less expensive devices. In these, the operating system and pre-installed applications (also known as bloatware) take up a large portion of this space. This limits device possibilities [7] and hinders the installation of new apps. This problem is worsened by a trend in the market towards the development of increasingly bigger apps.

According to a study carried out on Google Play, the size of the apps for Android devices has quintupled between 2012 and 2017 [8]. In iOS, the 10 most-installed applications in the US have increased their size 12 times between 2012 and 2017 [9]. This increase in the average storage space used by apps is largely due to the evolution of the market, requiring new features and better resources in apps.

In [8], it was shown that users monitor the space used by apps on their devices. The number of effective installations decreases by 1% for each 6 megabytes of increase in app size. Additionally, downloads are interrupted 30% more often in 100-megabyte apps than in 10-megabyte ones.

The need to optimize storage space use to meet the demands of a larger number of potential users is apparent. Researchers working in the field reacted with new proposals. In [10] and [11], elastic mobile app design models are proposed. These models use cloud computing technology to increase computation resources and storage space, splitting the apps into modules and migrating to the cloud those that require more resources. In addition to the obvious disadvantages, the excessive use of space can also negatively affect energy consumption [12].

To minimize the size of the apps built, the impact of the development approach chosen on power consumption should also be considered. In this article, the results of experimental tests quantifying how large this impact is based on the development framework used is presented. The frameworks analyzed were selected based on the various multi-platform development approaches available for mobile devices according to the classification presented in [4].

This article is an extension of [14], adding new tests and results to the experimentation discussed in that article. A new test scenario was defined considering access to the camera in the device, tests were carried out and the data obtained were analyzed. A study of Ionic, another multi-platform development framework, was also included in all test scenarios considered. Also, the tests previously presented in [14] were run once again using the latest versions of each framework, and the final results were reviewed. The introduction section was also expanded with updated data, more detailed information and relevant references. The level of detail to describe the experiments was also increased, adding information about the plug-ins used in each case.

In Sect. 2, the different approaches for developing mobile apps are discussed and described; Sect. 3 details the experiments carried out to compare the storage space used by applications developed with these approaches. In Sect. 4, the results obtained are presented and discussed. Finally, the conclusions and future lines of work are presented.

2 Types of Applications for Mobile Devices

In recent years, the mobile device market, especially that of smartphones, has seen a remarkable growth [13]. As regards operating systems, Android and iOS are the strongest in the market. Each has its own development infrastructure. The main challenge for mobile device application developers is being able to offer solutions for all market platforms; in these cases, development costs are so high that sometimes are hard to afford [15].

An appropriate solution to this problem is creating and maintaining a single application that is compatible with all platforms. The goal of multi-platform development is maintaining a single source code for several platforms. This results in a significant reduction of effort and costs.

In the following sections, different approaches are presented for the development of applications for mobile devices:

2.1 Native Applications

Native applications are developed to be run on a specific platform, considering the type of device and the operating system and its version. The source code is compiled to obtain executable code, similar to the process used for traditional desktop applications. When the application is ready for distribution, it is published in the app store specific for each platform. These stores have an audit process to check if the application meets the requirements of the platform on which it is going to be run. Finally, the application becomes available for download by end users.

One of the characteristics of a native application is that it allows unlimited interaction with all the functions and features offered by the device (GPS, camera, accelerometer, calendar, etc.). Additionally, Internet access may not be a requirement to run this type of applications. They are fast and can be run in the background, and they issue an alert when there is an event that requires user intervention.

This development approach has a high cost, since each platform requires the use of a specific programming language. Therefore, if the goal of a project is to encompass several platforms, a different application must be generated for each of them. This means that the coding, testing, maintenance and going live processes must be carried out more than once.

2.2 Web Applications

Web applications for mobiles are designed to be executed in the web browser of the device. They are developed using standard technologies such as HTML, CSS and JavaScript.

One of the advantages of this approach is that no specific component needs to be installed in the device, and no third-party approval is required before publication and distribution. Only Internet access is required. Additionally, updates are pushed directly to the device, since changes are applied on a server and enabled for immediate access by the users. In summary, they are easy and quick to implement. However, the greatest advantage of mobile web applications is that they are fully platform-independent. There is no need to adapt to a specific operating system, only a web browser is needed.

On the other hand, this approach can reduce execution speed, which can result in a somewhat less satisfactory user experience, and interfaces are more limited than those offered by native applications. Performance can also be affected due to connectivity issues, among others. Finally, some limitations could also be observed in relation to access to specific features offered by the device [16].

2.3 Hybrid Applications

Hybrid applications use web technologies (HTML, JavaScript and CSS), but are not run by a browser. Instead, they are run on a web container of the device that provides access to device-specific features through an API.

Hybrid applications offer great advantages, such as code reuse for the different platforms, access to device hardware, and distribution through application stores [17].

Hybrid applications have two disadvantages when compared to native applications. The first of these is that user experience suffers from not using the native components in the interfaces. The second disadvantage is that these apps may be slower due to the additional load associated to the web container where they are run.

Some of the more popular frameworks that use this approach are Apache Cordova [18] and Ionic [19], a complete SDK that uses Cordova to access device native features.

2.4 Interpreted Applications

Interpreted applications are built from a single project that is mostly translated to native code, with the rest being interpreted at runtime. Their implementation is non-platform dependent and uses several technologies and languages, such as Java, Ruby, XML, and so forth.

Unlike the web and hybrid multi-platform development approaches, with the interpreted applications approach native interfaces are obtained, which is one of the main advantages of this type of applications.

Some of the most popular interpreted development environments for these applications are Appcelerator Titanium [20] and NativeScript [21].

2.5   Applications Generated by Cross-compilation

These applications are compiled natively by creating a specific version for each target platform. Some examples of development environments used to generate applications by cross-compilation are Xamarin [22] and Corona [23].

Xamarin allows compiling fully native applications for iOS and Android by sharing the same base code written in C#.

Xamarin allows sharing the entire business logics code, but user interfaces must be programmed separately for each target platform.

Corona is a multi-platform framework that allows developers build both general-purpose applications and games for the main platforms. A single base code is used, which is then published for the different platforms. Unlike Xamarin, no specialized rewriting or projects are required. Programming is done with Lua, which is a simple scripting language.

3   Experiment

The development approaches analyzed in this article were the native approach and its multi-platform variations: hybrid, interpreted and cross-compilation (the mobile web approach is not relevant for the goals at hand). Each of these approaches has its own aspects in relation to how apps are built and run. These aspects can impact app size in a different manner and, therefore, they should be analyzed.

All tests detailed in this article were carried out using Android as a platform, which is the operating system that currently has the lion's share of the mobile device market. These same tests can be done in the future on iOS, so as to analyze the storage space required by these solutions on that platform.

3.1   Test Design

Even though in general terms the experiments revolve around the development approaches used, the tests had to be implemented using specific frameworks. There are several of these development frameworks for each of the approaches being considered. The ones chosen for this study are well known and very popular in the field. In all cases, the latest stable version of the framework at the moment of carrying out the experiment was used.

The frameworks used for the tests are:

1. Android SDK API 28 (Java, native)
2. Apache Cordova, version 8.1.2 (multi-platform, hybrid)

3. Ionic version 4 on Apache Cordova 8.1.2 (multi-platform, hybrid)
4. Appcelerator Titanium, SDK, version 7.5.0 GA (multi-platform, interpreted)
5. NativeScript, version 5.1.1 (multi-platform, interpreted)
6. Xamarin, version Xamarin Forms 3.4.0 (multi-platform, cross-compilation)
7. Corona, version 2018.3326 (multi-platform, cross-compilation)

In the tests, whose results are presented in the following section, the impact of these seven frameworks on the size of the applications built using them was assessed. To do this, the length of the APK file generated in each case was measured with a compiled version signed off in release mode (suitable for upload to Google Play Store). The APK (Android Application Package) file is a package containing the app to be installed in a device running Android as operating system. The size of this package is independent from the target device where the app will be later installed.

The inclusion of framework libraries, modules and plug-ins in the APK file can depend on the type of features implemented. For this reason, to assess the impact on app size, several observations are required considering different features.

Thus, 4 different types of apps were implemented, encompassing usual features: (1) text display, (2) audio playback, (3) video playback and (4) accessing device camera. Thus, there are 28 test cases:

For all tests, the applications were generated following the standard procedure recommended by the documentation for each framework. In all cases, it was specifically corroborated that no additional files, such as images or videos, were included. These files are usually added by framework tools when a new app is built. The source code for all the implementations developed for this work is available in [24].

The experiments were designed as follows:

Test scenario #1. Text Display. Seven versions were implemented, one for each framework being considered, for a simple app that shows the message "Hello World" on the screen of the device. This trivial feature allows identifying significant differences in the size of the app generated by the different frameworks under examination.

Test scenario #2. Audio Playback. Seven versions of the same app were implemented, one for each framework being considered, to play back a one-minute audio file. Audio was coded to a 1.32 Mb file. The most popular standard codec in the market was used, MP3 AC3, at a bit rate of 128 Kbps. For the implementation with Ionic, an audio playback plug-in [25] was required. Plug-ins were also needed for the implementation with NativeScript [26] and Xamarin [27].

Test scenario #3. Video Playback. Seven versions of the same app were implemented, one for each development framework being considered, to play back a one-minute video file on full screen. The video file used was coded into a standard, hi-def 89.2 Mb file (1280 × 720 pixels). The most popular standard codec in the market was used, H. 264, at a bit rate of 5585 Kbps. For audio track coding, AAC was used at a bit rate of 128 Kbps. For the implementation with Ionic, a video playback plug-in [28] was required. Plug-ins were also needed for the implementation with NativeScript [29] and Xamarin [30].

Test scenario #4. Device Camera Access. Seven versions were implemented, one for each framework being considered, of a simple app that allows opening the camera of the operating system, after managing the corresponding permissions. In the case of the implementation with Apache Cordova and Ionic [31], the use of a camera access plug-in was required. Plug-ins were also needed for the implementation with NativeScript [32] and Xamarin [33].

4   Results

Below, the results obtained for each of the test scenarios defined for the experiments are presented.

4.1   Text Display Application

Table 1 shows the results obtained for the text display app. It lists all frameworks with the corresponding value, in Mb, indicating the size of the APK file obtained. Data were sorted following the "most efficient first" criterion, efficiency being measured in terms of storage space requirements. Thus, the frameworks that produced the smaller apps are on the top of the table.

Table 1. App size – text display

Framework	Development approach	Size in Mb
Android SDK/Java	Native	1.4
Cordova	Hybrid	1.6
Ionic	Hybrid	4.53
Xamarin	Cross-compilation	4.72
Corona	Cross-compilation	6.79
NativeScript	Interpreted	11.9
Titanium	Interpreted	15.6

The native development approach turned out to be the most efficient in storage resource economy (smaller APK file). It is followed by the hybrid approach (Cordova and Ionic), cross-compilation (Xamarin and Corona), and finally, with the lowest performance, the interpreted approach (NativeScript and Titanium).

It should be noted that there are considerable differences among the various implementations, even when comparing two frameworks corresponding to the same development approach. Cordova produces an APK file that is only 14% larger than the native solution; this makes it an attractive solution that benefits from the advantages of multi-platform development with minimal increase in storage requirements. However, Ionic, the other hybrid framework used for the experiments, requires more than 3 times the space than the native app. The last position on the table is for the solution implemented with Titanium, which ended up being 11 times larger than the native solution. These significant differences can be clearly seen in Fig. 1a.

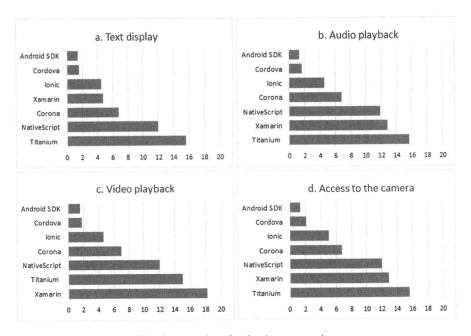

Fig. 1. App sizes for the 4 test scenarios

4.2   Audio Playback Application

Table 2 shows the results obtained for the audio playback app. The frameworks being tested are sorted from smaller to larger APK file.

Table 2. App size – audio playback

Framework	Development approach	Size in Mb
Android SDK/Java	Native	1.33
Cordova	Hybrid	1.67
Ionic	Hybrid	4.6
Corona	Cross-compilation	6.8
NativeScript	Interpreted	11.88
Xamarin	Cross-compilation	12.78
Titanium	Interpreted	15.68

The third column in Table 2 shows the size of the resulting app excluding the space used by the audio file that was packed together with the app.

The relation between framework and storage space is practically the same as the one seen in Table 1 (text display app). The native development approach is the most efficient one, closely followed by Cordova (hybrid) and further away by Ionic (hybrid).

Finally, the cross-compilation and interpreted frameworks yielded the lowest performances.

Again, Cordova represents the most attractive multi-platform solution (only 25% larger than the native implementation), and Titanium is the option that requires the most storage space (almost 12 times more than the native solution). Figure 1b shows a graphic representation of these differences.

4.3   Video Playback Application

Table 3 shows the results obtained for the video playback app. The frameworks being tested are sorted from smaller to larger APK file. The third column in this table shows the size of the resulting app excluding the space used by the video file that was packed together with the app.

Table 3. App size – video playback

Framework	Development approach	Size in Mb
Android SDK/Java	Native	1.6
Cordova	Hybrid	1.8
Ionic	Hybrid	4.7
Corona	Cross-compilation	7
NativeScript	Interpreted	12
Titanium	Interpreted	15
Xamarin	Cross-compilation	18.19

The same as in the case of the text display and the audio playback apps, the native approach produces the smallest app, followed by Cordova, Ionic and the other frameworks. Once again, Cordova represents the most attractive multi-platform option, increasing app size by only 12.5% vs. the native approach. On the opposite end, Xamarin is found on the last position of the table, with an app size that is 11 times larger than the native app. These differences are graphically represented in Fig. 1c.

4.4   Device Camera Access Application

Table 4 shows the results obtained for the app used to access the camera in the device. The frameworks are sorted from smaller to larger APK file.

Framework order in this ranking shows great similarities with the results obtained in the tests for the previous scenarios (see Tables 1, 2 and 3), and it is identical to the order obtained in the case of the audio playback apps (see Table 2).

Again, the best performance was recorded by the native development, followed by the hybrid approach represented by Cordova and Ionic frameworks, in that order. These are followed by the cross-compilation and interpreted frameworks, which are on the lower positions in the ranking with larger app sizes.

Cordova, which is on the second place in the ranking, represents the best solution of all multi-platform frameworks. The app generated with Cordova was 57% larger than the native app. This difference represents the biggest gap between both frameworks for the 4 test scenarios being considered.

Table 4. App size – device camera access

Framework	Development approach	Size in Mb
Android SDK/Java	Native	1.33
Cordova	Hybrid	2.09
Ionic	Hybrid	5.03
Corona	Cross-compilation	6.79
NativeScript	Interpreted	11.9
Xamarin	Cross-compilation	12.9
Titanium	Interpreted	15.6

The last position on the ranking corresponds to the app generated with Titanium, which is 11 times larger than the native app. The results presented on Table 4 are graphically represented in Fig. 1d.

4.5   General Result Analysis

Figure 1 presents a global view of the results obtained with the experiments. Chart bars represent the size of the apps developed with the frameworks under study. In all cases, the same distribution pattern is found, with minimal differences (see Figs. 1a, b, c and d).

In the 4 test scenarios that were considered, the first 3 positions in the ranking are always the same: (1) Android SDK, (2) Cordova and (3) Ionic. The native approach with Android SDK is the clear winner, always producing the smallest app. In second place, Cordova appears as the best multi-platform option, with minimal size difference versus Android SDK. Behind it, with apps that double the sizes obtained with Cordova, comes Ionic as the second best multi-platform development option.

Native apps are run directly by the underlying operating system. This helps avoid dependencies with interpreters or other tools that the multi-platform solutions usually pack within the app. Therefore, the native approach has a starting advantage and leads the ranking for smaller app.

The evidence obtained points to hybrid development (Cordova and Ionic frameworks) as the recommended multi-platform approach to obtain smaller apps. As opposed to this, interpreted development (Titanium and NativeScript) produces the largest apps. Interestingly, Xamarin (cross-compilation) is found on the lower end of the ranking in most of the scenarios that were tested. This is in contrast with the experiments carried out in [14], where a previous version of Xamarin was always among the upper end of the ranking.

5   Conclusions

In this article, the impact of development approaches on one of the non-functional requirements most relevant to mobile app users – device storage space – is analyzed. To this end, 4 different types of apps were considered, encompassing usual features.

It is concluded that the native development (Android SDK) is the most efficient one, saving storage space by generating smaller apps. Also of note are the good results obtained with the hybrid multi-platform development approach, in particular with Apache Cordova, which allows generating apps just slightly larger than the ones obtained with the native framework. On the other hand, cross-compilation and interpreted frameworks are the least optimal.

These considerations are applicable to reduced functionality apps, where the relative weight of the space used by framework libraries and tools is larger.

It should be noted that the results presented in this paper are linked to the development framework versions used for the experiments and, therefore, could change in the future as these frameworks evolve.

6   Future Work

In the future, our plan is to include other multi-platform development frameworks. A follow-up on future versions of the frameworks will also be carried out to find out how they evolve, either improving or worsening their use of storage space.

On the other hand, iOS application size will also be studied, since iOS is the second most widely used operating system in the market.

References

1. Joorabchi, M.E., Mesbah, A., Kruchten, P.: Real challenges in mobile app development. In: ACM/ IEEE International Symposium on Empirical Software Engineering and Measurement, Baltimore, Maryland, US (2013)
2. Delía, L., Galdamez, N., Corbalan, L., Pesado, P., Thomas, P.: Approaches to mobile application development: comparative performance analysis. In: 2017 Computing Conference, London (2017)
3. http://gs.statcounter.com/os-market-share/mobile/worldwide. Accessed Mar 2019
4. Xanthopoulos, S., Xinogalos, S.: A comparative analysis of cross-platform development approaches for mobile applications. In: BCI 2013, Greece (2013)
5. Delia, L., Galdamez, N., Thomas, P., Corbalan, L., Pesado, P.: Multiplatform mobile application development analysis. In: IEEE 9th International Conference on Research Challenges in Information Science (RCIS), Athens, Greece (2015)
6. Corbalan, L., et al.: Development frameworks for mobile devices: a comparative study about energy consumption. In: 5th IEEE/ACM International Conference on Mobile Software Engineering and Systems on (ICSE) MobileSoft 2018, Gothenburg, Sweden (2018)
7. Vandenbroucke, K., Ferreira, D., Goncalves, J., Kostakos, V., Moor, K.D.: Mobile cloud storage: a contextual experience. In: Proceedings of the 16th International Conference on Human-Computer Interaction with Mobile Devices & Services (MobileHCI 2014), pp. 101–110 (2014)

8. Tolomei, S.: «Shrinking APKs, growing installs» 20 November 2017. https://medium.com/googleplaydev/shrinking-apks-growing-installs-5d3fcba23ce2. Accessed Mar 2019

9. https://sensortower.com/blog/ios-app-size-growth. Accessed Mar 2019

10. Zhang, X., Kunjithapatham, A., Jeong, S., Gibbs, S.: Towards an elastic application model for augmenting the computing capabilities of mobile devices with cloud computing. Mob. Netw. Appl. 16(3), 270–284 (2011)

11. Christensen, J.H.: Using RESTful Web-services and cloud computing to create next generation mobile applications. In: Proceedings of the 24th ACM SIGPLAN conference companion on Object oriented programming systems languages and applications, New York (2009)

12. Lyu, Y., Gui, J., Wan, M., Halfond, W.G.J.: An empirical study of local database usage in android applications. In: IEEE International Conference on Software Maintenance and Evolution, Shanghai, China (2017)

13. http://gs.statcounter.com/platform-market-share/desktop-mobile-tablet/worldwide/#monthly-201403-201803. Accessed Mar 2019

14. Sosa, J., et al.: Mobile application development approaches: a comparative analysis on the use of storage SPAC. In: 2018 XXIV Congreso Argentino de Ciencias de la Computación CACIC 2018, pp. 631–641. Tandil (2018)

15. Raj, C.R., Tolety, S.B.: A study on approaches to build cross-platform mobile applications and criteria to select appropriate approach. In: 2012 Annual IEEE India Conference (INDICON), pp. 625–629. IEEE (2012)

16. Tracy, K.W.: Mobile application development experiences on Apple's iOS and Android OS. IEEE Potentials 31(4), 30–34 (2012)

17. Delia, L., Galdamez, N., Thomas, P., Corbalan, L., Pesado, P.: Multi-platform mobile application development analysis. In: 2015 IEEE 9th International Conference on Research Challenges in Information Science (RCIS), pp. 181–186. IEEE (2015)

18. http://cordova.apache.org. Accessed Mar 2019

19. https://ionicframework.com. Accessed Mar 2019

20. http://www.appcelerator.com. Accessed Mar 2019

21. https://www.nativescript.org/. Accessed Mar 2019

22. https://xamarin.com. Accessed Mar 2019

23. https://coronalabs.com/. Accessed Mar 2019

24. https://gitlab.com/iii-lidi/papers/apps-size.git. Accessed Mar 2019

25. https://github.com/apache/cordova-plugin-media. Accessed Mar 2019

26. https://market.nativescript.org/plugins/nativescript-audio. Accessed Mar 2019

27. https://www.nuget.org/packages/Xam.Plugin.SimpleAudioPlayer. Accessed Mar 2019

28. https://github.com/moust/cordova-plugin-videoplayer. Accessed Mar 2019

29. https://market.nativescript.org/plugins/nativescript-videoplayer. Accessed Mar 2019

30. https://www.nuget.org/packages/Plugin.MediaManager. Accessed Mar 2019

31. https://github.com/apache/cordova-plugin-camera. Accessed Mar 2019

32. https://market.nativescript.org/plugins/nativescript-camera. Accessed Mar 2019

33. https://www.nuget.org/packages/Xam.Plugin.Media. Access Mar 2019

Scrum Towards IRAM-ISO 9001:2015. Integrating Documentation Required

Julieta Calabrese[2] , Silvia Esponda[1(✉)] , Marcos Boracchia[1] ,
and Patricia Pesado[1]

[1] Computer Science Research Institute LIDI (III-LIDI),
School of Computer Science, National University of La Plata,
50 y 120, La Plata, Buenos Aires, Argentina
{sesponda,marcosb,ppesado}@lidi.info.unlp.edu.ar
[2] UNLP, La Plata, Argentina
jcalabrese@lidi.info.unlp.edu.ar

Abstract. On the road to achieving good process quality management in software-developing small and medium enterprises, there is a lack of documentation in methodologies that are currently very widely used (such as Scrum). A proposal to adapt Scrum documentation and recommended IEEE standards for development process stages to the documentation required by IRAM-ISO 9001:2015, defining a single integrating document, is presented.

Keywords: Scrum · Quality · IRAM-ISO 9001 · Documentation

1 Introduction

Currently, quality management is essential within any organization. This management may even become a competitive advantage that strengthens the organization by allowing it to provide a better service or offering a product that meets customer demands and expectations. Specifically, the software industry is one of the fastest-growing industries in recent decades, and even if software production uses a set of specific standards aimed at assessing various process- and/or product-related aspects, more often than not a Quality Management System (QMS) compliant with IRAM-ISO 9001 is required.

The standard IRAM-ISO 9001:2015 "Quality Management Systems. Requirements" [1] is based on the challenges that enterprises of any size and from any sector have to face today. It also focuses on the efficacy of the management system to comply with customer requirements. This standard promotes the adoption of an approach based on processes and **requires the existence of any documented information that the organization considers necessary for the efficacy of the QMS.**

Computer Science Research Institute LIDI (III-LIDI)—Partner Center of the Scientific Research Agency of the Province of Buenos Aires (CICPBA).

P. Pesado and C. Aciti (Eds.): CACIC 2018, CCIS 995, pp. 183–196, 2019.
https://doi.org/10.1007/978-3-030-20787-8_13

On the other hand, agile methodologies are a very commonly used alternative for the software system development process. It emphasizes the relation with the customer and an incremental development of the product. These methodologies offer an alternative to traditional software development processes, which are typically rigid and guided by the documentation generated during each of the stages in the process. Agile methodologies are based on frequent deliveries of functional software, allowing changes in requirements and customer direct participation throughout the development stage. One of the agile methodologies most widely used nowadays by software developing SMEs is Scrum [2], which is defined as an incremental, empiric iterative process to manage and control development tasks.

Working towards achieving good process quality management in small and medium enterprises that develop software and use Scrum, there is a need to bring the documentation used by the methodology up to code with the documentation required by the standard for QMS efficacy.

The documentation defined by Scrum is not enough to meet the requirements of IRAM-ISO 9001:2015. For this reason, additional documentation that is based on standards and presented as a single, integrating document, is required [8].

In the following section, the structure of IRAM-ISO 9001:2015 is described in detail, and a brief description of the guidelines included in ISO/IEC/IEEE 90003:2018 is added. In the third section, Scrum is presented and the agile methodology for development is discussed, indicating its drawbacks in relation to documentation. The fourth section describes the single, integrating document proposed to meet documentation requirements in IRAM-ISO 9001:2015 for SMEs that use Scrum in their development processes. It should be noted that only sections 6, 7 and 8 in the standard will be considered, since those are the sections that specifically consider the process to be certified. Finally, the conclusions and future lines of work are presented [8].

2   IRAM-ISO 9001:2015

2.1   Getting on the Road Towards Quality Management

An organization that plans on applying and implementing a QMS under ISO 9001 faces various barriers. Envisioning the starting point is critical for a large number of these organizations, especially if we consider that they usually do not have properly trained staff for carrying out such an endeavor and the costs of hiring consulting services are high.

Additionally, documentation is a highly important aspect. It is essential that users are able to obtain the maximum performance for the features offered by the product, and that stakeholders receive support so that they can understand product features and functions. To be good, documentation has to be specific, concise and relevant.

2.2   IRAM-ISO 9001:2015

In 2015, a new version of ISO 9001, identified as "ISO 9001:2015 - Quality Management Systems. Requirements" was published; this new version is restructured based on IRAM-ISO 9001:2008. The review came about as a response to the need to bring the standard up to date with modern times for organizations. It is structured as follows:

1. Scope: It details the goal for applying the standard in an organization, as well as its application field.
2. Regulatory References: This refers to standard ISO 9000:2015 "Quality Management Systems – Foundations and Vocabulary".
3. Terms and Definitions: Similarly, this refers to standard ISO 9000:2015 "Quality Management Systems – Foundations and Vocabulary".
4. Organizational Context: This lists the actions that the organization needs to carry out to ensure the success of its QMS, as well as information for understanding the context, needs and expectations, establishing the scope, processes and documentation, and so forth.
5. Leadership: It determines the involvement high management should have in the organizational QMS, quality management being part of the strategic decisions. Also, a customer-oriented approach and a quality policy suitable for the organization are mentioned.
6. Planning: It specifies the planning-related actions than need to be carried out within the organization to ensure the success of the QMS. It is aimed at identifying risks and opportunities, proposing quality objectives and considering how to plan for changes.
7. Support: It lists requirements for resources, competence, awareness, communication and documented information.
8. Operation: It lists requirements related to planning and control; as well as requirements for the production of products and services from inception to delivery.
9. Performance Assessment: It refers requirements pertaining to following up, measuring, analyzing and assessing the QMS.
10. Improvement: It lists the requirements for continued improvement.

With this new structure, some requirements have been modified, some have been removed, and some new ones have been added. For example, documents and records management, which so far was found on title 4.2, is now on title 7.5, under the concept of **documented information**.

In the new version, the process-based approach focuses on increasing management and control for existing interactions between processes and functional hierarchies in each organization. Also, the language used is simpler and easier to understand by any individual. Not only customers are mentioned now, but the necessary requirements to meet the demands of all interested parties are also identified.

There is a section within the standard that emphasizes the importance of the "organizational context". This section highlights how important it is to take into account and analyze the socio-economic context of the company and its existing links to stakeholders (internal and external). This analysis helps identify problems and needs that could potentially affect how the Quality Management System is planned. This is one of the most significant changes, since this is a concept that crosses the entire management system, i.e., it affects its implementation, deployment, maintenance and improvement.

Risks are a critical aspect that has been added to the standard, recommending their management throughout the process. To manage risks, the methodology that is most suitable to company needs can be used.

2.3   ISO/IEC/IEEE 90003:2018

Currently, there is a set of guidelines that provide guidance to organizations on how to apply ISO 9001 when acquiring, offering, developing, operating and maintaining software and related support services. These guidelines are compiled in ISO/IEC/IEEE 90003 [3], whose latest version was published in 2018. The ISO/IEC/IEEE 90003:2018 standard is used as guidance for software process certification under the IRAM-ISO 9001:2008 standard, and it includes an informational annex with instructions on how to use IRAM-ISO 9001:2015.

3   Software Development Process Under IRAM-ISO 9001:2015

Previous versions of IRAM-ISO 9001 required a quality manual. The current version of the standard no longer calls for one. The specific requirement of developing manuals, documented procedures that would be demanded during certification audits, work instructions, records, etc. is gone. However, organizations must establish the level of documented information **needed** to control the QMS. Also, access control is emphasized, indicating the importance of information protection.

When embarking on the journey towards certification under this standard, a large number of software development processes have **scarce documentation that is not enough to meet the requirements of the standard**. As already mentioned, we will focus on the agile development process known as Scrum.

3.1   Scrum

Scrum [6] is an agile framework for development software that is aimed at achieving continued control over the software that is produced. Customers can set priorities and the Scrum team auto-organizes to determine how best to deliver results. Work is done in cycles called *sprints* (short-duration iterations, typically lasting between 2–4 weeks). During each sprint, the team selects a set of requirements from a prioritized list, so that the features developed first in the project are those with higher value. At the end of each sprint, a software product that can be run on the environment required by the customer is delivered (Fig. 1).

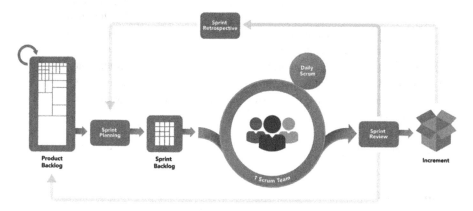

Fig. 1. Scrum methodology (from scrum.org).

The approach used in Scrum proposes functional software over excessive documentation. For medium-sized and large projects, maintaining such documentation was frustrating for team members due to the number of requests for changes and new requirements that were added throughout the project. As a result, documentation was usually outdated in relation to customer expectations.

Scrum uses a *product stack*, which is the heart of the documentation used by this methodology. This stack creates the list of all requirements, sorted by priority. This list is in constant evolution. All roles have access to the list, but it is the product owner the one responsible for prioritizing requirements and deciding over it. On the other hand, the team leader (Scrum Master) is responsible for monitoring the stack and selecting the project management tool that is more appropriate for this purpose.

Additionally, Scrum uses a *sprint stack* that includes only the requirements that will be worked on during the sprint at a given time. *Meeting minutes* are grouped under what is called *Retrospectives*, team chats that have a duration of 15 min after demonstrating the product to the customer. These chats are aimed at considering how the team worked throughout the sprint, the problems found, and the issues that could be improved for future sprints. Any changes in requirements that are deemed necessary moving forward can be made [7].

Table 1 shows the relation between items in the Standard where documented information is required and Scrum documentation.

Table 1. IRAM-ISO 9001:2015 documentation vs. Scrum documentation.

IRAM-ISO 9001:2015	Scrum documentation
6.1. Actions to approach risks and opportunities	Insufficient
6.2. Quality objectives and planning to achieve them	Insufficient
7.1.5. Tracking and measurement resources	Insufficient
7.2. Competence	Insufficient
8.2.3. Requirement review for products and services	Product stack Meeting minutes
8.3.2. Design and development planning	Product stack
8.3.3. Input for design and development	
8.3.4. Design and development controls	Insufficient
8.3.5. Design and development output	Insufficient
8.4.1. General aspects (controls for processes, products and services provided externally)	Insufficient
8.5.6. Change control	Insufficient
8.6. Product and service release	Insufficient

4 Integration

As seen in Table 1, Scrum documentation is insufficient to meet the documentation requirements mandated by the Standard. Based on this, a single, integrating document is presented, where a number of items are collected in accordance with known standards, in addition to Scrum documentation. Integration is aimed at providing all necessary documentation (during the requirement and planning stage) as defined in the requirements of Standard IRAM-ISO 9001:2015 for the creation of software products using the agile development methodology Scrum.

4.1 Existing Documentation

- **Documentation Based on Standards**
  There is a set of documents aimed at specifying different attributes (functional and non-functional) for the product to be developed and the project, which are defined in IEEE standards for the requirement specification and planning stages (Table 2).

Table 2. Documentation based on standards.

Document	Defined by
Software Requirements Specification (SRS)	IEEE-Std 830 [4]
Project Management Plan (PMP)	IEEE-Std 1058 [5]

Software Requirements Specification (SRS)

Requirements engineering is a specialized process that is carried out on a domain to document the features that a software product must have and transform those into a specification. Title 7.5 of the IRAM-ISO 9001:2015 standard states that the information that the organization considers necessary for the efficacy of the Quality Management System must be documented.

The *requirements specification* document must cover the representation and comprehension of the specific environment, and it must include all essential features (delimited functionality) of the software in a way that can be traced, is not ambiguous, and is independent from non-functional requirements and design restrictions.

In different organizations, this document is generated with various structures, although there are international standards that specify their structure, such as IEEE Std 830-1998. This Standard is a guideline for what should be included in such document, giving general content guidelines for each section.

The main sections of the document are presented in Table 3.

Table 3. Software requirements specification.

1. Introduction: This section provides an introduction for the Software Requirements Specification document. It consists of a number of sub-sections where the different attributes related to the document are defined.
2. Overview: This section describes those factors that affect the product and, consequently, its requirements. It consists of a number of sub-sections where the context for the product is defined, as well as various aspects of the context that need to be taken into account.
3. Specific Requirements: This section includes all requirements (functional and non-functional) described in thorough detail. It is the longest section in the document and it must be fully understandable to the customer and/or any other type of user related to the project. Functional requirements, such as performance, availability, reliability, security, maintenance and portability, are included.
4. Annexes: In this section, any type of information related to the document, but not part of it, can be included.

Project Management Plan (PMP)

The *Project Management Plan* defines project execution, supervision, and closing. Planning processes outputs are documented. The corresponding Standard does not specify the exact techniques that can be used for creating project plans nor does it offer examples; rather, each organization using this Standard should define practices and procedures to obtain a detailed guide for the creation and modification of software project management plans. These practices and procedures must necessarily consider environmental factors, both organizational and political, that could affect how the Standard is applied.

The main sections of the document are presented in Table 4:

Table 4. Project management plan.

1. Project Overview: In this section, a summary of the project is presented, describing its goal, deliverables and assumptions and/or restrictions. **2. References:** In this section, all documents related to the project management plan are listed. **3. Definitions:** This section is used to present the definitions of all necessary terms, abbreviations and acronyms necessary to understand the document. **4. Project Organization:** This section is used to define project roles, the internal structure of the organization, and external interfaces, if any. **5. Process Management Plans:** This section is related to process management. It is divided into sub-sections used to define the staff required for the project, project budget, the different activities to be carried out and the related effort in hours, and so forth. **6. Technical Process Plans:** This section is related to technical processes. It is divided into sub-sections used to define the lifecycle model that will be used for the project, acceptance levels agreed with the customer, and so forth. **7. Support Process Plans:** This section is devoted to support processes. It is divided into sub-sections detailing all project documentation, test plans, and so forth. **8. Additional Plans:** In this section, those plans that were not included in previous sections are described, such as security plans, backup plans, and so forth.

- **Scrum Documentation**

  As already mentioned, the agile methodology Scrum uses the *product stack*, which includes a number of elements that are mostly the functionalities required by the customer.

  A very well known practice is representing requirements through **user histories**, which provide clear and concise descriptions of the functionality in terms of their value for the end user of the product. A user history is written following a specific format: "As ROLE, I want FUNCTIONALITY to be able to BENEFIT".

  The following table defines the documents used with this methodology (Table 5):

Table 5. Scrum documentation.

Document	Defined by
Product stack	Scrum
Sprint stack (irrelevant for the article)	Scrum
Meeting minutes	Scrum

4.2   Existing Documentation vs. IRAM-ISO 9001:2015

The product stack (together with the meeting minutes) used by Scrum is not enough to meet the documentation requirements for IRAM-ISO 9001:2015. To overcome this, a way to integrate items from the Standards used nowadays was considered, so as to meet

Standard requirements. It should be noted that only sections 6, 7 and 8 in the Standard were considered, since those are the sections that specifically consider the process itself. Additionally, Standard ISO/IEC/IEEE 90003:2018 was used as reference and guidance for some sections.

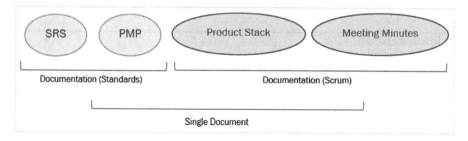

Fig. 2. Single document generation.

The single document represented in Fig. 2 includes items from various existing documents, and it was created to meet Standard requirements highlighting the development process (sections 6, 7 and 8).

The following table shows the sections in Standard IRAM-ISO 9001:2015 that require documented information, together with the items in existing documentation meeting those requirements (Table 6).

Table 6. Integration.

IRAM-ISO 9001:2015	Suggested documentation
6.1. Actions to approach risks and opportunities	PMP (5.4): Risk Management Plan
6.2. Quality objectives and planning to achieve them	PMP (5.3.4): Quality Control Plan
7.1.5. Tracking and measurement resources	PMP (7.2): Testing Plan
7.2. Competence	PMP (4.3): Roles and Responsibilities
8.2.3. Requirement review for products and services	(Scrum) Product stack - Meeting minutes (SRS) Section 3: Specific Requirements
8.3.2. Design and development planning	PMP (5.2): Work Plan
8.3.3. Input for design and development	(Scrum) Product stack PMP (5.1.2): Resource Acquisition Plan
8.3.4. Design and development controls	PMP (5.3): Control Plan
8.3.5. Design and development output	
8.4.1. General aspects (controls for processes, products and services provided externally)	PMP (5.1.2): Resource Acquisition Plan
8.5.6. Change control	PMP (7): Support Process Plans
8.6. Product and service release	PMP (5.5): Project Release Plan

4.3   Single Document for Sections 6, 7 and 8 in IRAM-ISO 9001:2015

To meet documentation requirements listed in these sections of IRAM-ISO 9001:2015, a single document is created based on the information listed in Table 7.

Table 7. Single document

a) Risk management
b) Quality Control
c) Roles and Responsibilities
d) User Histories (Product stack) – Specific requirements
e) Work Plan
e.i. Activities
e.ii. Effort allocation
f) Control Plan
f.i. Requirement control
f.ii. Calendar control
f.iii. Metrics collection
g) Resource acquisition
h) Support Process Plans
h.i. Verification and Validation (tests)
h.ii. Documentation
h.iii. Reviews and audits
h.iv. Troubleshooting
h.v. Third-party management
h.vi. Process improvement
i) Project Release Plan

Below, the items in the document are described:

(a) Risk Management

Every potential risk is detailed, accompanied by a strategy for mitigation and its contingency plan. Adding a note indicating if the risk affects the process, the product and/or the business is recommended, identifying also the likelihood of the risk and its impact.

For risk management activities, using a table as the one represented in Table 8 *is recommended.*

Table 8. Risk management.

Risk ID	Name	Likelihood	Impact	Responsible	State
[risk_id]	[name]	[likelihood]	[impact]	[responsible]	[state]

*Where "**risk_id**" is a code for identifying the risk, "**name**" is the detailed name of the risk, "**likelihood**" specifies the percentage chances of the risk happening (0–9% highly unlikely, 10–24% unlikely, 25–49% moderate, 50–74% likely, 75–100% highly likely), "**impact**" defines the relevance of the risk for the project, product and/or business (catastrophic: the project is canceled; serious: degraded performance, delayed deliveries; tolerable: minimal performance degradation; insignificant: minimal impact on development), "**responsible**" indicates the individual or group of individuals that will be in charge of responding to the risk, and "**state**" specifies if the risk has already happened or if it is latent.*

To handle the risks represented in the previous table, using a similar format to the one used for Table 9 *is recommended.*

Table 9. Handling risk.

Risk ID	Name:	Date:	
	Description:		
Likelihood:			
Impact:			
Responsible:		Class:	
Mitigation Strategy (Cancellation/Minimization):			
Contingency Plan:			

*The "**mitigation strategy**" must specify the set of activities that need to be carried out to AVOID the risk. If the risk has ALREADY HAPPENED, the "**contingency plan**" specifies the set of activities that should be carried out.*

(b) Quality Control
Quality objectives are described, detailing the actions to achieve them and how to check that they have been successfully completed.

(c) Roles and Responsibilities
The roles and responsibilities assigned to the individuals in charge of every feature in the project are detailed. The clearly defined roles in Scrum that should be included here are: Scrum Master, Scrum Team and Product Owner.

(d) User Histories – Specific Requirements
All system requirements are specified following the user history format. This must include a detailed and thorough list of all requirements that the system to be developed

has to meet. *The detail level must be enough for the development team to be able to design a system that meets these requirements, and for the team in charge of testing to be able to establish if the system does indeed meet the requirements. Non-functional requirements such as security, portability, reliability, availability, performance and maintenance must be included.*

To comply with the user history format, the header of each requirement should be worded as follows: "As ROLE, I want FUNCTIONALITY for a BENEFIT". The role indicates who is directly affected by the functionality (the requirement itself), whereas the benefit indicates what positive result, or benefit, is expected from the functionality.

(e) Work Plan

e.i. Activities
The activities to be carried out throughout the duration of the project are detailed, from the requirement elicitation stage to the testing and maintenance stage. Each task should be detailed, if appropriate.

Table 10. Effort allocation.

Activity	Number	Unit Effort (hs)	Effort (hs) Subtotal

e.ii. Effort Allocation
The activities to be carried out during the project (defined in e.i.) are detailed and the effort allocated to each of them, in unit hours and total, is specified. A Critical Path or PERT chart can be added.

For activity and effort specification, a table as the one shown in Table 10 *is recommended.*

(f) Control Plan

f.i. Requirement Control
Meeting minutes are created after every Sprint meeting, detailing the results of test cases in each user history for the product stack. The minutes should also include feedback from the Sprint, as well as possible improvements for future iterations.

f.ii. Calendar Control
Meeting minutes should record compliance with estimated timeframes for each Sprint.

f.iii. Metrics Collection
Scrum Master reports are presented in each Sprint meeting, detailing the status for the entire project (number of histories approved by the Product Owner vs. planned histories, number of histories whose execution is still pending, sprint compliance/non-compliance percentage, and so forth).

(g) Resource Acquisition

If there are external resources available for the project (hardware, software, service agreements, administrative services, etc.), a control table detailing each of this resources, how they were obtained, compliance date, and so forth, is created.

Using a table like the one shown in Table 11 *is recommended:*

Table 11. Resource management.

Resource	How it was acquired	Number	Time	Unit price	Total price
Example: Test server	*Rental*	*1*	*Monthly (18 months)*	*$500*	*$9000*
				Subtotal	*$9000*
				Total	*$9000*

(h) Support Process Plans

h.i. Verification and Validation (Tests)

The tests required to follow-up on each of the user histories are specified. Each test should be detailed indicating context, resources needed, expected results and results obtained.

h.ii. Documentation

All external documents used for the project must be listed and described.

h.iii. Reviews and Audits

The planning for reviews and audits is described, if the goal is to get certified.

h.iv. Troubleshooting

The Scrum Master is responsible for troubleshooting. The steps to be followed to solve any issues that may happen throughout development are described in detail.

h.v. Third-Party Management

The process for selecting and managing companies hired if any of the products in the project are provided by a third party.

h.vi. Process Improvement

In the meeting minutes for each sprint, the results obtained with each test case for each user history are defined, as well as potential changes throughout the project.

(i) Project Release Plan

Product Owner reports are submitted at the end of the project, describing any non-conformities with requirements and the actions that should be carried out in case of occurrence.

5 Conclusions

A description of Scrum and Standard IRAM-ISO 9001:2015 was presented, high-lighting the deficiencies of the agile methodology in relation to the documentation requirements included in the Standard, resulting in difficulties to obtain the corresponding certification under IRAM-ISO 9001.

In its current state, Scrum would not meet Standard requirements, so a single document was designed to match the documentation used in Scrum and the recommended IEEE standards for development process stages with the documentation required by IRAM-ISO-9001.

This prototype has been used in the course Software Engineering II at the School of Computer Science of the UNLP, where students work on a project applying the Scrum methodology.

References

1. IRAM-ISO 9001:2015: Quality management systems - Requirements
2. Pasini, A.C., Esponda, S., Boracchia, M., Pesado, P.M.: Q-Scrum: una fusión de Scrum y el estándar ISO/IEC 29110. In: Libro de Actas XIX Congreso Argentino de Ciencias de la Computación CACIC (2013). ISBN 978-987-23963-1-2
3. ISO/IEC/IEEE 90003:2018: Software engineering - guidelines for the application of ISO 9001:2015 to computer software
4. IEEE Std 830-1998: Software Requirements Specification
5. IEEE Std 1058-1998: Project Management Plan
6. Scrum Guide. https://www.scrumguides.org/docs/scrumguide/v1/scrum-guide-es.pdf
7. Scrum Documentation. http://metodologiascrum.readthedocs.io/en/latest/Scrum.html
8. Calabrese, J., Esponda, S., Boracchia, M., Pesado, P.M.: Hacia una mejora de calidad en Scrum. Integrando documentación requerida por IRAM-ISO 9001:2015. In: Libro de Actas XXIV Congreso Argentino de Ciencias de la Computación CACIC (2018). ISBN 978-950-658-472-6

Databases and Data Mining

.

.

Discovering Association Rules Using R. A Case Study on Retail's Database

Juan Manuel Báez Acuña⬤, Clara Anuncia Paredes Cabañas⬤,
Gustavo Sosa-Cabrera⁽✉⁾⬤, and María E. García-Díaz⬤

Universidad Nacional de Asunción, Asunción, Paraguay
{juanmanuelbaez,cparedescabanas,gdsosa,mgarcia}@pol.una.py
http://www.pol.una.py

Abstract. Today, the high competitiveness in retail businesses requires them to seek new strategies to ensure their survival. To this end, organizations have understood that the data located in their transactional databases can be used as raw material to boost business growth, if they can be exploited properly. The research's main objective is to apply Data Mining techniques for the discovery of association rules from purely commercial transactional data, taking as a study period *10-year* in a household appliances and furniture retail entity. The selection's phase and preparation data are described as well as its cost in man/hours. In the modeling phase, the *Apriori* and *Eclat* algorithms implemented in the *arules* package of the *R* tool were executed, where both the resulting associations and execution time were compared. The results show relevant patterns in the buying behavior of customers such as those that relate items and accessories' prices.

Keywords: Data mining · Association rules algorithm · Retail ·
Transactional databases · R tool

1 Introduction

In recent years, the unbridled growth of databases, especially those of the type of data on everyday activities such as customer choices, takes Data Mining at the forefront of new commercial technologies. Data that is analyzed in an intelligent way is a very valuable resource and can lead to new knowledge and, in commercial environments, to competitive advantages for companies.

In today's highly competitive, customer-centric and service-oriented economy, data is the raw material that drives business growth, if it can be properly exploited, creating an important added value in the business. Likewise, day by day the study of obtaining useful knowledge from data stored in large repositories becomes more relevant, since it is recognized as a basic need in many areas, especially those related to the businesses sector known as *retail* [1].

ⓒ Springer Nature Switzerland AG 2019
P. Pesado and C. Aciti (Eds.): CACIC 2018, CCIS 995, pp. 199–210, 2019.
https://doi.org/10.1007/978-3-030-20787-8_14

This case study involves a company from the retail sector that pioneered the sale of domestic appliances at a country level and has managed to position itself as one of the most recognized companies throughout its more than 6 decades of existence in the market [2]. This company started implementing the use of computer for its activities in the *1990s* and since then it has gone through 3 versions of retail management software, each with its own structure of relational database, recording its movements through transactions. Currently, the company has more than 16 stores so it has experienced a vertiginous growth both in sales and quantity of information. On the other hand, the need to look for new strategies to guarantee the survival of businesses has also grown, namely, because of globalization and the high competitiveness of the sector.

Therefore, there is a need for business intelligence that can transform data into knowledge, so that it can be used in a timely manner in decision making, promoting actions that result in a competitive advantage for the company [3,4].

The objective of this work is to present the results obtained from the application of techniques for the discovery of associations where the records belonging to the purely commercial transactions of the company, made over a period of *10 years*, are taken as the study period.

In the remainder of this paper, we briefly review in Sect. 2 the theoretical aspects. Materials and methods were documented in Sect. 3 to show the results achieved in Sect. 4. Finally, we summarize our conclusions in Sect. 5.

2   Theoretical Aspects

Data mining is the process of extracting useful and understandable knowledge from large amounts of data stored in different formats [5]. This process is part of an iterative sequence of stages discovering knowledge in databases [6]. Two types of tasks are distinguished: predictive (classification and regression) and descriptive (clustering and association rules) [7].

Through the discovery of association rules, it is intended to obtain interesting knowledge such as the purchasing habits of customers through, for example, the relation of the different items in their "shopping carts" [8].

It is well known that the algorithms essential in the search for association rules in databases are the Apriori, the Eclat and the FP Growth [9]. However, in [10] it is considered that only the Apriori and the Eclat are the two large families since FP Growth can be included as a member of the Eclat.

The Apriori algorithm [11] first looks for all frequent unit sets (counting their occurrences directly in the database), these are mixed to form the sets of candidate items of two elements and selects among them the frequent ones. Considering the property of the frequent item sets, these are mixed again, and the frequent ones are selected (until now all the sets of frequent items of three or less elements have already been generated). Thus, the process is repeated until in one iteration frequent item sets are not obtained.

In contrast, the Eclat algorithm [12] is based on grouping (clustering) between the items to approximate the set of maximal frequent items and then use efficient algorithms to generate the frequent items contained in each group. Two methods are proposed for clustering, which are employed after discovering frequent sets of two elements: the first, by equivalence classes: this technique groups item sets that have the same first item. The second, by the search for maximal cliques: an equivalence graph is generated whose nodes are the items, and the arcs connect the items of the frequent 2-itemsets, the items are grouped by those that form maximal cliques.

Finally, R is a programming language and an environment that provides a wide variety of statistical and graphical techniques. In addition, it is highly extensible through packages that are available on CRAN websites that cover a wide range of modern statistics.

3 Materials and Methods

3.1 Data

The company has started the use of management software in the *1990s*, generating since then large amounts of information that were stored in databases, that is, according to the different versions of software implemented and the resulting migration process of records. In addition, in the absence of a database dedicated to business intelligence, for this study, a "mirror" database was mounted to the transaction database. In this "mirror" database, movements corresponding to the sales of household appliances and furniture corresponding to the *2008–2017* period were taken into consideration, since from 2008 the retail company expanded its catalog of products, incorporating the sale of furniture [13].

Selection Phase. Entities registered in the history tables and that were identified as factors that intervene in the sale are shown along with their attributes in Fig. 1.

Preprocessing Phase. It is described below by entity:

– *Sellers.* It had as attributes name, surname, type of seller (seller, collector or both), for the study it was required to include variables such as gender, age, and more specific categories to the existing ones. Out of a total of 1292 vendor registries, 780 remained with movements in the study period. To assign gender, the gender of the name was taken into account, with an effectiveness of 90%, then an individual verification was applied until 100% of the records had a gender assigned. For the age variable, the vendors' data were cross-referenced with human resources records, identifying 132 vendors, then comparisons were made with social security payment records, a task that could not be completed due to lack of complete information, therefore that variable was discarded for the study, finally, bearing in mind the codes present in the seller's name, 11 new categories were manually assigned.

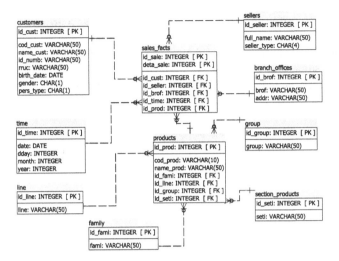

Fig. 1. Retail entity's database in star scheme.

– *Products.* Contains the data of the sold articles, classified in "family", "line" and "group" and distributed in 13 items of products. Out of a total of 37413 records, 26189 were in a "Discontinued" status, meaning that they did not have a valid classification for the study, which is why they should be re-categorized. It has been excluded 17037 records, for not having any movements in the period of study. 106 records have been excluded because they do not belong to the item "sale of appliances or furniture", leaving 20270 records for the sample. After having excluded the records, the number of items in "Discontinued" status was reduced to 14335. Considering the description of the product, a new classification was assigned to 14074 records. Due to the lack of standards in the loading of the products in the database, an individual verification was carried out, manually correcting 6971 records and finally 261 have been excluded for not belonging to the items of appliances and furniture leaving 20009 valid records for the study. Given that the products had very general categories, a comparison was made with the products exposed in the website of the retail company, in which it was found that the classification of "Family", "Line" and "Group" was not the same as the one available in the database. It could be observed that they were more specific and that way it was possible to extend such classification. Subsequently, using the description attribute, a new classification was assigned to all the preprocessed products.

– *Customers.* With 454737 records, 182449 records have been excluded, for not having movements in the period of study, leaving with 272288 records. Next, the attribute "Document Number" has been compared with the records of the database provided by the Identification Department of the National Police of Paraguay, finding 247766 coincidences, to which the attributes "date of birth", "type of person" and "sex" have been updated. Then, taking into account the attribute "RUC" [14], omitting the verification digit [14], we found 2247 records corresponding to physical persons, we have identified another 46 records with anomalous characters, to which the attributes were updated "date of birth", "type of person" and "gender". Then 14072 records corresponding to companies, diplomats and people with foreign documents, based on the RUC format, updated the "gender" and "type of person" data, discarding the attribute "date of birth" for these cases. In addition, taking into account the attribute "name of the customer", 490 records corresponding to companies [15], 126 customers registered as "Wedding List" have been identified. The same previous update was applied to the records, the same procedure used for the entity "Sellers" has been applied for the identification of gender by name gender to the 7541 records remaining, obtaining the following results: 3263 were female, 3758 were male, 25 records were corrected manually corresponding to companies, obtaining a success rate of 93.1% with the procedure. Finally, there were 495 records without an update, for which a manual and individual work was carried out using the names, comparing them with searches made in the *Google* search engine, identifying 162 records with female sex, 290 records with male sex and 20 records of business. Finally, only 23 records were discarded due to lack of adequate information to perform the update. Totaling 272265 optimal records for tests.

- *Sales.* For this entity there is a very small group of non-signaled transactions in the database, which would belong to grants in the form of gift items to customers for some promotion and not a sale as such, in this sense, we have interviewed the officers of the Marketing, Sales, Accounting and Audit departments of the company who have guaranteed that these occurrences were negligible for the purposes of the study. In addition, the relationship between the low number of variables and the sample size makes the statistical estimator consistent [16].

Remark. Although the traditional model of knowledge discovery in databases does not include activities for project management [17], in this work [18] it has been carried out a planning and measurement of time where the phases of selection and preprocessing of data had together an approximate cost of 880 man-hours.

Mineable Views. To finalize the preparation of the data, different combinations were made to obtain the mineable views (Table 1) where each contains the sales records with a detail for each product sold.

3.2   Induction of Association Rules

Firstly, the *Market Basket* technique (shopping cart) [19] used to discover associations between products was applied. The steps of the treatment applied to the mineable views to achieve the *basket* format necessary for the application of the Apriori and Eclat algorithms are described below (Table 2).

Table 1. Mineable views list.

Entities	Mineable views	
Prod	1. Family	3. Group
	2. Line	
Prod/Sellers	1. Gender/Group	7. Gender/SellerType/Group
	2. SellerType/Group	8. Gender/SellerType/Family
	3. Gender/Family	9. Gender/SellerType/Line
	4. SellerType/Family	10. Gender/Products
	5. Gender/Line	11. SellerType/Products
	6. SellerType/Line	12. Gender/SellerType/Products
Prod/Customers	1. Age/Group	7. Personality/Group
	2. Age/Family	8. Personality/Family
	3. Age/Line	9. Personality/Line
	4. Gender/Group	10. Age/Gender/Group
	5. Gender/Family	11. Age/Gender/Family
	6. Gender/Line	12. Age/Gender/Line
Prod/Time	1. Weekday/Group	4. Trimester/Group
	2. Month/Group	5. Semester/Group
	3. Sales' Peak/Group	6. Season/Group
Prod/Time/Customers	1. Age/Weekday/Group	4. Gender/Season/Group
	2. Age/Season/Group	5. Gender/Age/Weekday/Group
	3. Gender/Weekday/Group	6. Gender/Age/Season/Group
Prod/Customers/Sellers	1. Age/GenderSeller/Group	4. Personality/GenderSeller/Group
	2. Age/SellerType/Group	5. GenderCust/GenderSeller/Group
	3. Personality/SellerType/Group	6. GenderCust/SellerType/Group

```
> df.view <-read.csv("prod_cust_gral.csv", header=TRUE, sep=";")
> df.item.list <- ddply(df.view, c("id_sale","age_range_cust"),
    function(df1)paste(df1\$group, collapse=";"))
> df.item.list <- unite(df.item.list, items,
    c(V1, age_range_cust), sep=";",  remove=TRUE)
> df.item.list\$id_sale <- NULL
> write.csv(df.item.list, "ItemList.csv", row.names=TRUE)
```

Table 2. Transformation of records to the Basket format.

id_sale	age_range	group		id_sale	age_range	V1
100101	Adult	Stove				
100101	Adult	Coffee maker		100101	Adult	Stove; Coffee maker; Electric Oven
100101	Adult	Electric Oven ⟹		100102	Young	Cellphone
100102	Young	Cellphone		100103	Young	Coffee maker; TV
100103	Young	Coffee maker				
100103	Young	TV				

Subsequently, for the induction of association rules, the arules package was used [20] which contains the implementation of the algorithms "A PRIORI" and "ECLAT". To determine the degree of "significance" and "interest" of the rules, the known minimum thresholds of "support" (1) and "confidence" (2) respectively have been used, namely:

$$Supp(X) = \frac{|X|}{|D|} \tag{1}$$

$$Conf(X \implies Y) = \frac{Supp(X \cap Y)}{Supp(X)} = \frac{|X \cap Y|}{|X|}. \tag{2}$$

Remark. For this study, 5 support measures were used: 20%, 10%, 5%, 1% and 0.1%, due to the number of transaction records available in the retail company, a very low support was taken into account, so as to not discard frequent items that may be lost due to the number of existing records. Likewise, the percentage of the confidence used was 1%, so as not to exclude any rule, because for this study all the generated rules are worthy of being analyzed.

Execution of Algorithms. For the generation of the association rules, the runs of the algorithms were executed in the following way:

```
> m.data = read.transactions(file="ItemList.csv",
    rm.duplicates=TRUE, format="basket", sep=";",cols=1)
> m.rules <- apriori(m.data, parameter= list(supp=0.1,
    conf=0.01, target="rules"))
> m.rules <- ruleInduction(eclat(m.data,parameter=list(supp=0.1)),
    m.data, confidence=.01)
> inspect(m.rules)
```

4   Results

4.1   Rules Found

Given the main variable "Group" of the product, Table 3 shows the most relevant rules found, separated into groups of 10 years on one side and the last year on the other.

The results show that in both periods there is a strong relationship *[Mattress — Mattress Base]* and its different accessories, obtaining a confidence percentage higher than 95%, another rule that appears in both periods is *[Abdominals' Bench — Treadmills]*, with percentages of confidence greater than 50% in both cases, which indicates that there is a high probability of selling these items together.

In addition to mentioning that these combinations of products were maintained over time, the interesting thing about these data is that, considering the factor "price of sale of the product" and taking all the results shown in Table 3, it is reflected that the purchase of higher-cost items, induce the purchase of their respective accessories, as long as their price is less than or equal to 25% of the main item, this is a very valuable information that can be used by the marketing area to obtain benefits and increase the sales of products of lower cost, or the sale of products that have more accessories, carrying out promotions campaigns arming combos of said products. Its usefulness is extended to the commercial area, as a knowledge tool for sellers, when offering products to the customer.

Table 3. The 10 rules with the highest percentage of confidence per period.

2008-2017			2017		
Antecedent	Consequent	Confidence	Antecedent	Consequent	Confidence
Mattress Base, Mattress, Bedside Tables	Headboards	0.97	Mattress	Mattress Base	0.96
Mattress, Bedside Tables	Headboards	0.95	Mattress Base, Mattress, Bedside Tables	Headboards	0.96
Mattress	Mattress Base	0.93	Mattress, Bedside Tables	Headboards	0.95
Computer Desk	Webcam	0.85	Blenders	Blender Accs.	0.78
PC Screen, CPU	Computer Desk	0.73	Mattress Base	Mattress	0.74
PC Screen, CPU	Webcam	0.72	Mattress Base,		
Mattress	Bedside Tables	0.68			
Mattress Base, Mattress	Bedside Tables	0.62	Treadmills	Abs Bench	0.64
Mattress Base	Mattress	0.62	SMART TV	TV Support	0.59
Baby Cribs	Mattress	0.55	Table Ovens, Iron	Blenders	0.57
Treadmills	Abs Bench	0.53	Table Ovens	Kitchen Scale	0.55

Remark. These results have been interpreted and evaluated by specialized personnel from the sales area of the retail company.

Rules in Sale's Peak. In Fig. 2, a similar behavior is observed in the last 3 years of the study period, with respect to the sales trend, coinciding in 2 sales peaks. These peaks correspond to 2 festive dates, the first corresponds to May 14th, the day before "Mother's Day" in Paraguay and the second corresponds to *Black Friday* [21]. The rules obtained in the aforementioned dates are shown in Table 4, it can be noted that there is a strong relation of dependencies between the articles included in the rules, because a high degree of confidence is reached and even a case of 100% and it is also It emphasizes that these rules do not follow the same trend as those obtained in the periods of previous studies shown in Table 3.

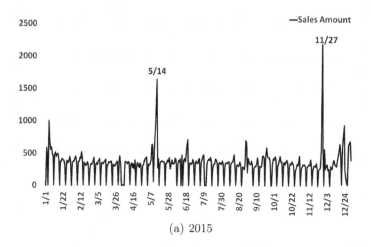

(a) 2015

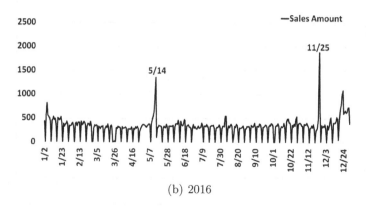

(b) 2016

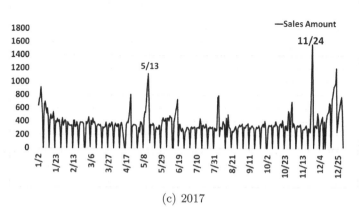

(c) 2017

Fig. 2. Sale's peak of the last 3 years of the study period

Table 4. The 5 rules with the highest percentage of confidence per sale's peak.

Mother's Day			Black Friday		
Antecedent	Consequent	Confidence	Antecedent	Consequent	Confidence
Pots and Pans	Kitchen Acc.	1	Pots and Pans	Kitchen Acc.	0.96
Treadmill	Abs Bench	0.97	LED TV	Table Ovens	0.94
Mattress Base	Mattress	0.96	Squeezer and Juicers	Blenders	0.82
Table Ovens	Hobs	0.74	Gas Stoves	Table Ovens	0.65
Table Ovens Irons	Blenders	0.63	Table Ovens	Coffee Makers	0.56

Algorithms Comparison. In Table 5, the comparison of the algorithms used for the experiment is reflected, taking into account parameters such as "Amount of Observations" and "Items", measuring the execution time and number of rules thrown.

Table 5. Performance in terms of execution time and rules found.

Description	Number Obs.	Number Ítems	Variables	Sup.	Conf.	APRIORI		ECLAT	
						Execution time (sec)	Number of rules	Execution time (sec)	Number of rules
Sales records for the 2017 period	124386	330	Product Group	0.001	0.01	2.97	218	3.36	185
				0.01	0.01	0.95	35	1.93	2
				0.05	0.01	0.69	3	0.71	0
				0.1	0.01	0.67	0	*	*
				0.2	0.01	0.68	0	*	*
Sales records for the period 2008 to 2017	1007064	543	Product Group	0.001	0.01	2.46	267	2.67	234
				0.01	0.01	2.25	33	2.14	0
				0.05	0.01	1.76	5	1.52	0
				0.1	0.01	1.41	0	*	*
				0.2	0.01	1.41	0	*	*
Sales records for the 2017 period	1125448	20265	Product	0.0001	0.01	4.78	478	384.6	476
				0.001	0.01	2.87	4	11.7	2
				0.01	0.01	2.29	2	10.2	0
				0.05	0.01	2.55	0	*	*
				0.1	0.01	2.4	0	*	*
				0.2	0.01	2.39	0	*	*

*No generation of rules because *ECLAT*, didn't find frequent ítemsets.

Execution time. All tests were performed on a hardware with Intel®Core(TM) I3-4005U CPU @ 1.70 GHz and 4 GB RAM. For 95% of the tests carried out, the Apriori algorithm has a shorter execution time compared to the Eclat in the generation of rules. In addition, in Table 4, it can be seen that the greater the number of items to be combined by the algorithms, the greater the gap in terms of execution time.

Number of Rules Found. The differences found are due to the fact that the Apriori algorithm generates rules with 1 frequent item that complies with the support specified as parameter, these rules do not have antecedents, they indicate that there is the probability of selling that product without taking into account another item involved.

5 Conclusion

This research has contributed to validate the results given by the application of techniques in the discovery of transactional databases in the retail sector using free software tools.

The association rules found for the sale of items in a group (with confidence measures above 50%) indicates the existence of relevant associations and that it can be considered as a valid pattern of customer behavior.

The second most important contribution has been the measurement of the great time invested for the preparation of the data. That is, due to the numerous preprocessing tasks that the transactional database has required, characterized by several version and migration updates since the *1990s*. This contribution is very valuable and should be considered for similar future research, such as the application of new techniques for the reduction of time in the preprocessing data phase.

6 Future Works

Given the results obtained in this work and the criteria and tasks that have been carried out to achieve them, we consider as future research, aspects related to the cost invested in the pre-processing of data, in analyzing other algorithms in the generation of association rules and the metrics and measures used in the analysis of those rules. Starting from the analysis of the great amount of time that has been invested in the pre-processing of data and in its transformations, it will be very important to analyze new techniques or improve existing ones, in order to reduce the time spent in that stage.

Regarding the algorithms used, we have analyzed the incorporation of FP-Growth or the Partition, in order to compare the results and verify whether or not they substantially improve the generation of rules, as well as the algorithms that allow us to generate association rules in time series. In this work, the exposed results were selected based on confidence measures as the main parameter, for other experiments the idea is to analyze other tools or measures that may give greater validity to the results for the evaluation of rules.

References

1. Douglas, H.: Retail—origin and meaning of retail by online etymology dictionary. https://goo.gl/zzwvu2. Accessed 25 May 2018
2. Giménez, G.G.: González giménez y cia. https://goo.gl/MY3oVv. Accessed 05 July 2018
3. Jiawei, H., Kamber, M.: Data Mining Concepts and Techniques. Morgan Kaufmann, San Francisco (2002)
4. Kim, J., Ale, J.: Descubrimiento incremental de las reglas de asociación temporales. In: X Congreso Argentino de Ciencias de la Computación (2004)
5. Witten, I., Frank, E.: Data Mining: Practical Machine Learning Tools with Java Implementations. Morgan Kaufmann, San Francisco (2000)
6. Fayyad, U., Irani, K.: Multi-interval discretization of continuous-valued attributes for classification learning. In: 13th International Joint Conference on Artificial Intelligence (IJCAI 1993), pp. 1022–1027 (1993)
7. Witten, I., Frank, E.: Data Mining: Practical Machine Learning Tools and Techniques, 2nd edn. Morgan Kaufmann, San Francisco (2005)
8. Agrawal, R., Imielinski, T., Swami, A.: Mining association rules between sets of items in large databases. ACM SIGMOD Rec. **22**, 207–216 (1993)
9. Heaton, J.: Comparing dataset characteristics that favor the Apriori, Eclat or FP-Growth frequent itemset mining algorithms. SoutheastCon, pp. 1–7 (2016)
10. Schmidt-Thieme, L.: Algorithmic features of Eclat. In: FIMI (2004)
11. Agrawal, R., Srikant, R.: Fast algorithms for mining association rules. In: Proceedings of the 20th International Conference Very Large Data Bases, VLDB, pp. 487–499 (1994)
12. Zaki, M., Parthasarathy, S., Ogihara, M., Li, W.: New algorithms for fast discovery of association rules. In: Third International Conference on Knowledge Discovery and Data Mining, pp. 283–286 (1997)
13. Ultima Hora, P.: González giménez expande sus productos y servicios (2008). https://goo.gl/LcmVvn. Accessed 17 June 2018
14. Martino, E.: Law num 1352/88. https://bit.ly/2ucWM1u. Accessed 18 June 2018
15. SET: Lista de pequenos contribuyentes. https://goo.gl/Fpqny5. Accessed 17 July 2018
16. Sosa-Cabrera, G., García-Torres, M., Gómez, S., Schaerer, C., Divina, F.: Understanding a version of multivariate symmetric uncertainty to assist in feature selection. In: Conference of Computational Interdisciplinary Science (2016)
17. Moine, J., Gordillo, S., Haedo, A.: Análisis comparativo de metodologías para la gestión de proyectos de minería de datos. In: Congreso Argentino de Ciencias de la Computación (2011)
18. Báez, J., et al.: Descubriendo reglas de asociación en bases de datos del sector retail usando R. In: Libro de Actas XXIV Congreso Argentino de Ciencias de la Computación, CACIC 2018, pp. 432–441. Red de Universidades con Carreras en Informática, RedUNCI. Facultad de Ciencias Exactas, Universidad Nacional del Centro de la Provincia de Buenos Aires (2018)
19. Han, J., Pei, J., Kamber, M.: Data Mining: Concepts and Techniques, 3rd edn. Morgan Kaufmann, Burlington (2012)
20. Hahsler, M., Buchta, C., Gruen, B., Hornik, K., Johnson, I., Borgelt, C.: arules: mining association rules and frequent itemsets. https://cran.r-project.org/package=arules. Accessed 03 May 2018
21. BBC: Black friday: por qué el viernes negro se llama así y otras 4 curiosidades sobre el famoso día de compras (2018). https://bbc.in/2AbApMP. Accessed 17 Jan 2019

D3CAS: Distributed Clustering Algorithm Applied to Short-Text Stream Processing

Roberto Molina[1,2], Waldo Hasperué[1,3(✉)] ⓘD,
and Augusto Villa Monte[1,4] ⓘD

[1] Facultad de Informática, Instituto de Investigación en Informática (III-LIDI),
Universidad Nacional de La Plata, La Plata, Argentina
rpmolina94@gmail.com,
{whasperue,avillamonte}@lidi.info.unlp.edu.ar
[2] CIN-EVC, La Plata, Argentina
[3] Comisión de Investigaciones Científicas (CIC),
Provincia de Buenos Aires, Argentina
[4] UNLP, La Plata, Argentina

Abstract. In this article, a proof of concept of a dynamic clustering algorithm based on density, called D3CAS, is presented. This algorithm was implemented to be run under the Spark Streaming framework, and it allows processing data streams. The algorithm was tested using a stream of short texts consisting of requirements generated by social media users, in particular, from a dataset called *Pizza Request Dataset*. The results, obtained in a virtualized environment, were analyzed with different configurations for algorithm parameters, which allowed establishing which are the configurations that yield the best results. Since the dataset used includes the label for each text in the stream, cluster purity could be measured and the results obtained could be compared to those presented by the authors of the dataset.

Keywords: Clustering · Spark · Streaming processing · Short text ·
Text analysis

1 Introduction

In recent years, the advance of technology has helped organizations and businesses generate and store large volumes of data. When these data are generated quickly and continuously over time, and storing them in their entirety becomes impossible, they are called "data streams".

Processing and analyzing data streams is a featured offered by many modern software systems and applications. Due to the growth of the Internet, system automation, increased social connectivity and technological progress, applications generate potentially infinite, volatile and continuous data streams, which requires real time, simple and fast processing.

In many cases, these large volumes of data can be mined to obtain relevant information of in a wide variety of applications, such as network intrusion detection, transaction streams, telephone records, social media, sensor monitoring, Internet of Things (IoT), medical applications, weather monitoring, and so forth.

© Springer Nature Switzerland AG 2019
P. Pesado and C. Aciti (Eds.): CACIC 2018, CCIS 995, pp. 211–220, 2019.
https://doi.org/10.1007/978-3-030-20787-8_15

A task that is commonly done on data streams is data clustering, which consists in splitting or grouping information in such a way that the data in each group are similar within the group and different from the data in other groups. With potentially infinite data streams, data clustering is an attractive challenge, since traditional clustering algorithms usually iterate over the set of data more than once. For this reason, runtime and memory use restrictions, in addition to the fact that the dataset is never complete, should be carefully considered in the context of data stream analysis. Also, the distribution of data in the stream is usually in constant change, which is known as concept-drift [1]. Thus, it would be interesting to have dynamic clustering algorithms, where the number of clusters at any given moment depends on the distribution of data in the stream [2, 3].

Nowadays, data generation accompanies human beings in almost every activity, and there is no indication that this will ever stop. Current technological advances help individuals communicate using digital text through the Internet. The volume of text information produced, in many cases exceeds the capacity of traditional methods used to capture, store and parse data. Tweets, e-mails, WhatsApp messages, Live Chat Support, and so forth, are constantly produced with no limits of any kind. These data are received as a stream that is usually parsed using clustering methods. Clustering texts is useful to identify topics, user profiles, interests, etc. For this reason, clustering text streams can be a challenging task.

In [4], a distributed, dynamic clustering algorithm for data stream processing called D3CAS (Distributed Dynamic Density-based Clustering Algorithm for data Streams) was presented. In this article, a systematic analysis of different parameter configurations for the D3CAS algorithm is carried out in an attempt to find the best configuration for handling text streams. The experiments were carried out by simulating a stream from real data where text labels are known. This is useful to measure the accuracy of the results obtained and thus identify the best configuration for the task at hand.

The remaining sections of this article are organized as follows: In Sect. 2, the state of the art is discussed in relation to text streams. In Sect. 3, the D3CAS algorithm is described. In Sect. 4, the experiments carried out are presented and the algorithm being studied is compared to one of the most relevant techniques used in the area. Finally, in Sect. 5, conclusions and future works are presented.

2   Short-Text Clustering

Nowadays, more than 80% of the data available in the world are stored as text, and automatically processing these data is a crucial task [5]. Text data stream clustering is one line of work where there is a current interest in reducing the problems generated by text information overload.

Unlike text streams formed by text documents such as scientific articles, news, clinical records or court files, the texts produced on social platforms are shorter and created in larger volumes. In the literature, there are several articles where short text streams are clustered with different goals. Some of the most recent ones are detailed below.

In [6], a popular food brand was selected to analyze a client comment stream in Twitter. They used K-means to group similar words found in tweets and a decision tree to discover terms used in positive and negative comments. Their goal was using this information to improve their marketing strategy. K-means was also used in [7] to sort short texts using additional semantic information, and in [8] to group text documents as new topics are identified within the corpus being considered. Finally, the authors in [9] successfully group short texts in data streams along time intervals by inferring changes in the distribution of words and topics.

2.1   The Data Stream Model

In the data stream model, input data are not permanently available for random access from memory or for retrieval from disc, but they arrive as one or more sequences of continuous, temporal data [3]. Data streams are potentially unlimited, which results in the use of an "on-the-fly" data processing method, i.e., once any given element is received, it is processed right then [2, 10].

There are two approaches when processing data streams. Incremental learning, where the model evolves incrementally to adapt to the changes in input data in the stream [11], and two-phase learning, also known as *online-offline learning*, where the basic idea is having a first phase (*online*) that generates a summary of the data that arrive in real time. In the second phase (*offline*), the mining process is carried out using the summaries generated during the online phase [12].

Since streams are potentially infinite, only a portion of them can be processed. The portion of data that are used is defined as the time window: $W[i,j] = (x_i, x_{i+1}, x_{i+2},..., x_j)$, where i and j are points in time with the property that $i < j$. Different types of time windows can be found in the literature: *landmark window* [13], *sliding window* [13], *fading window* [14], and *tilted time window* [12], each with its own advantages and disadvantages.

The problem of clustering data streams is a process that splits data continuously taking into account memory and time restrictions. In the literature, most of the data stream clustering algorithms use a two-phase scheme. Many of the existing data stream clustering algorithms are modifications of traditional clustering methods to use the two-phase approach proposed in [12]. For instance, DenStream [14] is an extension of the DBSCAN algorithm [15], StreamKM++ [16] is an extension of K-means++ [17], and StrAP [18] is an extension of AP.

3   D3CAS

D3CAS has turned out to be very efficient with simulated datasets, both for the detection of spherical clusters and clusters whose data form arbitrary or irregular shapes, obtaining better results than CluStream, another algorithm for handling data streams [4]. D3CAS can also detect and filter data representing noise, which is a very important feature. Figure 1 in [4] shows some results achieved with arbitrary shapes and their comparison with the results obtained with CluStream.

D3CAS is based on data structures (micro-clusters) and the online-offline processing methodology used by CluStream [12] and DenStream [14]. A micro-cluster is the data structure that represents and summarizes a dataset from the stream. A micro-cluster is a tuple of elements where the total volume of data in the micro-cluster and the linear and quadratic sums of the elements in the dataset are stored. The online-offline processing method is aimed at separating the clustering process into two phases – the online phase to generate the micro-clusters, and the offline phase to use them to carry out the clustering task.

The ultimate goal is implementing an algorithm that works on a distributed architecture, specifically, under the Spark Streaming model, which offers the most significant differentiating feature in relation to the techniques mentioned above, since both are designed to operate in a non-distributed environment.

To handle the data stream, the *fading window* model [14] is used, which offers the advantage of increasing data significance for more recent data, which is in turn useful for the early detection of changes in data distribution. To do this, each piece of data should store an attribute that determines its significance in time. This value is calculated using an aging function where the value of each piece of data decreases exponentially with time (Eq. 1).

$$f(dt) = 2^{-\lambda.dt} \tag{1}$$

where $\lambda > 0$ and dt is the difference between the timestamp at arrival and a moment in time greater than the time of arrival, usually represented by the current moment in time. As seen in Eq. (1) the higher the value of λ, the lower the significance of a piece of data compared to more recent data.

In D3CAS, the *online-offline* approach is used for handling the stream. The online phase is run in parallel on the Spark *workers* because the task of generating the micro-clusters is suitable for the type of processing carried out by *map* operations in Spark, whereas the offline phase is run on the *master* node, since knowledge of all generated micro-clusters is required to carry out the clustering detection task.

3.1   Online Phase

In this phase, the micro-clusters technique is used, which consists in reducing data volume to a smaller, more representative model. A micro-cluster at a moment in time t for a set P of n points with d dimensions $p_1, ..., p_n$ and their corresponding timestamps $T_1, ..., T_n$, is defined as a 7-tuple $MC = \{LS, SS, w, n, d, t_c, t_m\}$ where LS represents the weighted linear sum of the group of data, SS represents the weighted quadratic sum of the group of data, w represents the weight or significance of the micro-cluster in time, n represents the number of points in set P, d represents the dimensionality of the points in set P, t_c represents the timestamp at the moment in time when the micro-cluster was created, and t_m represents the timestamp of the last update to the micro-cluster.

When a new piece of data p_i is added to data partition P_k, a search for all points q_j whose distance to p_i is smaller than e (algorithm parameter that represents the radius of the micro-cluster) is carried out. If no point q_i is found, then a micro-cluster is created to represent point p_i. If a set of points close to p_i is found, then, being set Q formed by p_i and by the set of points close to p_i, a micro-cluster is created as follows: $MC(LS(Q),$ $SS(Q),$ $t_q,$ $cant(Q),$ $cant(Q),$ $timestamp(Q),$ $timestamp(Q))$.

After this process, *worker* nodes send the set of generated micro-clusters to the *master* node, which will be in charge of carrying out the update process and the cluster detection process.

3.2   Offline Phase

This phase of the clustering process is done by using a density-based technique, namely, DBSCAN [15], which allows detecting clusters without specifying how many. It also allows detecting clusters with arbitrary shapes, as well as noise or outliers present in the data.

For this process, the centers of all micro-clusters generated in the previous phase, whose end result is affected by two parameters from DBSCAN, are used. These parameters are *eps* and *minpoints*. *eps* represents the radius of point i where neighboring points are looked for, and *minPoints* represents the minimum number of neighboring points within radius *eps* that point i must have to be considered as a cluster.

During this phase, the process of updating micro-cluster weights is also carried out, since it is only now that all micro-clusters for the stream are available (*workers* are aware only of their own micro-clusters).

Micro-clusters are periodically updated, which includes updating weight w attributes and LS and SS attributes, which are also affected by time significance. Be t the current moment in time, t_m the timestamp of the last change to the micro-cluster, and dt the difference between t and t_m, then each micro-cluster updates its attributes using Eqs. (2) (3) and (4).

$$w = 2^{-\lambda.dt}.w \tag{2}$$

$$LS = 2^{-\lambda.dt}.LS \tag{3}$$

$$SS = 2^{-\lambda.dt}.SS \tag{4}$$

As it can be seen, given the decreasing nature of the aging function used, micro-clusters weights experience a gradual decrease. After the weight update process, a process to remove micro-clusters that are considered old based on their weights is carried out. A micro-cluster is considered to be old and has to be removed if its weight w is lower than a threshold μ, with $0 < \mu < 1$.

4   Experiments and Results

In [4], it was shown that D3CAS achieves very good results when processing number data streams with simulated datasets, both when processing clusters with spheric distributions as well as clusters with irregular ones. The results obtained with D3CAS were better than those obtained with CluStream.

In this article, a simulated stream of real short texts was used for experimentation. Experiments consisted in trying different parameter configurations for *e*, *eps* and *minpoints* in D3CAS and analyze their performance. The parameters controlling the sliding window were fixed ($\lambda = 0.25$ and $\mu = 10$), since these are the values typically used in *fading window* algorithms [14].

4.1   Text Flow Used

The text stream used for these experiments was created from the "Random Acts of Pizza" (RAOP) database presented in [19]. "Random Acts of Pizza" is an online community devoted to giving away free pizza to strangers that ask for one. Users can submit requests for free pizza and if their story is compelling enough a fellow user might decide to send them one.

This dataset contains the entire history of the Random Acts of Pizza Subreddit from December 8, 2010 to September 29, 2013 (21,577 posts total). From these, only 5671 posts were used; specifically, those posts where the authors of [19] were able to establish if the plea had been successful or not. Thus, this database has all the information for each post for which there is a known result (the "label" for the post), the number of downvotes and upvotes at the time the request was collected, number of comments for the request at time of retrieval, full text of the request, title of the request, number of days between requesters first post on RAOP and time of retrieval, total number of comments on Reddit by requester at time of request, and so forth.

The need to build a text stream from this dataset is given by the feature that each request has its own label, which allows measuring the level of purity for each cluster found and, therefore, measuring performance in each test carried out.

For the tests carried out in the context of this article, only text labels, full text, title and Unix timestamp of request were used for each post. The latter is used to sort posts chronologically. Even though posts correspond to a real period of almost three years, their timestamps were modified to simulate a stream of approximately 57 s, which translates as an arrival frequency of 100 posts per second.

As a result of their study, the authors of [19] identified five main topics (money, job, student, family and craver). Each of these topics is characterized by a set of words (110 in total). For the experiments carried out in the context of this article, the bag-of-words representation was used, using the dataset formed by those 110 words. From each post, a vector of length 110 was created using TF-IDF. Even though TF-IDF is not viable in text stream scenarios, there are alternatives that offer similar results, such as the one presented in [20].

4.2 Experiments

The stream of texts prepared for our tests was processed with D3CAS several times, using different configurations for parameters e, eps and $minpoints$. From each test, information about the number of clusters found and the number of micro-clusters in each cluster was stored.

After the clustering process was completed, the purity of each cluster was measured by assigning a label to each cluster as follows: Given a cluster C_i, be rp_i the number of posts in the cluster where the request was successful (positive class) and rn_i the number of posts where the request was not successful (negative class). Be TP the number of positive cases processed by the entire stream and TN the number of negative cases. Thus, the label for C_i will be positive if $(rp_i/TP) > (rn_i/TN)$, and negative otherwise.

Once the label representing each cluster is determined, the confusion matrix can be built for all clusters found. The ROC-AUC curve was calculated as follows: A weight w was established to calculate the distance from each piece of data to the clusters, punishing first those clusters representing one class, and then those representing the other.

Given a text t_j, be dp_j the distance to the closest positive cluster and dn_j the distance to the closest negative cluster in relation to t_j. Thus, distance weights w are calculated as follows:

$$DistP_j = dp_j \cdot w \tag{5}$$

$$DistN_j = dn_j \cdot (1 - w) \tag{6}$$

By changing w within interval $(0, 1)$, a widening or narrowing effect can be achieved in each of the clusters. With $w = 0$, positive clusters are wider, encompassing all data (minimum distance to each cluster, Eq. 5), while negative clusters have a radius of zero, which translates as the maximum distance to all data (Eq. 6). As w grows, positive clusters become narrower, while negative clusters become wider, until reaching the opposite end of the spectrum when w is 1.

The value of w was changed between 0 and 1 at steps of 0.01, measuring the confusion matrix in each step to build the ROC-AUC curve.

Table 1 shows the values used for each parameter, for a total of 12,500 combinations. The average AUC for all combinations is 0.585 with a deviation of 0.023. The best combination found corresponds to $e = 0.4$, $minpoints = 2$ and $eps = 0.2$, which resulted in a ROC-AUC of 0.671 (see Fig. 1). This value, which can be considered as low, is better than that found by the dataset authors themselves: 0,672 (see Table 4 in [19]). This shows the positive properties of clustering carried out by D3CAS.

Table 1. Values used for D3CAS parameters.

Parameter	Values used
e	0.2–10; step = 0.2
$minpoints$	2; 5; 10; 15; 20
eps	0.2–10; step = 0.2

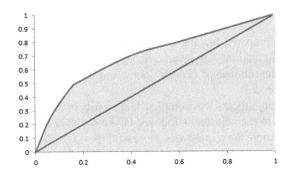

Fig. 1. ROC-AUC curve for the best configuration found.

Figure 2 shows the value of ROC-AUC for each run. As it can be seen, using a value of $e = 0.4$ (see Fig. 2a) achieved the best results. As regards *eps*, the best results were achieved using values closer to 0 (see Fig. 2b), while in the case of *minpoints*, there is no evidence that the use of any specific value achieves better results (see Fig. 2c).

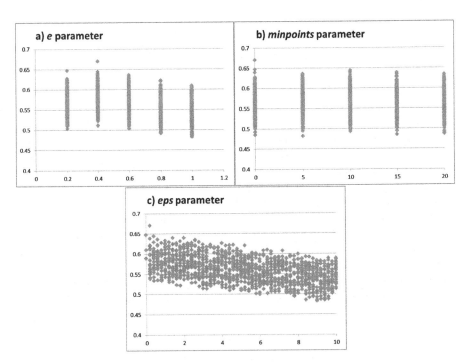

Fig. 2. AUC values obtained with the different parameter configurations. (a) *e*, (b) *minpoints* and (c) *eps*.

5   Conclusions and Future Work

In this article, D3CAS was presented, a proof of concept of a density-based dynamic clustering algorithm for data stream processing that can be run of the Spark Streaming framework.

The algorithm was tested with a simulated stream of short texts. This dataset consists in requests for free pizzas by users of reddit.com. TF-IDF was used for text representation, and the results obtained with the tests show that the configuration of D3CAS parameters requires special attention when a stream of texts is processed. In particular, the tests carried out allowed establishing that a value of 0.4 for parameter e and small values of eps yield the best results.

Experiments were carried out on a virtualized, non-distributed environment, measuring only the quality of the results obtained, not the efficiency in resource use while running the algorithm.

In the future, the algorithm will be run on a distributed environment to be able to measure and improve algorithm performance. Also, comparisons will be made both as regards results and the use of resources such as memory, communication overhead, power consumption, etc.

Additionally, tests will be run on a real environment, using a real data stream, such as the ones in Twitter or other social media.

References

1. Wang, S., Schlobach, S., Klein, M.: What is concept drift and how to measure it? In: Cimiano, P., Pinto, H.S. (eds.) EKAW 2010. LNCS (LNAI), vol. 6317, pp. 241–256. Springer, Heidelberg (2010). https://doi.org/10.1007/978-3-642-16438-5_17
2. Aggarwal, C.C.: Data streams: an overview and scientific applications. In: Gaber, M. (ed.) Scientific Data Mining and Knowledge Discovery. Springer, Berlin (2009). https://doi.org/10.1007/978-3-642-02788-8_14
3. Babcock, B., Babu, S., Datar, M., Motwani, R., Widom, J.: Models and issues in data stream systems. In: Proceedings of the Twenty-First ACM SIGMOD-SIGACT-SIGART Symposium on Principles of Database Systems (PODS 2002), New York, NY, USA, pp. 1–16. ACM (2002). https://doi.org/10.1145/543613.543615
4. Molina, R., Hasperué, W.: D3CAS: un Algoritmo de Clustering para el Procesamiento de Flujos de Datos en Spark. In: Proceedings of the XXIV Congreso Argentino de Ciencias de la Computación, pp. 452–461 (2018). ISBN 978-950-658-472-6
5. Miner, G., Elder, J., Hill, T., Nisbet, R., Delen, D., Fast, A.: Practical Text Mining and Statistical Analysis for Non-structured Text Data Applications. Academic Press, Cambridge (2012)
6. Halibas, A.S., Shaffi, A.S., Mohamed, M.A.K.V.: Application of text classification and clustering of Twitter data for business analytics. In: Majan International Conference (MIC), Muscat, pp. 1–7 (2018)
7. Li, P., et al.: Learning from short text streams with topic drifts. IEEE Trans. Cybern. **48**(9), 2697–2711 (2018). https://doi.org/10.1109/TCYB.2017.2748598

8. Jain, A., Sharma, I.: Clustering of text streams via facility location and spherical K-means. In: Second International Conference on Electronics, Communication and Aerospace Technology (ICECA), Coimbatore, pp. 1209–1213 (2018)

9. Duan, R., Li, C.: An adaptive Dirichlet multinomial mixture model for short text streaming clustering. In: IEEE/WIC/ACM International Conference on Web Intelligence (WI), Santiago, pp. 49–55 (2018)

10. Gama, J., Rodrigues, P.P.: An overview on mining data streams. In: Abraham, A., Hassanien, A.E., de Carvalho, A.P.L.F., Snášel, V. (eds.) Foundations of Computational, Intelligence Volume 6. Studies in Computational Intelligence, vol. 206. Springer, Berlin (2009). https://doi.org/10.1007/978-3-642-01091-0_2

11. Gepperth, A., Hammer, B.: Incremental learning algorithms and applications. In: European Symposium on Artificial Neural Networks (ESANN), Bruges, Belgium (2016)

12. Aggarwal, C.C., Han, J., Wang, J., Yu, P.S.: A framework for clustering evolving data streams. In: Proceedings of the 29th International Conference on Very Large Data Bases-Volume 29, pp 81–92. VLDB Endowment (2003)

13. Zhang, P., Zhu, X., Shi, Y., Wu, X.: An aggregate ensemble for mining concept drifting data streams with noise. In: Theeramunkong, T., Kijsirikul, B., Cercone, N., Ho, T.-B. (eds.) PAKDD 2009. LNCS (LNAI), vol. 5476, pp. 1021–1029. Springer, Heidelberg (2009). https://doi.org/10.1007/978-3-642-01307-2_109

14. Cao, F., Ester, M., Qian, W., Zhou, A.: Density-based clustering over an evolving data stream with noise. In: Proceedings of the SIAM International Conference on Data Mining, pp. 328–339 (2006)

15. Ester, M., Kriegel, H.-P., Sander, J., Xu, X.: A density-based algorithm for discovering clusters a density-based algorithm for discovering clusters in large spatial databases with noise. In: Proceedings of the Second International Conference on Knowledge Discovery and Data Mining, pp. 226–231 (1996)

16. Ackermann, M.R., Märtens, M., Raupach, C., Swierkot, K., Lammersen, C., Sohler, C.: StreamKM++: a clustering algorithm for data streams. ACM J. Exp. Algorithmics **17**(1), 173–187 (2012)

17. Arthur, D., Vassilvitskii, S.: k-means++: the advantages of careful seeding. In: Proceedings of the Eighteenth Annual ACM-SIAM Symposium on Discrete Algorithms, pp. 1027–1035 (2007)

18. Zhang, X., Furtlehner, C., Sebag, M.: Data streaming with affinity propagation. In: Daelemans, W., Goethals, B., Morik, K. (eds.) ECML PKDD 2008. LNCS (LNAI), vol. 5212, pp. 628–643. Springer, Heidelberg (2008). https://doi.org/10.1007/978-3-540-87481-2_41

19. Althoff, T., Danescu-Niculescu-Mizil, C., Jurafsky, D.: How to ask for a favor: a case study on the success of altruistic requests. In: Proceedings of ICWSM (2014)

20. Reed, J.W., Jiao, Y., Potok, T.E., Klump, B.A., Elmore, M.T., Hurson, A.R.: TF-ICF: a new term weighting scheme for clustering dynamic data streams, pattern recognition. In: Proceedings of the 5th International Conference on Machine Learning and Applications (ICMLA 2006) (2006)

Market Segmentation Using Data Mining Techniques in Social Networks

Eduin Olarte[1($\boxtimes$)], Marisa Panizzi[1], and Rodolfo Bertone[2]

[1] School of Information Systems,
Universidad Argentina John F. Kennedy, Bartolomé Mitre 1411,
Ciudad Autónoma de Buenos Aires C1037ABA, Argentina
eduinolarte@gmail.com, marisapanizzi@outlook.com
[2] School of Computer Science, Computer Science Research Institute LIDI
(LIDI-III), National University of La Plata, La Plata, Argentina
rbertone@lidi.info.unlp.edu.ar

Abstract. Social networks have gained great popularity during the last decade, due to the advance of new technologies and people's growing interest in generating content and sharing it with their contacts. This makes data generated in social networks grow exponentially over time.

These generated data contain information that can be analyzed, in order to discover patterns that can be of help in multiple disciplines. Marketing is one of these disciplines that is closely linked to understanding people's behaviors, tendencies and tastes. The aim of this study is to apply data mining (DM) to discover patterns in data coming from social networks. Obtaining patterns will enable to carry out different types of segmentations to help the marketing professionals direct their campaigns.

Keywords: Information exploitation · Data mining · Market segmentation · Social networks · Machine learning

1 Introduction

The concept of marketing was created to answer a question organizations often ask themselves: "Who are we trying to sell to?". Marketing is a social process by which groups and individuals satisfy their needs by creating and exchanging goods and services [1]. It is also a process that involves the identification of needs, relationships and desires of the target market.

The market is too broad and consists of different customers with different needs. Each company seeks to focus on individuals, according to their capacity, taste and age segments. To this end, companies conduct market strategies. The strategy of dividing the market into homogeneous groups is known as Segmentation. Market Segmentation consists of dividing a market into smaller groups with different needs, characteristics or behaviors that may require separate products or marketing mixes [2, 3].

Traditionally, data used to create segmentations come from collection processes such as surveys, sales history, etc. With the advent of social networks, a new source of information arose [4]. According to international measurements, it is estimated that

P. Pesado and C. Aciti (Eds.): CACIC 2018, CCIS 995, pp. 221–231, 2019.
https://doi.org/10.1007/978-3-030-20787-8_16

more than four hundred thousand Tweets are generated per minute, which represent a large amount of data to be analyzed [5]. At present, social networks provide developers with privileges to access information easily through web interfaces.

This large data set can be analyzed to identify patterns and relationships. This analysis can be done with data mining. Data mining is a multidisciplinary field that combines statistics, machine learning, artificial intelligence and database technology (Fig. 1) to establish relationships and find patterns in large datasets [6]. Identification of patterns and relationships allows the creation of different types of segmentations, thus offering solutions for companies.

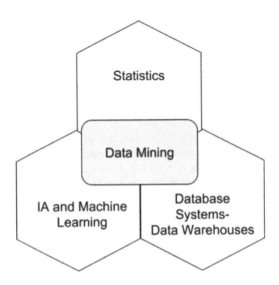

Fig. 1. Scientific disciplines that include data mining.

Data mining is the search for new, valuable and non-trivial information in large volumes of data. It is a cooperative effort of humans and computers. The best results are obtained by balancing the knowledge of human experts when describing problems and objectives with the search capabilities of computers.

In practice, the two main objectives of data mining are Prediction and Description. Prediction involves the use of some variables or fields in the data set to predict unknown or future values of other variables of interest. Description, on the other hand, focuses on finding patterns that describe the data that can be interpreted by humans.

The objectives of prediction and description are achieved through the use of data extraction techniques. Based on the type of patterns sought, different data mining techniques can be used: Classification, Clustering, Association and/or Trend Analysis [7, 12].

2 Analysis of Methodologies and Work Tools for DM Projects

This section firstly summarizes the comparative study of methodologies for data mining projects. The processes and methodologies considered for such analysis were: KDD (Knowledge discovery in databases) [8], SEMMA (Sample, Explore, Modify, Model, and Assess) [9], and CRISP-DM (Cross Industry Standard Process for Data Mining) [10]. Secondly, it synthesizes the comparative analysis of work tools used for data mining processes.

2.1 Comparative Study of Methodologies for Data Mining Projects

The process of data mining is often characterized as a multi-stage iterative process that includes data selection, data cleansing, application of data mining algorithms, evaluation, among others. A comparative study of the methodologies was carried out in order to identify whether they support equivalent stages (Table 1).

Table 1. Comparative study of methodologies for data mining projects.

Stages	KDD	SEMMA	CRISP-DM
Objectives	Pre KDD		Business understanding
			Data understanding
Preprocessing	Selection	Sample	Data preparation
	Preprocessing	Exploration	
	Transformation	Modification	
Model	Mining	Modeling	Modeling
Results	Interpretation/Evaluation	Assessment	Evaluation
Deployment	Post KDD		Installation

KDD methodology has nine stages for the process model, CRISP-DM has six and SEMMA, five stages. By examining the three data mining process models, it is observed that, at a certain point, they are equivalent to each other. Comparing them resulted in the following findings:

- The "Developing an understanding of the application domain" step of the KDD process can be identified with the "Business understanding" phase of the CRISP-DM process.
- The "Creating a target data set" and "Data cleaning and preprocessing" steps of the KDD process can be identified with the "Sample" and "Explore" stages of SEMMA, respectively, and/or can be identified with the "Data understanding" phase of the CRISP-DM process.

- The "Data transformation" step of KDD process can be identified with the "Data preparation" stage of CRISP-DM and the "Modify" stage of the SEMMA process, respectively.
- The three KDD process steps, "Choosing the right data mining task", "Choosing the right data mining algorithm" and/or "Data mining algorithm utilization" can be identified with the "Modeling" phase of CRISP-DM and/or "Model" stage of the SEMMA process, respectively.
- The "Interpreting mined patterns" step of the KDD process can be identified with the "Evaluation" phase of the CRISP-DM process and/or the "Assess" stage of the SEMMA process, respectively.
- The "Consolidating discovered knowledge" step of the KDD process can be identified with the "Deployment" phase of the CRISP-DM process.

The work methodology selected for this study is KDD, since it is currently the most widely used by experts; in addition, it represents the field related to Data Mining. This is because is considered more complete and precise, by providing steps specifically designed for the interpretation and evaluation of the results obtained after mining. By contrast, CRISP-DM and SEMMA do not implement an interpretation stage, which is crucial for the purpose of this study, since it seeks to detect useful relationship patterns among users and to interpret the impact of a marketing campaign aimed at those users.

2.2   Comparative Study of Work Tools

In this analysis, the tools were grouped into Licensed Software and Free Software (Table 2).

Table 2. Data mining tools.

Data mining tools	Free software	Weka
		RapidMiner
		KMine
		R
		Python and its data mining libraries
	Licensed Software	SAS data mining
		SPSS modeler
		Oracle data mining
		Microsoft SQL management studio

For the comparative study (Table 3), the most important characteristics of each tool were considered in order to identify whether they support equivalent characteristics.

Table 3. Comparative study of methodologies for data mining.

Characteristics	Weka	RapidMiner	R	Python	KMine	SQL
Clusterization	Yes	Yes	Yes	Yes	Yes	Yes
Mining association	Yes	Yes	Yes	Yes	Yes	Yes
Linear regression	Yes	Yes	Yes	Yes	Yes	No
Logistic regression	Yes	Yes	Yes	Yes	Yes	No
Bayesian classifiers	Yes	Yes	Yes	Yes	Yes	No
Decision trees	Yes	Yes	Yes	Yes	Yes	No
Time series analysis	Yes	No	Yes	Yes	Yes	No
Text analysis	Yes	Yes	Yes	Yes	Yes	Yes
BigData processing	Yes	No	Yes	Yes	No	No
Virtual flows	Yes	Yes	No	No	Yes	No

The language used in this study was Python, which was selected because it is dynamic, it offers a wide variety of libraries related to the machine learning field, and it is an open source. Additionally, it is widely used in science and engineering, thus users can rely on the Community's experience on data mining projects to clear up doubts about its development. For the purpose of this study, Python's Pytweet[1] library allows access to the Twitter API[2], which provides multiple access points that the social network has provided for developers.

3 Development of the Case Study

As part of the preliminary preparation, a series of interviews with marketing experts were carried out in order to acquire a general and specific knowledge of the problem. The sessions with experts were arranged in such a way that they participated in key steps of the development of this study. This is why three series of interviews were carried out for the problem posing, data review and selection, and solution validation phases. For surveying of information based on interviews, the model proposed by Martínez et al. [11] was used.

The selected technique was the Unstructured Interview. The following situations arose from the collected results:

1. A problem that a company can face is that by collecting data through surveys, interviews or observations, limited and structured data are obtained that provide a limited view of the market. On the other hand, taking into account the market's dynamism, these data can become quickly outdated, resulting in a less successful campaign, if launched time after.

---

[1] Pytweet is a pythonic library that provides a simple interface for the Twitter API. Values are normalized in Python types.

[2] "Application Programming Interface". In computer programming, an application programming interface is a set of subroutine definitions, protocols, and tools for creating software applications.

2. When generating a new digital marketing strategy through social networks, it is possible to find users who are not interested directly but represent a large number of cases for analysis. In these cases, the assertiveness of the campaign is considerably reduced. These users can be:

- Bot type or automatically created users.
- Users with scarce activity.
- Users who live in an area or country that is not targeted by the campaign.
- Users with few followers.

3. Since there is a whole universe of users of interest, it is necessary to analyze which of them generates a greater impact, and to understand those characteristics that relate them to other followers. This requires analyzing large volumes of data and it consumes a significant amount of time that can result in an outdated marketing plan. This study seeks to answer the following research enquiries:

- Is it possible to obtain social network data in real time?
- Is it possible to filter the content of those users who are not of direct interest for the Marketing campaign?
- Is it possible to make market segmentations of the followers of the account being studied using Data Mining methodologies and techniques?

According to the stated objective, an implementation instance will not be carried out; in other words, installing the development is not contemplated. However, this study does include a step by step conceptual development of the models, and the results are shown through graphs and figures that allow the marketing professional to measure their usefulness and applicability.

The analysis is limited to a single social network, because the complexity of the connection to the different APIs and the limited time available to make queries would make the data collection process excessively long. This is why it was decided to analyze a single account, since obtaining data from other accounts would require an amount of resources that are not available. In case of having such resources, the model could be scaled.

Finally, the purpose of the sample was to obtain the Tweets published in the Federal Capital area, where the variable "CapitalFederal" contains an array with the coordinates enclosing the city.

The development environment used was Anaconda[3], because it offers great benefits for handling packages and libraries. It also provides a control board that allows to manage and install the packages and applications to work on data analysis.

Twitter was chosen because it offers certain advantages that make it very interesting from the data analysis point of view. This study focuses on the analysis of an account of the above-mentioned social network with a large number of followers (Account under Study).

---

[3] It is an open source distribution of Python and R programming languages for large-scale data processing, predictive analysis and scientific computing, which aims to simplify package management and deployment.

Data extraction was performed using API REST. This application provides reading access to Twitter's public data. It does not require login information to access the accounts; therefore, data such as user tweets, users profile information and followers' information, among others, can be extracted in a very simple way. After a first analysis on Twitter, it was observed that relevant information such as age, sex, or physical characteristics, are not contained in the user profiles in the social network. Access to the users' location is limited, because they can choose whether to locate their tweets or not.

Therefore, the analysis on Twitter focused on existing data for each user that is publicly accessible through the API, such as the followers' activity, quality and interests.

A factor to be considered is the requests rate limit. The limit rate of the API is defined in 15 min intervals (or "windows") in which, depending on the method used, a certain number of requests can be made.

Initially, during the selection phase, the available data related to the selected Twitter account is analyzed. Afterwards, data from the Twitter API is obtained, selecting those that are considered relevant for the purpose of this study.

A Script is generated in Python, which includes the steps to follow to download the study data of the selected account. These steps are: (1) Authenticating and connecting to the Twitter API; (2) Obtaining profile data for each user using the GET users/lookup method; (3) Downloading and storing the last 200 tweets of each of the followers, based on the IDs obtained in step 2.

The account under study belongs to a well-known automobile manufacturer in Argentina that joined Twitter in October 2011; the reason for this is that it has published more than four thousand tweets and reaches more than fifty thousand followers. By using the API, more detailed data is obtained. Access to these data depends on having previously obtained the above described credentials, which provide a type OAuth 8 authorization.

During the data mining phase, possible scenarios associated with each type of segmentation (geographic segmentation, demographic segmentation, socioeconomic segmentation and behavioral segmentation) are set out; this seeks to solve the problem from each of these scenarios point of view, analyzing their characteristic attributes and applying the developed models with the data obtained from the previous stages. This allows to verify whether the market segmentation scenario is valid, and if it is possible to create segmentations based on the data obtained from Twitter.

In this article, we show the Geographical Segmentation Scenario. It involves dividing the analyzed information by countries, regions, cities, towns or neighborhoods. Twitter allows access to the user's location; nevertheless, some cases present drawbacks - incorrect or non-existent values.

To solve this problem, an algorithm was implemented previously, which allows to infer the user's location. Even in these cases, there are incorrect values that cannot be interpreted as a location. In order to do this, a data mining task is implemented, Rule Based Classification, which seeks to match or associate data to predefined groups (supervised learning).

These predefined data are the training set, which is prepared by humans (Experience). The model implementation requires building the training data set. For this purpose, we downloaded the Correo Argentino (Argentine Central Post Office) database. Once the training set is generated, the classifier uses it as shown in Fig. 2, where, according to the rule, it determines that the value "cap. fed" refers to the Federal Capital of Buenos Aires, Argentina.

The rule-based classifier uses a set of IF-THEN rules for classification. In the first instance, it is not necessary to generate a decision tree. In this algorithm, each rule for a given class covers many of the tuples of that class. According to the general strategy, the rules are learned one at a time. For each time rules are learned, a tuple covered by the rule is removed and the process continues for the rest of the tuples. The algorithm represented in Fig. 3 corresponds to the rule creation based on the training set.

Algorithm: Sequential coverage
  Input: data Training data
  Output: A set of IF-THEN rules
  Method: rule_set={ }; // the list of initial rules is empty for class in data
  Rule = Learn_Rule(class['location'], class['time_zone'].class['classification_location']);
  "Removes repeated rules generated by previous training
  Remove_Rules_Covered (rule_set, rule)
  # Adds a new rule
  Rule_set.apprend(rule) +
  return rule_set;

Fig. 2. Rule-generation algorithm

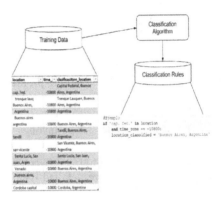

Fig. 3. Locative classifier

Evaluation phase of the model: Although the process carried out may provide an approach to the user's location, there may be cases in which the location is not obtained through the implemented classifier. For these cases, the field is left empty and is not considered for the geographical segmentation scenario. Figure 4 shows the results of the model execution. At least 70% of the data were successfully classified, while 30% could not be considered for creating the geographic segmentation.

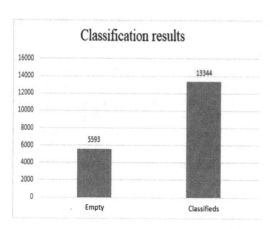

Fig. 4. Results of the model execution classification   **Fig. 5.** Concentration of followers

Finally, with the classified locations, it was possible to detect the location of 70% of the users of interest that follow the account. This information allowed to create the geographic segmentation of the followers and to create a heat map, which indicates the followers concentration density in certain regions (Fig. 5).

Generating this data also allows the creation of another geographical segmentation, a division by region, where it was observed that 80% of the account's important followers are located in the Pampa region (Fig. 6). On the other hand, as shown in Fig. 7, it is possible to create segmentations by province.

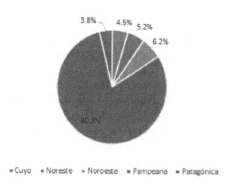

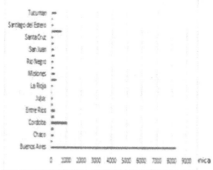

Fig. 6. Number of followers by region.   **Fig. 7.** Followers by province.

4 Conclusions and Further Work

The fundamental objective we have set for this project is to be able to create market segmentations from data obtained from social networks, through the use of Data Mining methodologies and techniques.

The choice of Twitter as the source of the data was satisfactory, because it provides a powerful API that allows data consumption, even though there were disadvantages at the data level, because Twitter shares a limited amount of user data. This did not allow segmentation with some attributes such as Age, Gender or Occupation.

It was necessary to select a development environment in order to connect to the interface supplied by the social network (API); Python was chosen for this purpose, which proved highly satisfactory, since this language currently has a lot of support from the community and has a great variety of open source libraries for multiple purposes.

One of these libraries turned out to be precise for abstracting the development of the complex implementation required for consuming an API and having to implement a pagination of its own.

The possibility of consuming the data directly from the Twitter servers provided an answer to the first problem question.

The KDD methodological process proposed was applied; through its processes, it allowed to troubleshoot the problems found. The pre-processing generated new data, based on those obtained and used as attributes to create the market segmentation.

Further works would need to be done in order to: (a) take advantage of NLP techniques (Neuro Linguistic Programming); for example, researching on emotions analysis; (b) create an application that allows analytics on any account and offer the results of the analytics in the same interface.

References

1. Kotler, P., Armstrong, G., Saunders, J., Wong, V.: Chapter 1: What is Marketing? Principles of Marketing, 3rd edn. Prentice Hall, Essex (2002). ISBN 0-273-64662-1. The European edition
2. Lamb, C.W., Hair, J.F., McDaniel, C.D.: Marketing. South-Western (2004)
3. May, P., Ehrlich, H.-C., Steinke, T.: ZIB structure prediction pipeline: composing a complex biological workflow through web services. In: Nagel, Wolfgang E., Walter, Wolfgang V., Lehner, W. (eds.) Euro-Par 2006. LNCS, vol. 4128, pp. 1148–1158. Springer, Heidelberg (2006). https://doi.org/10.1007/11823285_121
4. Chen, Z., Kalashnikov, D.V., Mehrotra, S.: Exploiting context analysis for combining multiple entity resolution systems. In: Proceedings of the 35th SIGMOD International Conference on Management of Data, SIGMOD 2009 (2009). https://doi.org/10.1145/1559845.1559869
5. Digital in 2017: Global Overview - We Are Social. (2017). https://wearesocial.com/special-reports/digital-in-2017-global-overview. Accessed 4 October 2017
6. Ashton Acton, Q. (ed.): Issues in General Science and Scientific Theory and Method, 2011 Edition (2011). ISBN: 978-1-4649-6346-9

7. Chen, M.-S., Han, J., Yu, P.S.: Watson IBM Research. Data Mining: An Overview from Database Perspective (1996). http://hanj.cs.illinois.edu/pdf/survey97.pdf

8. Fayyad, U., Piatetsky-Shapiro, G., Smyth, P.: From data mining to knowledge discovery in databases. AI Mag. **17**(3), 37–54 (1996)

9. SAS Institute Inc.: SAS Institute. White Paper, From Data to Business Advantage: Data Mining, The SEMMA Methodology and the SAS® System, Cary, NC: SAS Institute Inc (1998)

10. Chapman, P., et al.: CRISP-DM 1.0 Step by step BI guide (2000)

11. Martínez, R.G., Britos, P.V.: Ingeniería de Sistemas Expertos. Editorial Nueva Librería, Buenos Aires (2004)

12. Olarte, E., Panizzi, M., Bertone R.: Segmentación de Mercado Usando Técnicas de Minería de Datos en Redes Sociales. In: XXIV Congreso Argentino de Ciencias de la Computación. UNCPBA, Argentina (2018). ISBN 978-950-658-472-6

Hardware Architectures, Networks, and Operating Systems

Heuristic Variant for the Travelling Salesman Problem. Application Case: Sports Fishing Circuit

Ana Priscila Martínez[✉] and Lidia Marina López

Facultad de Informática, Universidad Nacional del Comahue,
Neuquén, Argentina
martinezanapriscila@gmail.com,
lidia.lopez@fi.uncoma.edu.ar

Abstract. The present work focuses on the construction of an algorithm to solve a sport fishing circuit, applying combinatorial optimization techniques in order to generate the best solution to the problem of the route for sport fishing in the province of Neuquén. The planning and management of roads for routes with preferences requires efficient systems for route optimization. Its complexity is exponential. For the resolution of this type of problems, heuristics must be used to allow feasible solutions. To model a tourist circuit associated with sport fishing, the exploration of a restricted graph is used. It is framed within the Travelling Salesman Problem. A metaheuristic Taboo search algorithm, based on a local search, is proposed to find a solution to the problem [1].

Keywords: Graph · Heuristic · Travelling Salesman Problem ·
Taboo searching · Algorithm

1 Introduction

The present work focuses on the construction of an algorithm to solve a touristic circuit with certain characteristics, applying combinatorial optimization techniques in order to generate the best solution to the problem of the route for salmon fishing in the province of Neuquén, which has two important basins: the Limay river in the south, and the Neuquén river in the north [2].

The main objective of this work is the study, construction and implementation of an algorithm that solves the assembly of a specific tourist circuit, in this case for sport fishing, using graph exploration techniques. That is, given a *start date* and an *end date* of the route, the type of fishing and the city of origin, returns an optimal path with all fishing accesses enabled for that period and that type of fishing. Departing from the origin city and ending therein.

The design of optimal routes or with restrictions on geographical routes involves the application of graph exploration algorithms and geographic information systems. Since these roads are not modified, the problem of route design, with certain preferences, fits into the variations of the classic Travelling Salesman Problem.

© Springer Nature Switzerland AG 2019
P. Pesado and C. Aciti (Eds.): CACIC 2018, CCIS 995, pp. 235–248, 2019.
https://doi.org/10.1007/978-3-030-20787-8_17

The planning and management of routes with preferences requires efficient route optimization systems that can not be addressed with exact resolution techniques, except for small problems. Heuristics must be used to find feasible solutions.

In this paper an algorithm based on graphs represented by adjacency matrix is presented, and a heuristic for obtaining the result graph.

2   Travelling Salesman Problem (TSP)

A travelling salesman wants to visit n cities, once and only once, starting with any one of them and returning to the same place from which he left. Suppose you know the distance between any pair of cities. How should you travel if you intend to minimize the total distance? [3].

This problem is known as Travelling Problem or TSP and it is one of the most prominent in the field of combinatorial optimization.

It is a complexity problem NP - difficult. Despite its apparent simplicity has not yet been able to find an algorithm that is able to solve it in a reasonable time (polynomial).

Mathematically the TSP corresponds to the problem of finding a Hamiltonian cycle of minimum distance in a complete graph $G = (V, E)$ where $V = \{1, 2, ..., n\}$ is the set of nodes and represent the cities, E is the set of branches that denote the connection between them and $d: E \rightarrow R^+$ a function that gives each $(i, j) \in E$ the distance d_{ij} between cities i and j.

A Hamiltonian cycle is the path that passes through all the vertices of a graph exactly once.

The TSP problem can be represented by graphs. The vertices are the places to visit and the arches the roads.

3   Heuristics Methods

The heuristic methods are applied procedures to solve optimization problems for which a computable algorithmic solution is not available; They seek to reach the solution from approximations.

In *combinatorial optimization*, an optimization problem is posed as a pair (F, h) where F is the set of feasible solutions of an instance of an optimization problem and $h: F \rightarrow R^+$ is the cost function [4].

The objective is to find a $f_0 \in F$ such that $h(f_0) \leq h(f)$ for all $f \in F$. The basis of the method is to assign to each $t \in F$ an environment of t, that is, a subset $N(t) \in F$ that contains atya whose elements we consider neighbors of t.

The *local search problem* belongs to the combinatorial optimization and consists of starting from an initial solution t_0, finding a $s \in N(t)$ with lower cost, in order to decrease $h(t)$, and repeat this procedure until reaching a t in which environment it is impossible to reduce the cost. If this happens, it is a local minimum. There are at least two ways to define s in each iteration. One is finding the first s that improves the cost, or another option, is to find an s that minimizes the cost especially $N(t)$ [5].

In this context, a heuristic is a mathematical function $h(f)$ defined in the nodes of a *search tree* - a data structure that allows an efficient search - which serves as an estimate of the cost of the most economical path of a given node, the target node. Heuristics are used in those local search algorithms such as egoistic search.

The egoistic search chooses the node that has the lowest value in the heuristic function. The search tree will expand the nodes that have the lowest value for $g(f) + h$ (f), where $g(f)$ is the (exact) cost of the path from the initial state to the current node. When $h(f)$ is admissible, that is, if $h(f)$ never overestimates the costs of finding the goal; the search tree is probably optimal [6, 7].

The following reasons can be mentioned to use heuristic methods:

- The problem is of such nature that no exact method is known for its resolution.
- Although there is an exact method to solve the problem, its use is computationally very expensive.
- The heuristic method is more flexible than an exact method, allowing, for example, the incorporation of difficult modeling conditions.
- The heuristic method is used as part of a global procedure that guarantees the best solution to the problem.

Heuristic methods are algorithms that do not guarantee an optimal solution, but usually find approximate solutions to the optimal result.

4 Approach of the TSP with Heuristic Algorithms

In order to enunciate the TSP through heuristic methods, different types of heuristic categories are presented. For this work, the following are studied:

Constructive Heuristics. The nearest neighbor algorithm [8] (NN) behaves like a greedy algorithm, allowing the travelling salesman to choose the nearest unvisited city as the next move.

This algorithm quickly returns a short route. For N cities randomly distributed on a plane, the average algorithm returns a path 25% longer than the smallest possible path. However, there are many cases where the distribution of cities makes the NN algorithm return the worst path.

The NN algorithm has an approximation factor[1] of order $log|V|$, where V is the number of cities, for instances that satisfy the triangular inequality.

A variation of the NN algorithm, called the Nearest Fragment Operator (NF), connects a group (fragment) of nearest unvisited cities, and can find the shortest route with successive iterations [9].

The main problem with NN is that at the end of the process there will probably be vertices whose connection will force to introduce edges of high cost. This is what is

---

[1] A well-designed approximation algorithm shows that the difference between your solution and the optimal solution is a constant factor. This factor is called the approximation factor, and is "<1 for maximization" or "> 1 for minimization". It depends on the application how close the approximate solution should be to the optimal solution.

known as *myopia* of the procedure since, in an iteration, it chooses the best available option without "seeing" that this can force to make bad choices in later iterations.

To reduce the myopia of the algorithm and increase its speed, the *candidate subgraph* concept is introduced, together with some modifications in the exploration. A candidate subgraph is a subgraph of the complete graph with the n vertices and only the edges considered "attractive" to appear in a low-cost Hamiltonian cycle. One possibility is to take, for example, the subgraph of the nearest k neighbors; that is, the subgraph with the n vertices and for each of them the edges that join it with the k nearest vertices.

Iterative Improvement. The basic idea is to start with an initial solution and make changes to improve its quality. The objective of this technique is to iteratively explore the state of solutions to find the optimal solutions. Some techniques are detailed below:

Peer-to-peer exchange [8]: Peer-to-peer exchange involves in each iteration the elimination of two edges and their replacement, with two different edges that reconnect the fragments created by the elimination of edges producing a shorter new path. This is a special case of the *k-opt* method.

Heuristic k-opt or *heuristic Lin-Kernighan* [8]: Take a given path and eliminate k edges. Reconnect the fragments forming the path, without leaving any disjoint subway (that is, not connect the two ends of the same fragment). This simplifies the TSP considerations by making it a simpler problem. Each end of a fragment has *2k-2* possibilities to be connected: from the total of *2k-ends* of fragments available, the two ends of the fragment being considered are discarded. Such a *2k-cities* restriction can be solved with a brute force method to find the lowest cost of reconnecting the original fragments. The *k-opt* technique is a special case of the *V-opt* or *variable-opt* technique.

Heuristic V-opt [8]: The *variable-opt* method is related and is a generalization of the *k-opt* method. While the *k-opt* method removes a fixed number *k* of edges from the original path, the *variable-opt* method does not set the size of the set of edges removed. Instead, this method increases the set as the search process continues. This method is considered the most powerful heuristic for the problem.

5   Case Study: Sports Fishing Circuit

The search for the optimal route of a circuit corresponds to the classic approach to the travelling salesman problem. In particular, the construction of a touristic circuit for salmonid fishing in the province of Neuquén, is the case study selected for the development of an algorithmic solution applying the preceding techniques.

5.1   Problem Statement

The TSP corresponds to a path of a graph where the origin is determined. For the case study presented it was decided to implement a heuristic algorithm, since it is demonstrated that these algorithms are very efficient finding solutions close to the optimum.

Model. The map M of the region to be studied, where the fishing accesses are geo-referenced, is modeled as a graph $G = (V, E)$. This graph complies with: The set of non-directed edges $E \in (V \times V)$ represents the segments of routes or paths between two fishing accesses. The set of vertices V represents the fishing accesses, associated with their respective geographic coordinates.

Requirements. The main objective is to start from a specific region, define only the points where there are fishing accesses of salmonids according to the needs of amateur fishermen, and return to the starting point. This stage of modeling requires first of all a process of obtaining the digital cartographic information associated to each one of the fishing zones to be worked and the pre-processing done on it.

5.2 Stages of Obtaining Requirements

The task is organized in the following stages:

Stage 1: Contact with the staff of the Undersecretariat of Tourism and the Chamber of Fisheries of the province of Neuquén.
Stage 2: Processing of the geographic information obtained.
Stage 3: Transformation of the data in structures for its computation.

The Adjacency Matrix (MA) is made, the generating base of the graph that graphically shows all the information of the fishing accesses.

This matrix has the information in kilometers, of all the distances that exist between the different points of the map, as long as there is a physical path that unites them.

Once the MA is drawn, the non-directed and labeled graph is constructed, where the weight of each edge is the distance in kilometers between each vertex, and as a vertex, the regions detailed in the aforementioned tables.

The resulting graph is the one shown in Fig. 1. Corresponds to a dense graph, difficult to follow. The same was made with the Pajek free application for network representation [10].

5.3 Taboo Search

This algorithm is attributed to Fred Glover who in 1986 states [11]:

"A bad decision based on information is better than a good random decision, since, in a system that uses memory, a bad choice based on a strategy will provide useful keys to continue the search. A good choice as a result of chance will not provide any information for further actions".

The taboo search [11] is a metaheuristic algorithm, that is, a heuristic method to solve a general computational problem type, using the parameters given by the user about generic and abstract procedures in a way that is expected to be efficient, and that can used to solve combinatorial optimization problems, such as the TSP.

A metaheuristic algorithm is applied, generally, to problems that do not have a specific algorithm or heuristic that gives a satisfactory solution; or when it is not possible to implement an optimal method, such is the case of the problem of finding an optimal salmonid fishing circuit.

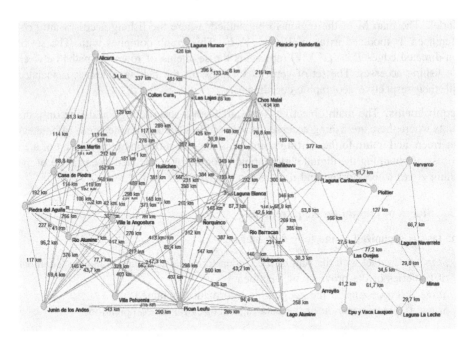

Fig. 1. Graph with Neuquén fishing access used

The taboo search uses a local search procedure or neighborhood search procedure to move iteratively from a solution x to a solution in the neighborhood of x, and even satisfy some stopping criteria. The taboo search modifies the neighbor structure for each solution as the search progresses. The supported solutions for $N^*(x)$ - the new neighborhood of x, are determined by the use of memory structures. The search then progresses by iteratively moving from a solution x to a solution x^* in $N^*(x)$.

The most important memory structure used to determine the allowed solutions to an $N^*(x)$, is the *taboo list*, which allows you to leave local optima to reach a global optimum.

In its simplest form, a taboo list is a short-term memory that contains the solutions that were visited in the recent past (less than n iterations back, where n is the number of previous solutions that are going to be stored, also called the *taboo possession*). The taboo search excludes the solutions in the taboo list of $N^*(x)$. The selected attributes of the recently visited solutions are called *taboo-active*. Possible solutions containing taboo-active elements are taboo.

Taboo lists that contain attributes may be more effective for some domains, even though they present a new problem. When only one attribute is marked as taboo, it usually results in more than one solution being marked as taboo.

Some of these solutions, which should now be avoided, could be of excellent quality and would not be visited. To mitigate this problem, the *aspiration criteria* are introduced: these can modify the taboo status of a solution, therefore including the previously excluded solution in the set of allowed solutions. A widely used aspiration criterion is to admit solutions that are better than the best known solution at the moment.

6   Algorithmic Solution Achieved

To find a solution to the problem, we decided to develop and implement a *meta-heuristic search algorithm taboo* based on a local search.

This solution is computable in a time and with an acceptable efficiency.

In the search for the solution, as the first instance, an algorithm is encoded with the taboo search method: better neighbor and then *iterative improvements* were made.

The proposed algorithm starts looking for the solution based on a possible solution previously entered. This is, from an initial arrangement with a possible solution, whose initial and final node coincide.

The initial data are: the number of nodes, name of the nodes and their description, the distances between the nodes, the type of fishing, the start and end dates of the season according to the type of fishing and the region.

The initial data structures are: the distance matrix: *distancia*, the matrix of start and end season dates: *fechaTemp*, the matrix of fishing types: *tipoPesca*, and the arrangement with the initial solution: *posibleSol*.

To fill with the initial content the arrangement *posibleSol* is performed an algorithm that searches in the matrix of fecha *fechaTemp*, and the matrix of fishing types, *tipoPesca*, fishing accesses (vertices/nodes) that meet the criteria entered by the user, which are: -City in which you want to start your journey, -Date of start and end of the planned route, -Type of fishing that you will perform, which can be: Spinning (bait cast or pot), Fly (Fly Cast), Drag (Trolling) or Spinning Exclusively with fly.

This algorithm returns the *posibleSol* with all the nodes corresponding to the fishing accesses that meet the given condition as the first solution.

6.1   Coding and Resolution of the TSP Using the Taboo Search Algorithm

This section shows how the *Travelling Salesman Problem* (TSP) is solved using a heuristic variation of the *Taboo Search algorithm*.

The *Taboo Search algorithm* [12] is an improvement over the basic local search, which attempts to overcome local search problems by not getting caught in a local minimum. In this way it allows to contemplate more results and compare them; it is achieved by allowing the acceptance of movements that do not improve the result. This implementation also allows the escape of sub-optimal solutions, through the use of a *Taboo List*.

The Taboo list is a list of possible movements that could be incorporated into a solution. These movements are *swap* operations. In the case where a movement is accepted (that is, a new better solution is found), that movement becomes taboo for a certain number of iterations.

When a movement becomes taboo, it is added to the list of taboos with a certain value called Taboo (Tabu Length). With each iteration, taboo tenure is decreased. Only when the taboo possession of a movement is zero, the movement can be realized and accepted.

A taboo list is represented as a matrix, where each cell represents the *taboo possesion* of an swap operation, if two cities are exchanged. For example, the city (1) and the city (2), the movement will become taboo in the matrix in both "(1) (2) and (2) (1)". This prevents a movement before exploring a bit.

To allow a taboo movement, it is necessary to apply criteria that allow selecting a taboo movement based on certain restrictions. For example, if a movement allows a new global solution, it is better accepted, and its taboo tenure is renewed.

In summary, the *taboo search* performs the following steps:

1. Create an initial solution, possible solution, then call it a better solution.
2. Find the best neighbor, based on the possible solution by applying certain swap operations.
3. If the best neighbor is reached by making a non-taboo movement, it is accepted as the new best solution, if not, find another better neighbor.
4. If the maximum number of iterations is reached (or some other stop condition), go to step five, otherwise, continue iterating from step two.
5. The best global solution is the best solution that we find throughout the iterations.

This heuristic method is designed to escape local optimality; it is based on the management and use of a collection of principles that serve to solve the problem in an "intelligent" way, that is, making use of flexible memory to involve two processes: -the acquisition and, -the improvement of the information; thus, by having a certain "history" of the roads already traveled and of the optimum ones found, one can avoid remaining in the same regions, and travel through new regions to find other better solutions [13].

Resolution and Coding. The code starts in the top-level class or *main*. This class contains the main method that initializes the problem data and performs the taboo search.

The algorithm tries to find the best neighbor solution in each iteration that does not imply a taboo movement. The solution is always accepted.

Each iteration starts from the solution given by the previous iteration. During the iterations, each generated solution is tracked and stored. The best solution is the one that is achieved when the predefined number of iterations has finished.

When implementing the algorithm, the issue of the number of non-existent paths between two pairs of cities or fishing accesses arises. For these cases, Dijkstra is applied.

For this, two options are contemplated: - apply Dijkstra to the best of all the paths returned by the *getMejorVecino* algorithm, or - apply Dijkstra in each iteration, after each call to *getMejorVecino*. Although, doing the latter is less efficient, it implies extra computability in each iteration, it is possible to reach optimal solutions for difficult paths to join.

Next, the algorithm Java coding of the best neighbor.

```java
public static int[] getMejorVecino(ListaTabu tabuList,
AmbienteTSP ambienteTSP,int[] solInicial) {
    int[] mejorSol = new int[solInicial.length];
    System.arraycopy(solInicial, 0, mejorSol, 0,
mejorSol.length);
    int mejorCosto = ambienteTSP.getValorFuncion(solInicial);
    int ciudad1, ciudad2 = 0;
    boolean primerVecino = true;

    for (int i = 1; i <mejorSol.length - 1; i++) {
        for (int j=2; j<mejorSol.length-1; j++){

            int[] newMejorSol = new int[mejorSol.length];
            System.arraycopy(mejorSol, 0, newMejorSol, 0,
newMejorSol.length);
                newMejorSol = intercambio(i,j, solInicial);
                int newMejorCosto =
ambienteTSP.getValorFuncion(newMejorSol);
```

| It allows a movement that doesn't improve | if (newMejorCosto > mejorCosto \|\| primerVecino) && tabuList.listaTabu[i][j] == 0) { primerVecino = false; ciudad1 = i; ciudad2= j; System.arraycopy(newMejorSol, 0, newMejorSol.length); mejorCosto = newMejorCosto; } | It isn't a taboo movement. Only when "listaTabu" is zero, the movement can be accepted. |

```java
                }
            }
        }

        if (ciudad1 != 0 ) {
            tabuList.decrementaTabu();
            tabuList.moverTabu(ciudad1, ciudad2);
        }
        return mejorSol;
}
```

"ListaTabu" decreases with each iteration.

When a movement becomes taboo, it's added to the list of taboos. (TabuList)

The algorithmic solution found combines adaptations of iterative heuristic algorithms: peer-to-peer exchange, Taboo search and Dijkstra search. It also uses auxiliary arrays with useful information to build the route and a stack structure.

Test Data

Date from: 02/07/2017 - Date until: 01/08/2017

Initial City: Neuquen (Nodo 28)

Fishing Type: Spinning (Int 0)

Result:

- Initial path: {28 29 27 13 9 6 3 1 0 28}
- Path before Dijkstra: {28 29 27 13 9 6 3 1 0 28}
- Final solution: {28 29 27 13 9 11 10 7 6 5 3 1 0 29 28}
- Cost: 1253 km

In Fig. 2 the final graph is shown. In red are the *nodoPaso (node 11, 10, 7, 5)*, these are the nodes that are only used to join two destinations, and in green the *nodoPesca*. The edges or paths are represented in the same way like the nodes. It can be seen with the naked eye that the path between the node 28 and the 29 is traveled twice.

This happens because: (1) there are no two different paths that join them, or (2) they are paths of passage, since the node 29 when visited for the first time is a node, but when visiting for the second time it is *nodoPaso*, this does not control that the nodes have already been visited.

As stated in previous paragraphs, the paths that serve to join two *nodoPesca* are not accessible through other *nodoPesca*, therefore it is not controlled if they were visited.

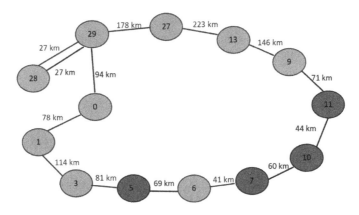

Fig. 2. Final graph of example, distinguishing the *nodoPaso* of the *nodoPesca*

7   Efficiency and Complexity

A TSP belonging to *NP-difficult* problems is modeled because the solution algorithm forms a polynomial time transformation of the generic TSP problem.

Figure 3 shows the workflow of the best neighbor algorithm along with the order of execution, which is $O(n^3)$.

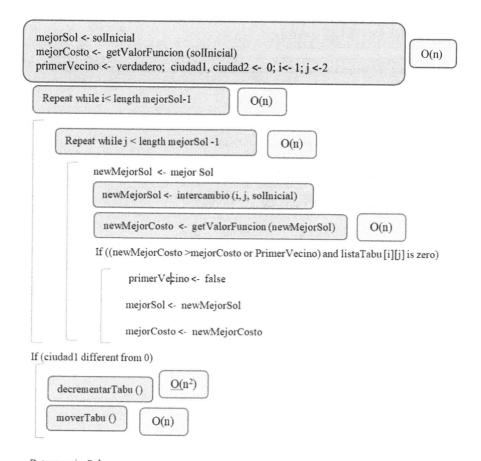

Fig. 3. Flow chart and execution orders of the final algorithm *getMejorVecino*

Figure 4 shows a general flow of the proposed algorithm. The algorithm's total execution time is calculated on it. This algorithm has a polynomial execution order, more precisely $O(n^4)$. This is mainly because the main algorithm, getBetterVeit is $O(n^3)$ and its call is within a repeating structure.

The order of an algorithm is used as a measure of its efficiency. An algorithm is considered efficient only in the polynomial case.

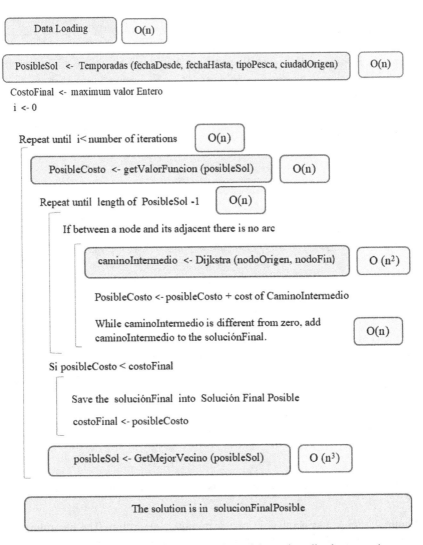

Fig. 4. Flow diagram and execution orders of the main call scheme, *main*

8   Conclusion

With this algorithm it is verified that the heuristics can find, in a reasonable time, approximate solutions to the optimum, for the Travelling Salesman Problem.

The *taboo search method* is effective for the realization of a cities circuit. Although the program exposes an indisputable effectiveness, its running cost is high, due to the number of checks and iterations that are made in its execution.

The present work presents and studies the possibility of giving a good heuristic that, from a map, the fishing accesses, a date and a type of fishing, would return an optimal fishing circuit that unites all the accesses of the province of Neuquén that meet the specified characteristic.

The way to achieve this is, first of all, by modeling the problem in the field of graphs, representing the initial map as a graph. The fishing accesses as nodes, and the routes that connect each of them as edges.

In the first place, in order to begin to solve the proposal, an algorithm is developed that generates as a result an arrangement containing those nodes that meet the condition that the user enters: type of fishing, dates and city of origin. This arrangement will be used as an initial solution to the problem.

Secondly, given the magnitude and the scope of the problem and *NP-Difficult* complexity, a heuristic algorithm with iterative improvements is constructed from adapting the *GetMejorVecino* algorithm to a metaheuristic taboo search algorithm, a method that provides good solutions for the scope of the problem raised.

This algorithm is an improvement over the basic local search, which tries to overcome the problems of the local search by not being trapped in a local minimum, allowing to contemplate more results, exchange them and compare them; accept movements that do not improve.

The solution provided is not optimal since it is only achieved by applying the brute force methodology, with a non-computable execution time.

A heuristic is then developed that proves to give good results in a short time. The immediate drawback is related to the inexistence of a path or edge that connects two consecutive nodes of the path resulting from being impracticable in real life, and therefore, makes the system not useful. This problem is solved by using a Dijkstra algorithm, to return the shortest path between two different nodes.

The final results are clearly affected by the initial solution entered. If the initial solution is bad, your final result will not be optimal, because you do not get to perform all the necessary exchanges to obtain a solution close to the optimum.

Regarding the requirements, through the developed heuristics, it is possible to fulfill the objective, the realization of an optimal fishing circuit based on the restrictions proposed at the beginning.

The results obtained are simple, clear and close to the optimum; cities that are only used to connect with other cities that are fishing ports are included, and not by pass. Concluding, the proposed algorithm is framed within the Iterative Heuristic Algorithms, and its complexity is $O(n^4)$.

References

1. Variante Heurística para el Problema del Viajante. Caso de Aplicación: Circuito de Pesca Deportiva. In: Congreso Argentino de Ciencias de la Computación. Libro de Actas, CACIC 2018. ISBN 978-950-658-472-6
2. Turismo Pesquero provincia de Neuquén. http://neuquentur.gob.ar/. Accessed 30 May 2016
3. Stockdale, M.L.: Tesis de Licenciatura - El problema del viajante: un algoritmo heurístico y una aplicación. Universidad de Buenos Aires. Facultad de Ciencias Exactas y Naturales (2011)

4. García, M.S.: Las Matemáticas del Siglo XX. Optimización Combinatoria. http://www.sinewton.org/numeros/numeros/43-44/Articulo22.pdf. Accessed 20 July 2016
5. Christofides, N.: Worst-case analysis of a new heuristic for the travelling salesman problem. Technical report 388, Graduate School of Industrial Administration, Carnegie-Mellon University, Pittsburgh (1976)
6. Pigatti, A.A.: Modelos e Algoritmos para o Problema de Alocação Generalizada (PAG) e Aplicações. Dissertação de mestrado departamento de informática. Programa de Pós-graduação em Informática, Rio de Janeiro (2003)
7. Rego, C., Gamboa, D., Glover, F., Osterman, C.: Traveling salesman problem heuristics: leading methods, implementations and latest advances. Eur. J. Oper. Res. **211**(3), 427–441 (2011)
8. Johnson, D.S., McGeoch: The traveling salesman problem: A case study in local optimization. In: Local Search in Combinatorial Optimization (1997)
9. Ray, S.S., Bandyopadhyay, S., Pal, S.K.: Genetic operators for combinatorial optimization in tsp and microarray gene ordering. Appl. Intell. **26**(3), 183–195 (2007)
10. Batagelj, V., Mrvar, A.: Pajek—analysis and visualization of large networks. In: Mutzel, P., Jünger, M., Leipert, S. (eds.) GD 2001. LNCS, vol. 2265, pp. 477–478. Springer, Heidelberg (2002). https://doi.org/10.1007/3-540-45848-4_54
11. Glover, F.: Búsqueda Tabú. In: Revista Iberoamericana de Inteligencia Artificial, pp 29–48. Melián, B. (2003)
12. Void Exception. http://voidexception.weebly.com/. Accessed 13 Sept 2016
13. El método de Búsqueda Tabú. http://tesis.uson.mx/digital/tesis/docs/18920/Capitulo2.pdf. Accessed 10 Mar 2017

Contention Analysis of Congestion Control Mechanisms in a Wireless Access Scenario

Diego R. Rodríguez Herlein[1]([⊠]), Carlos A. Talay[1],
Claudia N. González[1], Franco A. Trinidad[1], María L. Almada[1],
and Luis A. Marrone[2]

[1] Universidad Nacional de la Patagonia Austral, Río Gallegos, Argentina
{dherlein, ctalay, cgonzalez}@uarg.unpa.edu.ar,
tfracoalejandro@gmail.com, mluzalmada@gmail.com
[2] Universidad Nacional de La Plata, La Plata, Argentina
lmarrone@linti.unlp.edu.ar

Abstract. Studying the interaction between two or more flows competing for shared resources in a network, has helped in the understanding of how the congestion control mechanisms of different TCP variants, interact with each other. In these cases, it's essential to understand how such interactions come to be and to determine, under certain parameters, if it is possible for the flows to coexist in the same environment. On the other hand, it's interesting to analyze the preponderance which one might have above the others, in reference to bandwidth usage. In this paper, these aspects are analyzed in order to establish how such coexistence could be achieved, determining in what way two data flows of TCP variants might achieve a balanced state in a channel. This is done considering that nowadays, most networks present scenarios with heterogeneous paths due to mixed technologies, meaning that one might find routes that use wired and wireless mediums.

Keywords: TCP · Congestion control · WLAN · Fairness

1 Introduction

The vast majority of applications in the Internet use the Transmission Control Protocol (TCP) [1] to send data in a reliable way throughout the network. One of the more relevant aspects of TCP is congestion control. Although it wasn't part of the original implementation, it currently defines, in great part, its performance. Through congestion control [2], TCP regulates the rate of data injection in the network, utilizing a congestion window (CWND), whose size is regulated by the algorithms implementing such control.

The lack of algorithms for congestion control in the original version of the TCP standard, derived in an effect that came to be known as 'congestion collapse' [3]. Over time, various strategies were developed, the best of which are reflected on the different variants of the protocol. In this way, several methods and moments can defined in which the size of the CWND can be adjusted, and as many ways to detect and deal with congestion situations [4].

© Springer Nature Switzerland AG 2019
P. Pesado and C. Aciti (Eds.): CACIC 2018, CCIS 995, pp. 249–263, 2019.
https://doi.org/10.1007/978-3-030-20787-8_18

Internet is an heterogeneous environment, which implies that a segment transporting information might pass through diverse network conditions. Currently there isn't a single approach for congestion control in TCP that can be applied universally to all of them. One of the main causes for this, is that the diversity of network settings comes along with distinct characteristics that require optimization of different parameters [5]. The first proposal, Tahoe, introduced the basic technique of gradually probing network resources and relying on packet losses to detect that a limit has been reached. Unfortunately, this technique creates an inefficient use of the network. Some solutions to the problem of efficiency include algorithms that refine the principle of congestion control by making more optimistic assumptions about the network (Reno, New Reno) [6]; by improving TCP to include the capability for extended reports to the receiver (SACK); or by allowing the sender to estimate the state of the network in a more precise way (FACK). Another approach is to introduce alternative metrics for evaluating the state of the network, recurring to proactive methods, which are based on estimating the length of the queue through the observation of packet delays (Vegas, Veno).

The basic principles of congestion control from host to host may not only solve the problem of direct congestion, but also provide a property for prioritizing simple traffic. For instance, LP-TCP (Low Priority) aims to provide a chance to send non-critical data in a trusted way without interfering with other data transmissions.

Another group is focused on solving the problem of bad utilization of high velocity/high latency channels (hight BDP). The firsts proposals to tackle this problem (HS-TCP, H-TCP) introduced simple, but highly optimistic and aggressive policies, to poll networks in search of available resources. Subsequent proposals employed smarter techniques to make use of aggressive congestion control only when the network is considered free from it and conservative during a state of congestion. CUBIC uses packet loss to establish a limit for network resources, which is used to estimate its current state. Other group of proposals (C-TCP, Illinois) [7] deduces the state of the network based on secondary estimation techniques analyzing delays.

Due to TCP being thought of as a protocol for wired networks, its development was guided by the idea that packed loss was caused only by network congestion and estimating a near-zero loss rate in transit. With the emergence and demand for mobility, the TCP standard developed for wired networks was used in devices with wireless links. However, the properties of such links were different from those of the wired ones.

When using wireless connections, packet losses and packet delays are not caused exclusively by congestion. They are produced also by packet damage in transit [8], which might lead to an inefficient behavior from the protocol in such environments. The losses or damages to the information in transit, are fundamentally due to the nature of the wireless medium, which is the main one used in networks with mobile nodes. Device mobility may produce a path change, packet reordering, packet loss in transit and out-of-range disconnections. Wireless channels are prone to a higher error rates (BER) due to signal attenuation, interference, obstacles and fading through multiple tracks, which could generate packet loss or the reception of damaged packets by the receiver. Also, wireless channels are shared, which limits the capacity of an node to send packets due to the competition for the use of the medium shared by several nodes.

Due to its characteristics, TCP can't react adequately to packet losses that are not related to congestion, which is why wireless networks pose such challenges in terms of performance. If a data packet is lost because of interference in the transmission channel, even if there isn't a buffer overflow (congestion), TCP reduces the CWND in an incorrect manner. Instead, it should only recover from the loss and continue with the transmission at the same rate. This behavior produces an important decrease in performance.

To solve this problem, there are two different approaches: The first one maintains the original concept of TCP from host to host and thinks of the network as a black box, implying that no explicit information about it is received. This paper tackles some of the solutions that implement this approach. As an example, TCP Westwood uses packet loss combined with end-to-end bandwidth estimation, establishing the size of the CWND and the slow start threshold in order to improve the use of the link.

Other approaches use explicit information about the state of the network, or give up entirely on the idea of *host to host*, choosing to use completely different strategies. Some of these are: the use of intermediary nodes that divulge the state of the network, link layer retransmissions, or the isolation of wireless transmission routes prone to error from the wired ones by using an intermediary host.

An efficient use of the network doesn't rely only upon a TCP flow that can take advantage of the resources, but also on how well it interacts with others in the same network. Efficiency isn't the only important parameter for congestion control algorithms; they must also enforce a fair use of shared resources, specially bandwidth. This means that each flows shares an equitable portion of the resources.

It's because of this that contention analysis between two data flows, whether they use the same congestion control algorithms or not, can provide a vision about how bandwidth is distributed when different strategies are confronted. Studying the confrontation of protocols under these conditions gives rise to what's known as fairness. It's interesting to explore in detail the variants and the effects derived from this phenomenon [9]. Fairness is a measure of how a TCP flow affects other flows and how it's affected by them, in terms of bandwidth utilization.

Exploring this path, it was chosen a simple model with only two competing flows, sharing a node to generate bottleneck effect, in an heterogeneous scenario. This model could represent a wireless access network.

Of the TCP variants analyzed here, there are some papers about contention analysis of flows [10], including some with contention of different variants of congestion control for TCP [11]. However, the case study is based on a hybrid scenario, adding the complexity with which different congestion control mechanisms would have to deal in such networks.

2   Case Study

In order to perform the tests from which the data was extracted, a scenario like the one showed on Fig. 1 was created. This model was implemented through a discrete events simulator, called Network Simulator 2 (version 2.35) [12]. As it can be seen, the model represents a scenario with mixed links, with two fixed nodes with wired connections, a base station, and two nodes with wireless connections. This setting could represent a WLAN access network.

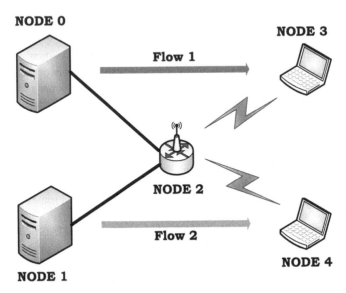

Fig. 1. Study model.

The wired links connecting the fixed nodes (0) and (1) to the base station (2) have a full duplex connection, a bandwidth of 10 Mb/s and a delay of 2 ms. The link that connects the base station (2) to the wireless nodes (3) and (4) has a 1 Mb/s bandwidth, with MAC 802.11. Each test was executed under the assumption that wireless nodes have no movement.

In each simulation, the first TCP flow was established from the node (0) (sender/source) to the node (3) (receiver/destination), while the second flow was set to go from node (1) to node (4). In order to avoid external influences that might affect the results, only two protocols are confronted at a time.

Each simulation was done independently. In every one of them, different TCP variants were confronted, including each against itself. The variants used were: Reno, New Reno, SACK, FACK, Vegas, Veno, LP (Low Priority), Westwood, HS (High Speed), H-TCP, Hybla, BIC, Cubic, C-TCP (Compound) and Illinois.

For each pair of variants, there were two independent simulations, interchanging the beginning and ending order of each flow. The first flow begins its transmission at 5 s after the simulation starts and it ends at 105 s. The second flow starts at 15 s and ends at 120 s.

These simulations and results are based on the paper "*Un análisis de comportamiento entre distintos mecanismos de control, de congestión ensayados sobre una topología mixta*", published at the *XXIV Congreso Argentino de Ciencias de la Computación* [13].

For each simulation, the average throughput and the Packet Delivery Ratio (PDR) were obtained from the corresponding trace files, with the use of AWK scripts. The average throughput was calculated by adding the instant throughput of all of the outgoing packets from the source node of a flow, within the interval going from 40 to 100 s. The PDR for each flow was obtained by calculating the quotient between successfully received packets in the destination and the total of packets sent in the same time interval. Analogously, the values of instant throughput and CWND were obtained for each flow.

The reasoning behind only taking samples in the time interval between 40 and 100 s, is being able to analyze network resource utilization by the competing flows, in a relatively stable state. In this way, the typical oscillations of transient states can be avoided, to analyze the behavior in a common track for a established communication.

For the comparison of competing TCP variants, a metric resulting from the product of the average throughput and the PDR corresponding to each simulation and each flow was used.

$$TPP = \text{Average Throughput} * PDR \tag{1}$$

Based on this metric, it's possible to do an evaluation of the behavior of two protocols coexisting in the same track. The metric in the Eq. (1) gives an idea of how each intervening protocol utilizes a percentage of the bandwidth, but doesn't provide any more data about the instantaneous throughput variations from the time the transmission begins until it gets to a balanced state [13]. Because of this, it's convenient to resort to other metrics in order to be able to evaluate this behavior in a more exhaustive way, such that it provides more information about it.

The measurement of fairness or justice between a set of x_j flows disputing the bandwidth, can be accomplished by a fairness index (FI), defined as follows:

$$f(x1, x2, x3. \ldots xn) = \frac{\left[\sum_{j=1}^{n} xj \right]^2}{n \sum_{j=1}^{n} (xj)^2} \tag{2}$$

Where, the terms of the Eq. (2) correspond to:

f is the Fairness Index, $0 \leq f \leq 1$;
n is the number of simultaneous flows;
x_j is the throughput of flow j.

On the other hand, if one takes two flows, where flow A begins, and a few moments later, flow B begins, the convergence time (CT) can be defined as the time it takes for flow B to achieve 80% of the throughput of flow B. CT can be calculated using the following equation:

$$Tc = T_{80} - T_{f2} \tag{3}$$

Where, the terms of the Eq. (3) correspond to:

T_c is convergence time (CT);

T_{80} is the time in which flow A's throughput is equal to 80% of flow B's throughput;

T_{f2} is the start time for flow B.

Incorporating these metrics, a series of tests were done, obtaining the results that will be discussed next.

3   Tests and Result Discussion

Taking into account the design of the study model (Fig. 1), some tests were conducted that allowed for the construction of four matrices. This is the result of confronting 17 TCP variants, which can be observed in the Tables 1, 2, 3 and 4, where the rows and columns represent the ones that were analyzed.

In the first matrix (Table 1), each cell shows the TPP of the confrontation between the TCP variant of the row and the one from the column, being the former the one that starts transmitting first.

Table 1. TPP obtained for the flows that start their transmission first, showed in rows.

	Bic	Compound	Cubic	Fack	Highspeed	HTCP	Hybla	Illinois	LowPriority	NewReno	Reno	Sack	Tahoe	Vegas	Veno	Westwood	YeAH
Bic	0,311	0,317	0,315	0,314	0,317	0,319	0,274	0,314	0,317	0,318	0,314	0,314	0,318	0,538	0,316	0,316	0,280
Compound	0,316	0,316	0,317	0,315	0,316	0,316	0,256	0,315	0,316	0,313	0,315	0,315	0,313	0,520	0,315	0,314	0,287
Cubic	0,317	0,314	0,315	0,310	0,314	0,315	0,270	0,318	0,314	0,315	0,312	0,312	0,315	0,564	0,315	0,314	0,293
Fack	0,320	0,317	0,316	0,322	0,317	0,312	0,255	0,314	0,317	0,315	0,322	0,322	0,315	0,562	0,315	0,318	0,303
Highspeed	0,316	0,316	0,317	0,315	0,316	0,316	0,256	0,315	0,316	0,313	0,315	0,315	0,313	0,520	0,315	0,314	0,287
HTCP	0,311	0,317	0,315	0,314	0,317	0,319	0,273	0,314	0,317	0,318	0,314	0,314	0,318	0,538	0,316	0,316	0,279
Hybla	0,339	0,347	0,345	0,367	0,347	0,345	0,296	0,382	0,347	0,389	0,353	0,356	0,389	0,571	0,445	0,347	0,344
Illinois	0,320	0,316	0,316	0,317	0,316	0,319	0,264	0,315	0,316	0,315	0,317	0,317	0,315	0,539	0,319	0,316	0,266
LowPriority	0,316	0,316	0,317	0,315	0,316	0,316	0,256	0,315	0,316	0,313	0,315	0,315	0,313	0,520	0,315	0,314	0,287
NewReno	0,312	0,315	0,318	0,315	0,315	0,318	0,230	0,316	0,315	0,318	0,318	0,318	0,318	0,444	0,321	0,317	0,305
Reno	0,320	0,317	0,316	0,322	0,317	0,312	0,269	0,314	0,317	0,315	0,322	0,322	0,315	0,562	0,315	0,318	0,264
Sack	0,320	0,317	0,316	0,322	0,317	0,312	0,265	0,314	0,317	0,315	0,322	0,322	0,315	0,562	0,315	0,318	0,307
Tahoe	0,312	0,315	0,318	0,315	0,315	0,318	0,230	0,316	0,315	0,318	0,318	0,318	0,318	0,444	0,321	0,317	0,305
Vegas	0,061	0,063	0,063	0,063	0,063	0,062	0,034	0,068	0,063	0,062	0,063	0,063	0,062	0,313	0,062	0,066	0,049
Veno	0,317	0,313	0,320	0,317	0,313	0,306	0,213	0,315	0,313	0,318	0,317	0,317	0,318	0,590	0,318	0,317	0,258
Westwood	0,315	0,314	0,317	0,319	0,314	0,322	0,290	0,315	0,314	0,313	0,319	0,319	0,313	0,564	0,313	0,322	0,263
YeAH	0,335	0,318	0,311	0,320	0,318	0,317	0,311	0,317	0,318	0,317	0,315	0,313	0,317	0,479	0,317	0,328	0,329

In order to facilitate the interpretation of the obtained values, they've been grouped according to their TPP values within certain intervals. These can be seen in the Tables 1 and 2 in a gray scale, defined as: (0 to 0,200), (0,201 to 0,300), (0,301 to 0,400) and (0,401 to 1).

In the second matrix (Table 2), it's used the same criteria as in Table 1, with the difference that the value of the cell represents the TPP value of the TCP variant that starts transmitting second.

Table 2. TPP obtained for the flows that start their transmission second, showed in columns.

	Bic	Compound	Cubic	Fack	Highspeed	HTCP	Hybla	Illinois	LowPriority	NewReno	Reno	Sack	Tahoe	Vegas	Veno	Westwood	YeAH
Bic	0,311	0,318	0,316	0,317	0,318	0,317	0,355	0,312	0,318	0,318	0,317	0,317	0,318	0,106	0,318	0,314	0,349
Compound	0,316	0,317	0,316	0,316	0,317	0,321	0,372	0,316	0,317	0,315	0,316	0,316	0,315	0,126	0,314	0,315	0,340
Cubic	0,319	0,314	0,313	0,314	0,314	0,319	0,352	0,315	0,314	0,316	0,314	0,313	0,316	0,086	0,317	0,313	0,337
Fack	0,321	0,319	0,317	0,325	0,319	0,315	0,378	0,315	0,319	0,315	0,325	0,325	0,315	0,086	0,314	0,319	0,331
Highspeed	0,316	0,317	0,316	0,316	0,317	0,321	0,372	0,316	0,317	0,315	0,316	0,316	0,315	0,126	0,314	0,315	0,340
HTCP	0,311	0,318	0,316	0,317	0,318	0,317	0,354	0,312	0,318	0,318	0,317	0,317	0,318	0,106	0,318	0,314	0,346
Hybla	0,285	0,279	0,281	0,262	0,279	0,290	0,334	0,248	0,279	0,249	0,271	0,280	0,249	0,078	0,184	0,281	0,285
Illinois	0,317	0,320	0,312	0,317	0,320	0,317	0,364	0,313	0,320	0,315	0,317	0,317	0,315	0,104	0,319	0,317	0,361
LowPriority	0,316	0,317	0,316	0,316	0,317	0,321	0,372	0,316	0,317	0,315	0,316	0,316	0,315	0,126	0,314	0,315	0,340
NewReno	0,314	0,315	0,316	0,317	0,315	0,316	0,405	0,315	0,315	0,319	0,319	0,319	0,319	0,191	0,317	0,313	0,334
Reno	0,321	0,319	0,317	0,325	0,319	0,315	0,355	0,315	0,319	0,315	0,325	0,325	0,315	0,086	0,314	0,319	0,369
Sack	0,321	0,319	0,317	0,325	0,319	0,315	0,369	0,315	0,319	0,315	0,325	0,325	0,315	0,086	0,314	0,319	0,326
Tahoe	0,314	0,315	0,316	0,317	0,315	0,316	0,405	0,315	0,315	0,319	0,319	0,319	0,319	0,191	0,317	0,313	0,334

To understand the values detailed in Table 1, one can take as an example the confrontation between Cubic and Hybla. If their corresponding TPP values are analyzed, in the case that Cubic begins, one gets a value of 0,207. On the other hand, the value when Hybla begins, is 0,345. These would be found as the intersection between the row corresponding to the protocol that starts first and the column for the protocol that starts second. In both cases, the TPP value in Table 1 corresponds to the protocol that starts first. If one desires the corresponding value for the protocol that starts last, one should do an analogous search on Table 2.

When these two TCP variants compete for resources, one can observe a certain preponderance from Hybla.

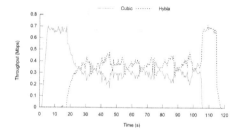

Fig. 2. Throughput vs. Time

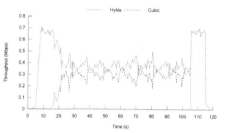

Fig. 3. Throughput vs. Time

As it can be seen on Figs. 2 and 3, Hybla tends to hog the bandwidth available, trying to transmit the most amount of data possible in detriment of Cubic. The following figures of CWND vs. Time can help to understand this phenomenon:

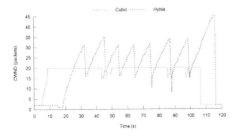
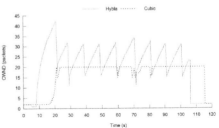

Fig. 4. CWND vs. Time   **Fig. 5.** CWND vs. Time

In the Figs. 4 and 5, one can see the way in which the congestion control algorithms of both variants, adjust the size of the CWND through time. It can be seen that the slight preponderance of Hybla over Cubic, is reflected on the aggressiveness of the former, due to the constant attempts to increase the transmission rate, incrementing the size of the CWND. This is only limited when it reaches a state of congestion. Hybla's aggressive behavior provokes periodic congestion states that influence the function of Cubic's congestion control, that also reacts to them and tends to reduce its CWND to avoid a collapse in the channel.

It can be seen that the use of TPP values alone can't explain the behavior of the protocols, reason why the figures of Throughput vs. Time were used: to appreciate the instantaneous variations for each flow. On the other hand, through the CWND vs. Time figures, one can analyze the protocol's aggressiveness to position itself on top for the transmission of data in the channel.

Analyzing the values for the instantaneous throughput and the size of the CWND, one can be appreciate, in a qualitative manner, the evolution in time for the data flows. On the other hand, through variations in the CWND, one can appreciate how the congestion control algorithms attempt to deploy their strategies in order to adapt to the available bandwidth. In this way, one can approximate the aggressiveness manifested by certain protocols and the way in which they try to acquire the biggest amount of available bandwidth to transmit data.

With the objective of quantifying the results of the strategies used by the congestion control algorithms of the 17 tested variants, another two matrices were build (Tables 3 and 4). These tables represent the fairness index and the convergence time respectively.

Table 3. Fairness index values

	Bic	Compound	Cubic	Fack	Highspeed	HTCP	Hybla	Illinois	LowPriority	NewReno	Reno	Sack	Tahoe	Vegas	Veno	Westwood	YeAH
Bic	0,999	0,999	0,999	1,000	0,999	1,000	0,998	0,999	0,999	1,000	1,000	1,000	1,000	0,777	0,999	0,999	0,996
Compound	0,999	0,999	0,999	1,000	0,999	1,000	0,996	0,999	0,999	1,000	1,000	1,000	1,000	0,805	0,998	0,999	0,999
Cubic	0,999	0,999	0,999	1,000	0,999	1,000	0,999	0,999	0,999	1,000	1,000	1,000	1,000	0,749	0,999	0,999	0,999
Fack	1,000	1,000	0,999	1,000	1,000	1,000	0,990	0,999	1,000	1,000	1,000	1,000	1,000	0,747	0,998	1,000	1,000
Highspeed	0,999	0,999	0,999	1,000	0,999	1,000	0,996	0,999	0,999	1,000	1,000	1,000	1,000	0,805	0,998	0,999	0,999
HTCP	0,999	0,999	0,999	1,000	0,999	1,000	0,999	0,999	0,999	1,000	1,000	1,000	1,000	0,777	0,999	0,999	0,997
Hybla	0,991	0,986	0,988	0,978	0,986	0,994	0,998	0,960	0,986	0,970	0,976	0,989	0,970	0,725	0,899	0,986	0,986
Illinois	0,999	1,000	0,999	1,000	1,000	1,000	0,997	0,999	1,000	1,000	1,000	1,000	1,000	0,775	0,999	1,000	0,993
LowPriority	0,999	0,999	0,999	1,000	0,999	1,000	0,999	0,999	0,999	1,000	1,000	1,000	1,000	0,805	0,998	0,999	0,999
NewReno	0,999	0,999	0,999	0,988	0,999	0,999	0,985	0,999	0,999	0,987	0,987	0,987	0,987	0,904	0,999	0,999	1,000
Reno	1,000	1,000	0,999	1,000	1,000	1,000	0,999	0,999	1,000	1,000	1,000	1,000	1,000	0,747	0,998	1,000	0,992
Sack	1,000	1,000	0,999	1,000	1,000	1,000	0,997	0,999	1,000	1,000	1,000	1,000	1,000	0,747	0,998	1,000	1,000
Tahoe	0,999	0,999	0,999	0,988	0,999	0,999	0,985	0,999	0,999	0,987	0,987	0,987	0,987	0,904	0,999	0,999	1,000
Vegas	0,705	0,704	0,714	0,703	0,704	0,707	0,696	0,714	0,704	0,705	0,703	0,703	0,705	1,000	0,707	0,710	0,680
Veno	0,999	0,999	0,999	1,000	0,999	1,000	0,979	1,000	0,999	1,000	1,000	1,000	1,000	0,704	0,998	1,000	0,988
Westwood	0,999	0,999	0,999	1,000	0,999	1,000	0,999	0,999	0,999	1,000	1,000	1,000	1,000	0,743	0,999	0,999	0,994
YeAH	0,992	0,996	0,997	0,999	0,996	0,998	0,996	0,996	0,996	0,998	0,997	0,999	0,998	0,842	0,994	0,992	0,998

Table 3 shows the fairness index. This metric evidences the way in which two protocols negotiate available bandwidth usage. According to the definition, this value varies between 0 and 1. When it takes the value of 1, both protocols have used the available bandwidth in an equitable manner; as it gets closer to 0, the distribution of bandwidth gets more and more inequitable.

Table 4. Convergence time values

	Bic	Compound	Cubic	Fack	Highspeed	HTCP	Hybla	Illinois	LowPriority	NewReno	Reno	Sack	Tahoe	Vegas	Veno	Westwood	YeAH
Bic	5,900	5,400	5,300	1,400	5,400	3,300	8,900	5,400	5,400	1,800	1,400	1,400	1,800	N/C	7,800	5,800	5,900
Compound	6,400	5,900	5,450	1,900	5,900	3,900	8,900	5,900	5,900	2,400	1,900	1,900	2,400	N/C	10,450	6,450	6,900
Cubic	6,400	3,450	5,400	1,850	3,450	3,900	8,400	3,450	3,450	1,900	1,850	1,850	1,900	N/C	9,400	6,400	6,450
Fack	5,650	5,150	4,850	1,850	5,150	3,150	7,350	5,150	5,150	1,850	1,850	1,850	1,850	N/C	11,150	4,650	5,650
Highspeed	6,400	5,900	5,450	1,900	5,900	3,900	8,900	5,900	5,900	2,400	1,900	1,900	2,400	N/C	10,450	6,450	6,900
HTCP	5,900	5,400	5,300	1,400	5,400	3,300	8,900	5,400	5,400	1,800	1,400	1,400	1,800	N/C	7,800	5,800	5,900
Hybla	9,850	13,100	6,600	4,250	13,100	5,850	14,650	27,000	13,100	3,600	13,250	4,250	3,600	N/C	70,012	13,150	14,150
Illinois	5,900	5,550	4,900	0,900	5,550	3,050	8,400	5,550	5,550	0,900	0,900	0,900	0,900	N/C	8,400	6,400	5,550
LowPriority	6,400	5,900	5,450	1,900	5,900	3,900	8,900	5,900	5,900	2,400	1,900	1,900	2,400	N/C	10,450	6,450	6,900
NewReno	6,350	6,900	5,350	15,550	6,900	3,400	9,100	6,900	6,900	16,050	16,050	16,050	16,050	N/C	7,900	5,350	6,350
Reno	5,650	5,150	4,850	4,850	5,150	3,150	7,350	5,150	5,150	1,850	1,850	1,850	1,850	N/C	11,150	4,650	5,650
Sack	5,650	5,150	4,850	1,850	5,150	3,150	7,350	5,150	5,150	1,850	1,850	1,850	1,850	N/C	11,150	4,650	5,650
Tahoe	6,350	6,900	5,350	15,550	6,900	3,400	9,100	6,900	6,900	16,050	16,050	16,050	16,050	N/C	7,900	5,350	6,350
Vegas	N/C	N/C	N/C	N/C	N/C	N/C	N/C	N/C	N/C	N/C	N/C	N/C	N/C	0,850	N/C	N/C	N/C
Veno	5,400	4,400	4,950	1,150	4,400	2,950	4,900	4,400	4,400	1,150	1,150	1,150	1,150	N/C	10,950	5,450	4,950
Westwood	6,350	6,350	5,350	1,700	6,350	3,350	3,900	6,350	6,350	1,700	1,700	1,700	1,700	N/C	7,850	5,350	6,350
YeAH	5,800	10,900	11,500	2,900	10,900	5,400	12,900	10,900	10,900	3,400	2,900	2,900	3,400	N/C	14,400	4,900	9,800

Table 4 shows the convergence time. When flow B starts transmitting, flow A is using the entire channel capacity without any challenge. Every network resource is available to it, so the bandwidth utilization depends only on its efficiency. Once the second flow is introduced, it starts demanding bandwidth to transmit its own data. At this point, a transient state is produced, and in the case of fairness, flow A starts to yield bandwidth as the flow B starts to gain it. In this way, one can think of this metric as the point in which the flow B reaches 80% of the throughput of flow A, who concedes the bandwidth.

In the same Table, some of the values are shown as N/C. This is because in some cases there isn't a time in which the differences between the instant values of throughput for both flows is less than 20% and, in which it maintains a fair and balanced state within that range.

To understand the different possibilities that can occur in the confrontation of protocols, below there's a series of figures representing 5 significant cases, chosen among the available data.

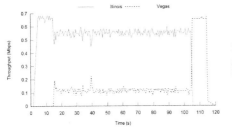

Fig. 6. Throughput - Illinois Vs. Vegas. FI = 0,775; CT = N/C

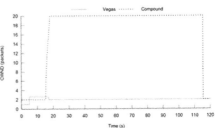

Fig. 7. CWND - Illinois Vs. Vegas

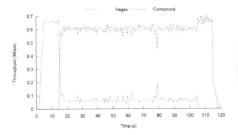

Fig. 8. Throughput - Vegas vs. Compound. FI = 0,714; CT = N/C

Fig. 9. CWND - Vegas vs. Compound

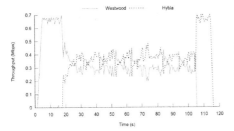

Fig. 10. Throughput - Westwood Vs. Hybla. FI = 1; CT = 0,39 s.

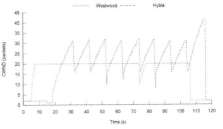

Fig. 11. CWND - Westwood Vs. Hybla

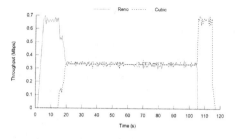

Fig. 12. Throughput - Reno vs. Cubic.
FI = 0,999; CT = 4,85 s.

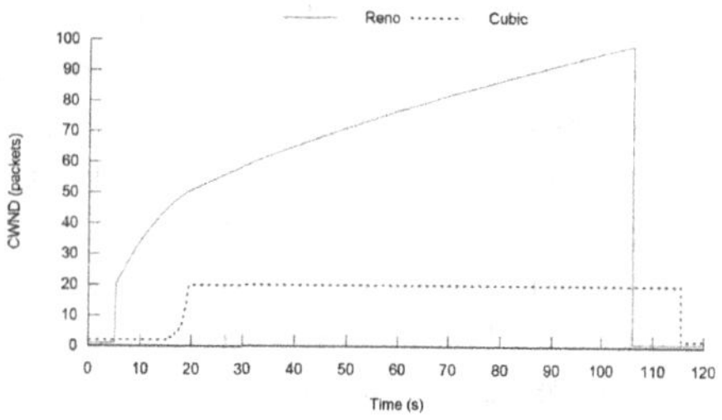

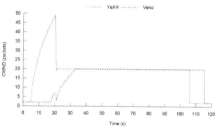

Fig. 13. CWND - Reno vs. Cubic

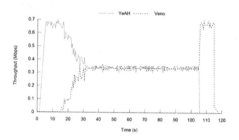

Fig. 14. Throughput - YeAH vs. Veno.
FI = 0,994; CT = 14,4 s.

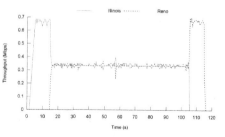

Fig. 15. CWND - YeAH vs. Veno

The previous figures (Figs. 2, 3, 4, 5, 6, 7, 8, 9, 10, 11, 12, 13, 14 and 15) correspond to representative cases on the totality of tests performed. They show how throughput and CWND vary through time in a qualitative manner. Each description has been accompanied with the corresponding values for CT and FI metrics. In this way, CT indicates how fast both protocols reach a balanced state in bandwidth distribution and FI signify how equable it is. To explain these concepts better, two extreme cases have been selected. In Fig. 16, it can be seen the confrontation between Hybla and Veno. It evidences that even though they reach a balanced state, it's only at the end of the test. On the other hand, FI shows that bandwidth distribution is not that equitable. Hybla dominates throughout the majority of the run-through and Veno only scales its throughput in the measure that its congestion control algorithms would allow to reach that balanced state.

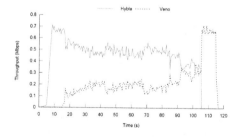

Fig. 16. Throughput - Hybla Vs. Veno.
FI = 0,899; CT = 70,012 s.

Fig. 17. Throughput - Illinois Vs. Reno.
FI = 1; CT = 0,9 s.

In the second case (Fig. 17), the opposing case is shown. CT is exiguous in comparison to other cases, reaching barely 0,9 s. At the beginning of the transmission, Veno reaches an equitable bandwidth distribution that is maintained until the very end, when Illinois finishes transmitting its data. When Illinois comes to conclude its transmission, Reno takes over the medium and transmits the remaining volume of data. At last, it can be seen a fairness index of 1 (with an error of 0,1%). Because of this, the distribution of bandwidth is strongly equitable.

Vegas represents a particular case. As it can be seen on Tables 1 and 2, it gets reduced bandwidth portions in relation to any other protocol that shares the same medium. This information can be confirmed through the analysis of the Tables 3 and 4, and it can be seen clearly on the Figs. 6 and 8. However, when an instance of Vegas shares a medium with another flow of the same kind, it reaches fairness in a reduced convergence time, as it can be seen on Fig. 18. Figure 19 shows the congestion window's size evolution for both flows. These considerations are take into account Vega's characteristic parameters (alpha and beta), defined by defect in NS-2. Nevertheless, its performance can be improved by adjusting their values [14].

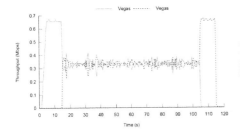
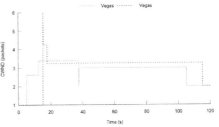

Fig. 18. Throughput - Vegas Vs. Vegas. FI = 1; CT = 0,85 s.   **Fig. 19.** CWND - Vegas vs. Vegas

The tests confronted all the protocols against each other, which implies the confrontation of their corresponding congestion controls. In this way, one can study the behavior of one protocol against every other, and even again itself. Considering the heterogeneity of the Internet and the fact that a TCP flow can pass through different types of connections between the sender and the receiver, it's interesting to evaluate the behavior of the named variants on a hybrid network. Also, one must take into account that not all of them are able to coexist with each other. In these cases, it's worth noting how the TPP measurements (Tables 2 and 3) show how some of the most aggressive variants hog all the bandwidth for their own data transmission, while others are left vulnerable against them.

Analyzing the obtained data and their figures, three kind of basic behaviors can be typified (taking into account two protocols A and B, where A starts first and after a certain time, B does). These are:

- Case 1: When protocol A starts, it uses the maximum amount of bandwidth available. When B starts, it's relegated to the possibility of growing in resource utilization, stabilizing itself in a value of throughput significantly less than that of A.

Here, Vegas, even being the one that starts, it's particularly sensitive in relation to others. As examples, Illinois vs. Vegas (Fig. 6) and Vegas vs. Compound (Fig. 8), are representative of this behavior. In them, one can see that Vegas, starting its transmission second (vs. Illinois) or first (vs. Compound), renounces its participation in the use of available bandwidth.

- Case 2: When the protocol A begins, it uses the majority of the bandwidth available, but when protocol B starts, it overcomes protocol A, acquiring a biggest portion of resources and reducing noticeably the amount used by the other. The simulation of Westwood vs. Hybla (Fig. 10) show Hybla's aggressiveness to hog bandwidth, endorsed by the evolution of its CWND (Fig. 11). This example is representative of this kind of behavior.
- Case 3: Protocol A starts transmitting and captures the biggest amount of bandwidth available. When protocol B starts, there are fluctuations where none of them appears to exercise a clear predominance over the other and gradually, they come to a equitable distribution of the bandwidth. Some examples are Reno vs. Cubic (Fig. 12) and YeAH vs. Veno (Fig. 14). In these cases, the evolution of the instantaneous throughput determines an almost equal utilization of bandwidth by both parts. Reaching this point of balances can be achieved in a relatively short span of time (as in Reno vs. Cubic), or gradually (as in YeAH vs. Veno). The latter is particularly interesting to analyze.

Analyzing different confrontations, one can see that Vegas's congestion control algorithm doesn't allow it to sustain a high bandwidth usage when it competes against the rest of the variants. In every case, Vegas resigns bandwidth and it's relegated to the background.

At the other end, protocols like Hybla and Illinois (with congestion control algorithms designed for high velocity networks) tend to be very aggressive and to dominate their counterparts in every run-through, trying to use as much bandwidth as possible.

Lastly, there's a third case in which congestion control algorithms negotiate their transit to a balanced state, distributing the available bandwidth in an equitable manner. This behavior appears on most confrontations observed. Particular examples of this are shown on the Figs. 12 and 14. As described before, even though their behavior is similar, it's not exactly the same. The main difference is in the time employed to get to a equilibrated state. Indeed, the case of Fig. 12 shows that the transition since the time protocol B begins, until it gets to a equitable state for the distribution of instantaneous throughput, is 4,85 s. Meanwhile, in the case of Fig. 14, the same time amounts to 14,4 s. These cases were selected from a wide range of values and forms, in which one can appreciate how the curves get to an equilibrium point.

4 Conclusions

As it can be seen, the metric defined as TPP gives an idea of how the protocols position themselves over the available bandwidth when they interact with other protocols, while sharing some of the links for transmission in a network. And yet, this metric on its own isn't enough to define the way in which such positioning is achieved. To be able to see in more detail, some figures like Throughput vs. Time and CWND vs. Time were included, because they provide more information about the events that take place. From these figures, two metrics are particularly interesting when it comes to quantify what's being observed: convergence time and fairness index. Through these 3 metrics, one gets a compact way to represent the information that defines the behavior of two protocols sharing networking resources. The values obtained for them, for every simulation, were presented on the Tables 1, 2, 3 and 4.

As on can appreciate, the 3 metrics provide enough information to do a behavior analysis about the confrontation between congestion control mechanisms. Based on this, and with the results provided in the tables, three general cases can be typified from a fairness perspective, which have been described in the discussion of the results.

On the other hand, the TCP variants with congestion controls developed for networks with high values of bandwidth-delay product (BDP) and algorithms with reactive character based in packet loss (e.g. YeAH and Hybla), present a noticeably aggressiveness when it comes to bandwidth usage. This characteristics determines the existence of instability in the negotiation of bandwidth and explains why they take a while to achieve a balanced state (as in the case of YeAH vs. Veno, in Fig. 14, and more notoriously, Hybla vs. Veno in Fig. 16).

In other cases, when protocols like Westwood intervene, that are also reactive but based on bandwidth estimation, it can be observed that its behavior is more friendly towards other variants when it's time to negotiate resources. In this way, most cases get to a balanced state in very little time.

As mentioned in the discussion, Vegas is a particular case. This protocol shows a clear weakness in the negotiation for use of the medium. Nonetheless, when it competes against another instance of the same type, the fairness index indicates a fair distribution of resources in a short time. Because of this, it can be said that Vegas does not present inter-protocol fairness (Figs. 6 and 8) but it does have intra-protocol fairness (Fig. 18).

At last, it's understood that this format of representation can be extended to analyze more than two flow competing for resources, being that a line of work for future investigations.

Acknowledgments. This project was financed by the Universidad Nacional de la Patagonia Austral, Unidad Académica Río Gallegos.

References

1. Postel, J.: Transmission Control Protocol, RFC 793 (1981)
2. Allman, M., Paxson, M., Blanton, E.: TCP Congestion Control. RFC5681 (Draft Standard) (2009)
3. Floyd, S., Fall, K.: Promoting the use of end-to-end congestion control in the Internet. IEEE/ACM Trans. Netw. 7(4), 458–472 (1999)
4. Jacobson, V.: Congestion avoidance and control. ACM SIGCOMM Comput. Commun. Rev. 25(1), 157–187 (1995)

5. Henderson, T., Gurtov, A., Nishida, Y., Floyd, S.: The New Reno Modification to TCP's Fast Recovery Algorithm. RFC 6582 (2012)
6. Liu, S., Başar, T., Srikant, R.: TCP-Illinois: a loss- and delay-based congestion control algorithm for high-speed networks. Perform. Eval. **65**(6–7), 417–440 (2008)
7. Lochert, C., Scheuermann, B., Mauve, M.: A survey on congestion control for mobile ad hoc networks. Wirel. Commun. Mob. Comput. **7**(5), 655 (2007)
8. Elaarag, H.: Improving TCP performance over mobile networks. ACM Comput. Surv. **34**(3), 357–374 (2002)
9. Rodríguez Herlein, D.R., Talay, C.A., González, C.N., Trinidad, F.A., Almada, M.L., Marrone, L.A.: Un análisis de comportamiento entre distintos mecanismos de control de congestión ensayados sobre una topología mixta. In: XXIV Congreso Argentino de Ciencias de la Computación (CACIC), Tandil, Argentina, pp. 725–734 (2018)
10. Rodgers, A., Kuznetsova, T.: TCP Reno and Vegas co-existence. Semantic Scholars (2015)
11. Esterhuizen, A., Krzesinski, A.E.: TCP congestion control comparison. In: Southern African Telecommunication Networks and Applications Conference (SATNAC), George, South Africa (2012)
12. Fall, K., Kannan, V.: The NS Manual, (formerly ns Notes and Documentation) ns-2.35. https://isi.edu/nsnam/ns/doc/ns_doc.pdf
13. Ahmad, M., et al.: End-to-end loss based TCP congestion control mechanism as a secured communication technology for smart healthcare enterprises **6**, 11641–11656 (2018)
14. Rodríguez Herlein, D.R., Talay, C.A., González, C.N., Trinidad, F.A., Marrone, L.A.: Performance of TCP Vegas According to Alfa and Beta Parameters in Hybrid Scenarios with Bursts Errors. In: International Conference on Information Systems and Computer Science (INCISCOS), Quito, pp. 217–223 (2017)

Innovation in Software Systems

Templates Framework for the Augmented Catalog System

Nahuel Mangiarua, Jorge Ierache[(✉)], Martin Becerra,
Hernán Maurice, Santiago Igarza, and Osvaldo Spositto

Department of Engineering and Technological Research,
Applied Augmented Reality Research Group,
National University of La Matanza, Florencio Varela 1903, La Matanza,
Buenos Aires, Argentina
jierache@unlam.edu.ar

Abstract. A novel system is presented for the augmentation of meta-contents, implemented over the existing virtual augmented catalog system (ACS), that shows positive results on improving the usability and lowering the entry barrier for non-expert users. It is introduced the concept of template of augmented reality, which allows the definition of amount and types of digital contents to be augmented together with their geometric transformations and visualization order. Once applied over a virtual catalog, the template helps to maintain a uniform format between its elements while simplifying the task for non-expert users by incorporating part of their domain vocabulary into the interface.

Keywords: Augmented reality · Augmented Catalogs System

1 Introduction

Augmented reality (AR) acknowledges people are used to living in a real world which cannot be played authentically on a computer, as AR augments the real world by using computational capacity [1]. RA combines real and virtual elements, interacts in real time and it is 3D registered [2, 3]. RA is a novel technology that arises from the virtual reality technology, it is widely extended and many examples and applications on different areas can be found, such as arts, education, medicine, engineering, among others. The possibilities of adapting RA to different everyday activities and business areas are countless and extensive. And at this point is where all its entire potential resides.

In the context of the augmented catalog system [4, 5] it is set the goal of simplifying the creation and content loading task for the end, non-expert user wanting to publish their custom content. This objective is born from the difficulties observed by Universidad de la Matanza Arts department during the Bienal de Arte Integral event to generate an augmented catalog with information about the exposed pictures and sculptures. It has been found that, despite the system GUI being relatively simple, the user was still under the need to know and understand the basic concepts of AR technology. Additionally, the work needed to create every AR marker with its contents

P. Pesado and C. Aciti (Eds.): CACIC 2018, CCIS 995, pp. 267–276, 2019.
https://doi.org/10.1007/978-3-030-20787-8_19

resulted tedious, repetitive and subject to small input errors. To solve this, it is proposed the development of a meta-content layer over the augmented catalog system.

An augmented catalog template allows a user with some knowledge of the system and AR concepts to define a structure for the elements, contents, to be augmented on each AR marker before actually uploading such content to the system. Once applied, a template helps to maintain a uniform format between the AR markers while simplifying the content loading task, abstracting the concepts of AR technology, by replacing them with vocabulary of the user's knowledge domain.

Figure 1 shows a conceptual diagram of the template layer for the augmented catalog system.

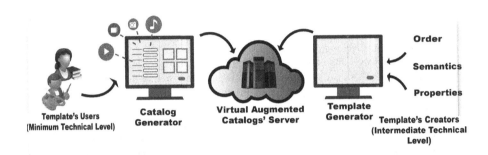

Fig. 1. Conceptual diagram of the template layer.

2 Augmented Reality Templates

Using the web interface in the Fig. 2, an augmented catalog template grants the ability to define the amount and types of content (text, image, video, audio) assigned to each marker of a catalog along with its geometric transformations (translation, rotation, scale), a name and display order. Furthermore, it allows to abstract away the AR technology term "marker" and replace it with something meaningful for the end user who will be loading the contents and working with the augmented catalog.

In Fig. 3 it is possible to see the GUI for the creation of an augmented catalog where it has been selected an existing template from a combo box. If selected, a template modifies the workflow of the system and the aspect of the GUI as shown on Fig. 4. The term "marker" is exchanged for that defined in the template and each content comes pre-allocated with a proper order and meaningful name which makes it easier for the end user to understand what goes where. This shortened workflow not only saves the end user time but also the burden of understanding and applying the correct geometric transformations to each content to achieve the desired visualization on the AR environment. Figure 4 details and contrasts the differences in the workflow when using a template versus not using one. In Fig. 4a it is observed the reduced workflow exemplified with the template used for the Bienal de Arte Integral art event. In Fig. 4b it is observed the regular workflow of the system where the additional steps are highlighted in black.

Fig. 2. Web interface of template editor for text content called "name" with order and position values.

The implementation of the augmented catalog template layer incorporates several new elements into the Augmented Catalog System responsible for the creation and maintenance of the templates. In Fig. 5 it is possible to see how the server module of the system hosts the web editor interface allowing the creation of augmented catalogs and their templates by user or user group.

Fig. 3. Template selection to modify catalog creation workflow.

The REST API grants access to the stored information as a serialized and then compressed protocol buffer message, serving as the bridge between the server and the mobile application responsible for the visualization of AR content.

As seen in Fig. 6 the new "Templates" component includes several classes. The MarkerTemplate class is responsible for the amount and order of ContentTemplate instances which store the relevant information about the type and geometrical transformations of each content that will be pre-allocated for each new marker. There is also the Content, ContentType and Marker classes responsible for the information loaded by the end user to a catalog. Additionally, each Marker instance holds a picture to help identification by humans. The User and AccessGroup classes are responsible for the identification of users and sharing of catalogs. Finally, the Catalog class in the top of the hierarchy puts every element together.

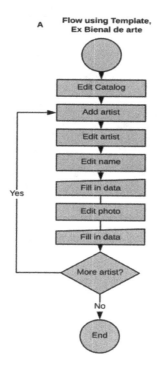

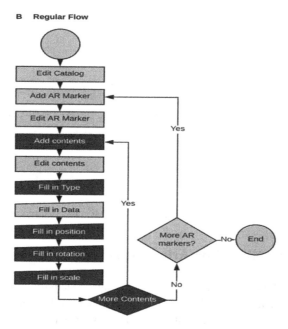

Fig. 4. a. Catalog workflow creation using templates. b. Regular flow without it.

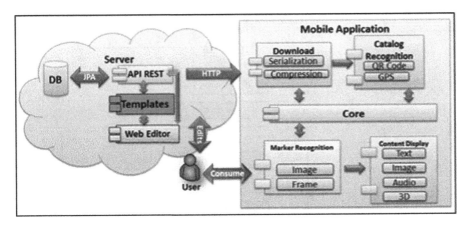

Fig. 5. Augmented catalog system architecture diagram

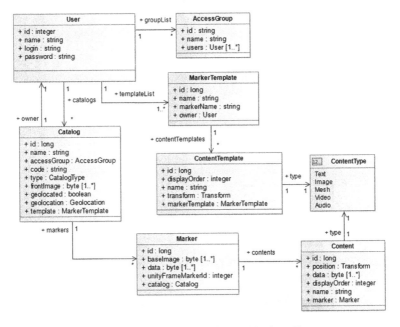

Fig. 6. Template implementation UML class diagram

3   Case Study: "Bienal de Arte Integral"

An early version of the Augmented Catalogs Template System [6], implementation was tested during the Bienal de Arte Integral [7], event held by Universidad de La Matanza as an extension effort of the research group. This event required a virtual catalog to augment each artwork piece in exhibition and its regular, paperback art catalog adding up a total of about 30 markers with multiple contents each. To test the system, it was generated a template in collaboration with a representative of the Arts Department, defining the amount, name and types of each content with their transformations, setting the term "artist" to replace the concept of "marker" in the editor GUI.

Fig. 7. Editor Interfaces at every step of the template edition process.

Next the steps used to create the template were detailed. From the main screen of the editor GUI the button is pressed to add a new template as seen in Fig. 7a. Once there it is filled in a name for the template and the term to replace "marker" in the catalog creation GUI, in this case "artist" is input as seen in Fig. 7b. After saving the changes a new button to add contents appear (Fig. 7c) and by pressing it, it was proceeded to add the contents that each future marker of the template must pre-allocate (Fig. 7d). For example, a content of type text with name "Artwork name" was added to be displayed as the second content of the marker. The transformations are adjusted and repeated for each content to be added to the template.

By applying this template on a new augmented catalog, it was effectively lowered the entry barrier of the system, allowing the staff of the event, with no previous knowledge of AR, to successfully create and load all the required markers (now called

"Artists" in the GUI) after a short verbal introduction, without any further intervention by members of the research group. In Fig. 8 it is possible to see a work in process catalog with 3 artists already loaded[1].

Fig. 8. Template created for the event "Bienal de Arte Integral".

In Fig. 9 it is possible to see the end result where an artist information in the paper catalog is augmented with additional multimedia content and access to social networks.

---

[1] Marker images used in Fig. 8 are artists pictures published on the Bienal de Arte Integral 2016 Catalog. Artist N°1: Guillermo Mac Loughlin – Art: Yuxtaposición, Artist N°2: Eugenio Monferran - Art: 12 Xurmadi, Artist N°3: Mirta Narosky - Art: Salón arcano.

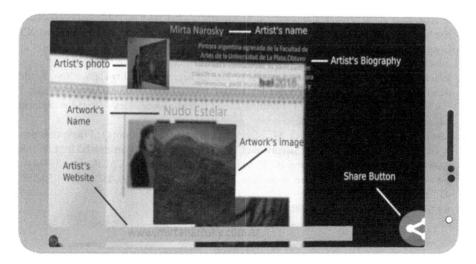

Fig. 9. Mobile application of the event Bienal de Arte Integral.

4 Conclusions and Future Work

The Augmented Catalog Templates layer was successfully integrated to the Augmented Catalogs System, providing a significant reduction in the entry level of the system. A template allows end users with no knowledge about AR concepts to create augmented catalogs with significant amounts on content and significantly reduces the time needed.

From the experience obtained from the tests of the system, as future lines of work, the addition of dynamic and interactive content types are considered as such. The former allowing the visualization of real time information such as social network feeds or remote sensors data while the interactive content, such as question-answer would allow the input of actions or information by the consumer of a catalog, opening a communication channel with the creator.

Acknowledgement. Thanks to the Department of Engineering and Technological Investigation of the National University of La Matanza for funding the present work under the PROINCE program.

References

1. Beaudouin-Lafon, M.: Beyond the workstation: mediaspaces and augmented reality. In: Cockton, G., Drapery, S.W., Weir, G.R.S.: People and Computers. Cambridge University Press, Glasgow. IX (1994)
2. Azuma, R.T.: A survey of augmented reality. Presence: Teleoperators Virtual Env. **6**, 355–385 (1997)
3. Craig, A.B.: Understanding Augmented Reality Concepts and Applications. Elsevier, Amsterdam (2013)

4. Ierache, J., et al.: Sistema de Catálogo para la Asistencia a la Creación, Publicación, Gestión y Explotación de Contenidos Multimedia y Aplicaciones de Realidad Aumentada. In: XX Congreso Argentino de Ciencias de la Computación, Red de Universidades con Carreras de Informática (RedUNCI), Buenos Aires (2014). http://hdl.handle.net/10915/42339

5. Ierache, J., et al.: Development of a catalogs system for augmented reality applications. World Acad. Sci. Eng. Technol. Int. Sci. Index 97, Int. J. Comput. Electr. Autom. Control Inf. Eng. **9** (1), 1–7 (2015). http://waset.org/Publications/development-of-a-catalogs-system-for-augmented-reality-applications/10000077

6. Mangiarua, N., Ierache, J., Becerra, M., Maurice, H., Igarza, S., Spositto, O.: Framework para la Generación de Templates en Sistema de Catálogos de Realidad Aumentada. In: Libro de Actas XXIV Congreso Argentino de Ciencias de la Computación CACIC, pp. 837–846. Universidad Nacional del Centro de la Prov. de Buenos Aires (2019). ISBN 978-950-658-472-6

7. BAI2016. http://ra.unlam.edu.ar/BAI2016.apk

Smart Assistance Spots for the Blind or Visually Impaired People

Guillermo Arispe[1,3]([✉]), Claudio Aciti[1,2], Matías Presso[1,2,3], and José Marone[2]

[1] Universidad Nacional de Tres de Febrero, Sede Caseros I,
Valentín Gómez 4828, B1678ABJ Caseros, Buenos Aires, Argentina
guillermo.arispe@gmail.com, matiaspresso@gmail.com
[2] Universidad Nacional del Centro de la Provincia de Buenos Aires, Pinto 399,
7000 Tandil, Buenos Aires, Argentina
{caciti,marone}@exa.unicen.edu.ar
[3] Comisión de Investigaciones Científicas de la Provincia de Buenos Aires,
Calle 526 entre 10 y 11, 1900 La Plata, Buenos Aires, Argentina

Abstract. This paper describes the design and development of a system whose main purpose is to guide blind or visually impaired people through different environments in a city. The system consists in a mobile application that orients the user with audio messages and a set of geolocated electronic devices distributed at strategic points of an urban center. These electronic devices send environment information to the mobile app through wireless communication, providing accessibility and simplicity. A fully functional prototype was implemented, with a mobile application developed for Android and devices created on the Arduino platform.

Keywords: Visual disability · Smart cities · Inclusive cities

1 Introduction

With economic development and the massive urbanization process, the percentage of the world population living in cities is increasing. How cities are designed impacts on how their residents relate with one another and how economic and social activities are organized. In other words, urban design affects the quality of life of city dwellers. The concept of smart cities, that is, the cities that use technology to increase the efficiency and sustainability of their services, is currently gaining considerable significance.

Yet, it is also necessary to consider inclusive and accessible cities because the design and functionality of a city will facilitate or hamper the inclusion, job opportunities, and independence of physically or intellectually disabled residents. [1–3].

In this sense, three fundamental characteristics of cities affect the lives of disabled people: physical, economic and social facilities [4].

© Springer Nature Switzerland AG 2019
P. Pesado and C. Aciti (Eds.): CACIC 2018, CCIS 995, pp. 277–293, 2019.
https://doi.org/10.1007/978-3-030-20787-8_20

The physical facilities allow people to move from one place to another in the city. These facilities are essential for people to be able to go to work, study, engage in leisure activities, see a doctor, that is, carry out everyday activities. For example, disabled people can move easily when the city provides smooth, wide sidewalks with wheelchair ramps, elevators or escalators at train stations, traffic lights with voice instructions, Braille on information signs and simple images, and no poles in unusual places. This provision enables people with disabilities to move freely and safely throughout the city.

The economic facilities of a city take into account disabled people in the design of job opportunities and consumer spaces and products. Examples of such design include adapted workplaces, accessible buildings, disability-friendly bathroom layouts, spaces in soft colors and soundproof areas, shopping centers with information points and simple signs. These services allow people with different abilities, either physical or intellectual, to contribute to society as workers and consumers.

The social facilities of a city enable all residents to share the public places, fostering interaction and participation in the community. Some social services are parks with adapted hammocks, disability training for museum guides, integration of disabled students into schools.

While adapting a city to people with disabilities involves large investments, the benefits can be enjoyed by all residents. For example, ramps on sidewalks and easy access to buildings will allow easier mobility for the elderly and for parents with baby carriages. Sound signaling and simple images will allow children and elderly people to orient themselves easily. Accessible and adapted public places will contribute to greater social wealth and to the enjoyment of all residents.

Blind or visually impaired people have enormous trouble getting around a city and hence limited autonomy, which means that they rarely leave the environments that they are most familiar with. This limitation affects their quality of life and their interaction with the world around them[1]. For them, getting around an urban center can be a daunting and sometimes overwhelming task. The anxiety, stress, and frustration involved in walking in a city that is not adapted to their needs lead thousands of blind people worldwide to stay at home for as long as possible. Even when they do go out with a cane or a guide dog, blind or visually impaired people encounter obstacles that they cannot always detect easily. For example, planned or unplanned construction sites in city streets are a major obstacle altering the environment that blind people are familiar with [5].

In 2014, the WHO (World Health Organization) conducted a study [6] showing that there are about 285 million visually impaired people in the world, 39 million of whom are blind and 246 million of whom have low vision. For these people, ordinary daily tasks can become difficult and even dangerous. They must face challenges like

---

[1] https://www.livestrong.com/article/241936-challenges-that-blind-people-face.

avoiding unexpected bumps on sidewalks, making a purchase at a supermarket, entering or leaving a subway station, getting on and off a bus at the correct bus stop, crossing a street, or simply walking to their destinations.

As technology advances, more and more cities will become smart by incorporating technology in different areas and making more efficient use of their resources and services. Smart cities aim at solving the main problems that residents face every day and improving their quality of life. It is precisely in this context that the motivation for the present study lies. Its initial version [7] shows how the idea originated and began to be developed, while the present work shows in greater detail and depth the original content as well as existing applications and tools for the visually impaired, a description of the system development and functionalities, the tests conducted, and future works.

2 Applications and Assistive Devices for the Visually Impaired

Different current developments aim to assist blind or visually impaired people. Some of them translate digital texts into Braille by means of a device, such as MyDot[2], which raises and lowers a series of dots allowing the user to read digital texts. Other applications provide help through mobile devices such as Blind Communicator[3], which informs the user of events that occur in the device. Another type of application allows objects to be recognized. For instance, TapTapSee[4] uses a camera to recognize the objects in front of a person and has a voice guide saying what the objects are. In addition, products like Sunu Band[5] help visually impaired people to move more freely. This device is an intelligent bracelet with an ultrasonic sensor that detects obstacles at a distance and notifies the person through vibrations on the wrist. It is a very useful device offering real-time information about the environment where the person moves and complementing basic tools such as the cane and guide dog. Its discreet and sophisticated design makes the device go unnoticed. Despite these advantages, the utility of this device is limited by its short battery life, high cost, and unavailability in some countries.

While these developments assist people with visual disabilities, they differ from the proposal of the present study, whose objectives are more associated with applications like Lazarillo[6]. Lazarillo is a tool for mobile devices with voice notification telling the users where they are and what is around them: parking lots, ATMs, stores, schools, restaurants, etc. While the users move around, the application lets them know what

---

[2] http://mydot.com.mx/.

[3] https://play.google.com/store/apps/details?id=ar.com.lrusso.blindcommunicator&hl=es_419.

[4] http://taptapseeapp.com/.

[5] http://sunu.io/.

[6] https://www.lazarillo.cl/.

services are nearby. Despite some similarities between this tool and the one proposed in this work, they differ in substantial ways. To start, Lazarillo requires registering with a Google account and shows a message with two options: manually enable Google Talkback[7] or continue without using this tool. When activated, the device automatically detects the users touches on the screen, tells them what they are touching, and asks them to press again to confirm the action. Although Google Talkback is recognized as one of the great applications assisting blind people in using their mobile devices, it is tedious and slow and it reduces the overall performance of the device. Another important difference is that once the Lazarillo application is closed, it does not continue to run in the background, forcing the user to always run it in the foreground. In addition, its interface is too complex for the target users. For the guide to be useful, the users must interact with too many elements: action buttons on the top menu bar, a small-sized menu at the bottom, lists of places to search from, different sections within the application, among others. The present work offers certain advantages over Lazarillo in terms of application use, since it has no graphic interface and requires no interaction.

Another current application is Lazzus[8]. This tool also uses GPS and the phone compass to help the person navigate through different interest points. It uses information from Google Places[9] and Open Street Data[10] and possesses two search devices, 360th mode and Flashlight mode. The former mode searches throughout a 100-m radio for places close to the user. The latter allows the user to point the mobile device to search for places in the pointed direction. At present (October, 2017), Lazzus is not available in many countries and where it is, it has a trial period of seven days after which users are required to pay for a license. Like Lazarillo, this application has an interface where the users must configure the mode and the points of interest which they want to receive information about as well as a list of nearby places. If no configuration assistance is provided to the users, this task can be complex for them. Besides, the application requires an Internet connection and is therefore limited to areas with good network coverage of both 3G/4G and WiFi signals. Another important difference from the present study is that Lazzus is not distributed for free and, although it is reasonably priced, the user is faced with the complexity of making online purchase and payment.

Another interesting project is an application developed in mid-2016 in Buenos Aires, Argentina, by a group of highschool students and teachers. Named Semáforos inteligentes (Intelligent Traffic Lights), it helps visually disabled people to cross the street safely and reduces the noise made by current traffic lights. The application communicates with the network of available traffic lights to offer the user contextual information, via voice notification, about the available crossing time and the name and

---

[7] Screen reader that allows user interaction with a device.

[8] http://www.lazzus.com/es/.

[9] https://developers.google.com/places/?hl=es-419.

[10] https://www.openstreetmap.org/.

location of the street where the user is. This application is similar to the one proposed here but only involves traffic lights. Their prototype is applicable anywhere since all the information to be communicated to the user is stored inside a board, which can be placed anywhere.

3 Objectives

3.1 General Objective

The main objective of this work was to provide visually impaired people with a tool that guides them through different environments, be they familiar or unfamiliar to the users, by means of information obtained from geolocation and devices placed in strategic points in a city. The purpose is not to replace conventional tools such as the cane or guide dogs but to complement them.

3.2 Specific Objectives

The specific aims of this work were as follows:

To develop as simple an application as possible, with an interface that can be used by the blind or visually impaired person.

To continuously detect the location of the user in order to determine when nearby boards must be searched for.

To connect the Android phone with the Arduino board, when both devices are near each other.

To process the information obtained in order to offer location information and guidance to the blind or visually impaired person.

4 Scope and Limitations

The prototype was developed on Android, and Arduino boards were used in different strategic points. The mobile device requirements are Bluetooth, GPS system, and a version of the operating system ranging from 4.0.3 to 7.1.2. Therefore, the users do not need a costly, high-end device.

The main limitations of this prototype are its inability to connect, at the same time, multiple mobile devices to the Bluetooth of the Arduino board located at a strategic point, the low intensity of the GPS signal from satellites, and the duration of the battery life of the device.

5 Proposed Solution

The proposed solution is an application for mobile devices with an Android operating system, which assists blind or visually impaired people by offering them guidance and location information from Arduino boards, or microcontrollers, located at strategic points in a city (Fig. 1).

Fig. 1. Example of application functioning at a traffic light strategic point.

Examples of strategic points:

Traffic lights. It is possible to obtain information about the current state of the light, timer, georeferentiation, street width, traffic direction, among others.

Construction site signaling. To signal works that require breaking the sidewalk or the street, the local government can place a board offering information to blind or visually impaired passers-by. This board is used at one site for as long as the construction lasts and may then be used at another site.

Supermarket aisles. The application can offer information about the products on display, location of check-out counters, exit, restrooms, among others.

Subway stations. The application can offer information about the entrance and exit, destination, waiting time until the next subway arrives, among others.

Bus stops. The application can offer information about the bus line, destination, waiting time until the next subway arrives, among others.

As shown in Fig. 2, the application communicates by means of Bluetooth with the boards located at strategic points in order to offer the user specific information about each of the places where these boards are placed. Once the information is sent from the board to the mobile device, it is processed by the device and transmitted to the user via voice notification.

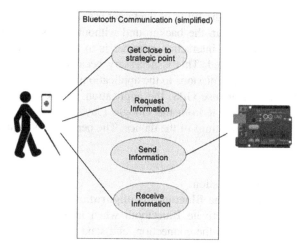

Fig. 2. Use case diagram: simplified communication between the mobile device and the hardware located at a strategic point.

Before establishing Bluetooth communication and interacting with the microcontroller, the application continuously detects the user's activity to know if the user is moving or not. When the user is not moving or returns to a rest state, the application deactivates Bluetooth, if it was activated, to reduce the device battery consumption. By contrast, when the application detects that the user begins to move, it obtains the individual's location. After taking at least two distance measurements, the application compares the distance covered by the user and if the difference is smaller than a configurable reference distance (set at ten meters), it activates Bluetooth and starts searching for a nearby board to connect to and request information from. If it does not find any board, it tries again after the following ten meters. Once a board is located at some strategic point, it initiates the connection process. In case of failure, it makes three more attempts to establish a connection. If, after these attempts, the application still fails to connect to a board, it notifies the user that an error has occurred and that it is not possible to offer information at that moment. If a successful connection is achieved, the application sends the first synchronization command to the board and waits for confirmation. Once the handshake is complete, the application requests the context information from the board and upon reception of this information - in JSON format – it interprets it and converts it into a message for the user.

In each of the communication stages, the application informs the user about what is happening via voice notification, from the first attempt to establish a connection to its finalization. This is done because an error can arise at some stage, such as the connection attempt, and if the user is not notified about the error, he or she may assume that the attempt is being conducted, and unaware of the error, may be kept waiting for the connection to be completed.

Bearing in mind the visual disability of the target users of this prototype, the whole process is done automatically in the background without the user having to interact with the application. The only interaction required is to allow the application to use GPS the first time it is executed. This is necessary because Android users have the option of not giving certain permissions to the applications installed in their devices. In addition to the permission to use GPS, the application requires users to give other permissions when they install it from the Google Play Store. It is also possible to modify from the permission settings of the device. The permissions required to operate the application are as follows:

Location via GPS
Permission to know the geolocation.

Access and management of the Bluetooth configuration
Permission to activate or deactivate Blueetooth when necessary, search for nearby
  Bluetooth devices, establish the connection, and send and receive data.

Recognition of activity
Permission to detect the user's movement or rest.

Detection of the moment when the system starts operating
Permission to automatically start the application together with the operating system,
  ensuring its availability when the user needs it so that he or she does not have to
  open the device manually.

The application also enables the user to search for nearby boards manually, by shaking the phone (Fig. 3), that is, if the user shakes it from one side to another, the application will start looking for nearby boards to connect to. Another important application feature is that it is automatically executed when the device is restarted, so it continues providing information to the users without them having to initiate it manually.

Fig. 3. "Shake" movement

Figure 4 shows a diagram summarizing the operation of the mobile application.

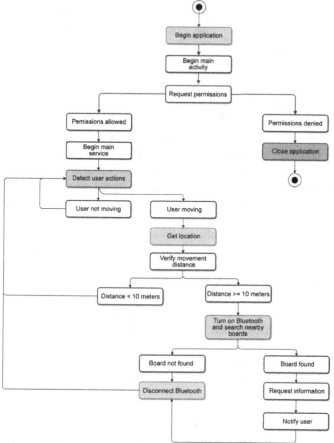

Fig. 4. Flow chart of the mobile application.

5.1 Hardware Configuration

The connection between the microcontroller, or Arduino board, and the Bluetooth HC-05 module is made according to the diagram shown in Fig. 5 and the sample connection description in Table 1:

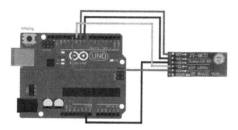

Fig. 5. Connection scheme between the board and the module.

Table 1. Description of connections between the Arduino board and the HC-05 module.

HC-05 Module	Arduino Uno
Tx – Transmitter	Pin 10 SoftwareSerial Receiver
Rx – Receiver	Pin 11 SoftwareSerial Transmitter
GND	GND
VCC	3,3 V

5.2   Software Embedded in the Microcontroller

Two software programs were developed for the Arduino board in the Processing programming language and using the official IDE provided by Arduino. One of the programs is responsible for configuring the Bluetooth module. After this first software component is installed and configured, it is replaced by the second component, which is responsible for the Bluetooth communication, for processing the commands from the Android application, and for sending the corresponding responses to it.

The program uses the SoftwareSerial library provided by Arduino and configures the Bluetooth module to work as a serial port, that is, the transmission is done sequentially, bit by bit. Once the serial port is established, the program sends the AT commands to the module to configure its different parameters. After sending a command, it waits for the module to respond and determine if the configuration has been done successfully. If so, it continues with the following command.

The second program mentioned above has two main and mandatory methods in every Arduino program. These are setup() and loop(). setup() is the first function to be executed, with an initial configuration of the Bluetooth module made as a serial port, in the same way as described for the first program. In this configuration, the network is named BLINDY_PARTNER, the password is configured, the role of the module is established as a slave so that the devices acting as masters may connect, and the modulation speed is changed to 115200 baud, since this is the speed needed to correctly receive the characters from the Android application. The second method, as its name suggests, is a loop that runs an infinite number of times until the microcontroller is turned off or restarted. During this loop, the program checks if there is something to read. When a character is found, the function processCommand (char command) is executed, which is responsible for taking the command from the application, processing it, and sending a response accordingly. This process is resumed in Fig. 6.

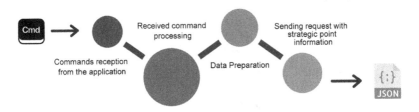

Fig. 6. Information service of the embedded software.

5.3   Android Application

The application was built in the environment or IDE Android Studio using mainly the Java and XML programing language for the few visual elements that the application has. Its main components are Main Activity, Main Service, and Broadcast Receiver. These components were developed following Android guidelines [8–10].

Main Activity. MainActivity is the home screen. It does not have any component with which the user can interact since it is designed to work automatically. When the users install the application and enter it for the first time, they are asked to grant permission to use GPS and manage the Bluetooth configuration. These are the only actions requiring the user to interact. Then, MainActivity decreases the screen brightness to the minimum to consume less battery and runs the MainService, which starts its background execution.

Main Service. MainService is run from MainActivity, and it continues its background run even if the user closes the application or switches to another one.

The following components and actions of MainService, considered the most important element of the application, are as follows in Fig. 7.

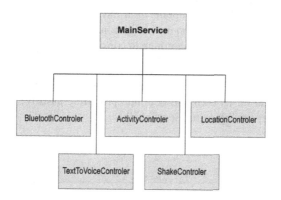

Fig. 7. MainService component diagram.

Each of the MainService controlers is assigned a specific responsibility. ActivityControler is responsible for detecting the user's activity, which, as mentioned above, consists in knowing when the user is moving. For this purpose, it uses Google Awareness API[11], which allows access to a variety of contextual signals such as the use of battery or memory, the current location of the device, the climatic conditions at the location, and among others, the user activity depicted in this project.

When the application detects that the user is moving, the MainService begins to obtain the device location through LocationController and then calculates the distance covered by the user. If this distance is at least ten meters, it activates he Bluetooth

---

[11] https://developers.google.com/awareness/.

function of the device using BluetoothControler and searches for nearby Arduino boards to which it will attempt to connect in order to obtain context information and notify the user.

The boards to which the application connects belong to the network called BLIN-DY_PARTNER. Figure 8 describes the communication process. When it finds a board, it starts the connection process and once the device is successfully connected, it sends a CMD_INIT (0) to start the communication. The Arduino board responds to this command with an EACK indicating that it is synchronized and ready to begin transmitting its information. The first character, 'E', stands for status and the second, 'I', for information. These characters are used for differentiating between responses associated with status or information message. Upon receiving the ACK, the application sends a second command: CMD_REQUEST_INF (1) to request information about the context where the board is located.

This information is sent to the application in JSON format and upon receiving it, the application parses it, converts it to voice, and transmits it to the user through the device speakers or headphones. This conversion is performed by the TextToVoiceControler. This information enables the blind or visually impaired person to learn about the surrounding context and make a decision based on it. Once the information has been transmitted to the user, the application sends the last command: CDM_FIN (9), which indicates to the board that the communication has ended. In reply to this, the board sends an EFIN, which the application uses to disconnect the communication. Bluetooth is then turned off so that it does not continue to consume battery power from the device, so it can be used it effectively.

Broadcast Receiver. This component is used when the device is rebooted, allowing the application to run on its own and continue providing assistive information to the user without the user having to run it manually.

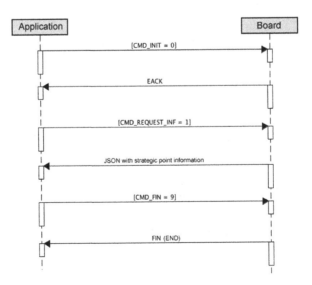

Fig. 8. Sequence diagram - communication protocol.

6   Prototype Testing

Different tests were performed to verify the correct functioning of the prototype.

6.1   The GPS is Off When the Application Starts

If the GPS is off when the application starts, the user is asked to turn it on so that he or she may receive assistance (Fig. 9). If the user does so, the application continues its execution. Otherwise, the application finishes its execution because it cannot obtain the user's location or search for nearby Arduino boards to request information. Before finishing the execution, the application informs the reason for closing it via voice notification. The next time the user enters the application, the GPS state is checked again.

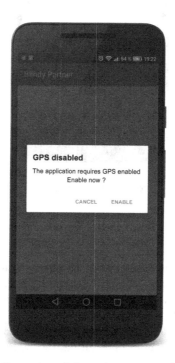

Fig. 9. Screenshot - informative message (GPS off)

6.2   The GPS is On When the Application Starts but Location Permissions are not Granted

After verifying whether the GPS is on, the application asks the user for permission to access the location of the device. If permission is given, the application is configured for use and for receiving assistance, and then it continues its execution. If permission is not given, it is requested again until the user decides not to receive the request anymore or allows access to his or her location (Fig. 10).

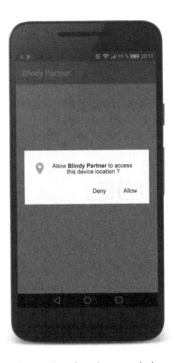

Fig. 10. Screenshot- location permission request.

6.3   Successful Connection Between the Device and the Arduino Board

When the user moves, the application verifies how far he or she has gone. The prototype's minimum distance is configured at ten meters. If this or a greater distance is measured, the application starts looking for nearby boards to connect to. When the device successfully connects to one of these boards, it sends the corresponding command to request the data of the strategic point in question. Once it receives the data in JSON format, it converts them and transmits the information to the user via voice notification. Figure 11 shows an example of the JSON structure with the data from a strategic point.

```
{
  "name": "Traffic Light",
  "description": "Traffic Light located at San Martín y Urquiza"
  "latitude": -34.123455,
  "longitude": -34.123455,
  "extra_info": {
    "remaining_time_seconds": 30,
    "street_width_meters": 7,
  },
  "nearby_places":[
    {
      "name": "Universidad Nacional de Tres de Febrero",
      "category": "Universidad",
      "latitude": -34.123455,
      "longitude": -34.123455,
    },
    {
      ...
    }
  ]
}
```

Fig. 11. Example of JSON with data from a strategic point

6.4 Failed Connection Attempt Between the Device and the Arduino Board

Once an Arduino board has been found, the application tries to establish the Bluetooth connection to request context information from it. There are two possible scenarios. The first one is a successful connection as described in Subsect. 6.3. The second one is a failed connection. In this case, the application makes three more attempts to connect and if the connection fails again in each attempt, it turns off the Bluetooth of the device and informs the user via voice notification that the connection has failed.

6.5 The Device Looks for Nearby Boards but Cannot Find Any

After verifying that the user has moved a distance greater than or equal to the minimum distance configured, the application activates Bluetooth and starts looking for nearby Arduino boards. If it does not find any in ten seconds, it notifies the user via voice notifications that "There are no nearby information devices".

6.6 Execution of the Application on Different Devices

The Firebase Test Lab[12] tool was used to execute the application on multiple different physical and virtual devices. Firebase Test Lab uses a Google data center to evaluate the application on different devices with different configurations. This makes it possible to find problems that only occur in configurations of specific devices (e.g., a Nexus 5 with a particular level of Android API and a specific regional configuration).

---

[12] https://firebase.google.com/docs/test-lab/?hl=es-419.

6.7   User's Movement Simulation

A user's movement was simulated. Using Google Maps, multiple points of a trajectory were obtained and then generated in a GPX file, where each point is composed of a pair of decimal values, corresponding to latitude and longitude. GPX files have been designed to transfer GPS data between applications and can be used to describe points, trajectories, and routes.

Once the GPX file was generated, it was loaded onto an Android emulator using the utility provided by IDE Android Studio to manipulate and configure different emulator sensors, including GPS. The simulation was then executed and it was found that when the user moves a distance greater than or equal to the minimum distance configured, the application also simulates the task of searching for nearby boards.

7   Conclusions

The mobile application was tested on different devices and it worked properly, regardless of the Android device used, if the minimum requirements mentioned in the Scope section were met.

During the tests, it was observed that the Bluetooth connection range does not pose a problem. The Bluetooth technology applied in most of the current devices has a coverage range from 60 m, in devices with Bluetooth 4.0, to 240 m in devices with Bluetooth 5.0. Every ten meters covered by the user, the application searches for a nearby board to connect to. The information stored on the board is fully editable, so it may loaded in different languages and the tool may be used in any city of the world. After developing the different stages of the prototype, we conclude that the tool developed is capable of providing contextual information for locating and guiding a person as he or she walks along city streets moves.

8   Future Works

Future works will be aimed at the following developments: controling the application through voice commands; allowing simultaneous Bluetooth connections to manage several requests at the same time; generating low-consumption Bluetooth communication with devices such as beacons; making a map of strategic points, allowing users to know where the closest point with an Arduino board is located, thus guiding the users to the point where they may obtain information about the environment and reach their destination; developing the "I got lost" functionality, whereby users can report via voice request that they are lost, obtain assistance to reach the nearest strategic point, and return to their destination. For this purpose, it will be necessary to register the strategic points where the users were connected to an Arduino board throughout their journey. Finally, implementing the system with numerous strategic points will require creating a remote system for loading and updating the information contained in the devices.

9 Acknowledgments

The authors thank CIC PBA, where M. Presso works as Research Support Professional.

References

1. Brady, E., Morris, M.R., Zhong, Y., White, S.C., Bigham, J.P.: Visual challenges in the everyday lives of blind people. In: Proceedings of the 2013 ACM SIGCHI Conference on Human Factors in Computing Systems. Paris, France (2013)
2. Hersh, M., Johnson, M.: Assistive Technology for Visually Impaired and Blind People. Springer, London (2008). https://doi.org/10.1007/978-1-84628-867-8
3. Claudio, B., Alejandra, A.: La movilidad y la ciudad inteligente: accesibilidad en la cadena de información y comunicación en el transporte público y su entorno, para la inclusión de las personas con discapacidad y adultos mayores. Universidad de Buenos Aires (2017)
4. Korngold, D., Lemos, M., Rohwer, M.: Smart Cities for All: A Vision for an Inclusive, Accessible, Urban Future. AT&T (2017)
5. World Access for the Blind. Blindness Challenge and Achievement. https://waftb.net/blindness-challenge-and-achievement
6. World Health Organization, Ceguera y Discapacidad Visual. http://www.who.int/mediacentre/factsheets/fs282/es/
7. Arispe, G., Aciti, C., Presso, M., Marone, J.: Prototipo de dispositivo de ubicación a través de puntos estratégicos para personas no videntes o con discapacidad visual. In: Proceeding of XXIV Congreso Argentino de Ciencias de la Computación, Tandil - Argentina, pp. 907–916 (2018)
8. Android Official Activities Documentation. https://developer.android.com/reference/android/app/Activity.html?hl=es-419
9. Android Official Services Documentation. https://developer.android.com/reference/android/app/Service.html?hl=es-419
10. Android Official Broadcast Receivers Documentation. https://developer.android.com/reference/android/content/BroadcastReceiver.html

Signal Processing and Real-Time Systems

Compound Interleaving Scheduling for SLM Transactions in Mode S Surveillance Radar

Oscar Bria[1](✉), Javier Giacomantone[1], and Horacio Villagarcía Wanza[1,2]

[1] Research Institute in Computer Science (III-LIDI) - School of Computer Science, National University of La Plata, La Plata, Argentina
onb@info.unlp.edu.ar
[2] Scientific Research Commission (CIC) - Province of Buenos Aires, La Plata, Argentina

Abstract. Mode S Secondary Surveillance Radar establishes selective and univocally addressed transactions with aircrafts while possible using efficiently the available budgets of time. Obtaining the last benefit is key to supporting high-traffic density within a coverage. Compound methods including different interleaving algorithms for the scheduling of Short Length Message transactions are presented and tested under a heavy load simulated scenario.

Keywords: Scheduling algorithms · Resource management · Mode S SSR

1 Mode S SSR and Resource Management

Mode S (Selective) is a Secondary Surveillance Radar (SSR) process that allows selective interrogation of aircraft according to the unique 24-bit address assigned to each aircraft. Such selective interrogation improves the quality and integrity of the detection, identification and altitude reporting with the addition of new reports from the aircraft and data-link capabilities. These improvements translate into benefits in terms of safety, capacity and efficiency, benefits which are key to supporting high-traffic density scenarios [1, 2].

The radar resource management function plays a critical role to maximize the radar resource usage for improving performance. In addition to the tracking tasks, the system also includes search and target confirmation tasks. A search task involves looking for new targets in the sky and a target confirmation task confirms the target after it is detected by the search task. Due to the multi-dimensional nature of radar resource allocation, the problem of optimally determining the process of resource allocations to maximize total system utility is NP-hard [3].

The radar resource management function includes a specific scheduling algorithm for the several transactions of the tracking task [4,5]. The scheduling algorithm considers waveform, beam shape, type of coding, dwell time, pulse repetition frequency, energy level, the time characteristics of the transactions and aircraft predicted positions. Since the targets move continually, and sometimes evasively, the resource allocation and scheduling decisions must be made frequently and in real-time.

Dwell time in a radar is the time that an antenna beam spends on a target. The beam dwell time of a 2D surveillance radar is derived from the antenna horizontal beam width and the turn speed of the antenna [6]. In Mode S SSR, during the beam dwell time, there is an alternation of two basic types of tasks, broadcasting and selective[1]. Broadcasting periods include Mode A/C searches and transactions (for compatibility with heritage radars and transponders), and Mode S searches. Selective periods include Mode S selective tracking transactions. Commonly, one-third of the beam dwell time is for broadcasting tasks.

Some characteristics of a Mode S SSR radar system of particular interest in resource management are [7,8]:

– Each Mode S selective transaction is compose of three phases in sequence: a transmission phase, a waiting phase and a receiving phase.
– Once a transmission or a reception starts, it cannot be preempted.
– The waiting phase is a wasting of time for a transaction.
– Transactions overlapping in the same beam can be interleaved by scheduling the transmit and/or receive phase of one transaction in the wait phase of another transaction.
– The longer the distance between the target and the radar, the higher the energy requirement.

Due to the selective nature of the Mode S transactions, interleaving is mandatory for high-traffic density [9]. The waiting time may change from one dwell to the next depending on the velocity vector of the aircraft relative to the radar. Therefore, the radar should be able to predict the approximate waiting time based on the previous tracking information about the aircraft.

The energy of the transmissions may be modulated by the distance, but this could result non-viable for some radar electronic implementations [10].

An interleaving scheduling algorithm for mode S was presented [11] and tested for a heavy load scenario. This article presents an extension by including two new algorithms that are compound with the earlier algorithm in various ways, tested and compared for the same heavy load scenario.

Section 2 shows the characteristics of SSR mode S transactions. Section 3 reviews an improper interleaving algorithm for transactions. Section 4 presents alternative interleaving techniques, decimated proper interleaving and broad interleaving. In Sect. 5 simulation results of the use of the improper algorithm are reviewed. Section 6 presents the simulations for compound methods using the three algorithms. Finally, Sect. 7 draws some comparisons and conclusions.

---

[1] In the literature [7] these types of periods are called SSR/all-call period and Mode S roll-call period, respectively.

2   Mode S SSR Transactions

Figure 1 shows the phases or time intervals of a transaction as part of a Mode S tracking task. The transmission interval is t_x while the reception interval t_r begins after a waiting time t_w. The cool-down interval, t_c, precedes the transmission interval of any transaction [3]. During this interval, there is no transference, and therefore it contributes to the evacuation of the heat from the active components of the radar. The interval time t_v represents the remaining time to the next transactions programmed for the current aircraft task. Even when the next transaction is normally programmed for the next antenna azimuth scan in a rotating surveillance radar, current transaction could be repeated in the present beam dwell for particular reasons.

Fig. 1. Transaction time intervals.

Transactions are characterized by the duration and coded features of the pairs transmission and response. From an scheduling point of view only the time intervals are relevant. Table 1 shows the possible pair combination encountered for Short Length Messages (SLM) [12].

Table 1. SLM transaction types

#	Transaction	t_x	t_r
1	Surveillance/Surveillance	20 μs	64 μs
2	CommA/Surveillance	34 μs	64 μs
3	Surveillance/CommB	20 μs	120 μs
4	CommA/CommB	34 μs	120 μs

3   Improper Interleaving for SLM Mode S

The phases t_x and t_r are non-preemptive, since a radar can only perform a single transmission or a single reception at a time. However, t_c of one task can be overlapped with t_r or t_w of another task, since the radar can cool down during the waiting and the receiving interval. Allowing the entire duration of a transaction (from transmission start to reception end) to be a non-preemptive job wastes resources and decreases the schedulability of the system [3]. Transactions can be interleaved to improve schedulability. The constructed interleaving may not be optimal in some restricted sense [13–15], but it must be effective for the target application, and preferably simple and with well-known properties.

Transactions can be interleaved in two ways: (a) properly nested interleaving and (b) improperly nested interleaving. Two transactions are said to be properly nested if one transaction fits inside the waiting time (t_w) of another, as in the left transactions in Fig. 2. Two transactions are said to be improperly nested when one transaction only partially overlaps with another as illustrated by the right transactions in Fig. 2.

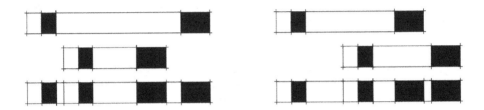

Fig. 2. Proper (left) and Improper (right) Interleaving.

Suppose that transaction T1 is improperly interleaved with transaction T2, where T1 starts first. Transaction T1 is called the leading transaction and transaction T2 is called the trailing transaction. Based on the phasing illustrated in Fig. 2, the necessary conditions for the interleaving to occur are given by Eqs. (1) and (2),

$$t_{w1} \geq t_{c2} + t_{x2}, \tag{1}$$

$$t_{c2} + t_{x2} + t_{w2} \geq t_{w1} + t_{r1}. \tag{2}$$

A phase offset for an improper interleaving is defined in (3) [16]. The value of the phase offset determines how tightly two nested tasks fit together. The aim is to minimize this offset in reception because it is a useless wasting of time,

$$o_i = t_{c2} + t_{x2} + t_{w2} - (t_{w1} + t_{r1}). \tag{3}$$

Cool-down time t_{c2} could have any positive value larger than a prescribed or derived minimun. For SLM $t_r > t_x$; if $t_{w1} \geq t_{w2}$ is taken, then o_i can be fixed to 0 and the following is derived,

$$t_{c2} = (t_{w1} - t_{w2}) + (t_{r1} - t_{x2}) > 0, \tag{4}$$

$$t_{c2} \geq \min(t_{c2}) = t_{r1} - t_{x2} > 0. \tag{5}$$

It means that for SLM, when interleaving condition are satisfied, the algorithm can forces offset $o_i = 0$ because the value of t_{c2} remains > 0 for any other condition.

The algorithm implemented in [11] starts with the transaction of the largest waiting time t_{w1}, and attempts to interleave it, avoiding overlapping, with the transaction with the largest possible t_{w2} smaller than that of the leading transaction based on the stated conditions (1) and (2) with $o_i = 0$. Cool-down time t_{c2} is a non conditioned variable derived in the process.

The algorithm repeats the process[2] taken the actual trailing transaction as the next leading transaction until it reaches the transaction with the smallest t_w that can no longer be interleaved, or all transactions are interleaved to form a single virtual transaction called a cycle [7].

If there is a backlog of transactions, the process is repeated until all transactions are included in as many cycles as necessary.

The improperly nested algorithm ensures that in any cycle the transmissions and receptions are equally sequenced. That is not the case for the properly nested alternative.

As was mentioned, for any type of SLM transaction t_x is shorter than t_r. As a consequence of that condition, it was demonstrated that the sequence of receptions of any cycle does not have gaps[3]. Meanwhile the sequence of transmissions of any cycle has transmission silences that contribute to cool down the active components of the radar[4].

4   Alternative Interleaving Techniques

Two alternative interleaving techniques to improper interleaving are presented. They are called decimated proper interleaving and broad interleaving. In the first technique the set of transactions to be scheduled is divided in a convenient way into two subsets; one subset is processed using proper interleaving and the other using improper interleaving. The second technique expands the concept of interleaving as proper or improper to a more general definition that include all the time intervals available in a multiple transaction or cycle.

4.1   Decimated Proper Interleaving

Under certain conditions proper interleaving is more efficient than improper interleaving. Figure 3 shows and example of proper and improper interleaving. The bars from below are the transmissions while the bar from above are the receptions. The reception intervals are numbered sequentially in reverse order of distance of the aircrafts. In this case, the schedule is composed by as much as one cycle for proper interleaving and two cycles for improper interleaving. Relevant here is that the elapsed time consumed for the entire schedule for proper interleaving is two-thirds of the elapsed time for the improperly nested schedule.

Figure 3 also shows that time of the properly interleaving schedule is as long as the time of the simple transaction with the longest total time, this situation

---

[2] The conditions of Eqs. (1) and (2) have to be suitably modified.

[3] Except for the guards to cover the estimates of the trackers.

[4] The consideration of the constraints over the working cycle of the active components of the radar is beyond the scope of this work.

is impossible to occur when improper interleaving is used for any set of transactions. Elapse time of the schedule for improper interleaving is longer than the longest transaction not only because of the improper technique but also because two cycles are needed to complete the schedule. Note than the schedule for proper interleaving could be improved in the sense of relaxing t_c for all transactions in more than $50\,\mu$s without affecting total elapsed time. In Fig. 3, t_c is equal to t_x.

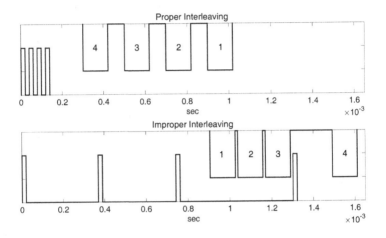

Fig. 3. Comparison of schedules for proper and improper interleaving.

Proper interleaving between two transactions is only possible when the total time of one of them is shorter than the waiting time of the other. If the preceding condition is not met, a new cycle must necessarily be created, but this is not always the case for improper interleaving. That disadvantage of proper interleaving was the main reason for not using this technique in [11], since the aircraft are densely grouped in the high density scenario used in the simulations [18].

Notwithstanding the foregoing, it is possible to divide in a convenient way the entire set of transactions to be scheduled into two subsets and use improper interleaving for one subsets and proper interleaving for the other subset. If the sum of the scheduling times for both subsets is shorter than the scheduling time for the entire set using improper interleaving, then the partitioned schedule is used.

For the subset to be properly interleaved it is convenient to choose transactions that produce a compact result in the sense of including the maximum number of transactions in the relatively shortest possible time minimize the sum of phase offsets (see Eq. (3) above). Experimentally it has been found that, for the heavy load scenario used in this work, a convenient way to select transactions for a compact proper subset is to decimate the original set with an appropriate decimation step which is found by comparing results for several alternatives.

4.2 Broad Interleaving

Classical proper and improper interleaving are not the unique suitable ways of nesting a new single transaction within a multiple transaction. A multiple transaction is the aggregate of two o more transactions already interleaved. In the following, a so called broad interleaving technique is proposed that takes into consideration all available time intervals remaining inside the multiple transaction rather than only the inner most one as in the classical algorithms [16]. In the classical interleaving algorithms the growing multiple transaction that end up in a cycle is view in each nesting iteration as a single transaction with enlarger transmission and reception intervals and shorter waiting interval, without considering the time intervals available among individual transmission and reception intervals.

The only conditions to be met for nesting a single transaction within a multiple transaction is to avoid the superposition of transmission and reception time intervals and to consider the restrictions for cooling. Broad interleaving can be used with all types of multiple transactions and cycles[5].

Figure 4 shows the time intervals for a single transaction and the available and unavailable time intervals for a multiple transaction with two available time intervals. The unavailable intervals include contiguous t_c and t_x if any and guard times when necessary. Without loss of generality, to nest a simple transaction into a multiple transaction with two available time intervals, one out of the three following conditions must be satisfied,

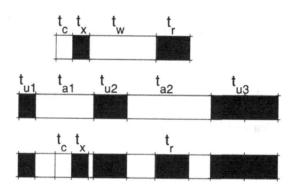

Fig. 4. Broad interleaving.

$$t_c + t_x + t_w + t_r \leq t_{a1}, \tag{6}$$

$$t_c + t_x + t_w + t_r \leq t_{a2}, \tag{7}$$

---

[5] A cycle is particular case of multiple transaction. A cycle is a saturated multiple transaction from the point of view of classical proper and improper interleaving algorithms.

$$t_c + t_x + t_w + t_r \leq t_{a1} + t_{u2} + t_{a2} \cup t_w \geq t_{u2} \cup t_r \leq t_{a2}. \tag{8}$$

Both Eqs. (6) and (7) are similar to the condition for proper interleaving. In the example of Fig. 4 the elapsed time is not incremented by the inclusion of the single transaction as in proper interleaving. If t_{u3} did not exist in Fig. 4 then t_{a2} is an open interval and if it were used for inserting the single transaction the result would be similar to improper interleaving, thus the elapsed time of the schedule would be extended.

The advantages of grouping in cycles are lost when using broad interleaving. In a cycle transmissions and receptions are sequentially grouped allowing reducing commutations and helping the control. Within a cycle, the sequential group of transmissions is received in the same order in improper interleaving and in reverse order in proper interleaving. In broad interleaving, the resource management function has to handle flow control accordingly.

When N_a is the number of available time intervals in a multiple transaction, the number of possible conditions N_{conds} for broad interleaving a single transaction is

$$N_{conds} = \sum_{i=1}^{N_a} i, \tag{9}$$

and only one must be fulfilled.

5   Improper Interleaving for Heavy Load Scenario

SLM are used in level 1 (CommA) and level 2 (CommB) data-link services in Mode-S SSR, particularly in the GICB (Ground Initiated CommB) protocol as used in the Mode S Enhanced Surveillance (EHS) [17].

Even when SLM includes different types of transaction, entirely GICB transactions are used for testing, as recommended by Eurocontrol; this corresponds to transaction #3 in Table 1. The distribution of aircraft in the high-traffic density scenario follows the non uniform histogram of Table 2 [18]. A uniform random distribution is applicable in each range band.

Table 2. Aircraft distribution in a beam dwell

Range NM	5–10	10–20	20–40	40–60	60–80	80–90	90–130	130–150
Distribution	1	3	12	7	7	2	6	10

Complementary parameters of the scenario are:

1. Beamwidth: the above 48 aircraft are distributed in a 3.5° sector.
2. GICB rate: 1 GICB per aircraft.
3. Minimum range: 5 NM.
4. Maximum range: 150 NM.
5. Scan rate: 4 s.

To relax the demand on the tracker accuracy, a guard of 12 μs is added between each response. The guard allows almost 1 NM error in the tracker estimation, which is loose.

The output of the improper interleaving algorithm for one realization of the scenario described is shown in Fig. 5. As before, the bars from below are the transmissions while the bar from above are the receptions. In this case, the schedule is composed by as much as 9 cycles. Relevant here is the elapsed time consumed for the entire schedule that is less than 14 ms.

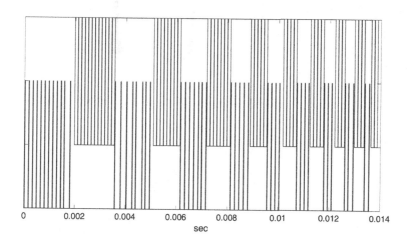

Fig. 5. Improperly nested scheduling for a 48 transactions scenario.

The left peak in Fig. 6 shows the normalized histogram of the elapsed time consumed by 10,000 random runs of the algorithm simulating 48 original transactions. The mean value of this data is 13.9 ms, the standard deviation is 148.5 μs, the maximum value is 14.4 ms, and the minimum is 13.4 ms.

Given: beamwidth, $\theta = 3.5°$; scan period, $\tau = 4$ s; fraction of dwell for Mode S transactions, $f = 2/3$. The available time for Mode S transactions in a dwell, A is,

$$A = f\tau \frac{\theta}{360°} = \frac{2}{3}\, 4\, \frac{3.5}{360}\, \text{s} = 25.9\,\text{ms}, \tag{10}$$

Roughly, it can be said that the schedule consumes more than 50% of the available time (the continuous vertical line in the right side of Fig. 6). As a consequence, two complete schedules are not allowed to be included in the same dwell.

Actually, the repetition of a transaction within the dwell is mandatory when not answer is received or any reception is pointed wrong as a consequence of a coding error detection [7].

Suppose that the initial probability of right reception of a transaction is $p_i = 68.38\%$. That means that 16 out of 48 receptions are misleading or wrong

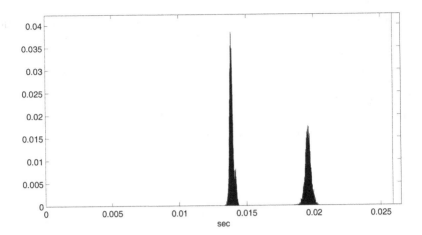

Fig. 6. Improper interleaving elapsed time histograms for 10,000 random run.

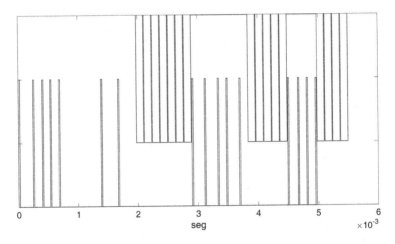

Fig. 7. Improperly nested 16 re-scheduled transactions from original scenario.

and the corresponding transactions have to be repeated during the present dwell in a new schedule. If that is possible, the final probability p_f for the transaction load in the dwell would be the prescribed [18],

$$p_f = p_i + (1 - p_i)p_i = 2p_i - p_i^2 = 90\% \tag{11}$$

The right peak of Fig. 6 shows the elapsed time consumed by 10,000 random runs of the algorithm for two consecutive schedules, i.e., a first schedule of original 48 transactions and a second schedule of 16 transactions peaked out randomly from the original. The mean value of this data is 19.5 ms, the standard deviation is 223.6 μs, the maximum value is 20.3 ms, and the minimum value is 18.5 ms. As can be seen in Fig. 6, the simulated data is far to the left of the available dwell time. Figure 7 is sample of a 16 transactions schedule consisting of 4 cycles and elapsing less than 6 ms. Also notice in Fig. 7 that at least some of the transactions of the last cycle could be broadly interleaved widely in the previous cycles that have adequate time periods available; see the example in the next Sect. 6 related to broad interleaving.

6   Compound Interleaving for Heavy Load Scenario

Besides the above simple improper interleaving, three more compound methods are defined for testing with the heavy load scenario already defined, given a total of four methods for build schedules:

A Improper interleaving.
B Improper interleaving refined with broad interleaving.
C Decimated proper interleaving complete with improper interleaving.
D Decimated proper interleaving complete with improper interleaving refined with broad interleaving.

Observe that A is a particular case of B when it is not possible to achieve any refinement with broad interleaving. For the same reason, C is a particular case of D.

The blocks for compound the methods are the interleaving techniques described in Sects. 3 and 4. The key characteristics of the three implemented interleaving algorithms are:

- The improper interleaving algorithm implemented for B, C and D is the algorithm described in Sect. 5.
- The decimated proper interleaving algorithm implemented for C and D has only one main variable parameter, the decimation step. The following seven decimation step have been used for the 48 transaction heavy load scenario, $\{6, 7, 8, 14, 15, 16, 17\}$; they have been selected after a preliminary analysis of the aircraft distribution in the scenario. The algorithm does not discard inefficient cycles that could possibly make it perform better. Special care have been taken in considering the cool-down time constraints, the minimum t_c has be taken equal to t_x for the simulations. The after decimation proper algorithm is similar to that presented in [16].
- The broad interleaving algorithm implemented for B and D is a simple version of many possibilities. Departing from the already schedule given by the improper algorithm, the last transaction is taken as the one to be broadly interleaved in the remains of the schedule considered as a multiple transaction. If the single transaction is embedded in some place of the multiple transaction, the process is iteratively repeated as many times as possible over the modified scene. Observe that both, departing from a improper schedule and taken the last transaction iteratively to be the one to be embedded in the remainder, constitute an arbitrary heuristic restriction of the algorithm. Special care have been taken in considering the cool-down time constraints, making it as large as possible (see details of Fig. 4) even when this practice undermines the performance of the algorithm itself.

Let consider an example taken from the simulations where a set of 48 transactions is scheduled:

- From the reverse ordered set of growing distances 8 transactions are picked with decimation step 6 to build a compact proper partial schedule composed by 8 transactions similar to that shown in Fig. 3.
- The remaining 40 transactions are improperly scheduled. The upper subpart of Fig. 8 shows only the first cycle of the schedule that comprises 11 transactions.
- The lower subpart of Fig. 8 shows the broadly interleaving of the last 2 transactions of the improper schedule. Observe how the interval of transmission of transaction number 39 is located equidistantly from its neighbors for the purpose of distributing equitably the time available, while for transaction number 40 it is not possible to do the same.
- Once the broad interleaving is complete, in this case interleaving transaction number 38 in the second cycle (not showed in Fig. 8), both partial schedules are grouped into one. As mentioned, the algorithm can be improved, observe that may be better to interleave the lower order numbered transaction first into the larger available intervals (e.g., transaction 38 in the place of transaction 40), but with the constraint that the higher order numbered transactions have to find room to be interleaved necessarily.

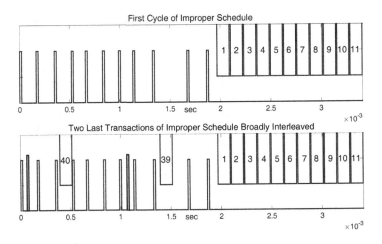

Fig. 8. Improper interleaving refined with broad interleaving.

The schedule times for the four methods are computed for each sample of 10,000 random runs of the algorithm simulating 48 transactions, and the schedule with the shorter time is peaked as the best for that sample. Observe that if method C is better than method A it does not imply that method D is better than method B. The best method distribution for 10,000 runs is given in Table 3.

Table 3. Best method distribution for 10,000 runs

Method	A	B	C	D
48 original transactions	1	2626	5	7368
16 Re-scheduled transactions	45	9557	358	40

The distribution of the second row of Table 3 justifies the use of both alternative interleaving techniques presented in Sect. 4 for the heavy load scenario with 48 transactions. Broad interleaving is effective almost every time while decimated proper interleaving contributes almost 3 out of 4 times. For a more detailed analysis of Table 3 see Sect. 7.

The left part of Fig. 9 shows the normalized histogram of the elapsed time consumed by 10,000 random runs of the load presented by 48 original transactions when the best method is peaked. Even though the distribution has apparently two modes, the mean value of the entire data is 12.9 ms, the standard deviation is 252.7 μs, the maximum value is 13.8 ms, and the minimum is 12.1 ms.

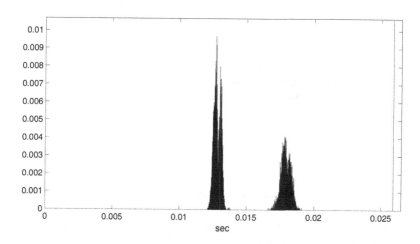

Fig. 9. Best interleaving elapsed time histograms for 10,000 random run.

The right part of Fig. 9 shows the elapsed time consumed by 10,000 random runs of the algorithm for two consecutive schedules, a first best schedule of original 48 transactions and a second best schedule of 16 transactions peaked out randomly from the original. The mean value of this data is 18.0 ms, the standard deviation is 339.3 μs, the maximum value is 19.1 ms, and the minimum value is 16.7 ms.

For 16 transactions the best method distribution shows that broad interleaving is effective most of the time with a small contribution of decimated proper interleaving and a tiny contribution of the simplest improper interleaving (see third row of Table 3).

7   Conclusions

In Sect. 4 two algorithms named decimated proper interleaving and broad interleaving are given. Four methods for scheduling are defined compounding those two algorithms with the improper interleaving algorithm already presented in [11].

Section 5 and Fig. 6 show results from the use of the first method, i.e., the improper interleaving algorithm only, and Sect. 6 and Fig. 9 show results when the best among the four methods is selected; both in the context of a heavy load simulated scenario for mode S SSR prescribed in [18].

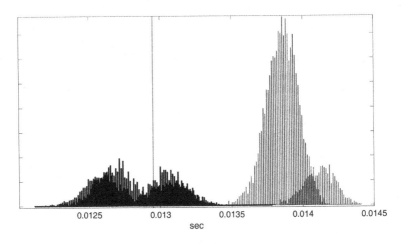

Fig. 10. Comparison of best and improper interleaving elapsed time histograms.

Figure 10 is a selected interval and superposition of Figs. 6 and 9. The darker part shows the best interleaving elapsed time histogram for a 10,000 simulation of 48 transactions with the range distribution given in Table 2, and the lighter part shows the improper interleaving elapsed time histogram for the same 10,000 transactions. The vertical line in Fig. 10 is half the available time in a dwell given by Eq. (10). As was expected, the results for the best method are shift to lower values compared with those of method A or improper interleaving. As a consequence, two complete schedules are allowed to be included in the same dwell 56% of the time according to the simulated data when the best method is used for scheduling. The scattering into two modes is not caused by the methods but by the simulated heavy load data.

Related to the algorithms developed and the way they are compound for the heavy load scenario, it can be concluded (see Table 3):

- Improper interleaving as a single option is best adapted to the heavy load scenario than proper interleaving. When used compound with the other algorithms, its performance is improved almost every time.

- Decimated proper interleaving is a good alternative for complementing improper interleaving for the heavy load scenario. Even a preliminary version as the one developed here contributes more than 73% of the time to improve performance for the heavy load scenario composed of 48 transactions, almost every time when it is refined by broad interleaving.
- Even the simple version of broad interleaving implemented here improves performance more than 26% when used alone, method B, for the high density load condition of the 48 transactions. When broad interleaving is used after decimated proper interleaving, method D, the performance is improved in 73% of the load. Totally, broad interleaving improves performance almost every time. For a less demanding load, as the represented by the 16 re-scheduled transactions, the best performance is given by the broad interleaving algorithm alone, method B, 95% of the time.

All three interleaving algorithms conform a library for using alone or compound in other scenarios. Intend to refine every schedule with broad interleaving is a recommended practice when possible.

References

1. ICAO (International Civil Aviation Organization): Annex 10, 3rd edn, vol. IV (2014)
2. ICAO (International Civil Aviation Organization): Manual on the secondary surveillance radar (SSR) sytems. In: Doc 9684 AN/951 (2004)
3. Ghosh, S., Hansen, J., Rajkumar, R., Lehoczky, J.: Integrated resource management and scheduling with multi-resource constraints. In: IEEE International Real-Time Systems Symposium, Lisbon, Portugal (2004)
4. Ding, Z.: A survey of radar resource management algorithms. In: IEEE Canadian Conference on Electrical and Computer Engineering - CCECE - Niagara Falls, ON, Canada (2008)
5. Mir, H., Wilkinson, J.: Task scheduling algorithm for an air and missile defense radar. In: IEEE Radar Conference, Rome, Italy (2008)
6. Richards, M.P., Scheer, J., Holm, W.: Principles of Modern Radar, Basic Principles. Scitech Publisher (2015)
7. Orlando, V., Drouilhet, P.: Functional description of mode s beacon system. Project Report ATC-42 Revision B, Lincoln Laboratory, MIT (1982)
8. Moo, P., Ding, Z.: Adaptive Radar Resource Management. Elsevier Academic Press, Cambridge (2015)
9. Xie, X.-X., Zhang, W., Chen, M.-Y.: A novel time pointer-based fast radar pulse interleaving algorithm. In: IEEE 5th International Congress on Image and Signal Processing (2012)
10. Shih, C.-S., Gopalakrishnan, S., Ganti, P., Caccamo, M., Sha, L.: Template-based real-time dwell scheduling with energy constraint. In: The 9th IEEE Real-Time and Embedded Technology and Applications Symposium (2003)
11. Bria, O., Giacomantone, J., Villagarcía Wanza, H.: Interleaving scheduling algorithm for SLM transactions in Mode S Surveillance Radar. In: Actas del XXIV Congreso Argentino de Ciencias de la Computación (2018). ISBN 978-950-658-472-6

12. Stevens, M., Ding, Z.: Secondary Surveillance Radar. Artech House, Norwood (1988)
13. Shih, C., Gopalakrishnan, S., Caccamo, M., Sha, L.: Template-based real-time dwell scheduling with energy constraints. In: Proceedings of the IEEE Real-Time and Embedded Technology and Applications Symposium, Toronto, Canada (2003)
14. Charlish, A., Nadjiasngar, R.: Quality of service management for a multi-mission radar network. In: IEEE 6th International Workshop on Computational Advances in Multi-sensor Adaptive Processing (CAMSAP), Cancun, Mexico (2015)
15. Sgambato, P., Celentano, S., Di Dio, C., Petrillo, C.: A flexible on-line scheduling algorithm for multifunctional radar. In: IEEE Radar Conference, Philadelphia, PA, USA (2016)
16. Ghosh, S., Rajkumar, R., Hansen, J., Lehoczky, J.: Integrated QoS-aware resource management and scheduling with multiple-resource constraints. Real-Time Syst. J. **33**, 7–46 (2006). Springer
17. ICAO (International Civil Aviation Organiztion): Manual on Mode S specific services. In: Doc 9688 AN/952 (2003)
18. EUROCONTROL (European Organisation for the Safety of Air Navigation): European Mode S station functional specification. In: SUR/MODES/EMS/SPE-01 (2005)

Position and Deformation-Checking Method Based on Structured Illumination. External Radiotherapy Use

Leopoldo Garavaglia[1,2(✉)], Liliana Mairal[2,4], and Jorge Runco[2,3]

[1] Instituto de Investigaciones Fisicoquímicas Teóricas y Aplicadas
(CCT-CONICET, La Plata and Universidad Nacional de La Plata),
1900 La Plata, Argentina
lgaravaglia@inifta.unlp.edu.ar
[2] Departamento de Física, Facultad de Ciencias Exactas,
Universidad Nacional de La Plata (UNLP), 1900 La Plata, Argentina
lmairal@gmail.com, runco@fisica.unlp.edu.ar
[3] Instituto de Física La Plata (CCT-CONICET, La Plata and UNLP),
1900 La Plata, Argentina
[4] Mevaterapia Centro Médico, C1198AAW Buenos Aires, Argentina

Abstract. The main goal of a radiotherapy treatment is to provide the prescribed radiation dose to the tumor while minimizing healthy tissue irradiation. During every fraction of treatment, correct placement of the patient on the treatment couch as well as early detection of any shape changes that the patient´s body may undergo are crucial, because both affect the dose distribution. Structured illumination by fringe projection is typically used for finding an object's spatial dimensions by projecting a pattern on it and taking a photo from a specific location. In this paper we propose a different approach for this technique: given an object's 3D surface, an image can be computed and projected with the objective of locating this object at a specific location; only when the object is at the exact previously chosen position and preserves its original shape and form, an undistorted fringe pattern will be observed. Verification of patient's correct position on the treatment couch and the detection of shape changes nearby the radiation field are feasible using the structured illumination based method presented in this work, a potentially useful tool for external radiotherapy treatments.

Keywords: Structured illumination · External radiotherapy · Signal processing

1 Introduction

Radiotherapy is the use of ionizing radiation for cancer treatment. It forms part of three main medical modalities for this aim among surgery and chemotherapy [1]. External radiotherapy is based on irradiating malignant tissue from outside the patient's body with the linear accelerator of electrons (LINAC) being the most used equipment for this treatment [2].

© Springer Nature Switzerland AG 2019
P. Pesado and C. Aciti (Eds.): CACIC 2018, CCIS 995, pp. 313–324, 2019.
https://doi.org/10.1007/978-3-030-20787-8_22

Ionizing radiation can modify the normal behavior of living tissue, affecting cell proliferation and even producing cell death [3]. For this reason, the main goal of radiotherapy relies on delivering the prescribed dose to the tumor while minimizing normal tissue irradiation [4].

External radiotherapy implies reproducibility of the patient position on the couch established during the tomographic imaging acquisition procedure for treatment planning. It is imperative that this position be precisely repeated for every treatment fraction according to the specified tolerances of the particular radiotherapy technique (typically on the order of one millimeter) [4]. It is customary to mark fiducial points on the patient's skin for reference between tomography and treatment positions. Radiotherapy technicians are responsible for positioning the patient on the treatment couch generally by means of three lasers (one on top and two at each side of the couch) that need to be aligned to the fiducial marks.

Structured illumination allows getting an object's spatial dimensions by projecting a pattern on it and taking a photo from a specific site. This photo is later processed to obtain spatial information [5]. The fringe projection technique has already been explored in the external radiotherapy field for obtaining a patient's 3D information [6, 7]. In this paper we present an alternative approach to this technique: positioning an object of known dimensions object at a specific place and also detecting changes in the objects form.

The spatial dimensions of a patient are known from the tomographic data set obtained in the early stages of the treatment planning. Also head, trunk, and extremities positions relative to the couch are registered. Then, a system of specific shaped fringes for the patient can be made from the data set containing spatial information of his/her exact position at the scanning machine. The image projection of this specific system of fringes on the patient can be used to verify closeness to correct position during irradiation and detect shape changes like the ones produced by adjuvant chemotherapy or corticosteroids effects.

Thermoplastic masks are usually used as immobilizer devices on head and neck treatments. This kind of device should perfectly fit the patient's skin surface. The treatment plan is aware of its dosimetric impact. Air gaps between the mask and patient's skin alter dose distribution, and consequently, the prescription would not be correctly achieved [8]. Some patients can gain or lose weight during the course of therapy and sometimes even a mask does not perform as an immobilizer at all.

In terms of radiological protection, fringe projection is a safe technique, meaning that there is no ionizing radiation involved, so its application can be made without restriction (many strategies make use of X rays for monitoring the patient's position) [9]. Even real-time position checking during irradiation is feasible for the structured illumination method proposed. This could be particularly useful in the case of using fringe projection as an alternative to immobilizer devices.

2   Technique

2.1   Structured Illumination: Typical Use Basic Description

By means of structured illumination, the spatial dimensions of an object can be obtained. A reference surface must be set and two positions must be chosen: one for the projector and the other for the camera. The object placed in front of the reference surface must be illuminated with a pattern coming from the projector's fixed position and then observed by the camera (also fixed in space). Many different kinds of patterns, projections schemes and posterior data analysis are used [5, 10–12]. We used a Ronchi grid pattern that consists of uniformly spaced fringes of step intensity distribution, meaning that in a black and white grid of this kind, there is no grayscale present.

Fig. 1. Photo of a Ronchi grid pattern projected on a plane surface (a wall in this case). Note that there is no perfect white fringes because of the wall paint tonality. The image projected was made in black and white.

Figure 1 shows a computer made pattern illuminating a wall using a projector. The object to be measured should be positioned in front of this reference plane. As a result of this, the fringes illuminating the object change its pattern shape while the fringes on the wall remain unaltered (Fig. 2).

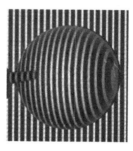

Fig. 2. Photo of a hemisphere located against the wall with projector at the left side and camera at the right (reader point of view). Note at the left side of photo the finger holding the object.

The shape of the fringes projected on an object is unique for that object and the chosen experimental geometry (pattern, reference surface, location of projector and camera). Thus, the reshaped fringes contain the topographical information of the object. The merit of this technique relies on finding the spatial dimensions of an object with no need of making contact with it.

The procedure for finding the object's spatial information can be made using a simple geometrical analysis (among other ways [5]) that takes into account the relative displacement of each fringe (and each point of it). Looking at the situation of Fig. 1 from above allows this analysis (Fig. 3) where P indicates the projector position and C the camera position.

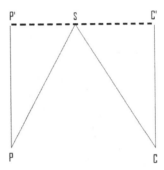

Fig. 3. Top view of typical experimental setup geometry.

P′ and C′ lie on the reference plane such that P-P′ line stands for the minimum distance between projector and plane (the wall in this case) and C-C′ line for the minimum distance between camera and plane. Fringes seen in this way are represented as a thick dashed line from P′ to C′. An arbitrary fringe point (pixel) named s is projected from P and observed from C as P-s and C-s rays depict. Now Fig. 4 represents what happens with an object placed in front of the plane while fringes are projected.

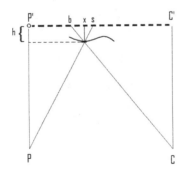

Fig. 4. An object placed in front of the plane while fringes are projected.

It can be seen that the projected point s is observed by C as it were on position b on the plane and it shows that the consequence of placing an object into the illuminated zone is to modify the actual pattern.

The displacement of point s towards b captured by the camera allows finding object's height h at position x. Figure 4 depicts a reference point O at P' for point displacement measure purposes. Now the point s, b and x are associated to its distance from O. Also, $\overline{PP'}$ is defined as the distance from P to P' and $\overline{CC'}$ as the distance from C to C'. These are experimentally measured parameters that remain fixed.

Recalling Fig. 4 and triangle similarity one has:

$$\frac{s-x}{h} = \frac{s}{\overline{PP'}}, \quad x = s - \frac{hs}{\overline{PP'}} \tag{1}$$

$$\frac{x-b}{h} = \frac{C'-b}{\overline{CC'}}, \quad x = \frac{h(C'-b)}{\overline{CC'}} + b \tag{2}$$

Eliminating x from (1) and (2) and rearranging terms:

$$h = (s-b)\left[\frac{(C'-b)}{\overline{CC'}} + \frac{s}{\overline{PP'}}\right]^{-1} \tag{3}$$

Values for s and b are found by counting pixel displacement on reference photo (pattern photo) and measurement photo (photo of modified fringes shape due to object), respectively.

2.2   Structured Illumination: Novelty Use Basic Description

It has been shown how the shape of the fringes is unique when a pattern is projected on a particular object. Then, there is only one specifically shaped fringe system made for a known 3D surface that when used for illuminating this object at a chosen position, makes the observation of the unmodified pattern possible. So, if the object is not placed in the chosen position nor conserves its shape, it won't be possible to see the unaltered pattern. This idea, already mentioned in our previous work [13], is going to be carefully explained here so as to show the algorithms implemented for signal processing.

The idea behind a positioning fringe projection is being able to watch the pattern only when the known object preserves its shape and occupies the chosen position in front the reference surface. Figure 5 shows the P-s and the C-b thin dashed rays for the situation of a projected pixel towards s being observed by the camera as if it were reflecting from b due to the object's presence.

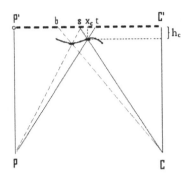

Fig. 5. Geometric description for a positioning fringe projection.

To observe the pattern grid (with the illuminated object in front of the plane) it is necessary to redirect the P-s ray to the t position. This way, the camera can record the point s in the same reference position as with no object present (Fig. 5). Now, the point projected towards t lies on the object's surface where it has a height h_c. This height is known and chosen to be at the x_c position.

In the same manner as before, one has from Fig. 5:

$$\frac{C'-s}{\overline{CC'}} = \frac{x_c-s}{h_c}, \quad x_c = s + h_c\frac{C'-s}{\overline{CC'}} \tag{4}$$

$$\frac{t}{\overline{PP'}} = \frac{t-x_c}{h_c}, \quad t = x_c\left[1 - \frac{h_c}{\overline{PP'}}\right]^{-1} \tag{5}$$

Once the h_c point of the object's surface is chosen to be at the x_c position of the reference plane (this is the previously established position), the s point in Eq. 4 has to be redirected towards t according to Eq. 5.

Briefly, it can be said that:

The structured Illumination technique allows finding tridimensional space information from two-dimensional space information, the knowledge of experimental setup geometry and projection and image acquisition characteristics.

Moreover, if tridimensional space dimensions of an object are known, it is possible to compute a two-dimensional image that serves as a position-checking and also a deformation-checking device.

3   Experimental Arrangement and Materials

The experimental setup was designed in order to have a projected pixel size of 1 mm × 1 mm on the reference plane and a 50.6 pixels/mm relation on the digital photos. The projected reference pixel has no more than 0.1% error (projecting the 800 pixels on 80 cm of plane surface and performing careful measurement). Illumination was performed on a SONY VPL-ES5 projector having three LCD panels (one per RGB component) of 800 × 600 pixels (0.48 Mp) resolution each. Photos were taken with a Canon PowerShot A590 IS, 3264 × 2448 pixels (8 Mp) and 4x optical zoom. Photo processing was made by programming the geometric algorithms based on formulas presented here in Sect. 2. These routines running on ACER ASPIRE 4310, Intel® Celeron® M 530, 1.73 GHz, 1 GB DDR2 laptop under Windows VistaTM Home Basic operative system.

Support and alignment of the camera was carried out on Thorlabs Multi-Axis Stages. Polypropylene 5 cm radius hemicylinder and 10.7 cm radius hemisphere were used as representative testing objects for the experiments among other simply shaped objects (Fig. 6).

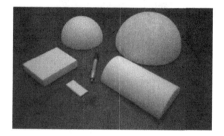

Fig. 6. Polypropylene testing objects.

4 Results

4.1 First Stage: Fringe Projection Typical Use for Finding Tridimensional Data

Typical use of this technique was performed mainly for geometric setup checking purposes needed for further experimental stages. Figure 7 shows a 3D plot of the data set obtained from a photo of projected fringes on a hemicylinder. Figure 8(a) comes from the hemisphere's photo processing but the data acquired was interpolated before plotting. Differences between known and acquired dimensions were on the order of one millimeter for all testing objects. Figure 8(b) is a plot of the hemisphere's mathematical formula using the same radius as the testing polypropylene hemisphere. Artifacts turned out to be more pronounced at the hemisphere's base.

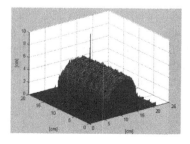

Fig. 7. 3D plot of data set obtained from illuminated hemicylinder.

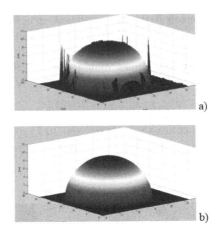

Fig. 8. (a) Topographical reconstruction from illuminated hemisphere. (b) Plot generated from hemisphere's mathematical formula.

4.2   Second Stage: Fringe Projection Novelty Use for Known Objects Positioning

From the hemisphere's known dimensions (recall Fig. 8b), positioning images were computationally generated using algorithms based on Eqs. 4 and 5. These images also can be used for deformation detection purposes. One image of this kind is shown in Fig. 9. It can be seen from this Figure that the first curved white fringe on the left side is not complete.

Fig. 9. Digital positioning image to be projected specifically shaped for the hemisphere.

Due to the projector's low resolution, every curved fringe also has a staircase aspect: the available pixel size is not small enough to smoothly achieve this sort of curved lines. Obviously, as the curved fringes get thinner, this undesired effect is more evident, as can be seen on the right side of Fig. 9.

Figure 10 is a series of four photos taken during a positioning procedure belonging to our original work [13]. Figure 10(a) is a photo of the hemisphere's positioning image continuously projected on the reference plane. Figure 10(b) is a photo showing one of the first approaches to achieve correct position; as can be seen in this photo and the next two, the object is being held with one finger against the wall (center left side of photos).

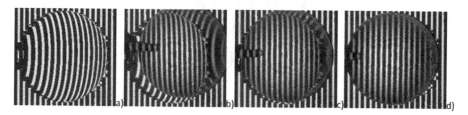

Fig. 10. Four photos taken during positioning procedure: (a) Positioning image projected. (b) The hemisphere arriving from the top right. (c) The hemisphere reaching the correct position. (d) Correct position achieved: Ronchi grid pattern is visible.

As compared to our previous work [13], a more exhaustive description of the experimental methodology together with new results about precision in repeatability of positioning procedures is given next.

All positioning procedures were performed using the human visual sense (as radiotherapy technicians do) and by iteratively displacing the object until locating it at a place where the unaltered pattern appeared clearly. This last position is called the final position and is the closest to the previously established position (the position that was chosen to locate the object) within the limitations imposed by visual acuity and the exactitude of all the experimental components. After many repetitions of this procedure, optimum skill is achieved for these purposes.

Approaching the previously established position is evidenced by the gradual appearance of the unaltered fringe pattern shape, as can be seen in the sequence from Fig. 10(a) to (d).

Although the closeness to correct position depends on the goodness of the computed positioning image in conjunction with projector resolution (these two being limiting factors in our case), the final position and the previously established position were on the order of one millimeter apart. Refinement in all experimental aspects allows us to achieve this improvement as compared with previous results [13].

We measure the standard deviation from the mean final position of a series of seven different positioning procedures in terms of the horizontal and vertical components of position. This new result reveals the virtue of this technique for repeatability, which is of great importance in external radiotherapy as was already mentioned. The horizontal deviation turns out to be 0.19 mm while vertical deviation was 0.41 mm. The difference between these values is related to the fact that fringes were vertically set: horizontal displacements alter the pattern more evidently than vertical displacements for this hemisphere case. A detailed region of a final position photo is shown in Fig. 11. The hemisphere borderline was used to measure distances from the final position to the previously established position.

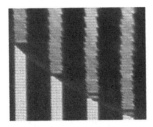

Fig. 11. Left inferior region of a "final position" photo. Object borderline and projected pixels can be seen. Also evident is the staircase aspect of fringes projected on the hemisphere.

4.3   Third Stage: Fringe Projection Novelty Use for Deformation Detection

This experimental stage constitutes an advance in our work, exploiting the properties of a positioning image. We made use of image subtraction strategy as an instrument for verifying the correct position and detecting shape changes based on black color content of the image. Figure 12 shows two photos and its corresponding subtraction images. The reference (unaltered pattern) photo is subtracted from every positioning photo. Figure 12(a) is a photo of a position not quite satisfactory; its corresponding subtraction image in Fig. 12(b) also confirms this fact. Figure 12(c) is a photo of the object held as near as possible to the previously established "correct position".

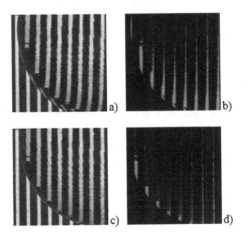

Fig. 12. Hemisphere's bottom left region photo series. (a) Relatively close to "correct position" placement of the object and its subtraction image (b). (c) As close as possible to "correct position" placement and its subtraction image (d).

The subtraction images visually reveals more clearly the weaknesses of the computed positioning image we achieved, already mentioned in previous Sect. 4.2.

 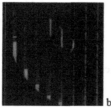

Fig. 13. Photo of hemisphere with protuberance (a) and its subtraction image (b).

The deformation detection test was carried out by attaching a 4 mm high small polypropylene piece at the bottom left of the hemisphere surface. Figure 13(a) is a photo of this "reshaped" hemisphere illuminated by the original positioning image. Figure 13(b) is a subtraction image of actual hemisphere with protuberance.

5   Discussion and Future Work

Even though a protuberance would be evident in a photo, e.g. Figure 13(a), the subtraction image strategy can be used to reveal more clearly and quantitatively if desired, any shape changes. Suppose having a much more precisely computed positioning image, then the subtraction of a satisfactory positioning procedure photo from the reference photo would result in an almost fully black image (e.g. Figure 12d would be almost black); then, the protuberance appearance would be easier for an observer to detect. This could be of particular interest if a real time application of this method is intended during an irradiation, because the black color content of the photo (or video) is a measure of deformation and distance to correct position.

Subtraction images have more clearly revealed the weaknesses of the computed positioning image we achieved; also there might be another effect to be studied that the last fringes on the right side of the hemisphere reveal, conditions outside the paraxial zone. Recall the projector was on the left and camera on the right, and the algorithms implemented were deduced by geometrical optics.

6   Conclusions

The outcome of an external radiotherapy cancer treatment strongly depends on the correct placement of the patient on the treatment couch at time of irradiation and early detection of any shape changes that the patient may undergo. In this way, the position-deformation-checking method presented here is potentially useful.

Although the closeness to correct position depends on the goodness of the computed positioning image in conjunction with projector resolution (these two being limiting factors in our case), the final position and the previously established position were on the order of one millimeter apart.

Experimental results for the novelty positioning structured illumination method have shown great results in terms of repeatability. The horizontal standard deviation of 0.19 mm and vertical deviation of 0.41 mm from the mean in a series of seven distinct positioning procedures confirm this fact. This particular performance feature could be of great interest in external radiotherapy. It is obvious that these applications can have potential uses far beyond the external radiotherapy field. Yet is in this particular medical area where they could improve the outcome of a cancer treatment.

The deformation-checking experiment reveals effectiveness by successfully detecting the relatively small 4 mm height protuberance.

The possibility of using our method in conjunction with a real time monitoring subtraction image was also pondered.

References

1. Podgorsak, E.: Radiation Oncology Physics: A Handbook for Teachers and Students. International Atomic Energy Agency, Vienna (2005)
2. Khan, F.: The Physics of Radiation Therapy, 3rd edn. Lippincott Williams & Wilkins, Philadelphia (2003)
3. Tubiana, M., Dutreix, J., Wambersie, A.: Introduction to Radiobiology. Taylor and Francis, London (1990)
4. Webb, S.: The Physics of Three Dimensional Radiation Therapy: Conformal Radiotherapy, Radiosurgery and Treatment Planning. Institute of Physics Publishing, Bristol (2001)
5. Gorthi, S., Rastogi, P.: Fringe projection techniques: whither we are? Opt. Lasers Eng. **48**(2), 133–140 (2010)
6. Moore, C., Burton, D., Skydan, O., Sharrock, P., Lalor, M.: 3D body surface measurement and display in radiotherapy part I: technology of structured light surface sensing. In: Clapworthy, G., Moore, C. (eds.) Third International Conference on Medical Information Visualisation-BioMedical Visualisation (MediVis 2006), pp. 97–102. IEEE (2006)
7. Lilley, F., Lalor, M., Burton, D.: Robust fringe analysis system for human body shape measurement. Opt. Eng. **39**(1), 187–195 (2000)
8. Webb, S.: Intensity-Modulated Radiation Therapy. Institute of Physics Publishing, Bristol (2001)
9. Mundt, A., Roeske, J.: Image-Guided Radiation Therapy: A Clinical Perspective. People's Medical Publishing House-USA, Connecticut (2011)
10. Fu, Y., Luo, Q.: Fringe projection profilometry based on a novel phase shift method. Opt. Express **19**(22), 21739–21747 (2011)
11. Yagnik, J., Siva, G., Ramakrishnan, K., Rao, L.: 3D Shape extraction of human face in presence of facial hair: a profilometric approach. In: Proceedings of the TENCON 2005 IEEE Region 10 Conference, pp. 1–5. IEEE, Melbourne (2005)
12. Cortizo, E., Years, A., Lepore, J., Garavaglia, M.: Application of the structured illumination method to study the topography of the sole of the foot during a walk. Opt. Lasers Eng. **40**(1–2), 117–132 (2003)
13. Garavaglia, L., Mairal, L., Runco, J.: Reconstrucción topográfica a partir de iluminación estructurada. Su aplicación en Radioterapia Externa. In: Proceedings of the XXIV Congreso Argentino de Ciencias de la Computación CACIC 2018, pp. 957–966. RedUNCI, Buenos Aires (2018)

Computer Security

Deep Convolutional Neural Networks for DGA Detection

Carlos Catania[1(✉)], Sebastian García[2], and Pablo Torres[3]

[1] LABSIN, Facultad de Ingeniería, UNCuyo, Mendoza, Argentina
`harpo@ingenieria.uncuyo.edu.ar`
[2] CTU - Czech Technical University, Prague, Czech Republic
`sebastian.garcia@agents.fel.cvut.cz`
[3] Universidad de Mendoza, Mendoza, Argentina
`pablo.dtorres@gmail.com`

Abstract. A Domain Generation Algorithm (DGA) is an algorithm to generate domain names in a deterministic but seemly random way. Malware use DGAs to generate the next domain to access the Command & Control (C&C) communication server. Given the simplicity of the generation process and speed at which the domains are generated, a fast and accurate detection method is required. Convolutional neural network (CNN) are well known for performing real-time detection in fields like image and video recognition. Therefore, they seemed suitable for DGA detection. The present work provides an analysis and comparison of the detection performance of a CNN for DGA detection. A CNN with a minimal architecture complexity was evaluated on a dataset with 51 DGA malware families and normal domains. Despite its simple architecture, the resulting CNN model correctly detected more than 97% of total DGA domains with a false positive rate close to 0.7%.

Keywords: Deep neural networks · Network security · DGA detection

1 Introduction

A domain generation algorithm (DGA) is used to dynamically generate a large number of pseudo random domain names and then selecting a small subset of these domains for the Command & Control (C&C) communication channel. The idea behind the dynamic nature of DGA was to avoid the inclusion of hard-coded domain names inside malware binaries, complicating the extraction of this information by reverse engineering [8]. The first DGA detection attempts depended on published lists of domains already detected as DGA. However, given the simplicity and velocity associated to the domain generation process, detection approaches that relied on static domain blacklists were rapidly rendered ineffective [6]. Nowadays, DGA detection methods can be classified in two main groups: (A) Context-based or (B) Lexicographical-based. The so-called context-based approaches mostly rely on the use of context information such as the

© Springer Nature Switzerland AG 2019
P. Pesado and C. Aciti (Eds.): CACIC 2018, CCIS 995, pp. 327–340, 2019.
https://doi.org/10.1007/978-3-030-20787-8_23

responses from the DNS servers. A typical example would the fact that DGA domains are not usually registered and therefore the DNS response is usually *NXDomain*. On the other hand, lexicographical approaches classify the domains by studying the statistical properties of the characters conforming the domain name.

Regarding Lexicographical approaches, Natural Language Processing (**NLP**) emerged as one of the most useful techniques for detecting DGA, specially in the analysis of the n-gram frequency distribution of domain names. An n-gram is defined as a contiguous sequence of n items from a given sequence of text. It is possible to use greater values for n than 1. In the simpler form, when $n = 1$, the single character frequency distribution is generated. The assumption is that DGA domains will have a different n-gram distribution than normal domain names. An example of n-gram based DGA detection are [10,14] that compares uni-grams and bi-grams distribution using the Kullback-Leibler (K-L) divergence.

Several other DGA detection approaches extended the idea of using the information provided by domain names properties (including n-gram distributions) to train a machine learning classifier such as Random Forest [1] or Linear Regression [14]. Recently, to avoid the need of designing the right set of features for training machine learning classifiers, some authors explored the application of Deep Learning (DL) techniques. In particular the application of Long-Short-Term-Memory (**LSTM**) networks [3]. When applied to the text analysis problem, the internal design of LSTM cell is capable to capture combinations of characters that are important to discriminating DGA domains from non-DGA domains. This flexible architecture generalizes manual feature extraction like n-grams, but instead learns dependencies of one or multiple characters, whether in succession or with arbitrary separation.

Despite the good results reported, LSTM networks have proved to be difficult to train under some particular cases [7]. The aforementioned issue together with the considerable time required during training could be the major obstacle for the massive adoption of LSTM networks in DGA detection. The fact is that DGA techniques change over the time and the periodical retraining of the network becomes mandatory. However, if the presence of long-term dependency patterns in DGA domain names is ignored, it is possible to apply another well-known Deep Learning technique: Convolutional Neural Networks (**CNN**). CNN are simply neural networks that use convolution in place of general matrix multiplication in at least one of their layers. CNN have been successfully applied in a many practical applications mainly related to image and video recognition. When applied to text analysis the convolution is applied over one dimension and denoted as 1D-CNN. The main advantage of 1D-CNN are they can be trained much faster than LSTM (up to 9X times faster than LSTM) and similarly to LSTM, 1D-CNN are capable of learning representations for groups of characters without being explicitly told about the existence of such groups. However, they can't deal with patterns with arbitrary separation.

In the present work we focus on analyzing the DGA detection performance of a 1D-CNN. Similarly to [13], we are interested in evaluating the performance of a network with a minimal architecture complexity. Hence, the considered network architecture consists of just a minimal extra layers in addition to the Convolutional Layer. Evaluation is conducted on a dataset containing 51 different DGA families as well as normal domain names from the Alexa corpus and the Bambenek feeds. Two different DGA schemes, including the recent word-based scheme, are included in the dataset. Word-based DGA consists of concatenating a sequence of words from one or more wordlists, resulting in a domain that appears less random and thus may be more difficult to detect [8].

The hypothesis of this work is that despite the known limitations of 1D-CNN, they can learn the common properties from different DGA generation schemes. The evaluation also verifies that the detection performance is within the range required for real-world scenarios.

The main contributions of the present article are:

- An analysis of the advantages and limitations of a simple 1D-CNN learning model for detecting DGA.
- A detailed evaluation of 1D-CNN on a extended dataset that includes domain names from 51 different real malware DGA following different generation schemed as well as normal domains from two different sources.
- A comparison with another well known deep learning technique. In particular, LSTM networks, which have been successfully applied to the DGA problem before [13]. This last set of experiments provides a significant addition to our previous work on the topic [2].

The rest of this paper is organized as follows: Sect. 2 describes the network architecture, Sect. 3 details the experiments design and results while Sect. 4 discusses the importance of the results obtained by 1D-CNN. Sect. 5 compares the performance of 1D-CNN with a LSTM network with a minimal architecture complexity. Finally, Sect. 6 presents the conclusions.

2   The Neural Network Architecture

The Neural Network Architecture model used in this paper is a 1D-CNN. This CNN is composed of three main layers. The first one is an *Embedding* layer, then there is a *1D Convolutional* layer, and finally a Dense fully connected layer. The first two layers are the most relevant components of the architecture regarding the problem of detecting DGA domains. Both layers are responsible for learning the feature representation in order to feed the third Dense and fully connected layer. Beside the three layers previously described, the complete Neural Network Architecture includes some other layers for dealing with the dimensions output of the *1D Convolutional* layer as well as layers for representing the input domain and the output probability. A detail of the complete architecture together with the used activation functions is shown in Table 1, whereas the three main layers are described in the following subsections.

Table 1. The complete network architecture of the CNN, including the corresponding output dimensions and activation function used in each layer

Layer (type)	Activation function
input (Input Layer)	–
embedding (Embedding)	–
conv1d (1D Convolutional)	relu
dense_1 (Dense)	relu
dense_2 (Dense)	sigmoid

2.1 Embedding Layer

A character embedding consists in projecting l-length sequences of input characters into a sequence of vectors R^{lxd}, where l has to be determined from the information provided by the sequences in the training set and d is a free parameter indicating the dimension of the resulting matrix [13]. By using an *Embedding* layer in the architecture, the neural network learns in an efficient manner the optimal set of features that represent the input data.

2.2 1D Convolutional Layer

The *1D Convolutional* layer refers to a convolutional network layer over one dimension. For the DGA detection problem, such dimension consists of the length of the domain name sequence. The convolutional layer is composed of a set of convolutional filters that are applied to different portions of the domain name. A visual example of the feature extraction process for a *1D Convolutional* layer is shown in Fig. 1. The figure depicts a *1D Convolutional* layer constructing 256 filters (features) ($nf = 256$), with a window (kernel) size of 4 ($ks = 4$) and a stride length value of 1 ($sl = 1$). The layer selects from groups (also referred as patches) of 4 characters to apply the convolutional filters, and continues shifting one character at a time (stride value) applying the same convolutions filter over the rest of the sequence. Consequently, the neural network generates 4-g features. These features represent the discriminative power of these group of letters in the domain names.

By applying the same filter all over the sequence the required computation time is considerable reduced when compared with traditional Multilayer Perceptron layers. Additionally, since a convolutional kernel independently operates on each 4-gram it is possible to go over the entire input layer concurrently. This paralellization and its consequent low computing time is one of the major benefits of using convolutional networks instead of other deep learning approaches usually used for text processing such as Long Short Term Memory (LSTM) [4,12,13].

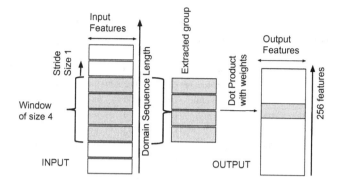

Fig. 1. Feature extraction process of the 1D Convolutional layer

2.3 Dense Layers

The features extracted by the two previous layers are used by a traditional Multilayer Perceptron Network (MLP), in order to output the probability of a given domain belonging to the *DGA* or *Normal* class. The MLP is composed of two layers: A first fully connected layer of size *hn* (*Dense* layer) connected to a second *Dense* layer of size 1 used for actually giving the probability output about the considered domain.

3 Experimental Design

The experiments done in this paper focused on the detection performance of the algorithms from two points of view. First, considering the detection of DGA and normal domains. Second, considering the detection performance on the different malware families included in the dataset.

Several standard performance metrics for network detection evaluation were used. These metrics are the True Positive Rate (**TPR**) and the False Positive Rate (**FPR**). TPR is computed as the ratio between the number of correctly detected DGA domains and the total number of DGA domains. Whereas FPR is computed as the ratio between the number of normal domains that are incorrectly classified as DGA and the total number of normal domains.

The evaluation of the 1D-CNN DGA detection method was carried out following the usual machine learning methodology. A dataset containing both DGA and normal domains was split in a 70%/30% ratio. To guarantee the independence of the results, the 70% of the datasets was used for tuning the 1D-CNN hyper-parameters (training set). Whereas the remaining 30% (testing set) was used for testing the performance of the 1D-CNN DGA detection model on unseen domains.

3.1 Dataset Description

The 1D-CNN detection method was evaluated on a dataset containing both DGA and normal domain names. The normal domain names were taken from the Alexa

Table 2. Episode frequency and generation scheme for the DGA Malware Families in the dataset used for training and testing the 1D-CNN for DGA detection method. (A) stands for Arithmetic generation scheme while (W) for word-based

Family	Scheme	Freq.	Family	Scheme	Freq.	Family	Scheme	Freq.
bamital	(A)	904	cryptolocker	(A)	112,809	padcrypt	(A)	1,920
p2p	(A)	4,000	proslikefan	(A)	100	murofet	(A)	49,199
bedep	(A)	706	dircrypt	(A)	570	necurs	(A)	81,920
post	(A)	220,000	dyre	(A)	26,993	newgoz	(A)	1,666
chinad	(A)	256	fobber	(A)	600	nymaim	(A)	20,225
conficker	(A)	99,996	gameover	(A)	12,000	pushdo	(A)	94,278
corebot	(A)	840	geodo	(A)	1,920	pykspa	(A)	25,727
goz	(A)	1,667	hesperbot	(A)	192	qadars	(A)	1,600
kraken	(A)	9,660	locky	(A)	9,028	qakbot	(A)	60,000
ramdo	(A)	102,000	ramnit	(A)	91,978	ranbyus	(A)	23,167
rovnix	(A)	53,632	shiotob	(A)	12,521	symmi	(A)	4,448
shifu	(A)	2,554	virut	(A)	11,994	sisron	(A)	60
zeus	(A)	1,000	vawtrak	(A)	300	simda	(A)	28,339
tinba	(A)	193,912	tempedreve	(A)	225	$pykspa_v1$	(A)	18
pykspav2F	(A)	800	pykspav2R	(A)	200	banjori	(W)	439218
suppobox	(W)	8185	matsnu	(W)	100127	volatile	(W)	996
beebone	(W)	210	cryptowall	(W)	94	madmax	(A)	2

top one million domains. An additional 3,161 normal domains were included in the dataset, provided by the Bambenek Consulting feed. This later group is particularly interesting since it consists of suspicious domain names that were not generated by DGA. Therefore, the total amount of domains normal in the dataset is 1,003,161. DGA domains were obtained from the repositories of DGA domains of Abakumov[1] and Bambenek[2]. The total amount of DGA domains is 1,915,335, and they correspond to 51 different malware families. The list of malware families and the amount of domains selected can be seen in Table 2.

The DGA generation scheme followed by the malware families includes the simple arithmetical (A) and the recent word based (W) schemes. Under the arithmetic scheme, the algorithm usually calculates a sequence of values that have a direct ASCII representation usable for a domain name. On the other hand, word-based consists of concatenating a sequence of words from one or more wordlists.

3.2   Hyper Parameters Tuning

Adjusting the network hyper-parameters is perhaps the most difficult task in the application of neural networks. For the proposed 1D-CNN architecture several hyper parameters needed to be adjusted. Among all the possible hyper-parameters, we particularly focused on finding the optimal values related to the

---

[1] https://github.com/andrewaeva/DGA.
[2] http://osint.bambenekconsulting.com/feeds/.

Embedding, *Conv1D* and *Dense* layers. In the case of the Embedding layer, two values need to be set: l and d. The parameter l is the length of the input sequence. This parameter was set by following the common approach of fixing it to the maximal domain length found in the dataset [13]. Therefore, only the matrix dimension d needed to be adjusted.

For the *Conv1D* layer, the parameters to adjust were the number of filters nf and the size of the kernel ks. The stride length sl was fixed to 1. In the first *Dense* Layer the number of neurons hn was the parameter to optimize. Finally, Since a low FPR is a requirement of DGA detection models, the decision boundary threshold (*thres*) in the second Dense layer was set to 0.90 instead of the more common 0.5. Therefore, only those domains names with a very high probability would be detected as DGA.

Table 3. Best hyper-parameters of the proposed architecture. Only the first parameter combination is shown. The parameters combination with the higher average F1-Score was chosen for the remaining experiments.

avg. F1	sd	nf	ks	sl	d	l	hn	Parameters
0.9797	**0.0050**	**256**	**4**	**1**	**100**	**45**	**512**	**5,612,705**

A traditional grid search was conducted through a specified subset on the training set. For a robust estimation, the evaluation of each parameter combination was carried out using a k-fold cross validation with $k = 10$ folds. The 1D-CNN layer was trained using the back propagation algorithm [9] considering the *Adaptive Moment Estimation* optimizer [5]. The 1D-CNN training was carried out during 10 epochs.

Table 3 shows the parameter combinations with the better performance detection in terms of the F1-Score.

3.3   Evaluation on Unseen Domains

The present section describes the experiment results after evaluating the 1D-CNN with the hyper-parameters selected from previous section. For this experiment complete training set was used for training the 1D-CNN and the evaluation was done on the testing dataset which was a 30% of the original dataset. The metrics described in Sect. 3 were calculated on the testing set with a decision boundary threshold set to 0.90. In terms of the two considered classes (i.e Normal or DGA), the resulting TPR value was around 97% while the FPR was 0.7%.

Regarding the FPR discriminated by normal domains types, the 1D-CNN DGA detection algorithm has correctly detected as normal almost 100% of total Alexa domains. However, for the case of the Bambenek domains, the false positive rate increased to 16%.

Figure 2 shows the TPR per DGA malware family and its DGA generation scheme (red for arithmetic and blue for word based). The diameter of the circle around each point provides a visual idea about the absolute frequency of DNS requests that belong to that malware family in the training set. In general, most of the DGA were detected, having a TPR close to 0.75 no matter which was the DGA generation scheme used. The only three exceptions were `Cryptowall` with TPR value of 0.16, `Virut` with 0.39 and `Suppobox` malware with 0.47.

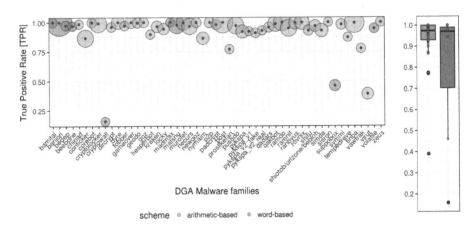

Fig. 2. True positive rate per DGA malware family for 1D-CNN (Color figure online)

4   Discussion

According to our experiments, the 1D-CNN detection method was capable of extracting common patterns present in arithmetic-based DGA generation algorithms of the different malware families. The previous claim could be an explanation of the good results observed in malware families with very low episode frequency. That is the case of families such as `chinad` and `bamital`, which with less than 1000 examples showed a TPR greater than 90%.

The situation was different for the word-based DGA schemes. As can be seen in the boxplot located at the right of Fig. 2, 75% of TPR for arithmetic-based DGA were concentrated between 1 and 0.92. On the other hand, in the case of word-based, 75% of TPR values were between 1 and 0.70. It seems clear that the TPR for malware families using the arithmetic-based generation scheme were significantly better than word-based. These results may be explained by the fact that word-based generation schemes aim at imitating the look of the normal domains.

There was, however, some unexpected results that deserved a deeper analysis. In particular, results showed for the `Matsnu` malware family, a word-based DGA with a 0.92 TPR and the case of `Virut`, an arithmetic-based DGA with a 0.39 TPR.

In the case of `Virut`, the poor performance can be explained by the Frequency Character Distribution (**FCD**) of the generated DGA domains. The Fig. 3 shows the FCD for the `Virut` DGA malware (in black) and compare them with FCD for normal domains (in white). Notice that for ease of comparison only characters present in DGA domains were included in the normal FCD.

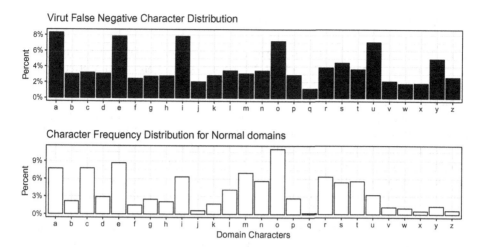

Fig. 3. Character frequency distribution for not detected DGA malware

Despite not being a word-based DGA, Virut vowels frequency is considerable higher when compared with the rest of the characters. Moreover, such vowel frequency in DGA domains shows similarities with the normal FCD. The similarities with normal FCD could difficult the discrimination process carried out by the 1D-CNN detection method. Such process is even more complicated since Virut a small number of episodes included in the dataset.

In the case of Matsnu, the high TPR could not be explained by the FCD, since, as expected, Matsnu FCD shared similarities with normal FCD. After inspecting several aspects of the DGA, we found that domain name length was the discriminative feature between normal and Matsnu domain names. Domains names generated by Matsnu were considerable larger than normal domains. In Fig. 4 we compare the Character Length Distribution (**CLD**) of Matsnu and normal domains. As can be seen, the Matsnu domains are significant larger than normal domains. On the other hand, the suppobox malware (shown also in Fig. 4) has a CLD close to normal domains. Since not only CLD but also FCD are similar to normal domains, suppobox domains become very difficult to detect.

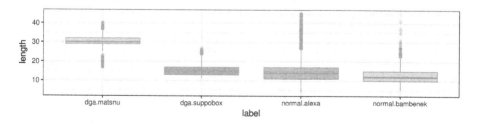

Fig. 4. Character length distribution of Matsnu, Suppobox and normal domains names

5   A LSTM Network Architecture for Detecting DGA

The present section presents a performance comparison on DGA detection using a simple LSTM network and the 1D-CNN previously presented. In particular, the network architecture of the LSTM was implemented as described by Woodbridge et al. [13].

Long Short-Term Memory (LSTM) networks are a special type of Recurrent Neural Network (RNN) first introduced by Hochreiter & Schmidhuber in 1997 [4] that has been successfully applied to Natural processing Languages (NLP) problems. The main benefit of LSTM, when compared to convolutional networks and densely connected networks, is that each input has to be processed independently, with no state kept in between inputs. This lack of memory complicates the processing of sequences or temporal series of data. On the other hand, LSTM are capable of memorizing information previously seen on a sequence. Such capability translates into learning character patterns that are not necessary contiguous in the sequence. An example of this capability, and the difference pattern with 1D-CNN, can be observed in Fig. 5.

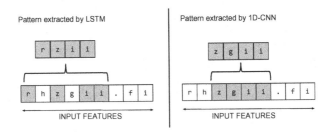

Fig. 5. Pattern extraction capabilities of LSTM and 1D-CNN networks

Similarly to convolutional networks, LSTM networks have to include at least one layer of LSTM cells. A LSTM cell consists of a state that can be manipulated via a set of programmable gates that allow the cell to remember or forget a particular input. An additional output gate modulates the contribution of the cell's state to the output, which propagates to the input gates of LSTM cells across the layer, as well as to subsequent layers.

In this case, the neural network architecture is composed by an *Embedding* layer and then a *LSTM* Layer. Finally, a Dropout layer is added before the output layer. Dropout [11] consists of randomly removing a random subset of edges between layers of a network during each iteration of training, but restoring their contribution at test time. The detailed architecture of the LSTM network is described in Table 4.

According to [13], the network hyper-parameters for the *Embedding* layer were $d = 128$ and $l = 75$, while the number of *LSTM* cells in the *LSTM* Layer was set up to 128. Finally, the *Dropout* Layer was setup to 0.5. Similarly to the 1D-CNN, LSTM network was trained during 10 epochs on the 70% of the dataset described in Sect. 3 and tested in the remaining 30%.

Table 4. The complete network architecture including the corresponding output dimensions and activation function used in each layer

Layer (type)	Activation function
input (Input Layer)	–
embedding (Embedding)	–
lstm (LSTM)	relu
dropout_1 (Dropout)	–
dense_1 (Dense)	sigmoid

The resulting model showed a TPR value around 94% of total DGA present in the dataset while the FPR value is close to 3% of total normal domains. According to previous results, the LSTM network performed considerable worse than 1D-CNN. Specially, if we consider the importance of low false positive rate for real-world scenarios.

The TPR per DGA malware family and its DGA generation scheme is shown in Fig. 6. Similarly to Fig. 2, most of the DGA were detected with TPR values close to 0.75. Moreover, as can be seen in the boxplot located at the right of Fig. 6 the 75% of TPR for arithmetic-based DGA are concentrated between 1 and 0.92. However, the 75% of TPR values for word-based scheme are between 0.97 and 0.12, results that are considerable worse than 1D-CNN.

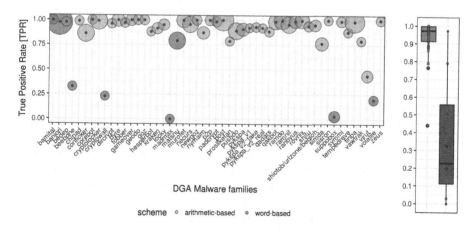

Fig. 6. True positive rate per DGA malware family for LSTM

A detailed comparison considering not only malware families but also normal requests is shown in Fig. 7. As can be observed the detection performance of LSTM was better than 1D-CNN for the case of the `Cryptowall` malware (a word-based DGA) and the `Virut` malware. On the other hands the 1D-CNN significantly outperformed LSTM for most of the word-based DGA, such as `Beebone`, `Suppobox`, `Matsnu`, `Madmax` and `Volatile` malware. Such low performance for detecting word-based DGA was also observed [13].

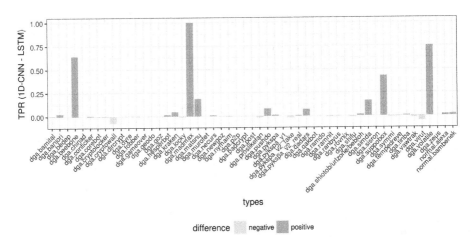

Fig. 7. Performance detection pero DGA malware families and normal requests

It is important to remember that the LSTM architecture presented in [13] is simpler than the 1D-CNN described in Sect. 2. Moreover, the additional *Dense* Layer present in the 1D-CNN could be the explanation of the poor performance in word-based detection for the LSTM network.

6   Concluding Remarks

In the present work, we explored the viability of 1D-CNN for lexicographical DGA detection. A network with a minimal architecture complexity was evaluated on a dataset containing domains names generated by 51 different malware families as well as normal domains. Malware families included two different DGA generation scheme: (1) the most common arithmetic-based and (2) the recent and more difficult to detect Word-based. The dataset was properly split in training and testing sets. A hyper-parameters grid search was conducted on training set and the best resulting model was then evaluated on the testing set.

Despite its simple architecture, the resulting 1D-CNN model correctly detected more than 97% of total DGA domains with a FPR around 0.7%. Such results make it suitable for real-life networks. Inspecting the malware family results, we observed that the 75% arithmetic-based DGA showed TPR values between 1 and 0.92. Such values were observed even in malware families with low frequency episode, confirming the hypothesis that a 1D-CNN can learn the common properties from the different DGA generation families, at least under the arithmetic-based generation scheme. On the other hand, in the case of word-based, the 75% of TPR values were between 1 and 0.70. Such high variability in the TPR results responds to the high TPR for malware such as Matsnu and the low TPR for malware such as Suppobox and Cryptowall. By analyzing the FCD and CLD we detected than even tough both shared the FCD with normal domains, Matsnu showed a significant increment in the length of the domains, a situation that makes it easily detectable. Different was the case of malware such as Suppobox, that shared both FCD and LCD with normal domains, and consequently was very difficult to detect.

The performance of 1D-CNN was compared with a simple LSTM network on the same dataset. The experiments showed the LSTM performance is worse compared to 1D-CNN in terms of TPR and FPR. In particular, the 4% of false positives obtained by the LSTM is a significant performance loss with high impact when applied to real-world networks. Such performance loss could be explained by the extremely simple architecture of the LSTM proposed by Woodbridge et al. [13]. The performance of LSTM networks with more complex architecture will be the subject of future work.

Despite the good results shown by 1D-CNN, we observed that it could be very difficult to detect word-based DGA that share the CLD and FCD with normal domains. Therefore, as the word-based generation schemes become more precise in imitating normal domains the detection could be extremely hard. Moreover, it is possible that such particular cases be outside the capabilities of detection methods based only on a lexicographical approach. Consequently, an alternative detection strategy could be necessary.

Acknowledgments. The authors would like to thank the financial support received by CVUT and UNCuyo during this work. In particular the founding provided by the Czech TACR project no. TH02010990 and the PICT 2015-1435 granted by ANPCyT. The authors would also like to specially thank Whalebone s.r.o., whose technical support and help have been fundamental to the complete research process.

References

1. Ahluwalia, A., Traore, I., Ganame, K., Agarwal, N.: Detecting broad length algorithmically generated domains. In: Traore, I., Woungang, I., Awad, A. (eds.) ISDDC 2017. LNCS, vol. 10618, pp. 19–34. Springer, Cham (2017). https://doi.org/10.1007/978-3-319-69155-8_2
2. Catania, C., Garcia, S., Torres, P.: An analysis deep convolutional neural networks for detecting DGA. In: XXIV Congreso Argentino de Ciencias de la Computación, Tandil (2018)
3. Goodfellow, I., Bengio, Y., Courville, A.: Deep Learning. MIT Press, Cambridge (2016). http://www.deeplearningbook.org
4. Hochreiter, S., Schmidhuber, J.: Long short-term memory. Neural Comput. **9**(8), 1735–1780 (1997)
5. Kingma, D.P., Ba, J.: Adam: a method for stochastic optimization. arXiv e-prints arXiv:1412.6980 (2014)

6. Kührer, M., Rossow, C., Holz, T.: Paint it black: evaluating the effectiveness of malware blacklists. In: Stavrou, A., Bos, H., Portokalidis, G. (eds.) RAID 2014. LNCS, vol. 8688, pp. 1–21. Springer, Cham (2014). https://doi.org/10.1007/978-3-319-11379-1_1

7. Pascanu, R., Mikolov, T., Bengio, Y.: On the difficulty of training recurrent neural networks. arXiv e-prints arXiv:1211.5063 (2012)

8. Plohmann, D., Yakdan, K., Klatt, M., Bader, J., Gerhards-Padilla, E.: A comprehensive measurement study of domain generating malware. In: 25th USENIX Security Symposium (USENIX Security 16), Austin, TX, pp. 263–278. USENIX Association (2016)

9. Rumelhart, D.E., Hinton, G.E., Williams, R.J.: Learning representations by back-propagating errors. In: Neurocomputing: Foundations of Research, pp. 696–699. MIT Press, Cambridge (1988)

10. Schiavoni, S., Maggi, F., Cavallaro, L., Zanero, S.: Phoenix: DGA-based botnet tracking and intelligence. In: Dietrich, S. (ed.) DIMVA 2014. LNCS, vol. 8550, pp. 192–211. Springer, Cham (2014). https://doi.org/10.1007/978-3-319-08509-8_11

11. Srivastava, N., Hinton, G., Krizhevsky, A., Sutskever, I., Salakhutdinov, R.: Dropout: a simple way to prevent neural networks from overfitting. J. Mach. Learn. Res. **15**, 1929–1958 (2014). http://jmlr.org/papers/v15/srivastava14a.html

12. Torres, P., Catania, C., Garcia, S., Garino, C.G.: An analysis of recurrent neural networks for botnet detection behavior. In: 2016 IEEE Biennial Congress of Argentina (ARGENCON), pp. 1–6 (2016)

13. Woodbridge, J., Anderson, H.S., Ahuja, A., Grant, D.: Predicting domain generation algorithms with long short-term memory networks. arXiv e-prints arXiv:1611.00791 (2016)

14. Yadav, S., Reddy, A.K.K., Narasimha Reddy, A.L., Ranjan, S.: Detecting algorithmically generated domain-flux attacks with DNS traffic analysis. IEEE/ACM Trans. Netw. **20**(5), 1663–1677 (2012). http://jmlr.org/papers/v15/srivastava14a.html

Innovation in Computer Science Education

Computer Science and Schools: A Specific Didactics?

Claudia Queiruga[1]($\boxtimes$), Claudia Banchoff Tzancoff[1], Paula Venosa[1], Soledad Gómez[1], and Glenda Morandi[2]

[1] LINTI, Computer Science School, National University of La Plata,
La Plata, Argentina
{claudiaq, cbanchoff, pvenosa, sgomez}@info.unlp.edu.ar
[2] School of Journalism and Social Communication,
National University of La Plata, La Plata, Argentina
glenda.morandi@presi.unlp.edu.ar

Abstract. This paper presents the curricular proposal for the "Teaching Specialization in Computer Science Didactics" of the province of Buenos Aires, Argentina. The focus of this proposal is the training of high school teachers in the field of Computer Science, since there is a deficit in the training in this topic in compulsory school. The project arises in the framework of a call for national universities with Computer Science courses, launched by Fundación Sadosky of the Ministry of Science, Technology and Innovation. One of the main features is the acknowledgement of Higher Institutes for Teacher Training as referents of excellence in ongoing teacher training. The result is the consensual design and implementation, between these Institutes and the universities, of a curricular program of Computer Science.

Keywords: Computer science · High school · Teaching programming · Computational thinking

1 Introduction

The inclusion of Computer Science into formal educational systems at compulsory levels is a current and innovative topic in Argentina and the world [14].

There are multiple reasons and conditions meting its placement. On the one hand, the great opportunities provided by technologies and software as the driving force of economic and social development, and on the other, the need for citizens to understand its constitutive elements and adapt and modify them to fit their needs in an ever-connecting world, where computing is ubiquitous. Resolution 263 of the 2015 meeting of the Federal Education Council of Argentina declared the strategic importance of the Argentinean educational system of teaching and learning programming during compulsory schooling, in order to strengthen the economic and social development of the Nation. Simultaneously, in recent years, a set of federal initiatives and policies have helped to consolidate a perspective that strengthens the reasons why it is necessary to place the teaching of Computer Science as a disciplinary field. An example of this is the emergence of educational policies, such as "Program.AR" [1], "Programa Conectar

P. Pesado and C. Aciti (Eds.): CACIC 2018, CCIS 995, pp. 343–351, 2019.
https://doi.org/10.1007/978-3-030-20787-8_24

Igualdad", "Plan Nacional Integral de Educación Digital" (PLANIED) [2], among others, which allow us to situate, socially and historically, the need to think in terms of education, development, advancement and synergy in this field. More recently, in 2017, the project "Secondary 2030" [3] approved by the Federal Council of Education proposes to gradually incorporate a teaching approach based on transversal digital skills and competences.

The declaration of its strategic incorporation into compulsory formal education in Argentina makes it necessary to work in a sustained manner in the training of teachers in conditions that lead the learning processes of Computer Science. Currently, teacher training in this disciplinary field in the province of Buenos Aires is an area of relative vacancy. Although some teaching training courses in Computer Science in some universities are identified, such as those from UNICEN (National University of the Center of the Province of Buenos Aires) and the UBA (University of Buenos Aires), it is strategic to locate a graduate program in teaching of Computer Science which links with the higher education system of the province and deepens tying processes between national universities and the Higher Institutes for Teacher Training (ISFD) of the provincial jurisdiction. In turn, the emergence of the topic in public education agendas is characterized by the scarce references on which to base the organization of contents and methodology on how to teach them. That is why it is essential to train teachers in both aspects and jointly by interdisciplinary expert teams in Computer Science and didactics.

In response to address the need, Program.ar in 2016 made a call to national universities with programs in Computer Science that were interested in designing and implementing a specialization in teacher training in partnership with the ISFD of their jurisdictions. Out of the universities that were nominated, 8 were selected based on the quality of the proposals and the professional experience of their teams. In the province of Buenos Aires the UNLa (National University of Lanús) was chosen in association with the ISFDyT N° 24 "Dr. Bernardo Houssay", UNLP (National University of La Plata) in association with Escuela Normal Superior No. 1," Mary O. Graham"- ISFDN° 95 and UNICEN in association with ISFDyT N° 166" José de San Martín". The province of Buenos Aires will have 3 proposals aimed at different recipients: a training on the discipline and its didactics aimed at junior school level teachers (UNICEN - ISFDyT No. 166), one aimed at high school level teachers with basic training in the discipline or a related one such as mathematics, physics, chemistry and technology (UNLP - ISFD No. 95), and a last one aimed at secondary level teachers with training in other subjects, primarily in social sciences (UNLa-ISFDyT No. 24). Each of these offers proposes a cut of contents and a particular didactic for its approach according to the recipients of the training as well as the last beneficiaries -students- of each offer.

The remaining sections of this work are organized as follows. Section 2 discusses the disciplinary field of Computer Science in the school, Sect. 3 describes the curricular design of the "Teaching Specialization in Computer Science Didactics" prepared by the authors of this work and presents the current situation in relation to the implementation of the first cohort of the Specialization. Conclusions are presented in Sect. 4.

2 The Relevance of the Disciplinary Field of Computer Science at School

In our daily life, we are surrounded by digital objects, from the cell phone that accompanies us all the time, traffic lights and smart homes, to drones that fly over us and wearable technology, among other elements that are increasingly ubiquitous in our daily lives. These elements modify our habits, our way of relating to each other, to entertain ourselves, to study, and they enhance our cognitive abilities—that is why it is necessary to understand what happens inside there. This reality poses a challenge in the educational field: the training of citizens who can know, understand and operate on the world around them, including their digital environment, placing them as critical subjects and creators of innovations with digital technologies, over passivity and mere technological consumption. That is why it is necessary that computer skills are incorporated into the school designs of national education systems.

Computer education is currently a global concern. Countries such as New Zealand, Estonia, Japan, Finland and the United Kingdom, among others, have updated their school curricula including the teaching of programming in schools [4, 5]. Several states in the United States have also implemented active policies in response to the needs of the technology industry through the "LearnToCode" movement, led primarily by the global code.org and codeacademy initiatives. In Argentina, over the last decades, the use of ICT has been incorporated into educational practices at different levels of compulsory schooling. As an example, in the province of Buenos Aires exists a new curricular design of primary education [6], which contains a module on the inclusion of ICT that tries to transversally incorporate the use of digital technologies in the different curricular areas and the NTIC curricular space [7] of high school where concepts related to the Computer Science discipline are being included. However, Computer Science as a discipline has not yet been legitimized in the field of school education. Although there are some cases where this is changing, the field has not yet reached the necessary consensus for its inclusion in school curriculums at the federal level. The technical high schools are the only ones that have training courses in Computer Science. In this way, the study of the discipline does not occur transversally, nor is it an integral part of the content that most students access during their time at school. The incorporation of the computer science discipline in the school's curricula constitutes an achievement and the certainty of a space for the development of cognitive processes linked to the logical reasoning that allows to predict, analyze and explain the formulation of algorithms, the decomposition of problems in simpler parts, the abstraction to handle the complexity, the generalization by means of the discovery of patterns and similarities and, finally, the evaluation. These ideas, which identify "computational thinking" [8, 9], are widely applied in solving problems using computers and in understanding systems beyond the school space. In turn, the teaching and learning of "programming" is an aspect of Information Technology that is perceived as the most challenging in the school. That is why it is necessary for teachers to be trained in concepts, practices and approaches to computational thinking, so that they are accessible and attractive to students and fundamentally allows them to appropriate them to understand how the digital world works and how to use this knowledge to program.

The curricular design presented here recovers the relevance of teacher training in the teaching and learning of Computer Science with special attention to "programming". The transversal intentionality that guides the approach of "programming" is oriented to develop a work with the teachers that place them in the situation of getting involved in a practice of "programming" that reflects around each one of the cognitive processes that this development supposes. Likewise, a situated and non-abstract approach to programming is proposed, addressing the problems of daily life that this practice helps to solve and improve. The focus of attention is on taking advantage of the possibilities offered by "programming" in relation to its creative uses, promoting that the subjects overcome the condition of only consumers of software.

3   Teacher Specialization in Computer Science Didactics

3.1   Proposal

The Specialization is aimed at teachers and professionals teaching computer science in high school. It covers both teachers of Technologies and Informatics and those who work in the areas of Mathematics, Physics and Chemistry. These teachers had previous training in topics such as propositional logic, models and abstraction, problem solving, and use of scientific language, required as basic training for the Specialization. The first topics to be addressed correspond to the political and pedagogical aspects that come with the teaching of Computer Science. In this framework, issues such as the potential and the scope of the teaching of this discipline in the current socio-historical context are traversed by technological development and innovation in this field, highlighting the analysis of the concept of technological sovereignty and its relations with the ideas behind free software and proprietary software. These issues, together with the analysis of social, political and ethical aspects linked to technology and its use in daily life make up the foundation related to the training of digital citizenship, as well as good practices in the safe and responsible use of data networks and digital technologies.

As mentioned in the previous section, the content of the Specialization pays special attention to the teaching and learning of computer programming, which is why a large number of hours are dedicated to this topic and the sense of it is transversally related to all the modules. It starts with the most basic aspects such as the understanding and analysis of algorithms, and ends with the development of a software project using different computer tools. Some of them are based on block programming and others use textual programming languages. In this sense, four modules of increasing complexity are proposed, in which both the basic aspects of programming and sequencing, control and abstraction structures are worked on, such as propositional logic concepts and free software developments. During the first year of the Specialization, aspects related to the internal functioning of computers and the role of operating systems are also developed, and in the second year the fundamental concepts on data networks are worked on. These topics are addressed not only from the theoretical point of view of their operation but also with practical activities that promote the use of resources available in schools: computer rooms, educational robots, netbooks and/or smart phones and tablets.

The approach of these subjects applied to two practices will allow to form graduates that can design, coordinate and evaluate innovative didactic situations focused on the development of computational thought and to incorporate, in the educational practices, a focus on programming that recovers strategies favoring processes of creation of applications and digital contents.

This approach promotes the exchange with teachers of different disciplinary areas of the school curriculum, in the search for a linkage between computational thinking strategies and their teaching and learning processes.

3.2 Articulation with ISFD

The proposal of the Specialization recognizes the ISFDs as referents for excellence in continuous teacher training, and national universities with programs in Computer Science as the creators of specific knowledge of the field. That is why the teaching specialization presented here responds to the need to create sustainable teacher training devices by linking both institutions. Likewise, the development of the Specialization was conceived in terms of adaptation to the needs and possibilities of the jurisdiction in which it is subscribed. In the case of our proposal, it was developed in association with Escuela Normal Superior No. 1, "Mary O. Graham" - ISFD No.95 and is aimed at high school level teachers with training in the discipline, or in related subjects such as mathematics, physics and chemistry.

3.3 Teaching Methodology

The implementation of the development of the curriculum of the Specialization forced the team to rethink the ways of teaching each one develops daily, in our role as teachers. In this sense, interdisciplinary accompanied the process, given that the team is composed of professionals from Computer Science, Education and Communication Sciences. The project proposes to teach from a specific didactics the contents of Computer Science, aimed at teachers in the secondary level. These teachers may or may not have computer training and may or may not have pedagogical training in the field, which was a great challenge. Our proposal aims to teach something potentially unknown and those who know it may not have the tools to teach it. The decision was based on the consensus of the work team that aims to break apart from some classroom work dynamics that do not strengthen the development of computational thinking, but rather promote work practices conducive to the development of technological knowledge from a purely instrumental perspective. Problem-based learning and the inquiry-based work methodology [10] proved to be coherent options to enhance work with technologies and promote production practices with them.

The methodology of work proposed by problem-based learning (PBL), closely linked to new perspectives on the teaching of Computer Science [11], solves the problem of teaching with certain difficulties, as we are concerned about ignorance on the proposed topics. In this sense, for the team, this form of classroom work forced us again to rethink the ways in which knowledge is produced and the cognitive processes that it aims to help produce. The teachers, in most cases, will be faced with the challenge of knowing the technology and its possibilities, although the concern of the team lies in the possibilities of resignifying it and putting it into practice. From this perspective it would seem that the concern of the work team is the mere use and application. However the starting point is the belief that in the stages of a critical process of appropriation of knowledge it is necessary first to know and then transform into praxis [12]. Returning to the ABP methodology, its incorporation into the different proposals of the curriculum was linked to the path students take from the original approach of the problem to its solution. The collaborative work in small groups enables the students to share in that learning experience the possibility of practicing and developing skills, of observing and reflecting on attitudes and values that could hardly be put into action in the conventional expository method. In this sense, we agree with Guevara Mora [13] when she explains that "the work experience in a small group oriented to the solution of the problem is one of the distinguishing characteristics of PBL. In these group activities, the students take responsibilities and actions that are basic in their formative process".

Inquiry, central and constitutive practice of the PBL, is strongly linked to technological development as it is increasingly favored by access to information and the era of flows. The students recognize themselves in these practices because they are constitutive of their daily technological uses, which strengthen their capacities to inquire, investigate and create. It is important to understand that this capacity for creation and discovery defined as inquiry is the basis for the development of critical and meaningful thought processes. Understanding this in a broad way allows us to conceive technology as a possibility and a fundamental tool, not only because of the current context that surrounds us and conditions it, but because of the access to knowledge and the networks that it generates. To be able to think the way in which, for what and why teaching Computer Science constitutes a daily challenge for this team, which considers that technologies cross us and condition our ways of living, therefore their approach in formal education must be ensured, not only in the curriculum but from the promotion of creation with technologies.

3.4 Curricular Organization

The program is structured in ten modules, with a workload of 320 h of disciplinary modules and 80 h of teaching practice located, with two semesters in each year. The modules that make up the curriculum are articulated around three areas of knowledge, which make it possible to group specific teaching objects of Computer Science, and develop them gradually in levels of increasing complexity, starting from a sequence that is articulated with the learning processes that students of high schools are expected to develop.

The delimited knowledge areas are:

- Computer Science, digital citizenship and education, which includes the modules "Pedagogical-political framework of the teaching of Computer Science" and "Safe and responsible use of technology and Internet services".
- Architecture, operating systems and networks in secondary education, which includes the modules "Computers and operating systems", "Data networks and Internet" and "Situated Professional Practice I".

- Programming and its teaching, which includes the modules "The algorithm as an object of learning and form of organization of thought", "The teaching of programming through visual languages", "The teaching of programming in real software production languages with special attention to free software", "The process of teaching the development of a software project" and "Situated Professional Practice II".

This curricular organization offers an axis of supervised practical training - Situated Practice I and Situated Practice II -, which takes place in two different curricular spaces, in each one of which the students elaborate a project or teaching design in which they must include the strategies and content addressed in the program. Table 1 summarizes the organization of the program in 2 years.

Table 1. Organization of the program into years.

First year			
Pedagogical-political framework of the teaching of Computer Science (30 hs.)	The algorithm as an object of learning and form of organization of thought (30 hs.)	Computers and operating systems (40 hs.)	The teaching of programming through block-based visual languages (50 hs.)
Situated Professional Practice I (30 hs.)			
Second year			
Data Networks and Internet (40 hs.)	The teaching of programming in real software production languages with special attention to free software (50 hs.)	The process of teaching the development of a software project (40 hs.)	Safe and responsible use of technology and Internet services (40 hs.)
Situated Professional Practice II (50 hs.)			

3.5 Implementation of the Specialization

The specialization here presented has been approved by the General Council of Culture and Education of the province of Buenos Aires in March 2018 and has a resolution by the General Director of Culture and Education of the province. This resolution establishes the beginning of its implementation in the year 2018, to a closed cycle, and the provision of points to the teachers who complete the program. It is currently in the process of being implemented, and for this reason, a good teacher-student relationship is being considered in each of the modules, given that the activities will focus mainly on workshops methodologies. Likewise, attention will be paid to the follow-up of the development of the modules, in order to encourage retention, propitiating the completion of the training. The aim is that this federal training policy can act as soon as possible in the training of our adolescents during their high school years. The faculty of the specialization comprises specialists in the disciplinary field and teachers in the area of communication and education for modules that require a clear understanding of the policies that accompany the development of the discipline in the field of education.

4 Conclusions

The development of this specialization is the result of an interdisciplinary work in which a team composed of teachers from UNLP and ISFD No. 95 of La Plata coordinated effort and experience in a work that covers an area of vacancy in teacher training.

State plans and programs, such as Schools of the Future of PLANIED, which among its initiatives propose to distribute technological resources in Argentinean schools, require specific training to promote significant learning, placing students as creators of digital artifacts. In addition, teachers and managers are inquired by these new materials and require training such as that presented in this paper that allows them to organize and plan their activities with these technologies that add to the classroom space.

It is relevant to recover that the Specialization in Didactics of Computer Sciences presented in this paper is promoted by a federal program, which in turn promoted the implementation of seven other specializations oriented to teacher training in Computer Science in the school setting, to be taught in other provinces of the country during the year 2018. This speaks of a federal perspective in relation to the teaching and learning of Computer Science in compulsory schooling, resulting in a great advance in relation to the inclusion of Computer Science in the classroom. It also proposes a starting point for the reformulation of the curricular contents of compulsory schooling in the Argentine educational system.

References

1. Program.AR: programa de la Fundación Sadosky, Ministerio de Ciencia, Tecnología e Innovación Productiva de la Nación Argentina (s.f). https://bit.ly/2HoCCdI
2. PLANIED: Plan Integral de Educación Digital del Ministerio de Educación y Deportes de la Nación Argentina (s.f). https://bit.ly/2GQYi16
3. Secundaria 2030: Transformar la Secundaria para transformar vidas (s.f). https://bit.ly/2XcmXmt
4. National curriculum in England: computing programmes of study (2013). https://bit.ly/1gmCybj
5. Dirección General de Cultura y Educación de la Provincia de Buenos Aires. Diseño curricular para la educación primaria: primer ciclo y segundo ciclo; coordinación general de Sergio Siciliano. - 1a ed (2018). https://bit.ly/2sGcbqb. ISBN 978-987-676-095-9
6. The New Zealand Curriculum on-line (s.f). https://bit.ly/2XYUQaM
7. Dirección General de Cultura y Educación de la provincia de Buenos Aires. Diseño Curricular para la Educación Secundaria Ciclo Superior. ES4: Nuevas Tecnologías de la Información y la Conectividad. Coordinado por Claudia Bracchi. -1a ed. (2010). https://bit.ly/2zUfQ7b. ISBN 978-987-1266-98-2
8. Wing, J.M.: Computational thinking. Commun. ACM 2006 **49**(3), 33–35 (2006)
9. Wing, J.M.: Computational thinking and thinking about computing. Philos. Trans. R. Soc. A **366**, 3717–3725 (2008)
10. Morales, P., Landa, V.: Aprendizaje Basado en Problemas. Theoria, 13(2004). http://www.redalyc.org/articulo.oa?id=29901314. ISSN 0717-196X

11. Echeveste, M.E., Martínez, M.C.: Desafíos en la enseñanza de Ciencias de la Computación. Virtualidad Educación y Ciencia **7**(12), 34–48 (2006)
12. Freire, P.: Pedagogía de la autonomía: saberes necesarios para la práctica educativa. Siglo XXI, México (2004)
13. Mora, G.G.: Aprendizaje Basado en Problemas como Técnica Didáctica para la Enseñanza del Tema de la Recursividad. InterSedes: Revista de las Sedes Regionales, XI (2010). http://ucsj.redalyc.org/articulo.oa?id=66619992009. ISSN 2215-2458
14. Queiruga, C., Banchoff Tzancoff, C., Venosa, P., Gomez, S., Morandi, G.: Ciencias de la Computación y escuelas ¿una didáctica específica?. In: XXIV Congreso Argentino de Ciencias de la Computación. Red de Universidades con Carreras en Informática (RedUNCI) (2018). ISBN: 978-950-658-472-6

Digital Governance and Smart Cities

Open Government Assessment Models Applied to Province's Capital Cities in Argentina and Municipalities in the Province of Buenos Aires

Ariel Pasini$^{(\boxtimes)}$, Juan Santiago Preisegger , and Patricia Pesado

Computer Science Research Institute LIDI (III-LIDI) - Center of the Scientific
Research Agency of the Province of Buenos Aires (CICPBA),
Universidad Nacional de La Plata, 50 y 120, La Plata, Buenos Aires, Argentina
{apasini,jspreisegger,ppesado}@lidi.info.unlp.edu.ar

Abstract. With an increase of digital government policies and citizens that demand more of their governments, a new public management paradigm appeared, which became known as *open government* and is supported by three basic principles: *Transparency*, *Collaboration* and *Participation*. These are found in multiple different strategies, depending on the country, province or city adopting an open government, but all of them sharing two common pillars: *open public data* and *open processes*. Lately, various initiatives were promoted on various government levels to allow all citizens to have access to public information.

In this context, this document proposes an assessment model to establish the progress made towards that goal in the capital cities of the different provinces of Argentina and a select group of municipalities in the province of Buenos Aires through the various open government tools offered to citizens by such cities through their official websites to improve their services.

Keywords: Software engineering · Open government · Open data ·
Government portals

1 Introduction

Our modern society expects increasingly more from its government and government officials. These demands include transparency and an efficient management of public goods, as well as society collaboration and participation in the decision-making process. Based on these requirements, and assisted by new technologies, a new type of government with greater citizen inclusion came to be, allowing citizens to contribute to public policies and participate in the government's decision-making process [1]. This new type of government is called *open government*, and is defined as "*... an institutional and technological platform that turns government data into open data to allow their use and protection, as well as citizen collaboration in the decision-making, accountability and public service improvement processes.*" [2]. It is based on three well-defined principles: **Transparency**, **Collaboration** and **Participation**. [3, 4] These

P. Pesado and C. Aciti (Eds.): CACIC 2018, CCIS 995, pp. 355–366, 2019.
https://doi.org/10.1007/978-3-030-20787-8_25

principles can be approached from different perspectives, and their application varies based on the actual interest of government officials to promote the concept of open government. For this reason, defining a model that allows assessing open governments is a very complex task, especially if such model is to be extrapolated to any governmental structure.

Using the ecosystem proposed by Ramírez-Alujas and Dassen [5] as a starting point, an assessment model that allowed reviewing the websites of a set of municipalities in the province of Buenos Aires and assigning scores describing their data and processes openness was developed.

The model consists of eight attributes (2 for transparency, 3 for participation, and 3 for collaboration) that can have predefined, discrete values based on the information surveyed on the corresponding municipal websites.

Argentine is organized as a decentralized federal state, with 24 self-governed states – 23 provinces and the Autonomous City of Buenos Aires (CABA), which is the federal capital of the country. The 23 provinces keep all of the powers that are not delegated to the national State, and ensure the autonomy of their municipalities.

The province of Buenos Aires has 135 municipalities, from which a sample based on population was taken. This criterion only allowed assessing large cities, but it did not provide a good representation of the province as a whole. To obtain a more homogeneous sample, the five more populated municipalities in each electoral section were included.

The assessment model proposed was applied to the 24 self-governed states (national level) and the 36 selected municipalities from the province of Buenos Aires (provincial level) to analyze their progress in relation to the three principles for an open government.

In Sect. 2, the general concepts of open government are presented. Then, in the following section, the assessment model is described. In Sect. 4, the model is applied to the selected municipalities and the results obtained are discussed. Finally, the conclusions drawn from the analysis are presented.

2   Open Government Concepts

Lately, government portals have become a tool for the dissemination of financial information towards the promotion of government transparency. This practice is commonly mistaken with the concept of "*open government*". However, transparency is not just a characteristic of open governments, it is also the consequence of open government policies that make information available to citizens [6, 7].

2.1   Open Government

To define the concept of "*open government*", we should first analyze the concept of "*government*", which is defined as the act or *process of governing*. This involves the administration of public resources based on several laws or regulations that are applicable to the government. Following this approach, the concept of *"open"* is linked to the free availability of the information related to the administration of public resources. This expected "freedom" in relation to the concept occurs on two planes – data and government processes. That is, it acts as a complex system of technology processes used both by the government and the community to manage information.

Sandoval [2] defines it as follows: *"An open government is understood as an institutional and technological platform that turns government data into open data to allow their use and protection, as well as citizen collaboration in the decision-making, accountability and public service improvement processes."*

From this definition, it can be inferred that an *open government* is not only about "data" on a website to promote government transparency, but rather, that information and communication technologies (including social media) should be provided to ensure data protection and promote community participation [6–8].

2.2 Open Government Principles

In [5], a new approach to the principles proposed by Obama in [9] is presented.

Transparency. *A transparent government provides information about what it is doing, its plans of action, its data sources, and everything for which society can hold it accountable. This fosters and promotes administrative accountability to its citizens and permanent social control.*

Participation. *A participative government promotes the right of its citizens to actively collaborate in formulating public policies, and paves the road for public administrations to benefit from the knowledge, ideas, and experience of their citizens. It promotes the creation of new meeting spaces that favor citizen leadership and involvement in public affairs.*

Collaboration. *A collaborative government engages and involves its citizens and other social agents in its efforts for working together to solve national problems. This requires cooperation and coordinated actions not only with citizens, but also with businesses, associations and other agents. Similarly, it leverages joint work within administrations themselves, and among them and their employees, transversally.*

The application of these concepts is based on two key pillars:

1. **Opening data:** using public data (*transparency*) for innovation, generating new applications by turning governments into service managers (allowing communities to generate new services that add value).
2. **Opening processes:** facilitating communication for open decision-making processes (*participation*), citizen knowledge and experience in the design of public policies (*collaboration*).

The same authors [5] propose an ecosystem based on the three principles for the development of an open government, which is represented in Fig. 1 below.

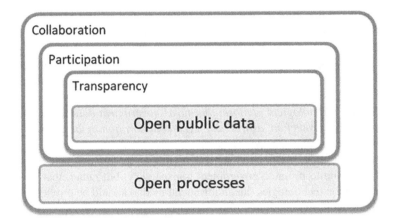

Fig. 1. Relationship between the three principles for an open government

2.3 Open Government Portal

A *portal* is a website that offers its users, in a simple and integrated way, access to a number of resources and services related to a specific topic. An *"open government portal"* is a website that offers citizens a number of resources and services related to data opening. It is a key component in the process of opening data. These portals are digital platforms that are used to store, share, connect and view databases [10].

2.4 Data Catalog

The data catalog is the core of an open data portal. It contains a list of all published tables with a description of the database contents, the name of the agency responsible for such content, update frequency, number of visits, technical information to plug it into software applications, and a space for user comments. Some portals also add a database quality assessment area [10].

3   Open Government Assessment Model

To survey all municipalities in the province of Buenos Aires, a model based on the three principles mentioned before was defined, as seen in Table 1. For each principle, a set of attributes and a corresponding set of possible values for those attributes are established. ***Transparency*** is related to the ability of accessing the data and automation level of the medium making such data available. Therefore, the attributes *Data Visualization Level and Information Display Level* were defined. In the case of ***participation***, the possibility of having citizen participation in specific proposals, in the design of policy proposals and in public debates was measured, which required defining the following attributes: *Citizen Participation Level, Participation Level in Public Policy Design, and Public Debate Level.*

Table 1. Assessment model attributes and values

	Attribute	Description	Values
Transparency	Information Display Level – IDL	It categorizes how data are presented	0 - It does not have an open data portal/catalog 1 - It has an open data portal/catalog 2 - It has an open data portal
	Data Visualization Level - DVL	It categorizes data format	0 -There are no data available 1 - Data are available on the Web, in any format (PDF) 2 - Structured, proprietary (Excel) 3 - Non-proprietary format (CSV) 4 - Using URI (Uniform Resource Identifier) 5 - Linked to other data to provide context (Junar)
Participation	Citizen Participation Level - CPL	It categorizes the possibility for citizens to be part of the decision-making process (for instance, participatory budget)	0 - It does not allow participation 1 - It only offers information on opportunities to be part of the decision-making process (physical presence required) 2 - It allows remote participation
	Participation Level in Public Policy Design - PLPPD	It categorizes those policies that were designed based on citizen contributions	0 - There is no evidence of citizen participation in public policy design 1 - There is evidence that some public policies originally come from citizen contributions 2 - There is evidence that some public policies originally come from citizen contributions and participation
	Public Debate Level - PDL	It categorizes government openness to discuss policies with its citizens	0 - There is no information about public debates 1 - There is information about public debates (physical presence required) 2 - There is a discussion forum for public debate
Collaboration	Interaction Level - IL	It categorizes interaction with citizens	0 - There is no information about services 1 - There is a roadmap of formal procedures or information about services 2 - It allows basic communication operations 3 - It allows basic transactional operations

(*continued*)

Table 1. *(continued)*

Attribute	Description	Values
Level of Relationship with SMEs – LRS	It categorizes government relationship with SMEs from the perspectives of assistance offered to SMEs, tenders, private job boards	0 - There is no relationship with SMEs 1 - There is only information addressed to SMEs (assistance offered/tenders/job boards) 2 - It allows online enrollment to SME assistance plans, tenders and/or job boards 3 - It allows online management for the entire process of SME assistance, tenders, and/or job boards
Citizen Contribution Level - CCL	It categorizes how suggestions, observations, requirements and claims presented by citizens are handled	0 - No contributions are possible 1 - It allows citizens to submit their contributions 2 - It allows citizens to submit their contributions and follow up on them 3 - Citizen contributions resulted in policy plans

In the case of **Collaboration**, citizen participation and relation with private organizations, specifically SMEs, that can potentially develop commercial activities in the municipality were considered. As main participation option, interaction with citizens through the municipal portal, suggestions, observations, requirements and claims submitted by the community to the municipal government were analyzed, as well as considering if there was any evidence of any of these contributions becoming government policies. Relationship with SMEs was also included as part of collaboration, specifically, whether there are any SME assistance programs offered by the municipal government, if there is any information about tenders and job boards where private companies can post job offers open to the community. To do this, the attributes *Interaction Level, Level of Relationship with SMEs and Citizen Contribution Level* were defined. [11].

To achieve a level of *Transparency (T)*, there is a very strong interdependence among the attributes defined. For instance, if IDL is 0 and DVL is 0, it means that there are no data available and there is no portal or catalog, meaning that transparency is also 0. If IDL is 1, i.e., there is an open data catalog, the value of DVL differentiates whether those data can be linked to generate context or not. Finally, if IDL is 2, this means that DVL will have a value of 4 or 5. This can be seen in Table 2.

In the case of *Participation (P)*, if CPL has a value of 0, whatever value the other variables have is irrelevant, since no participation is considered to exist. If CPL has a value of 1 (physical participation required) or 2 (remote participation), the existence of participation or contributions for public policy design (PLPPD) is analyzed and, then, whether the public debate methodology is applied. In this case, the highest level is characterized by those municipalities that offer the highest level of participation to their citizens through public debates in a forum, generating public policies based on citizen contributions and allowing remote voting on such policies. This can be seen in Table 3.

In the case of *Collaboration (C)*, the level of citizen interaction (IL) is analyzed. If the value for this attribute is 0, any other attributes are automatically disregarded, since no collaboration is considered to exist. If there is interaction with citizens, the Level of Relationship with SMEs (LRS) and the Citizen Contribution Level (CCL) are considered to measure existing collaboration between the government and the private sector and between the government and its citizens. In this case, the highest level is characterized by those municipalities that allow carrying out transactions with the parties, resulting in policy plans based on their contributions and allowing them to actively participate in creating and disseminating information about job opportunities with SMEs. This can be seen in Table 4.

Table 2. Transparency

T	IDL	DVL
0	0	0
1	0	1–5
2	1	1–3
3	1	4–5
4	2	4–5

Table 3. Participation

P	CPL	PLPPD	PDL
0	0	–	–
1	1	0–1	0–1
2	1	1–2	0–1
3	2	1–2	0–1
4	2	1–2	2

Table 4. Collaboration

C	IL	LRS	CCL
0	0	–	–
1	1	1	–
2	1	2	1–2
3	2	2–3	2–3
4	3	3	3

4 Assessing Municipalities

4.1 Criteria for Selecting Municipalities

Municipal portal assessment was done on both national and provincial levels. On the national level, the capital cities of the 24 self-governed states (Table 5) were considered, while on the provincial level, a selection of municipalities in the province of Buenos Aires was analyzed.

The population of the Province of Buenos Aires is 15,625,000, which is almost 40% of the total population of Argentina (2010 census). It has a surface of 307,571 km divided into 135 municipalities with government autonomy. Populational density in municipalities ranges between 1 and 9167 inhabitants per km^2. The province is divided in eight electoral dependencies. To obtain a cross section sample of the municipalities in the province, for each electoral dependency, the 5 municipalities with the largest percentage of population in relation to the population of the entire province were considered [11].

Table 5. Capital cities

	Province	Capital city		Province	Capital city
1	Buenos Aires	La Plata	13	Misiones	Posadas
2	Catamarca	San Fernando del Valle de Catamarca	14	Neuquén	Neuquén
3	Chaco	Resistencia	15	Río Negro	Viedma
4	Chubut	Rawson	16	Salta	Salta
5	Córdoba	Córdoba	17	San Juan	San Juan
6	Corrientes	Corrientes	18	San Luis	San Luis
7	Entre Ríos	Paraná	19	Santa Cruz	Río Gallegos
8	Formosa	Formosa	20	Santa Fe	Santa Fe
9	Jujuy	San Salvador de Jujuy	21	Santiago del Estero	Santiago del Estero
10	La Pampa	Santa Rosa	22	Tierra del Fuego, Antártida e Islas del Atlántico Sur	Ushuaia
11	La Rioja	La Rioja	23	Tucumán	San Miguel de Tucumán
12	Mendoza	Mendoza	24	Argentina	City of Buenos Aires

Table 6 below lists the municipalities that were selected.

Table 6. Municipalities selected

Dependency	Municipalities
1	General San Martín, Merlo, Moreno, San Miguel and Tigre
2	Baradero, Pergamino, San Nicolás, San Pedro and Zárate
3	Almirante Brown, La Matanza, Lanús, Lomas de Zamora and Quilmes
4	Chacabuco, Chivilcoy, Junín, Nueve de Julio and Trenque Lauquen
5	Balcarce, General Pueyrredón, La Costa, Necochea and Tandil
6	Bahía Blanca, Coronel de Marina Leonardo Rosales, Coronel Suárez, Tres Arroyos and Villarino
7	Azul, Bolívar, Olavarría, Saladillo and Veinticinco de Mayo
8	La Plata

4.2   Applying the Model

The model was initially applied to the municipalities in the province of Buenos Aires. The web sites of the 36 municipalities were analyzed, considering the different sections offered to see how they met the requirements for the attributes proposed in the model.

Data were processed, and 56% of the cases (20 municipalities) obtained a value of 56% for *Transparency*. This corresponds to level 1, i.e., they offer open data in any format, but there is no catalog or portal that structures these data. This was followed by 17% of the cases with no open data. On the other hand, there is a 14% (5 municipalities) that offer open data portals, being on the vanguard. As regards *Participation*, 78% of the municipalities does not offer the possibility. This is followed by 14% of the municipalities that only offer information about how to participate. There are only 2 municipalities (6%) on level 3. Finally, there is only 1 municipality (3%) on the highest level of participation. As regards *Collaboration*, 31% (11 municipalities) does not offer any collaboration options. Three percent have some collaboration with the private sector. Eleven percent (4 municipalities) have an acceptable level of collaboration with citizens and the private sector. Finally, 56% (somewhere between levels 3 and 4) offer collaboration options with citizens and SMEs through communications and transactions.

Table 7 below lists individual values.

Table 7. Results obtained for the province of Buenos Aires

Level	Transparency		Participation		Collaboration	
0	6	17%	28	78%	11	31%
1	20	56%	5	14%	1	3%
2	4	11%	0	0%	4	11%
3	1	3%	2	6%	11	31%
4	5	14%	1	3%	9	25%

A similar analysis was carried out on the 24 provincial capital cities; the values listed on Table 8 were obtained. As regards *Transparency*, the same as in the province of Buenos Aires, the highest percentage is on level 1 (10 cities, 42%), followed by level 0 (8 cities, 33%). There are 2 cities (8%) that are on level 4. As regards *Participation*, 14 cities (58%) are on level 0 (no participation is possible), followed by 4 cities (17%) that are on level 2 (there is evidence of participation mechanisms), and 1 city on level 4. *Collaboration* is where a greater difference is found versus municipalities. All provincial capitals offer some type of collaboration option – 18 cities (75%) offer information on different services and some level of interaction, 1 city is on level 4 for offering collaboration options through communication and transactions with its citizens and private sectors, all remaining cities are on level 2 or 3.

Table 8. Results obtained for capital cities

	Transparency		Participation		Collaboration	
0	8	33%	14	58%	0	0%
1	10	42%	3	13%	18	75%
2	4	17%	4	17%	3	13%
3	0	0%	2	8%	2	8%
4	2	8%	1	4%	1	4%

As it can be seen, the application of open government principles is an area of particular interest for governments and society. Its implementation is starting to roll both nationally and provincially.

In the province, it should be noted that everything starts with *Transparency*, where a large portion of the municipalities that were surveyed are taking steps towards consolidating this principle. As regards *Collaboration*, there is an increase in the lack of application of this principle, as well as progress towards its consolidation since, when it is applied, this is done on higher levels. In comparison, the principle of *Participation* is where municipalities show the least progress or greatest lack of interest. Close to 80% of the municipalities do not have any measures in place to allow citizen participation, and only 9% applies it on the two highest tiers of the scale.

Figure 2 below shows these results in more detail.

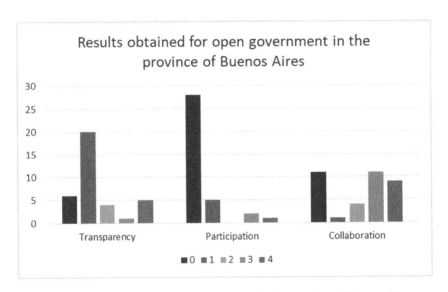

Fig. 2. Results obtained for open government in the province of Buenos Aires

In relation to capital cities, as seen in Fig. 3, the highlight is *Collaboration*, which is present in all cities as information about the services provided to citizens or the private sector as a starting point to strengthen collaboration between government and society. As regards *Transparency*, there is an emerging interest by the governments in publishing information. In the case of *Participation,* the same as on the provincial level, there is less progress, although there is more growth when compared with the province.

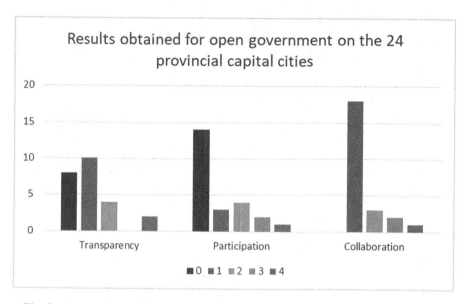

Fig. 3. Results obtained for open government in capital cities of provinces in Argentina

5 Conclusions

In this article, the basic concepts of open government were introduced, focusing on the principles of *Transparency, Participation* and *Collaboration.*

Based on these principles, an assessment model consisting of eight attributes was designed.

The 24 capital cities in the country and 36 municipalities in the province of Buenos Aires, selected based on population in relation to the electoral district to which they belong, were used as case study.

This municipal survey allowed analyzing the current status for provincial capitals and the province of Buenos Aires in relation to the application of the three open government principles. It was concluded that the issue is being approached using various methods, initially through actions pertaining to Transparency, followed by Collaboration and Participation. The municipalities that evidenced a higher level of progress offer transference services to their citizens, offering them channels to be part of the decision-making process and positively affecting society and quality of life.

References

1. Chun, S.A., Shulman, S., Sandoval, R., Hovy, E.: Government 2.0: making connections between citizens, data and government. Inf. Polity **15**(1–2), 1–9 (2010). City University of New York, College of Staten Island
2. Gil-García, J.R., Criado, J.I., Téllez, J.C.: Tecnologías de Información y Comunicación en la Administración Pública: Conceptos, Enfoques, Aplicaciones y Resultados. Infotec, primera edición (2007). ISBN 978-607-7763-24-6
3. Calderón, C., Lorenzo, S.: Open Government: Gobierno Abierto. Algón Editores, España (2010)
4. Naser, A., Ramírez-Alujas, Á.: Plan de gobierno abierto Una hoja de ruta para los Gobiernos de la región, Libros de la CEPAL (2017)
5. Dassen, N., Vieyra, J.C.: Gobierno abierto y transparencia focalizada: Tendencias y desafíos para América Latina y el Caribe. IADB (2012)
6. Ramírez-Alujas, Á.V.: El Gobierno Abierto Y Los Desafíos Tecnológicos En Latinoamérica. Goberna, América Latina - Instituto Universitario de Investigación Ortega y Gasset (2013)
7. Cruz-Rubio, C.N.: ¿Qué es (y que no es) gobierno abierto? Una discusión conceptual. Eunomía. Revista en Cultura de la Legalidad (8), 37–53 (2015). ISSN 2253-6655
8. González, S., Juan, J.: La participación ciudadana como instrumento del gobierno abierto. Revista Espacios - Universidad Autónoma del Estado de México (2015)
9. Obama, B.: Transparency and Open Government: Memorandum for the Heads of Executive Departments and Agencies (2009)
10. Moneo, A.: IADB Portal (2014). https://blogs.iadb.org/conocimiento-abierto/es/que-es-un-portal-de-datos-abiertos-y-para-que-sirve/
11. Pasini, A.C., Preisegger, J.S.: Modelos de evaluación de gobiernos abiertos, aplicado a los municipios de la provincia de Buenos Aires. In: Libro de Actas XXIV Congreso Argentino de Ciencias de la Computación CACIC 2018 (2018). ISBN 978-950-658-472-6

Combining Artificial Intelligence Services for the Recognition of Flora Photographs: Uses in Augmented Reality and Tourism

Guillermo Feierherd[1]([⊠]) [ID], Federico González[1], Leonel Viera[1], Rosina Soler[2], Lucas Romano[1], Lisandro Delía[3], and Beatriz Depetris[1]

[1] Instituto de Desarrollo Económico e Innovación, Universidad Nacional de Tierra del Fuego, Hipólito Irigoyen 880, 9410 Ushuaia, Tierra del Fuego, Argentina
{gfeierherd, fgonzalez, lviera, lromano, bdepetris}@untdf.edu.ar
[2] Centro Austral de Investigaciones Científicas, CONICET, Houssay 200, 9410 Ushuaia, Tierra del Fuego, Argentina
rosinas@cadic-conicet.gob.ar
[3] III-LIDI - Universidad Nacional de La Plata, 50 y 120, 1900 La Plata, Buenos Aires, Argentina
ldelia@lidi.info.unlp.edu.ar

Abstract. Tourism information services are evolving rapidly. With Internet, tourists organize their trips by managing information before arriving at their destination. Nature is the main tourist attraction in Argentina. However, the information tools as field guides, have had few improvements in their digital version compared to printed ones. This work compares and combines machine learning services that includes deep learning, artificial intelligence and image recognition, to evaluate the app development for mobile phones that offer recognition of flora species in real time, in natural areas with low or no internet connectivity. Recognition of three *Nothofagus* tree species (with a dataset of 45 photos per species) were evaluated in the Tierra del Fuego National Park, using IBM Watson, Google Cloud and Microsoft Azure. Finally, we defined an algorithm combining those services to improve the results. Google Cloud was the service with the best performance recognizing all the tree species (83% effectiveness in average). The accuracy of Watson and Azure was lower than Google Cloud, and varied according to tree species. Combined algorithm improved the recognition with a 90% effectiveness in average. A next iteration of this work expects to increase the accuracy of recognition to get a total of 150 photos per specie into the dataset. We also expect to use assisted learning to improve the efficiency of the neural network obtained to know the adaptation capacities for each evaluated service.

Keywords: Smart tourist destinations · Computer vision · IBM Watson · Microsoft Azure · Google Cloud

© Springer Nature Switzerland AG 2019
P. Pesado and C. Aciti (Eds.): CACIC 2018, CCIS 995, pp. 367–375, 2019.
https://doi.org/10.1007/978-3-030-20787-8_26

1   Introduction

1.1   Background

The present work is an extension of the one presented at the XXIV Argentine Congress of Computer Science (CACIC 2018) [1]. Both are part of the project "Virtual and Augmented Reality, Big Data and Mobile Devices: Applications in Tourism" that since 2017 is developed in the National University of Tierra del Fuego, Antarctica and South Atlantic Islands. The project seeks to reveal the uses that the tourism industry is making of these emerging technologies individually or in combination, to propose alternatives for application in the area of Tierra del Fuego.

In the previous work, machine learning and artificial intelligence services offered in the cloud by IBM and Microsoft were used in order to generate the bases for an application that would allow recognizing in real time the three most common *Nothofagus* species in the National Park of Tierra del Fuego.

In the current one, Google services have been added to the comparison and an algorithm has been proposed that, by combining the results of the three aforementioned services, substantially improves the recognition capacity.

1.2   Technical Rationale

Considering that the main tourist attraction of Tierra del Fuego is wildlife (flora and fauna), tourists often enrich their trip with field guides, species guides or information brochures about the local flora and fauna. However, it would be much more interesting if they could recognize a species at the same moment of taking a photograph and in this context, the potential of augmented reality and the recognition of images associated with artificial intelligence, is promising.

Biological organisms are not always easy to photograph. Animals, whether they are walkers, fliers or swimmers, besides being mobile (and some of them very fast) are elusive to human presence or have cryptic behavior. Photographing plants, on the other hand, is much easier, accessible and attractive for anyone without technical knowledge of photography, even when they have only a smartphone. Moreover, throughout the world, the proportion of identified plant species is greater than any other biological group [2].

Despite this greater knowledge about plant species, in some cases the interspecific morphological differences are minimal and difficult to recognize with the naked eye. Even in herbaria that contain a large number of specimens, their identification is being carried out with artificial vision and machine learning approaches applied to scans of leaves or images of plants in the field [3]. The trees of the genus *Nothofagus* are the most representative of the forest of Tierra del Fuego, but the specific differences of their leaves are difficult to recognize when comparing them without expert human eye, which represents an ideal difficulty to test the augmented reality together with computer vision.

Considering the complexity and constant evolution of the technologies related to machine learning, deep learning, artificial intelligence and image recognition, we decided to use the services provided in the cloud to train the neural network from a database of photos to identify tree species typical of the forest of Tierra del Fuego. The ultimate goal is to use that knowledge and to develop an offline app in the future to recognize flora and fauna without connectivity, which is a peculiarity of the protected areas.

2 Information in Smart Tourist Destinations

Tourist information systems have traditionally been organized in three chronological stages: promotion, planning and stay. In this way, the person who deals with the management of a tourist destination, first makes marketing, then provides information tools to plan the itinerary and, finally, guides the tourists with useful information to help them know the destination during their stay. In recent years, the concept of stay was reoriented to that of experience and a fourth component was added to the stages: sharing what was lived.

This work focuses on the stage of the experience, particularly when it takes place in Protected Areas. In those cases, the traditional methods to provide information were based on printed brochures (which could be obtained at a visitor center), on strategically located posters, signage of the trails, etc.

This scheme, with its advantages and disadvantages, but the only one possible until a few years ago, must be complemented and enriched with the resources that technology offers today. This also allows adapting them to the characteristics of younger visitors, digital natives, accustomed to using new technological resources to obtain the information they need.

Lansky [4] questions the role of visitor centers. Their questions take into account the investment that many of them represent and the increasingly scarce utility of their services. In his opinion its strategic location makes many tourists visit them with the idea of collecting some free maps and brochures, or maybe get an air-conditioned space, shelter from rain or cold, or the need for toilets. But, if they were not there, that does not mean tourists could not get the same information services using their phones and other mobile devices.

Obviously there will be some people who do not carry a smartphone with them, but they are becoming a limited minority. And it is likely that the "analogue" visitors will already arrive prepared with a printed guide, newspaper clippings or the advice they have requested from the hotel receptionist.

It is known that smartphones have been replacing several useful old devices for tourists, such as photo cameras, video recorders, GPS among others. It is also true that many visitors consider the Protected Areas as a symbol of nature and feel that it is worthwhile to remain "disconnected" while they go through them.

People over 50 only use the telephone (Fig. 1) to perpetuate moments and understand the place -take pictures, look at a map- while younger generations incorporate communication tools to interact with social networks and for other recreational uses such as listening music while they visiting the protected area [5].

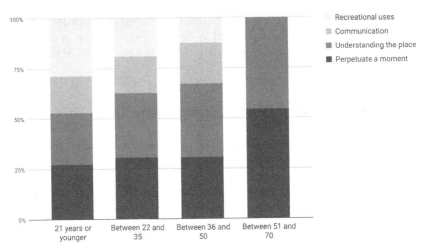

Fig. 1. Uses of the smartphones according to generations grouped by activity [4].

The biggest difference between young and old generations is linked to recreational use and communication (with the outside world of the protected area). This mean that older generations are prone to disconnect themselves within protected areas, while digital natives prefer to remain connected and give intensive use to all the analyzed functions of the telephone when visiting protected areas.

From the above, it is clear that interactive identification of species using a smartphone can be a motivation against traditional brochures or guides with descriptions and figures.

3 Methodology

3.1 Morphological Aspects of the Compared Species

For this work three tree species of the genus *Nothofagus* were selected, which predominate in the Fuegian forest: Lenga (*N. pumilio*), Ñire (*N. antarctica*) and Guindo (*N. betuloides*). The first two are deciduous and phylogenetically closest species [6], so hybridization between them is possible [7]. While the third species is an evergreen tree with morphological characteristics that differentiate it from its congeners. The main foliar characteristics of these trees (Table 1) allow to recognize with an ordinal eye, with a minimum of botanical knowledge, what kind of species they are [8, 9].

Table 1. Main foliar characteristics of the *Nothofagus* species considered in the study

Foliar characteristic	Lenga	Ñire	Guindo
Habit	deciduous	deciduous	evergreen
Shape	oblong-elliptical	oblong	oval
Length	2–3 cm	2–3 cm	1–2.5 cm
Width	1.5 cm	1.5 cm	1 cm
Apex	blunt	rounded	sharp
Edge	crenate	irregular lobed	regular serrated
Base	slightly asymmetric	asymmetric	symmetric
Petiole length	0.5 cm	0.5 cm	0.3 cm

3.2 Visual Recognition Services

Neural networks have proven effective at solving difficult problems but designing their architectures can be challenging, even for image classification problems alone. Different provider services aim to minimize human participation, employing evolutionary algorithms to discover such networks automatically [10]. Despite significant computational requirements, it is now possible to develop models with high accuracies.

Different complex artificial intelligence and machine learning services are being offered in the cloud by companies such as IBM, Microsoft, Google or Amazon. With different levels of complexity regarding its implementation, this paper compares the services of IBM Watson (Visual Recognition), Google Cloud (Vision), and Microsoft Azure (Custom Vision), since they are the only ones that incorporate integral products based on visual platforms that facilitate its implementation in great measure.

3.3 Collection of Photographs

For each species of *Nothofagus* trees, 45 photographs of leaves or branches with different level of clearly differentiable leaves were provided, to be used as machine learning models. The photos were taken at different seasons of the year (except winter) by people without specific knowledge of photography, but with knowledge of plant species.

In addition to the datasets created and categorized, a stock of 30 photos (10 for each specie) that did not belong to the database and were used to verify the certainty of the results offered by Watson, Google and Azure was established.

The quality of this 30 photographs (Table 2) was variable to represent different situations into the database, all of them in jpg format.

Table 2. Main characteristics of photographs for each species used to verify the model for this study. Nb: Guindo (*Nothofagus betuloides*), Np: Lenga (*N. pumilio*), Na: Ñire (*N. antarctica*)

Photo	Leaves/branches	Noise	Human recognition	Photo quality	Colour
Nb1	35/10		easy	good	green
Nb2	70/10		easy	good	green
Nb3	50/5	fruits	easy	medium	green
Nb4	45/2		easy	good	green
Nb5	30/10	gall	easy	good	green
Nb6	60/5		easy	good	green
Nb7	80/10		easy	good	green
Nb8	50/15	fence	easy	good	green
Nb9	55/10		medium	good	green
Nb10	20/5	stems	easy	medium	green
Np1	85/2		easy	good	green
Np2	50/10		easy	good	yellow
Np3	20/5		easy	bad	green
Np4	60/15		easy	good	green
Np5	80/2		medium	medium	red
Np6	40/5		tricky	good	green
Np7	10/2		tricky	good	green
Np8	75/5		easy	good	green
Np9	60/2		easy	good	green
Np10	55/20		medium	good	green
Na1	60/10		tricky	bad	yellow
Na2	35/10		easy	good	green/yellow
Na3	80/0		easy	medium	green
Na4	75/2		easy	bad	green
Na5	55/5		easy	good	green
Na6	50/20	fruits	easy	good	green
Na7	75/2		easy	good	green
Na8	45/15		easy	good	green
Na9	20/15	flowers	easy	good	green
Na10	15/20	hand	easy	good	green

3.4   Combination of Recognition Services

After having generated the neural networks in each platform, the results obtained individually with each service were combined, with the aim of evaluating whether the results improved. A simple algorithm was developed which is described below:

1. If all 3 predictions matched, that result was considered valid.
2. If only 2 predictions matched (i.e., the majority), that result was considered valid.
3. If the predictions did not matchet, the one with the greatest accuracy reported was considered valid. This, as long as that accuracy is greater than the lower confidence reported by the models.
4. Otherwise the result was indeterminate and the species unknown.

4 Results

In general terms, the three services had good results when evaluating Guindo and Ñire. With Lenga the case was different since Watson and Azure had more problems than Google Cloud.

Figure 2 summarizes the results obtained with a confusion matrix. The diagonal marked in gray shows the percentage of hits for each platform, while the white cells indicate the degree of error and what was the confusion. For example: when evaluating Lenga (Np), Azure confused 20% of the samples with Guindo (Nb); Something similar happened to Google with Ñire and Guindo.

	Watson			**Azure**			**Google**		
	Nb	Np	Na	Nb	Np	Na	Nb	Np	Na
Guindo (Nb)	90%	0%	10%	80%	0%	20%	90%	0%	10%
Lenga (Np)	20%	40%	40%	20%	40%	40%	0%	70%	30%
Ñire (Na)	20%	0%	80%	30%	0%	70%	20%	0%	80%

Fig. 2. Confusion Matrix with recognition probability of tree species between Watson, Azure and Google Cloud services. Match cases are highlighted in gray over the diagonal. Nb: Guindo, Np: Lenga, Na: Ñire

A quick analysis of the confusion matrix makes it easy to see that Google Cloud was the service with the best performance. It equaled Watson with a 90% effectiveness when analyzing Guindo images, was highly superior to Watson and Azure in evaluating Lenga (70% against 40% in the other two platforms), and finally equaled Watson by recognizing Ñire correctly in 80% of cases.

The combination of the three models improved the individual results (Fig. 3). Analyzing the results obtained, it can be seen that the performance for Guindo and Ñire reached 100% effectiveness, while for Lenga it was not possible to improve the results previously achieved with Google Cloud.

	Watson			Azure			Google			Combined		
	Nb	Np	Na	Nb	Np	Na	Nb	Np	Na	Nb	Np	Na
Guindo (Nb)	90%	0%	10%	80%	0%	20%	90%	0%	10%	100%	0%	0%
Lenga (Np)	20%	40%	40%	20%	40%	40%	0%	70%	30%	10%	70%	20%
Ñire (Na)	20%	0%	80%	30%	0%	70%	20%	0%	80%	0%	0%	100%

Fig. 3. One matrix has been added to preliminary results, combining those models with the described algorithm.

5 Conclusions

Watson and Azure services had similar performance, but Google was more successful in recognizing two of the three analysed tree species. Guindo (Nb) and Ñire (Na) seem to have more defined morphological characteristics, while Lenga (Np) had intermediate and similar morphological characteristics to other species and this generated high confusion for the systems.

Considering that the knowledge base was generated from 45 photographs for each species, we believe that the results have been highly satisfactory. A next iteration of this work will add 315 more *Nothofagus* photographs to be included into the dataset to compare the evolution capacity that each service has to improve their models. We expect to add 105 photos for each species, so the database will be a set of 150 photos per species. Regarding this last point, it is important to refine the recognition capabilities of the machine learning for the current database (but mainly for Lenga), manually correcting the errors of the first iteration and testing a new group of photographs. At that time, the combination algorithm will be applied again to evaluate its potential in a more refined model than the current one.

This work focused on the interpretation of images in the foreground (leaves, branches) since for tourist purposes it is of great value for the visitors to be able to know what they have at their fingertips. Beyond this objective, it would also be interesting and possible in future studies to broaden the point of view towards the interpretation of specimens at medium distances to answer questions like "what kind of trees are those?" or to count "how many individuals of each species are there?" in a determined group.

It is necessary to incorporate new species in the training process in the near future to generate a database with knowledge about local flora of high interest for tourists. The three species studied in this work are the most representative trees of the Tierra del Fuego National Park, and also the best known by people. The recognition of other plants as forbs, grasses, or ferns is a major challenge from a technical point of view, since a greater variety of species very similar among them could potentially generate more confusion in the recognition or less accuracy of results.

Finally, and as final outcome of our project "Virtual and Augmented Reality, Big Data and Mobile Devices: Applications in Tourism" we expect to develop a public offline app that incorporates image recognition and offers results from the compared platforms, while generating at the same time new databases to refine knowledge with assisted machine learning. Offline mode is a key feature for the usefulness of apps in countries such as Argentina, where the main destination of international tourism are the National Parks (Perito Moreno Glacier, Iguazú Falls). Although Argentina is one of the countries with higher access to the internet in Latin America, such connectivity occurs in cities or urban areas where population is concentrated [11]. The protected areas do not have any type of internet connection and in most cases, no access to mobile phone network [12]. To achieve this, the application must be able to identify the species offline without external services. With the previous training of a neural network based on machine learning services, we hope to have enough potential to achieve it.

References

1. Feierherd, G., et al.: Comparison of services for the recognition of flora images. Uses in augmented reality and tourism. In: Proceedings of the XXIV National Congress of Computer Science, Tandil, Buenos Aires, Argentina, pp. 1152–1159 (2018)
2. Mora, C., Tittensor, D.P., Adl, S., Simpson, A.G.B., Worm, B.: How many species are there on earth and in the ocean? PLoS Biol. **9**(8), e1001127 (2011)
3. Carranza-Rojas, J., Goeau, H., Bonnet, P., Mata-Montero, E., Joly, A.: Going deeper in the automated identification of herbarium specimens. BMC Evol. Biol. **17**(1), 181 (2017)
4. Lansky, D.: Has the Smartphone Killed the Tourist Office? Digital Tourism Think Tank (2016). http://thinkdigital.travel/opinion/has-the-smartphone-killed-the-tourist-office/
5. González, F.: Digital tourist information tools in protected areas for Millennials and Gen Z. Master thesis, University of Girona, Spain (2017)
6. Jordan, G.J., Hill, R.S.: The phylogenetic affinities of Nothofagus (Nothofagaceae) leaf fossils based on combined molecular and morphological data. Int. J. Plant Sci. **160**(6), 1177–1188 (1999)
7. Lilian, B.S., et al.: Descripción de posibles híbridos naturales entre Nothofagus pumilio y N. antarctica en Patagonia Sur (Argentina). Bosque (Valdivia) **31**(1), 9–16 (2010)
8. Moore, D.M.: Flora of Tierra del Fuego. Anthony Nelson, England (1983)
9. Donoso, C.: Las especies arbóreas de los bosques templados de Chile y Argentina. Autoecología. Marisa Cuneo Ediciones, Chile (2006)
10. Real, E., et al.: Large-scale evolution of image classifiers. In: Proceedings of the 34th International Conference on Machine Learning, Sydney, Australia, PMLR, vol. 70 (2017)
11. Open Signal: Global cell coverage maps, Argentina (2018). https://opensignal.com/networks?z=4&minLat=-56.9&maxLat=-16.6&minLng=-109.7&maxLng=-18.3&s=&t=4
12. APN: Mapa oficial con polígonos de las Áreas Protegidas Nacionales de Argentina. Administración de Parques Nacionales (2018). http://mapas.parquesnacionales.gob.ar/layers/geonode%3Aapn_areasprotegidas_01

Author Index